OECD Urban Policy Reviews: Kazakhstan

OECD
BETTER POLICIES FOR BETTER LIVES

Please cite this publication as:
OECD (2017), *OECD Urban Policy Reviews: Kazakhstan*, OECD Publishing, Paris.
http://dx.doi.org/10.1787/9789264268852-en

ISBN 978-92-64-26884-5 (print)
ISBN 978-92-64-26885-2 (PDF)

Series: OECD Urban Policy Reviews
ISSN 2306-9333 (print)
ISSN 2306-9341 (online)

Photo credits: Cover illustration © Jeffrey Fisher

Corrigenda to OECD publications may be found on line at: *www.oecd.org/about/publishing/corrigenda.htm*.

Foreword

By 2050, the world urban population is expected to nearly double. Urbanisation will be one of the most important transformations of the 21st century. The importance to the national economy of cities and their corresponding metropolitan areas makes them critical players in the international marketplace. Throughout OECD member and non-member countries, governments have renewed their support to cities and have adopted policies to solve traditional urban problems such as urban sprawl, abandoned districts and poverty, as well as newer issues such as competitiveness, city marketing, environmental sustainability and innovation. The adoption of the New Urban Agenda at Habitat III in October 2016 provides governments with a set of global standards in sustainable urban development and the way cities are built and managed.

The OECD Urban Policy Review of Kazakhstan highlights that, while the country is modernising, its urban centres still show a number of weaknesses that need to be addressed if they are to achieve their full potential as the main engines of economic growth. As urbanisation progresses, the country's economic performance will be more closely linked to the functioning of its cities and its urban governance system. The review suggests that Kazakhstan needs to invest in the quality of its urbanisation if it is to achieve national development objectives. Urbanisation is a necessary, but not sufficient, condition for economic development. Developing an attractive and well-managed system of large and medium-sized cities is thus of particular importance for Kazakhstan. This requires an urban development framework that clearly formulates policy direction, concepts and strategies for urban and spatial development, and a comprehensive land-use planning system.

OECD Urban Policy Reviews are conducted by the OECD Regional Development Policy Committee (RDPC) through its Working Party on Urban Policy, a unique forum for international exchange and debate. The OECD reviews follow a consistent methodology that features cross-national comparisons and recommendations on the integration of sectoral policies into urban development policy, planning and programmes. The reviews provide a comprehensive assessment of a country's urban policies as seen through multiple lenses, including economic, social and environmental. First, the reviews focus on the policies designed and introduced by the central government that directly address urban development challenges. Second, the reviews analyse how national spatial planning for urban regions, along with specific sectoral policies, affect urban development directly and indirectly. Third, the reviews address issues of governance, including intergovernmental fiscal relationships and the various institutional, fiscal and policy tools aimed to encourage co-ordinated urban development among different levels of government and different administrations at the central level.

Lamia Kamal-Chaoui

Director, Centre for Entrepreneurship, SMEs, Local Development and Tourism, OECD

Acknowledgements

This review of Kazakhstan is part of a series of Urban Policy Reviews produced by the OECD Centre for Entrepreneurship, SMEs, Local Development and Tourism and its Regional Development Policy Division, led by Joaquim Oliveira Martins. The review was made possible through the financial support of the Ministry of National Economy of the Republic of Kazakhstan.

The OECD Secretariat is grateful to Kuandyk Bishimbayev, Minister of National Economy of the Republic of Kazakhstan; Roman Sklyar, Vice Minister of National Economy; Zhaiyk Sharabassov, Director General of Regional Policy, Assessment and Analysis of the Regions; and the co-ordinating team at the Ministry of National Economy led by Dauren Zhambaibek and with excellent support from Arslan Bissembayev, Sholpan Baimagambetova, Nurlan Seitkhanov, and Dauren Zakumbayev. The Secretariat would also like to acknowledge the numerous representatives from the public and private sectors, civil society and academia who shared perspectives with the OECD delegation. In particular, the Secretariat would like to thank Anara Makatova, Yelena Yerzakovich, Malika Tukmadiyeva, Mats Andersson, Meruert Makhmutova, and Aigul Kosherbayeva. Special thanks go to the authorities of Astana, Almaty City, South Kazakhstan *oblast*, Shymkent, Turkestan and Kentau for the organisation of the interviews and the valuable information provided. Kazakhstan's Committee on Statistics provided valuable data and assistance for this review. Thanks also go to the Asian Development Bank local office in Astana for sharing their perspectives with the OECD delegation. The Secretariat is grateful to the governments of Canada and Turkey for acting as leading peer reviewers.

This report was co-ordinated by Oscar Huerta Melchor and drafted by Antoine Comps, Madina Junussova and Oscar Huerta Melchor. Rüdiger Ahrend, Head of the Urban Programme, supervised this review and provided critical guidance throughout the process. Valuable comments and input were provided by Daniela Glocker, Isabelle Chatry, Karen Maguire, Monika Sztajerowska, Tierra McMahon, Michael O'Neill, and Andrea Uhrhammer. The Secretariat is grateful to Dan McCarthy, Director of Energy and Environment Policy at the Atlantic Canada Opportunities Agency, for his useful comments and advice. This report was elaborated within the framework of the Kazakhstan Country Programme and benefitted from the support of colleagues from the OECD Eurasia Programme at the Global Relations Secretariat. Special thanks to Pilar Philip, Joanne Dundon, Vicky Elliott and Cécile Cordoliani for preparing the review for publication.

Table of contents

Tables

Figures

Acronyms and abbreviations

BANOBRAS	National Bank of Works and Public Services (*Banco Nacional de obras y Servicios Publicos*)
BEEPS	Business Environment and Enterprise Performance Survey
CDP	Comprehensive Development Plan (*Комплексный план развития*)
CPI	Consumer Price Index
CREM	Committee for Regulation of Natural Monopolies
CSOT	Territory Development (*Комплексные схемы градостроительного планирования территорий областей*)
DAUP	Department of Architecture and Urban Design
DEBP	Department of Economy and Budget Planning
DLP	Detailed Local Plans (*Проект застройки*)
ECA	Eastern European and Central Asian
ECP	Eurasia Competitiveness Programme
EIA	Environmental Impact Assessment
EPCI	Établissements Publics de Coopération Intercommunale
ERDF	European Regional Development Fund
ERI	Economic Research Institute
FSCD	Forecast of Socio-Economic Development (*Прогноз социально-экономического развития*)
FUA	Functional Urban Area
GPEEC	Employment, Workforce and Competency Planning (*Gestion prévisionnelle des emplois, des effectifs et des compétences*)
GSOT	General Scheme of Organisation of the Territory of the Republic of Kazakhstan (*Генеральная схема организации территории Республики Казахстан*)
HESA	Higher Education Statistics Agency

IAU	The Greater Paris Region Institute for Urban Planning and Development (*Institut d'Aménagement et d'Urbanisme de la région Île-de-France*)
INEGI	Mexican National Statistics Institute (*Instituto Nacional de Estadística y Geografía*)
INS	Identification Number System
IP	Innovation Policy
IPPUC	Urban Research and Planning Institute of Curitiba in Brazil
ISTD	Interregional Schemes of Territorial Development (*Межрегиональные схемы территориального развития*)
KPIs	Key Performance Indicators
LRT	Light Rail Transit
MNE	Ministry of National Economy
MoU	Memorandum of Understanding
MRD	Ministry of Regional Development
NAC	National Analytical Centre
NAMA	Nationally Appropriate Mitigation Actions
NDIT	Northern Development Initiative Trust
NHSCR	National Health Service Central Register
NO_2	Nitrogen Oxides
O&M	Operations and Management
PADD	Urban Sustainable Development Plan (*Plan d'Aménagement et de Développement Durable*)
PM_{10}	Fine particle concentration
$PM_{2.5}$	Ultra-fine particles
PPPs	Public-Private Partnerships
PRP	Performance–Related Pay
PTD	Programmes of Territorial Development (*Программа развития территории*)
RDP	Regional Development Programme
REFINA	Reduction of Land Consumption and for Sustainable Land Management

SCoT	Territorial Coherence Programme (*Schéma de cohérence territoriale*)
SDGs	Sustainable Development Goals
SEZs	Special Economic Zones
SMEs	Small and Medium-sized Enterprises
SNGs	Subnational governments
SO_2	Sulfur
SOEs	State-Owned Enterprises
SPAIID	State Programme on Accelerated Industrial and Innovative Development
SPCE	School of Continuous and Professional Education
TTOs	Technology Transfer Offices
UGBs	Urban Growth Boundaries
UNFCC	UN Framework Convention on Climate change
UPC	Urban Design Council (*Градостроительный совет*)
UZR	Urban Zoning Registry (*Государственный градостроительный кадастр*)
VAT	Value Added Tax
VUF	Viet Nam Urban Forum

Executive summary

The context

- Kazakhstan aims to become one of the 30 most developed countries by 2050, with an urbanisation level of 70%. However, after a decade of urban population decline after independence, the urban population began to grow, but at a moderate pace. OECD estimates that between 1990 and 2001, the urbanisation level decreased from 54.8% to 50.3%, but rose to 55.6% by 2016. Kazakhstan has fewer densely populated areas and the percentage of its population living in metropolitan areas is lower than in most OECD countries. Indeed, the three largest urban agglomerations – the metropolitan areas of Astana, Almaty City and Shymkent – account for only 23.1% of the overall population, whereas in OECD countries, the average is 48.6%.
- The country has a complex urban and territorial structure. The *oblast* (regional) level comprises 16 regions, including Almaty City and Astana. The *rayon* (districts) level consists of 217 districts, of which 38 are cities of regional significance, 160 rural districts and 17 city districts. The third level is composed of 2 455 municipalities, of which 47 are cities of district significance, 26 are urban settlements and the rest are villages and rural communities. Cities are placed within the three levels of subnational government depending on their population level and political significance. Administrative status, however, does not always reflect demographic realities, since the criteria for granting urban status, and thus access to more resources, are not followed systematically.
- Subnational governments are politically, administratively and financially weak. Inter-governmental relations are based on the hierarchical subordination of lower levels of government to the level immediately above, which exercises considerable influence over local decisions. Mayors (*akims*) are appointed by the upper executive power, and cities are largely dependent on budget transfers from the upper level of government.

Key urban challenges

- Public urban transport is in decline. Urban transit is increasingly dominated by the private automobile. Moderate gasoline prices, road extensions and improvements in and around big cities, and the low quality of public transport services, have increased car ownership. This, in turn, has led to high pollution levels and congestion in the largest cities.
- Despite a growing housing stock, housing affordability is a problem. Rapid population growth in large and medium-sized cities has led to a shortage of affordable housing for low-income residents, incoming migrants and even middle-class households. Only 4% of the overall housing stock is social housing. The rental market is also underdeveloped.

- Utility networks are obsolete, and inadequate metering and low tariffs do not yield sufficient funds for modernising, maintaining and repairing them. Four-fifths of the heating network is inefficient, with high distribution heat losses and failures. Around 64% of water and sanitation networks need complete repair or replacement.
- Air pollution and waste management are becoming major health issues in large cities. The two main sources of air pollution are industrial or energy plants and individual motor vehicles. Municipal waste collection is not yet available in all communities, and solid waste is often dumped into sites without proper environmental protection systems.

Key policy recommendations

- Kazakhstan requires a specific urban development framework that clearly formulates policy direction, concepts and strategies for urban and spatial development. The creation of a Ministry for Urban and Regional Development and the installation of a National Urban and Regional Development Co-ordination Council, with the political support of the prime minister, would simplify horizontal co-ordination for urban policy.
- Since many of the urban challenges facing Kazakhstan's cities are related to a lax land-use planning system, authorities should develop a comprehensive land-use planning system to control disordered conversion of farmland into urban land and prevent urban sprawl. In addition, a more comprehensive land-use management method is needed that connects spatial planning with the implementation of closely related urban policy issues such as economic development, social well-being, housing, utilities and transport planning.
- Policies to bridge the housing affordability gap are needed. Avoiding restrictive land-use regulations, using the planning system to create affordable housing, and stimulating the development of the rental market are some options for bridging the gap.
- Forging closer links among land-use planning, transport, tax policy, and urban infrastructure planning will require a shift towards a broad, strategic approach to planning based on networks. To achieve this, Kazakhstan needs to improve the capacity for cross-sectoral planning, for example through the creation of urban planning institutes.
- The infrastructure and management of public utilities need to be reinforced. Setting clear priorities and enhancing the effectiveness of programmes to rehabilitate municipal infrastructure assets could help to bridge the infrastructure gap. To make the financing sustainable, there is a need for tariff reform that allows cost recovery, and for a more active participation of the private sector in public utilities, including through public-private partnerships where appropriate.
- Internal migration should be facilitated. Urban development planning needs to take internal migration into account. Possible measures include developing a registration system that makes it easier for migrants to register, delinking the provision of public services from registration status and instead using the existing single identification number of each citizen.
- Subnational capacity for urbanisation needs to be strengthened. A fairer and more flexible public financial system would include a reform of the property tax and

modernisation of the cadastre to increase revenue. An unambiguous assignment of expenditure responsibilities across levels of government would also help improve urban finances. More generally, investing in the strategic management of the public workforce to upgrade public servants' competencies and skills and ensure a well-structured workforce at all levels is essential.

Assessment and recommendations

After a decade of urban population decline following independence in 1991, Kazakhstan began urbanising, although at a moderate pace. As urbanisation progresses, the country's economic performance will be more tightly linked to the functioning of its cities and its urban governance system. Until 2015, Kazakhstan's average annual economic growth rate was 8%, largely boosted by its extractive industry (oil and gas). Since falling oil prices are likely to reduce the opportunities for economic growth, the urbanisation process will be essential for developing a more balanced economic model. The importance of cities for GDP has been growing consistently over the last five years. In 2015, Almaty City and Astana accounted for about 15% of the country's population, and produced one-third of national GDP, due to the concentration of high added-value activities. "Getting cities right" can provide a supportive environment for firms, entrepreneurs and institutions to innovate. Cities, under the right conditions, can increase the flow of ideas, facilitate the sharing of localised knowledge and enable innovation, which is a major drive for economic growth.

This review suggests that Kazakhstan needs to invest in the quality of its urbanisation if it is to achieve the development objectives established in its "Kazakhstan 2050" strategy. The experience of OECD countries shows that, while urbanisation is a prerequisite of economic development, it is not a guarantee. Adhering to the New Urban Agenda and pursuing the UN Sustainable Development Goals (SDGs) will help Kazakhstan transform its cities into an engine of economic and social development. To ensure its citizens' well-being, the country needs to find adequate responses to critical urban challenges such as housing, public utilities, land use, urban transport and internal migration. Current urban governance arrangements do not provide the necessary tools and incentives for cities to promote sustainable and inclusive development.

Kazakhstan's urban system

Kazakhstan, the ninth largest country in the world in terms of surface area, has a dispersed settlement pattern, with fewer densely populated areas than most OECD countries. Given its low population density, the development of an attractive and well-managed system of large and medium-sized cities is of particular importance for its economic development.

Kazakhstan's cities are still influenced by their Soviet past…

The government envisions making Kazakhstan one of the 30 most developed countries by 2050, with an urbanisation level of 70%. However, the country is still trying to shed the legacy of its Soviet past. Soviet central planning shaped the urban system that Kazakhstan inherited in 1991. City location and growth, and related infrastructure development, were largely determined by the growth of extractive industries and, to a lesser extent, by the needs of the agricultural economy. Cities thus reflected the ambitions of central planners rather than a naturally developed urban system. After independence, cities played a key role in the country's transition to a market economy. The dismantling of many elements of the Soviet system (e.g. the compulsory work placement of young graduates, and the heavily subsidised transport and energy tariffs) led to an increased concentration of population in large cities. However, even 25 years after independence, the large majority of Kazakhstan's cities have not yet finished adapting to new market conditions.

Over the past 20 years, Kazakhstan's urban development has followed two paths. The first was the development of two large cities of national importance – Astana and Almaty City. These metropolises are now expected to become important hubs in the Eurasian system of trade in goods, and for financial, technological and cultural exchange. The second is the development of a "backbone" of national and regional cities that concentrate local economic activity. The government has paid increasing attention to urban agglomerations, single-industry towns ("monotowns"), and small towns in recent years, while focusing on the two largest cities.

… as reflected in its complex urban structure

In the current territorial structure, Kazakhstan has 87 cities and 30 urban settlements (*posiolki*) located within the vicinity of cities. In 2016, there are 2 676 subnational governments (SNGs) in Kazakhstan, constituting three layers of territorial administration: regional (*oblast*) including Almaty and Astana, district (*rayons*), and municipal (*auls*). Cities are placed within those three levels. However, the administrative-territorial structure has not been fully updated to take into account recent social and demographic trends. Official population data in large cities is unreliable and underestimates the real number of urban dwellers, as many internal and external migrants live in big cities without being officially registered. Since budget transfers are based on official population numbers, discrepancies between official demographic statistics and true population numbers can present governance challenges and undermine the effective provision of public services. Such discrepancies also suggest that the official urbanisation rate is not a reliable indicator of the country's urbanisation level.

After a decade of urban decline, urbanisation is proceeding at a relatively moderate pace

Kazakhstan is the most urbanised country in Central Asia. However, the country experienced atypical demographic patterns after independence in 1991. Between 1991 and 2001, the country's population declined by 9.1%. The decline was somewhat more pronounced in the urban population than in the rural population, which led to a moderate drop in the urbanisation rate, from almost 55% in 1991 to 50.3% in 2001, according to OECD estimates. This decline was due to the return of urban dwellers of Russian and German origin to their places of origin, and to low natural population growth. In 2001, the urban population started growing again, and by 2011, the overall population exceeded its 1991 level. Demographic growth has stabilised at around 1.4%-1.5% annually since 2010. Since 2002, the urban population has expanded at a slightly faster pace than the rural population, allowing the official urbanisation rate to reach 57% in 2016. However, several large-scale administrative-territorial changes since 2002 have also affected official urban and rural population figures. Between 2010 and 2015, the urban population grew rapidly, by 1.8 percentage points annually, but growth rates remained below levels seen in China (3%) or Turkey (2%). The comparatively moderate pace of urbanisation has been due to low internal mobility and low rural-urban migrations. Internal migration contributed to only one-fifth of urban population growth between 2010 and 2015. Since

2006, natural population growth in cities has contributed much more to the expansion of the urban population than net migration.

Kazakhstan's level of urbanisation is comparable to OECD levels

In order to provide a meaningful comparison of Kazakhstan's urbanisation level with OECD countries and to correct for some of the weaknesses of the official urbanisation rate, this review used the OECD-EU methodology for defining functional urban areas (FUAs) – the first time this methodology had been applied to Kazakhstan. It identified 26 FUAs, accounting for 55% of the overall population. This is close to the median population share of FUAs in OECD countries (56%). The FUA analysis thus suggests that the country's urbanisation level is not as low as indicated by the comparison of national urbanisation rates, and that Kazakhstan is not "under-urbanised" compared to OECD economies. Nevertheless, the three Kazakhstani metropolitan areas (Almaty City, Astana and Shymkent) accounted for about 23% of the overall population in Kazakhstan in 2009. The percentage of the population living in metropolitan areas is lower than in most OECD countries (48.6%) and China (59%), which leaves considerable scope for increasing the population and economic concentration in large urban centres. Urban centres are typically better connected to regional and global markets and benefit from agglomeration, which suggests that concentration in metropolitan areas could be expected to boost economic growth.

The largest cities drive urban population growth, mainly due to low-density territorial expansion

Astana, Almaty City and Shymkent are growing at a faster pace than the other 23 FUAs in Kazakhstan. From 1999 to 2009, their share of the overall population rose from 18.2% to 23.1%. Their population increased, on average, by 3.1% a year in the same period. From 2009-2014, the population of the core municipality in metropolitan areas expanded at an annual rate of 3.2%, as compared to 1.6% for the cores of medium-sized cities and 1.8% for small urban areas. Astana's impressive growth during the period corresponds with the relocation to Astana of Kazakhstan's central administrative apparatus and the headquarters of large state-owned enterprises (SOEs). Its other fastest-growing cities, in the south and west of the country, are often involved in natural resources extraction. By contrast, the population of FUAs in the northeast of Kazakhstan has stagnated or even declined. The territorial expansion of large cities is common in Kazakhstan and has been a significant factor in the growth of the urban population. Cities such as Shymkent, Almaty City and Atyrau have extended their administrative borders and absorbed neighbouring municipalities. This was considered necessary to improve transport, build social infrastructure and develop housing projects.

Government is working to revitalise single-industry towns …

As a legacy of the Soviet era, Kazakhstan has 27 single-industry towns (monotowns) focused on mining or fishing activities. These face such challenges as declining competitiveness of the main industry, poor transport connectivity, low wages, emigration of qualified personnel and a lack of formal employment opportunities. In 2012, the central government introduced measures to support economic diversification in monotowns, for example by stimulating entrepreneurship and SMEs. However, due to budget constraints, the planned policy measures were only partially implemented. Monotowns are very diverse, and the top-down, "one-size-fits-all" approach adopted so far has not provided enough flexibility to adapt policy measures to local circumstances. The government conducted a diagnosis of the economic potential of each monotown based on a single methodology and found that only two monotowns have "low economic potential." Studies of socio-economic indicators in monotowns suggest that figure is too low.

... but this strategy could be fine-tuned with updated, more realistic analysis

Kazakhstan's monotown policy could be revised to better reflect current conditions. In any case, government support to industries located in monotowns should be temporary and focused on diversifying monotowns with reasonably good long-term economic prospects. Sustained government support to the main companies in monotowns, whether direct or through cross-subsidies, has proven to be fraught with risk. Not only can it prevent a more efficient spatial distribution of workers and businesses, it can hold back the modernisation of substantial parts of the country's manufacturing sector. Targeted support to SMEs and entrepreneurship and improved transport connectivity are efficient ways to boost the economies of large and medium-sized monotowns.

Urban challenges

Urbanisation will be crucial to the country's socio-economic development, but ensuring that cities become more inclusive, sustainable and prosperous is a major national challenge. Kazakhstan and its cities are modernising, but its urban centres still have issues to address before they can achieve their full potential as the engines of economic growth.

Urban public transport is in decline

Urban transport and transit are increasingly dominated by the private automobile. Kazakhstan inherited a legacy of low car ownership and extensive, but not always cost-efficient, urban public transport from the Soviet era. However, car ownership has risen rapidly since the 2000s, with the highest motorisation rate in Almaty and Astana (428 and 385 cars per 1 000 inhabitants, respectively, in 2015). Car ownership has been increased by the high demand for private automobiles, moderate gasoline prices, road extensions and improvements in and around big cities, and the low quality of public transport services. The urban public transport modes inherited from the Soviet era (i.e. trolleybuses and tramways) are in decline. Buses, operated by individual entrepreneurs or private companies, are the dominant means of public transport in large cities, but congestion on the roads reduces their efficiency. Astana and Almaty are developing policies to improve public transport through light-rail transit systems, but these are long-term projects.

Housing stock has been expanded, but satisfaction with housing conditions is relatively low...

Since 2000, the housing stock in Kazakhstan has expanded considerably, more than doubling in Astana and Almaty. In regions with strong economic and demographic growth, such as Atyrau, Kyzylorda and Mangystau, it has been growing rapidly. The average housing space per person has increased, but inequalities in housing space per capita remain. Despite quasi-universal access to basic sanitary facilities, satisfaction with housing conditions is low; many newly built family homes are not connected to the sewage system, for instance. Since 2001, rapid population growth in large and medium-sized cities has led to a shortage of affordable housing for low-income residents, incoming migrants and even middle-class households. After the massive privatisation of housing in the 1990s, owner-occupancy is the dominant tenure in Kazakhstan, as it is in Eastern European and OECD countries. Public housing accounts for less than 4% of the overall housing stock in almost all large cities, including Astana and Almaty, whereas in

OECD countries, it accounts for 8% on average. Given the extremely limited direct public provision of housing (including social housing), the private sector is best equipped to accommodate the rising demand for affordable housing in large cities.

… house prices are rising and the rental housing market is under-developed

The 2016 economic slowdown is pushing down prices and sales volumes of affordable, smaller flats, while demand for expensive housing units has not slowed. Affordable housing is in low supply, since real house prices rose almost sixfold between 2001 and 2015, for both newly built and existing dwellings. Kazakhstan has one of the world's highest home-ownership rates (97% of the housing stock was owner-occupied in 2011). This suggests that the rental market is underdeveloped, and much renting activity is probably informal and undocumented. The weakness of the rental market limits mobility, which not only depresses economic productivity but pushes up the cost of rents.

Utility networks are outdated, and low tariffs prevent their modernisation

Kazakhstan's municipal utilities (water supply, sewage and district heating) have deteriorated rapidly since 1991. During the transition period, little or no investment was made in the maintenance and repair of municipal networks. Four-fifths of the crucial district heating network is obsolete, with high distribution heat losses and failures. The modernisation of district heating and the thermal renovation of housing units present an opportunity to increase energy efficiency and reduce greenhouse gas emissions. Around 64% of water and sanitation networks need complete repair or replacement. Insufficient metering, which does not charge for actual consumption, and low tariffs discourage utility companies from making the substantial investments required to renew and modernise the networks.

Air pollution and waste management are becoming a major health issue in large cities

Air pollution is a rising concern in Kazakhstan's large cities. The two main sources of air pollution are industrial and energy plants and individual motor vehicles. Although concentrations of particulate matter were lower in 2011 than in other upper-middle income countries, they are expected to rise quickly in large cities, given the rapidly increasing motorisation rates. Environmental monitoring systems are underfunded, and environmental statistics do not always reflect the current pollution load on the environment. Kazakhstan plans to decrease the use of coal in electricity production and rely more on gas-fuelled power plants and alternative energy sources, such as solar panels and wind farms. Municipal waste collection services do not yet cover the whole population. Often municipal solid waste is dumped in sites with few, if any, engineered environmental protection systems, creating significant risks for ground water and the environment.

Responding to urban challenges

To make Kazakhstan's development vision a reality, it is essential to get urbanisation right. Addressing a number of interrelated urban challenges – housing, land-use planning, transport, public utilities and internal migration – would help make its cities more sustainable and inclusive.

The planning system needs to be further improved

In Kazakhstan, urban planning is still limited mainly to producing urban design projects. The "General Plan" is the main document that guides the physical development of a city. It usually includes a 30-year projection and is updated as required. Every level of government has to produce one general plan. To further improve the practice of urban planning, the general plan is to be based not only on technical norms, but on a local needs assessment. Planning and budget decision-making processes should be closely linked, to facilitate implementation of the general plan. Bridging the overall information gap in the sector of urban design and land-use management would increase transparency and informed public participation; the general plans should thus be based on high-quality information and citizens' input. Moreover, government needs to i) regularly monitor and evaluate progress; ii) ensure transparency; iii) assess not only compliance with technical norms but also the local financial, human and natural resources needed for actual implementation; and iv) engage the local community.

The land-use planning system needs to be updated

Most of the key problems facing Kazakhstani cities are related to a lax land-use planning system. Urban sprawl, pollution, poor public services (e.g. utilities), housing shortages, and weak intra-city connectivity are all problems that stem from a lack of proper land-use planning and deficiencies in implementing land-use regulation. Three strategies could address these problems. First, Kazakhstan should develop a comprehensive land-use planning system to regulate the conversion of farmland to urban land and prevent urban sprawl. This would require the national government to define the authority and competences for land-use planning across the different levels of government. Second, authorities could adopt a more comprehensive system of land-use management that connects planning and implementation of closely related urban policy issues, such as economic development, social well-being, housing, utilities and transport planning. National policies on housing and public utilities should be assessed from the perspective of land use and improving urban living conditions. The integration of the land registry and Urban Zoning Registry would make urban development more efficient. Investing in good zoning practices as an instrument for effective land-use management and in the capacity of the civil servants responsible for land-use management would promote a more efficient use of land. Finally, given rapid population growth in some areas of the country, authorities could employ land-use regulations and instruments to control urban sprawl. This could be achieved by integrating housing policy with city development plans, transport policy and better land-use management. Housing policy should be aligned with efforts to develop more compact cities. Using a mix of regulatory instruments to manage urban growth is recommended, as there is no single solution for managing urban growth without some negative side-effects.

Policies are needed to bridge the housing affordability gap

Kazakhstan needs to provide affordable housing options that encourage social inclusion while promoting sustainable urban development. One option to resolve the housing shortages is to ensure that the land-use regulations are flexible and do not increase housing prices. Another option is to take an inclusionary approach to the planning system, developing programmes or regulations that require or encourage private developers to include affordable or social housing in market-driven development. Affordable housing could be included in the same development or built elsewhere, or money or land could be set aside to build affordable housing. Such options should be feasible in Kazakhstan, as the private sector plays an important role in housing. However, it would require cities to develop the skills and resources in the local public administration to negotiate with developers to assess how viable the projects are.

Equally important is allocating affordable housing – that is, deciding between a broad-based or targeted system of social housing. Since demand for social housing has increased and the overall stock is limited, authorities may need to assess eligibility criteria frequently to free up social housing for needier households.

Expanding the rental market is another way of improving housing affordability. Options Kazakhstan could consider would include the design and implementation of a national rental housing policy, a revision of the regulatory framework to balance out the treatment of property owners and tenants, and offering tax incentives for rental properties. Housing projects should also prioritise safety considerations.

Land use, transport and investment should be linked

Ensuring sustainable, accessible modes of urban transport is a challenge for Kazakhstan's cities. Part of the problem is the lack of a strategic approach to planning and managing urban transport. To address this, authorities could clarify the role of cities in transport and housing planning and reinforce their technical capacities. In planning land use and new housing, cities should be required to consider the mobility and accessibility needs of future inhabitants, as well as the impact of new housing developments on traffic flows and mobility for the city as a whole. Authorities need to integrate the planning of land use, transport and other urban infrastructure, which will require shifting from the current ad hoc, technical, solution-driven planning to a broad, network-based, strategy-driven approach. To achieve this, Kazakhstan needs to improve the capacity for cross-sectoral planning. One solution would be to create urban planning institutes, alongside existing academic institutions, carefully considering their ownership and sources of funding. The advantage of urban planning institutes is that they work on a variety of topics with multidisciplinary teams. In addition, ensuring co-ordination across departments within the city *akimats* and promoting co-operation with other levels of government could facilitate more comprehensive planning. Cities could establish public-private partnerships and adopt a more commercial approach to the financing of transport projects.

The infrastructure and management of public utilities need to be reinforced

Public utilities are one of the major urban and investment challenges for authorities in Kazakhstan, since dated and inadequate infrastructure is a common feature of urban centres. Clear priorities could be established for programmes to rehabilitate municipal infrastructure, and financial modes must be found to support the utilities sector. The national government may conduct a reform of the sector, for example by giving local authorities the possibility to adopt tools that improve the management of existing infrastructure assets and allowing them to consider whether to contract out the running of public utilities to the private sector. Nonetheless, it is important to limit opportunities for abuse (e.g. high prices for consumers and poor service) and maintain sufficient incentives for investment. To ensure financing for maintenance and expansion, the private sector may be encouraged to participate in public utilities through public-private partnerships (PPPs). But this would make it necessary to build adequate capacity and experience in the utilities sector at subnational levels of government. Moreover, reform in the public utilities sector would need to ensure energy efficiency in construction. An Energy Building Code or minimum mandatory energy-efficiency standards or requirements for building components and equipment could be adopted to improve energy efficiency in new and old buildings alike.

Internal migration should be encouraged

In contrast to the Soviet period, the citizens of independent Kazakhstan enjoy greater freedom of movement. However, although residence permits are not required to obtain a job in a location that is not the employee's official place of residence, key public services (schools, the public health system, access to targeted social assistance and employment centres) in Kazakhstan are provided to people only in the district where they are formally registered. Moreover, the lack of adequate planning for migration has resulted in the emergence of squatter settlements, traffic congestion, urban poor and urban sprawl. It is important that Kazakhstani authorities recognise that internal migration can help to build the urban economy. Migrants to the cities may not all be highly educated, but the diversity of skills and competencies they bring to the urban economy is necessary for its development. A comprehensive migration policy and legislation could help cities prepare for and respond to emerging problems. Developing a system in Kazakhstan that makes it easier for migrants to register, and that allows for accurate data on migration flows for urban planning, should be a top priority. This could be done by using citizens' identification numbers rather than their registration status as the basis for access to public services.

Meeting the governance challenges of urbanisation in Kazakhstan

Urbanisation can be one of Kazakhstan's major assets for development, but this will require adjustments to existing institutions, state budgets, and administrative and cultural practices. Strengthening the public administration of subnational governments will be central to "getting cities right".

Subnational governments are politically, administratively and financially weak

As is typical of many countries in the region, local authorities in Kazakhstan have no clear division of functions, powers, competencies and responsibilities. Intergovernmental relations are based on hierarchical subordination of lower levels of government, so that the level immediately above exercises considerable influence over local decisions. This is evident both in the appointment of *akims* by the upper executive power and the degree of dependence on transfers from the upper level of government. Efforts to reform the intergovernmental structure have led to a significant deconcentration of administrative functions to subnational levels of government. In practice, the central government has delegated some authority and responsibility to subnational levels, but local units are still fully accountable to the central government ministry or agency. No incentives are in place to encourage horizontal co-ordination among cities or among regions. The governance arrangements – whether budgetary, administrative or political – prevent cities from working together on projects that could lead to economies of scale.

Increasing subnational governments' democratic basis can enhance urbanisation and decentralisation

Efforts to improve urban governance should focus on strengthening local self-governments and integrating urban communities into the decision-making process for urban development projects. One key to this process will be to give local *maslikhats* more responsibility for oversight of the *akim* and the local administration, making them more accountable to the public. Election of rural *akims* could be one positive step for strengthening local self-government, but this could be expanded to include the election, rather than the appointment, of *akimats* at all levels (including those of Astana and Almaty City). OECD countries' experience shows that such reforms could increase local governments' responsiveness to citizens through democratic institutions. Further decentralisation would give subnational governments more freedom to solve their own problems. One option would be an asymmetric approach to decentralisation, under which the central government devolves responsibilities to subnational governments, which may be better qualified to assume duties in certain sectors. Decentralisation could help SNGs assume control over the resources they administer and become more accountable to citizens. This needs to be a flexible process that allows the central/local dynamics to evolve. However, a clear plan for its implementation should be designed, with defined roles for the various management levels and linkages between them. Introducing co-ordination mechanisms among cities could facilitate joint investments and enhance metropolitan planning.

Kazakhstan lacks a framework for urban development

Urban development in Kazakhstan does not yet benefit from an overall vision for integrating economic, social, environmental and physical development policies. A comprehensive strategic document could help establish the priorities of urbanisation, the role cities will play in the development process and the institutional processes that will enable cities to build on their assets and potential to achieve long-term sustainability. Second, urban development is still largely based on sectoral plans. The Regional Development Programme for urbanisation policy is mostly a collection of existing sectoral policies. Lastly, the lack of co-ordination between central agencies responsible for urban development was exacerbated by administrative issues, since the Ministry of Regional Development was merged into the Ministry of National Economy just one year after its creation. This meant that urban and regional development issues were not given adequate consideration in the political agenda and in citizens' perception.

Urban development in Kazakhstan requires direction, co-ordination and data to inform decision-making

Kazakhstan could benefit from an urbanisation policy framework that clearly formulates a strategy for urban and spatial development aligned with the New Urban Agenda and the UN Sustainable Development Goals, in particular Goal 11, on "making cities inclusive, safe, resilient and sustainable". This would require increasing the authority of local authorities at the *oblast*, *rayon* and even town levels, which could co-ordinate investment to cities to promote growth. Kazakhstan needs to diversify the mechanisms for horizontal co-ordination (i.e. ministerial posts for cross-cutting issues, and rotations of government managers) at the central level for urban policy. Authorities might consider creating a Ministry for Urban and Regional Development charged with linking urban and regional policy objectives to broader governmental goals.

To facilitate cross-sectoral planning for urban development, each sector needs a comprehensive understanding of the other sectors' roles, responsibilities, legal authorities and assets. High-level committees, working groups or bilateral partnerships could be established, and the establishment of a National Urban and Regional Development Co-ordination Council could communicate top-level strategies on regional and urban development among ministries. Platforms for sharing best practices and promoting regional/urban development among subnational government authorities (i.e. an association of cities) might also be set up. Strengthening accountability for urban development is critical to shape incentives for collaboration and joint action. Developing policy proposals on collective ministerial responsibility could serve the public interest, so that it is possible to work across institutional lines to develop the best possible policy. To promote sustainable and inclusive urban development, Kazakhstan needs to improve the efficiency of data collection at the city level and provide reliable quantitative analysis of urban issues.

Cities have limited financial resources for urbanisation

The financing of public services in Kazakhstan is left to intergovernmental transfers and vertical programmes. This leaves SNGs with few internal financial resources and a lack of incentives to develop their own tax base. SNGs receive all kinds of transfers, including: intergovernmental grants, subsidies, donations and sharing of tax revenues. The most important taxes go to the central government's budget and are distributed to regional governments. Revenue that exceeds the forecast expenditure of a local budget is reallocated to the central government. Local governments do not have independent authority to determine tax rates or the basis for taxation. Because the tax receipts allocated to SNGs are stable, local authorities are unable to exert much influence over their own budget revenue. The amount of tax accruing to local budgets depends only indirectly on the extent of production and entrepreneurship, investment capacity or restructuring of regional economies. This limits their freedom to increase self-generated revenue. There are strict limits on borrowing by SNGs, and they can only borrow from the budget of the next government level. Astana and Almaty City are now allowed to issue bonds to cover budget deficits.

A fairer and flexible public financial system is needed to support urbanisation

The intergovernmental transfer system needs to be restructured to support a metropolitan strategy and monitoring earmarked grants in implementing national urban objectives. To reduce the level of dependence on transfers from higher levels of government, certain taxes could be allocated to the local level. Moreover, more efficient and clearer property taxation in rural and urban areas is essential. This will require reform of the property tax, so that SNGs, in particular cities, can benefit from increased revenue. Including rural land in this tax reform could also help villages and towns provide public services. Modernising the cadastre would be one way to increase property tax revenue. More options for borrowing are needed, so that SNGs can finance urban infrastructure, under the strict supervision of the national government.

The existing system of local finances does not encourage accountability in ensuring public service delivery. Fiscal decentralisation has been uneven: expenditure has been decentralised, but revenue has not. To build a financial system that supports urbanisation, the *maslikhats* should be able to encourage *akimats* to discuss urban development and a region or city's economic challenges in an open and informative manner. A clear assignment of budget responsibilities across levels of government should be made a priority, to increase efficiency and accountability. This would make it possible to assess the adequacy of the revenue and tax assignment to different levels of government and the need for a system of intergovernmental transfers. Avoiding an unwieldy mix of deconcentration and decentralisation of government activities is recommended. Careful review of how responsibilities are assigned in an adequately decentralised system of governance is also important, so that responsibility for the provision of services can be allocated to the lowest level of government appropriate to the area served.

Strengthening local governments' capacity requires strategic management of the public workforce

SNGs have a large share of the public workforce, much of which is under-skilled. They have little freedom to adapt their workforce to local needs. Local public administrations need to improve public servants' technical expertise and managerial capacity. A civil service reform has been instituted to create a "career-based system" at all levels of government, to professionalise the state apparatus. The aim is to give every citizen with the potential and skills an opportunity to enter into the civil service. Promotions are to be granted based on competition among internal candidates, who are given preference over external candidates.

To complement the current reform efforts, Kazakhstan needs to invest in capacity for strategic workforce planning, so that it can maintain a workforce of an appropriate size to meet the changing needs of the public service in general in a cost-efficient manner. To help SNGs adapt their workforce to better meet their needs, the central government could grant them authority over human resource management, to increase managerial flexibility and improve performance and responsiveness. This could include determining and managing pay levels. A performance management system, bearing in mind that effective performance depends on the contributions of activities at all levels, could be linked to the strategic goals of organisations and government as a whole. Possible options would be to enhance the training and skills of central and subnational civil servants; establish a periodic rotation of public employees to broaden their experience; define clear career paths and job categories; and ensure equal opportunity.

Citizens should be partners in the urbanisation process

Although authorities in Kazakhstan seem to be aware of the importance of public participation in developing the urban environment, opportunities for citizens to participate in planning decisions are limited. The issues can be highly technical, civil servants have no training in community engagement, and citizens are wary and not always engaged. National and subnational authorities may wish to promote more participatory urban planning processes, in which citizens participate in forums, public hearings or offer their opinions by mail or online. This should be part of the process of strengthening local self-governments and enhancing transparency. Free access to meetings of the *akimats* and *maslikhats* could be one way to build trust and inform citizens. Making public deliberation a key component of urban planning allows those concerned some influence over the decision process. Local communities need to be given a variety of tools to participate in resolutions adopted by the local authorities, but it is important to ensure that citizens' participation does not become an obstacle to urban projects. *Akimats* could help ensure that citizens have timely access to clear and reliable information on urban development plans.

Chapter 1

Kazakhstan's urban system and its challenges

This chapter provides an overview of the main trends and challenges of urban areas in Kazakhstan, with particular emphasis on the functional urban areas providing a new picture of urban agglomerations in the country. Specifically this chapter addresses: i) *the main features of the urban structure of the country;* ii) *the moderate pace of urbanisation at the start of the 21st century;* iii) *the range of policy challenges facing cities in areas such as housing, public urban transport, public utilities and migration; and* iv) *the opportunities to foster innovation in cities.*

Introduction

After 70 years of Soviet rule, Kazakhstan emerged as an independent nation in 1991. A disruptive period of transition ensued between 1991 and 2000 as it progressed from a centrally planned economy to a market-based economy. In the first decade of the 21st century, Kazakhstan experienced sustained economic and demographic growth. Economic growth was on average 8% per year from 2000 to 2013, before slowing to 4.2% in 2014 and to 1.2% in 2015 (Committee of Statistics, 2016a), propelled by the oil and gas sector. Between 2000 and 2005, this sector accounted for half of GDP growth, but domestic demand and services have been the main drivers since 2010. Positive developments in manufacturing, notably transport equipment, chemicals and pharmaceuticals, and knowledge-intensive services also played a part, but the overall size of the manufacturing sector remains small. This sector employs about 5% of the labour force and generates 11% of GDP, a relatively low level by comparison with both emerging economies and advanced resource-rich countries (OECD, 2016a). Overall, extractive industries still make up a large share of value added, and the majority of exports and foreign direct investments to Kazakhstan. The oil and gas sector alone still generates around 30% of GDP. Another key feature of Kazakhstan's economy is the high percentage of employment in agriculture, which accounts for 24% of the workforce, but only 5% of GDP. Shifting labour to more productive sectors could raise GDP per capita by some 30%, but would require boosting public, private and foreign investment (OECD, 2016a).

Kazakhstan is the ninth-largest country in the world, with an area of 2.74 million km^2. It has low population density and a dispersed settlement pattern, with fewer densely populated areas than most OECD countries (OECD, 2017a, forthcoming). Developing a well-managed system of large and medium-size cities is thus of paramount importance for the country's economic development. The three largest urban agglomerations are identified as key drivers of future demographic and economic growth in Kazakhstan's "Regional Development Programme Until 2020" (Government of Kazakhstan, 2014). This is an integral part of "Strategy 2050", the government's long-term development agenda, whose goal is to make Kazakhstan one of the 30 most developed countries in the world by 2050.

With an urban population of 55.6% at the end of 2014, Kazakhstan is the most urbanised country in post-Soviet Central Asia, where the typical share is around 40% of the overall population. Urbanisation rates are not directly comparable across countries, however. An analysis of functional urban areas (FUAs) suggests that, while urbanisation in Kazakhstan is close to that of most OECD countries, Kazakhstan stands out because of its small population share living in *metropolitan areas* (large urban agglomerations of more than 500 000 people).

Overall, the pace of urbanisation in Kazakhstan has been relatively slow by comparison with worldwide trends. In 1990, the year before independence, around 43% of the world's population lived in cities; by 2014, that figure had risen to 54% (United Nations, 2015). For that period, Kazakhstan's urbanisation rate was almost stable (rising from 54.8% to 55.6%, according to OECD estimates),[1] largely because of the economic recession and emigration of the 1990s. The bulk of urban growth in Kazakhstan's history occurred before 1990, during the Soviet era (Figure 1.1). According to official statistics, from 2001 onwards, the urban population has also grown faster than the rural population in every year but 2005.[2] But even during this more recent period, the rate of urbanisation process appears to have been slower than in most other middle-income countries like China and Turkey.

The Soviet central planning system shaped the urban system that Kazakhstan inherited in 1991. City location and growth, and related infrastructure development, were largely determined by the growth of extractive industries and, to a lesser extent, the needs of the agricultural economy. The exploitation of mineral resources and the creation of petroleum, chemical, metallurgy and coal industries were drivers of urbanisation, leading to the creation of "monotowns" (single-enterprise towns) such as Ekibastuz, Rudny, Temirtau, Kentau and Karatau (CER, ESCAP, UNDP, 2013). After 1991, the dismantling of many elements of the Soviet system (including the compulsory work placement of young graduates, heavily subsidised transport and energy tariffs) reshaped Kazakhstan's urban system, concentrating population in large cities.

Figure 1.1. **Urbanisation rate, Kazakhstan and selected countries (1950-2015)**

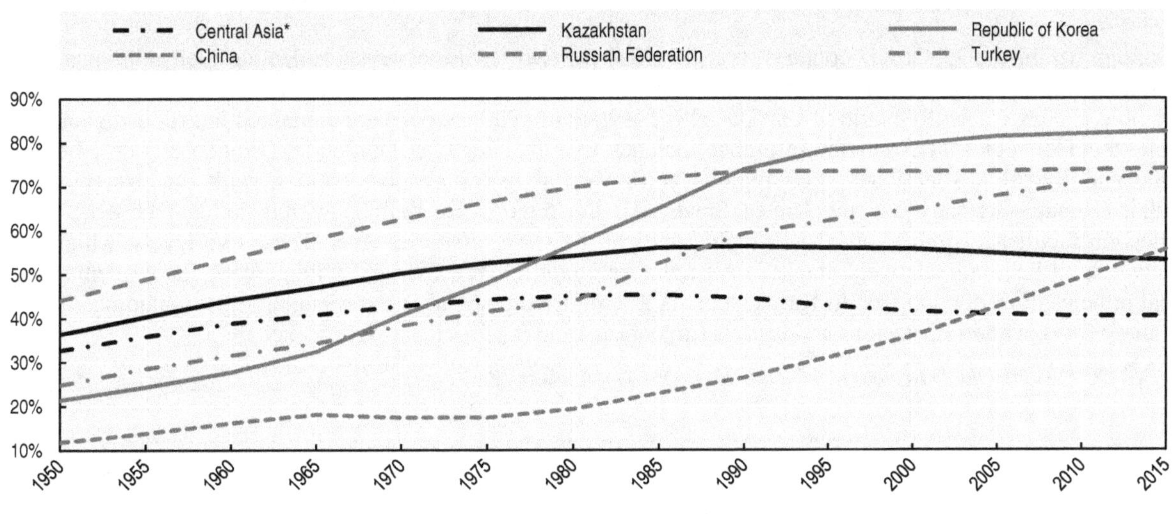

Note: * Central Asia comprises Kazakhstan, Kyrgyzstan, Tajikistan, Turkmenistan and Uzbekistan.

Source: UNDESA (2014), "World Urbanization Prospects: The 2014 Revision", United Nations Department of Economic and Social Affairs, June, https://esa.un.org/unpd/wup/ (accessed September 2016).

This chapter considers Kazakhstan's urban structure and recent urbanisation trends, including the dynamic growth of the country's largest urban agglomerations. Along with official data based on the administrative definition of urban areas, it introduces the functional urban areas (FUAs), which offer a new picture of its urban agglomerations, based on settlement patterns and travel-to-work commuting flows. This chapter then reviews the links between urbanisation and economic growth and key economic challenges related to cities (including single-industry towns and attracting foreign investments). It also reviews Kazakhstan's main urban challenges (urban mobility, housing, municipal utilities, air quality and municipal solid waste) and the links between economic growth, urbanisation and innovation.

Kazakhstan's urban structure

An administration based on three layers of subnational government

An analysis of urbanisation in Kazakhstan requires a basic understanding of the definition of urban and rural areas. City definitions vary widely across countries, because they are often based on political and historical criteria, as well as current policy priorities. A large urban area may consist of many subnational governments (SNGs), most often municipalities. In contrast, city boundaries sometimes extend well beyond dense urban population clusters. This is typically the case in Kazakhstan. Among the country's three metropolitan areas (Almaty City, Shymkent and Astana), only Almaty City (with 2 402 inhabitants per km^2)[3] had a higher density than the median of city cores in OECD metropolitan areas (1 474 inhabitants per km^2). Using built-up areas rather than statutory cities, Angel (2012) finds that Almaty City's density is in the medium range of large city densities worldwide, and lower than large city densities in most developing countries.

Box 1.1. **The OECD territorial classification of Kazakhstan**

Regions within the 35 OECD countries are classified on two territorial levels reflecting their administrative organisation. The 391 large (TL2) OECD regions represent the first administrative tier of subnational government, for example, the province of Ontario in Canada. The 2 197 small (TL3) regions are contained in a TL2 region. For example, the TL2 region of Aquitaine in France includes five TL3 regions: Dordogne, Gironde, Landes, Lot-et-Garonne and Pyrénées-Atlantiques. TL3 regions correspond to administrative entities, with the exception of Australia, Canada, Germany and the United States. All the regions are defined within national borders. This classification facilitates comparison of geographic units at the same territorial level. These two levels, which are officially established and relatively stable in all member countries, are used as a framework for implementing regional policies in most countries. In Kazakhstan, TL2 regions correspond to the regional level (including Astana and Almaty City), while TL3 regions are districts (rayons) and cities of regional significance.

Source: OECD (2016c), *OECD Regions at a Glance 2016*, OECD Publishing, Paris, http://dx.doi.org/10.1787/reg_glance-2016-en.

Table 1.1. **Territorial organisation in Kazakhstan (2016)**

	Regional level (TL2)	**District level (TL3)**	**Municipal level**
Unitary country (2016)	14 regions (*oblast*) and 2 cities of republican significance (Astana and Almaty city)	38 large "cities of *regional* significance"[1] 177 districts (*rayons*) (17 city districts and 160 rural districts)[2]	47 smaller "cities of district significance" 2 372 villages, rural communities and settlements (*selki okrug i posiolki*) and 26 urban settlements (*gorodskie posiolki*)
	16	**215**	**2 445**

1. Cities of regional significance have district-level administrative status and prerogatives, in addition to municipal-level tasks and prerogatives.
2. The four largest cities of Kazakhstan, Almaty City, Shymkent, Astana and Karaganda, are divided into city districts that are subdivisions of the municipal administration.

Source: OECD/UCLG (2016), "Subnational governments around the world: Structure and finance", www.uclg-localfinance.org/sites/default/files/Observatory_web_0.pdf, and Committee on Statistics of the Republic of Kazakhstan.

In Kazakhstan, the definition of urban areas is based on the 1993 Law "On Administrative and Territorial Structure of the Republic of Kazakhstan" (herein referred to as the 1993 Law), which gives urban status to the 87 Kazakhstani cities, as well as to 30 urban settlements (*posiolki*) in the vicinity of cities. As of 1 January 2016, Kazakhstan had 2 676 subnational governments (SNGs), constituting three layers of territorial administration (see Table 1.1 above).

One noteworthy feature of the system is the way in which the administration of cities fits into this scheme. Depending on population and political power, cities are placed in three levels:

- The regional (*oblast*) level includes 14 regions and the two main cities of Almaty City and Astana, defined as "cities of republican significance". Both cities enjoy a unique administrative position, since they enjoy the prerogatives of the regional, district and municipal levels.
- The district (*rayon*) level includes 170 rural districts, 38 cities of regional (*oblast*) significance, and 17 urban districts (Table 1.1). These cities, the largest in the country, enjoy district-level administrative capacity. The 1993 Law defines them as "major economic centres with a developed industrial and social infrastructure and a population higher than 50 000".
- The municipal level includes the 47 smaller cities defined as "cities of district significance" and 2 372 municipal entities, which sometimes group several rural settlements (*aul or selo*).

Article 3 of the 1993 Law "On the Administrative and Territorial Structure of the Republic of Kazakhstan" defines which type of settlement can be considered urban. Under this definition, urban areas are cities and some settlements (*posiolki*) located in the vicinity of large cities:

- Cities are settlements with at least 10 000 inhabitants and at least two-thirds of whose population employed outside the agricultural sector, i.e. as employees or factory workers.
- Settlements (*posiolki*) are small towns of at least 3 000 inhabitants, at least two-thirds of whose population is employed outside the agricultural sector, i.e. as employees or factory workers. Some settlements (*posiolki*) are considered urban if they are located on the territory of a city administration, usually in the vicinity of a major city (Box 1.2).

Box 1.2. **Cities and city administrations in Kazakhstan**

The 38 cities of regional significance have district-level administrative status, which corresponds to the second tier of subnational government (TL3) in the OECD classification. Of these, 32 have an administrative territory covering the city proper and the surrounding areas, including rural villages and urban settlements (*gorodskie posiolki*). This enlarged administrative territory (distinct from the city itself) is known as the "city administration" (*gorodskoï adkimat or G.A.).* The city mayor (*akim)* and his administration have the same responsibilities towards these areas as district (*rayon*) *akims* have in their district.

"City administrations" are not strictly equivalent to cities, since they include rural settlements surrounding the central city. Besides, they are highly heterogeneous: some include only around a thousand inhabitants in addition to the central's city population, while others extend to vast territories comprising dozens of settlements and up to 20 000 inhabitants (in the case of Ekibastuz*)* in addition to their central city.

Source: OECD research.

Administration status often no longer matches demographic realities

In the last 25 years, the administrative-territorial structure of Kazakhstan has not been fully updated to take into account recent social and demographic trends. Official population data for large cities are unreliable and underestimate the real number of the urban population in large cities, because many internal and external migrants live in big cities without being officially registered (Box 1.3). This discrepancy between official demographic statistics, on the one hand, and social and demographic trends on the other, could present issues for the effective provision of public services. Since budget transfers are based on official population numbers, some large cities whose population has been underestimated may not receive enough funding for public services and to cope with the growing burden on urban infrastructure.

Box 1.3. **Large city population and internal migrants: A downward bias**

In Kazakhstan, the Committee on Statistics gathers data on internal migration and on the urban population, based on official registration data collected by the migration police of the Ministry of Interior. According to the Law "On Migration", internal migrants must register at their new place of residence. In practice, however, as noted in the last Global Assessment of the statistical system of Kazakhstan by the UN Economic Commissions (UNECE and UNESCAP, 2008), "the registration accuracy of migrants is problematic".

The main issue is that many internal migrants live and work in cities without going through the registration procedure (Zimovina, 2009). According to an independent research survey conducted in Almaty City in 2012, 54% of young internal migrants (aged 15-29) were registered in the city (Makhmutova, 2012). Internal migrants face many hurdles before they can register in large cities: they must present a property title for their place of residence or involve their landlords. Landlords usually refuse to become involved in the burdensome procedure of registering their tenants, given the largely informal nature of Kazakhstan's rental market. In addition, registration of citizens living in informal housing units is not possible.

Field research confirmed that local *akims* (mayors) in large cities are aware of the underestimation of actual population in the official statistics, and sometimes refer to alternative (unofficial) population data. For instance, the *akim* of Astana recently recognised that many of Astana's current inhabitants are unregistered and therefore not accounted for in official statistics. While Astana's population was officially set at 880 000 at the beginning of 2016, according to Astana's *akim*, local hospitals serve around 940 000 people, and around one million people are commuting across the city.[1]

Little information is available on the extent of this undercounting of the urban population, which may vary from one city to another. Unofficial population estimates exist for large cities such as Astana, Almaty City and Shymkent. A systemic underestimation of actual population by official statistics in large urban centres has many potential adverse consequences. City and regional *administrations* need accurate population figures to plan for urban development and local services such as schools, hospitals and public transport. Moreover, current budgetary transfers to cities from higher levels of governments are to a large extent based on official demographic statistics. The discrepancies between official and actual population may compromise the allocation of budgetary transfers, probably in favour of smaller towns or rural areas. Indeed, internal migrants living (sometimes temporarily) in large cities are often still registered in their previous place of residence, which are typically smaller towns or rural areas.

1. See "Isekeshev ob"jasnil pojavlenie v Astane millionnogo zhitelja", Tengri news, available (in Russian) at https://tengrinews.kz/kazakhstan_news/isekeshev-obyyasnil-poyavlenie-v-astane-millionnogo-jitelya-298163/.

Sources: UNECE, UNESCAP (2008), Global Assessment Report of the statistical system of Kazakhstan, January 2008, www.unece.org/fileadmin/DAM/stats/documents/technical_co-op/GA_Kazakhstan_EN.pdf; Zimovina (2009), "Processy urbanizacii v Kazahstane v postsovetskij period i ih demograficheskaja sostavljajushhaja", *Demoskop Weekly*, Moscow, available (in Russian) at: www.demoscope.ru/weekly/2009/0363/analit02.php; OECD field research.

Since January 2016, Kazakhstan has officially listed 87 cities. However, the urban status does not always reflect current demographic realities. The legal criterion for defining urban status (population thresholds, share of factory workers and employees) are not systematically implemented. In many cases, the urban status reflects more the legacy of the Soviet past than current socio-economic realities. For instance, in 14 cities the population is under the 10 000 threshold (three cities have even less than 5 000 inhabitants). By contrast, 14 settlements (*posiolki*) have a population level of more than 10 000 inhabitants and five have more than 20 000 inhabitants. Of these last five settlements, only two have urban status, because they are located on the City Administrations (Aralsk and Kyzylorda) (Table 1.2).

The problem is that the official urbanisation rate is used to determine budget transfers from the national budget to regions (TL2 level) budgets, and subsequently from regions to districts and cities of regional significance. An urbanisation coefficient is applied to reflect the higher relative costs of public service delivery in urban areas regarding certain expenditure items, such as municipal utilities or health care (Ministry of National Economy, 2014). Thus, if the official urbanisation rate no longer reflects socio-demographic realities, it can arguably have a negative influence on budget transfers received by regions and districts where urbanisation is underestimated by official statistics.

Table 1.2. **Settlements (*posiolki*) with more than 20 000 inhabitants, 2016**

Name	Population	Proximity to next larger city	Administrative status	Part of
Ajteke bi	40 747	Isolated	Rural	Kazalinsk district
Zachagansk	36 300	2 km from Uralsk	Urban	Uralsk City Administration
Zatobolsk	24 513	3 km from Kostanay	Rural	Zatobolsk district
Tasbuget	24 415	9 km from Kyzylorda	Urban	Kyzylorda City Administration
Otegen batyra	21 275	3 km from Almaty city	Rural	Ilïiski district

Source: Committee on Statistics of the Republic of Kazakhstan (2016b), Demographic database, available (in Russian) at: www.stat.gov.kz/faces/wcnav_externalId/homeNumbersPopulation?_adf.ctrlstate=u5ioriyfd_4&_afrLoop=1653212230005672 (accessed 16 November 2016).

As with urban and rural status, the legal definition of cities of regional significance (i.e. a population of more than 50 000 inhabitants) is not always implemented in practice. For instance, four cities that have been undergoing rapid population decline in the 1990s are still designated as having regional significance, despite populations of well below 50 000. On the other hand, two cities with high population growth in recent years, whose population exceeds this threshold, were not granted regional significance (Kaskelen and Kulsary). As noted in Chapter 3, cities of regional significance have more administrative capacity than others (i.e. they have their own local administration), because they are on the district rather than the municipal level. The lack of administrative and budgetary capacity can potentially hold back their urban growth. The government may thus consider granting them regional significance in the near future.

Box 1.4. **Urban statistics in this Review and in Kazakhstan**

In the context of this Review, data on city population use both functional urban areas (FUAs) and statutory (administrative) cities. The data available is limited: population and employment data at the municipal level are available only for the last census years, and population data on FUAs only for 2009 and 1999. Any analysis using FUAs will thus clearly mention it. When not noted otherwise, city population and other city-level data in this chapter refer to statutory (administrative) cities. It may be noted that the core cities of Kazakhstan's FUAs are also statutory (administrative) cities.

In Kazakhstan, official statistics for units below the regional level (TL2) are sparse. Many indicators, such as the poverty rate (defined as the percentage of households with income below the national minimum living standard), are not available at the TL3 level (districts, or *rayons*, and cities of regional significance). More importantly, little data is available for the 2 445 municipalities (Table 1.1). No surface aerial data covering all municipalities is available.

More statistical information at district and municipal levels is needed both for international benchmarking and for the data users on the ground, such as local administrations. This is an urgent issue, because the national government plans to expand the responsibilities of the municipal level of government, but few territorial statistics are available at this level to assist local authorities in assessing or designing policies.

Source: OECD Research.

Municipal fragmentation is not significantly higher than the OECD average

The number of municipalities in Kazakhstan has increased by 5.3% since 2001, thanks to an increase in the number of rural municipalities. However, since 2009, municipal mergers have taken place both in rural and urban areas, and the number of municipalities is gradually dropping. Given Kazakhstan's size, the area of its average municipality is 10 965 km^2, higher than that of any OECD country except Australia. As part of efforts to strengthen the capacity of this lower tier of public administration, the government plans to promote more municipal mergers, mainly in rural areas (President of Kazakhstan, 2012). In 2009, the average population of a municipality in Kazakhstan was 1 724 inhabitants, a low range for OECD countries.[4] However, municipal fragmentation (as measured by the average number of municipalities per 100 000 inhabitants) is only slightly higher than the OECD average for 2015/2016. Box 1.5 briefly presents OECD country experience of municipal mergers.

Box 1.5. **Municipal mergers: experiences from OECD countries and China**

Municipal mergers have been adopted in some OECD countries (e.g. Denmark, Finland, Greece, Iceland, the Netherlands, Norway and Sweden) to reduce the number of municipalities and increase their area and population. China has also been moving towards administrative consolidation, especially in the lower tiers of government, where two or three (or more) towns have been merged to become a district, and counties merged into cities. In China, the primary motivation was to increase the pace of urbanisation. This is a positive step towards amalgamation of subnational authorities, which may have an impact in the reduction of costs associated with public service delivery, especially within a single functional urban area (FUA).

Source: OECD (2015a), *OECD Urban Policy Reviews: China 2015*, OECD Publishing, Paris, http://dx.doi.org/10.1787/9789264230040-en; OECD (2014a), *OECD Regional Outlook 2014: Regions and Cities: Where Policies and People Meet*, OECD Publishing, Paris, http://dx.doi.org/10.1787/9789264201415-en.

Figure 1.2. **Average number of municipalities per 100 000 inhabitants (2015-16)**

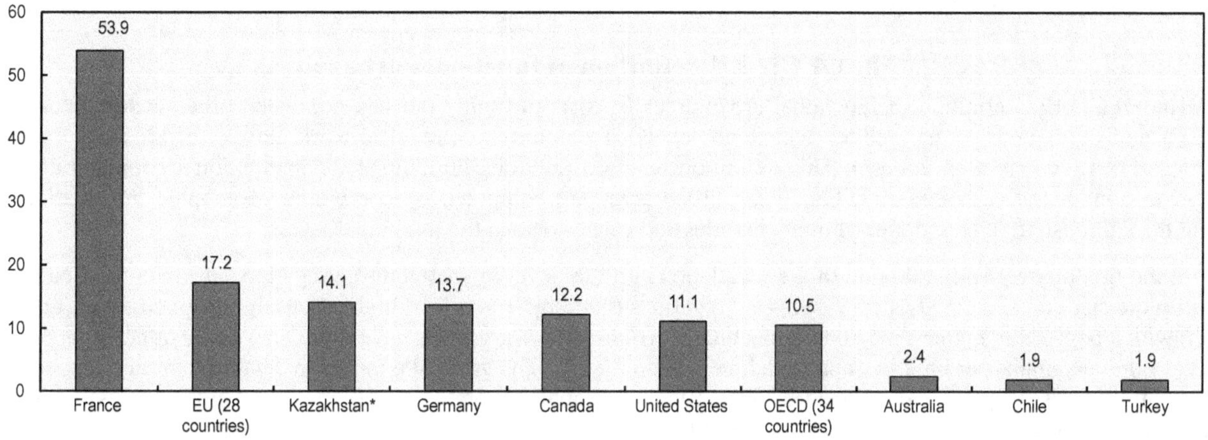

Note: * Municipalities comprise cities, rural communities (*selki okrug*) and urban and rural settlements (*posiolki*) with their own local *akim*.

Source: OECD (2016d), "Subnational governments in OECD countries: Key data" (brochure), OECD, Paris, www.oecd.org/regional/regional-policy; Committee on Statistics of the Republic of Kazakhstan (2016b), Demographic database, available (in Russian) at: www.stat.gov.kz/faces/wcnav_externalId/homeNumbersPopulation?_adf.ctrlstate=u5ioriyfd_4&_afrLoop=1653212230005672.

In considering further municipal mergers in urban areas or around large cities, the functional urban areas (FUAs) defined in this chapter can provide useful insights. Municipalities inside the same FUA typically need to co-ordinate policies at the level of the entire urban agglomeration, and excessive municipal fragmentation should thus be avoided.

Redefining urban agglomerations in Kazakhstan: functional urban areas (FUAs)

To provide a meaningful comparison of Kazakhstan's urbanisation level with OECD countries and to correct for some of the drawbacks of the official urbanisation rate (i.e. urban status sometimes does not reflect current demographic trends), this Review applies the OECD-EU methodology to define FUAs in Kazakhstan for the first time (Boxes 1.6 and 1.7). The methodology identifies urban areas as functional economic units, with densely inhabited city cores (i.e. central cities) and commuting zones whose labour market is highly integrated with the city cores. The FUAs define urban areas as functional economic units (rather than using official administrative boundaries): this can guide Kazakhstan's national authorities; regional and city administrations to better plan infrastructure, transport (particularly public passenger transport), housing and schools, as well as space for culture and recreation. Indeed, FUAs are the unit best suited to public services provided for the entire urban agglomeration.

Applying the OECD-EU methodology to Kazakhstan (with some minor adaptations, see Box 1.6), it is possible to identify 26 FUAs (Figure 1.3) that accounted for 54.5% of the overall population in 2009, which includes both the urban and rural population that live within the commuting zones of the 26 city cores. This is close to the median population share of FUAs in OECD countries (56%, see Figure 1.4). In 12 OECD countries, the FUA share of overall population is lower than in Kazakhstan. This suggests that Kazakhstan's urbanisation level is not as low as suggested by the comparison of national urbanisation rates,[5] and runs counter to the view that Kazakhstan is "under-urbanised" by comparison with most developed economies.

Box 1.6. **The OECD-EU definition of functional urban areas**

The OECD-EU definition of functional urban areas consists of highly densely populated urban centres ("city cores") and contiguous municipalities with high levels of commuting (travel-to-work flows) towards the core municipalities ("commuting zones"). This definition resolves previous limitations for international comparability linked to administrative boundaries. Functional urban areas are computed by combining geographic information about the administrative boundaries of municipalities and census data at the municipal level.

In the first phase, the distribution of the population at a fine level of spatial disaggregation – 1 km2 – is used to identify the city cores, defined as contiguous aggregations ("urban clusters") of highly densely inhabited areas (grid cells) with a population higher than 50 000 inhabitants. High-density grid cells have more than 1 500 inhabitants per km2 (1 000 inhabitants per km2 in Canada and the United States). The gridded population data used in this first step is from the Landscan project developed by Oak Ridge National Laboratory in Tennessee (United States). Core municipalities corresponding to these city cores are identified.

In a second phase, the commuting zones of these internationally comparable city cores are defined using information on travel-to work commuting flows from surrounding municipalities. Municipalities sending 15% of their resident employed population or more to the core are included in the commuting zones, which thus can be defined as the "worker catchment area" of the urban labour market, outside the densely inhabited core. The size of the commuting zones relative to the size of the core give a clear indication of cities' influence on surrounding areas.

In a third and last step, municipalities surrounded by a single functional area are included as part of the functional urban area, whereas isolated, non-contiguous municipalities (i.e. municipalities that are part of the commuting zone but geographically isolated from the rest of the FUA) are excluded.

The definition is applied to 30 OECD countries (of the OECD countries, data is not available for Iceland, Israel, New Zealand and Turkey) and identifies 1 198 urban areas of different sizes. Among them, 281 metropolitan areas (including 81 large metropolitan areas of more than 1.5 million inhabitants) have a population higher than 500 000 and are included in the OECD Metropolitan database. As of 2014, they account for 49% of the OECD overall population, 57% of gross domestic product and 51% of employment. Other functional urban areas include 411 medium-sized urban areas (with a population of between 200 000 and 500 000) and 506 small urban areas (50 000 to 200 000).

Source: OECD (2016c), *OECD Regions at a Glance 2016*, OECD Publishing, Paris, http://dx.doi.org/10.1787/reg_glance-2016-en; OECD (2012), *Redefining "Urban": A New Way to Measure Metropolitan Areas*, OECD Publishing, Paris, http://dx.doi.org/10.1787/9789264174108-en.

Box 1.7. **Identifying Kazakhstan's functional urban areas: methodology**

Kazakhstan is currently developing a modern system of geospatial data infrastructure, including a land cadastre based on GIS techniques (www.aisgzk.kz/aisgzk/ru/content/maps/) and an urban planning cadastre (http://nationalplan.kz/). However, the country does not yet have digital data for all administrative boundaries in the country. Many municipal boundaries are still not available in digital format, even in the vicinity of large cities. When they exist, digital maps with municipal-level administrative boundaries are considered a state secret1 and not available to foreign researchers and international organisations.

Given the low population density, a threshold of 1 000 inhabitants per km2 was used to identify city cores in Kazakhstan, as is the case for instance in Canada and the United States. Gridded population data from the Landscan project at a fine level of spatial disaggregation – 1 km2 – is used to identify city cores. The identification of core municipalities was made possible thanks to the derivation of municipal boundaries of the 26 FUA cores (i.e. the largest cities in Kazakhstan) from open cartographic resources, such as Open Street Map. The exact location of the FUA cores was cross-checked using several openly available digital maps and the official GIS map from Kazakhstan's land cadastre.

Box 1.7. **Identifying Kazakhstan's functional urban areas: methodology** (*cont.*)

Without an accurate digital map of municipal boundaries, adjustments had to be made to the last step of the OECD methodology for defining FUAs (i.e. include municipalities surrounded by a single functional area and dropping non-contiguous municipalities). After identifying municipalities in the commuting zone, thanks to travel-to- work commuting flows, the OECD listed all settlements in these municipalities based on their administrative code, or KATO (*Rus. Klassifikator administrativno-territorial'nyh obektov*). Geocoding these settlements made possible the location of isolated (non-contiguous) municipalities (i.e. municipalities that are part of the commuting zone but geographically isolated from the rest of the FUA), which were then excluded.[2] Given the limited data and the absence of municipal boundaries, no municipalities surrounded by a single functional area could be identified.

1. According to Law No. 349-1 "On State Secrets" adopted on 15 March 1999 (as amended), any information "disclosing the results of topographic, geodetic and cartographic activities, having an important defense or economic value" is considered a state secret (Article 12, paragraph 22).

2. A 50-kilometre circular buffer zone (corresponding to the area of the largest city) was used to identify isolated municipalities.

Figure 1.3. **Commuting zone settlements of Kazakhstan's 26 functional urban areas**

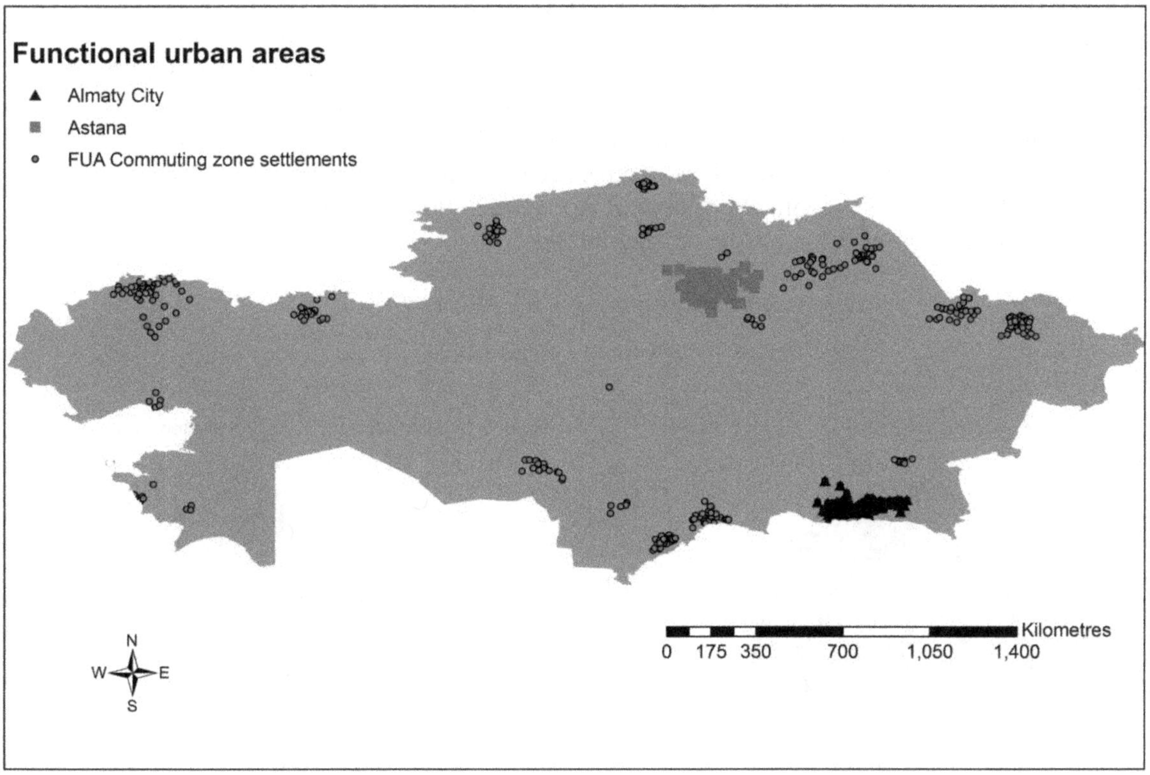

Note: This document and any map included herein are without prejudice to the status of or sovereignty over any territory, to the delimitation of international frontiers and boundaries and to the name of any territory, city or area.

Source: OECD research based on data from the Committee of Statistics.

Figure 1.4. **Share of overall population living in FUAs**

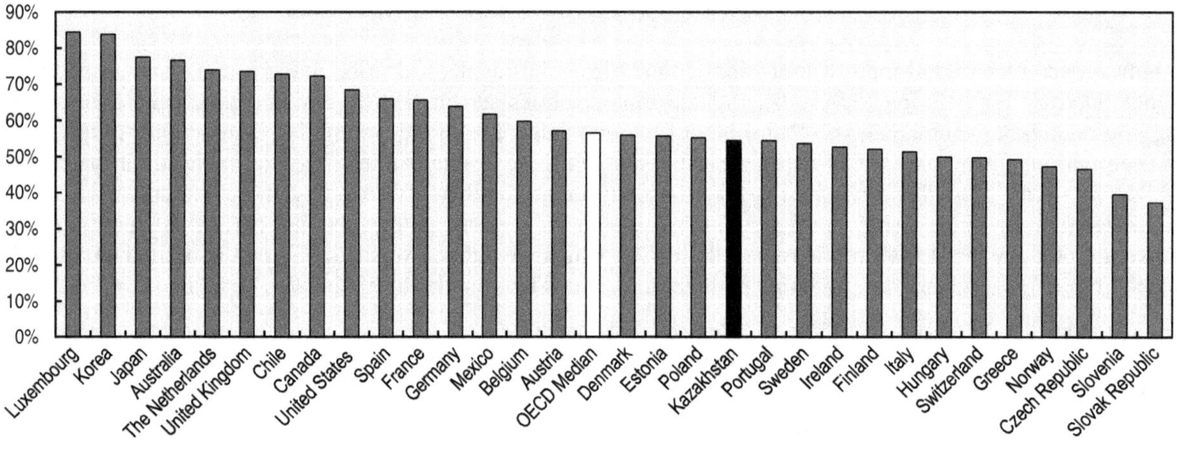

Source: OECD research based on data from the Committee of Statistics (unpublished).

Kazakhstan has only one large metropolitan area centred on Almaty City: it is by far the largest urban agglomeration in Kazakhstan, accounting for 14.4% of Kazakhstan's overall population. The size of the functional area of Almaty City is much larger than suggested by its administrative population. Almaty is also the only polycentric functional area, i.e. it consists of the two interrelated city cores of Almaty City and *Kaskelen*. Almaty City has the largest commuting zone among all Kazakhstan's FUAs. Among Kazakhstan's FUAs, only three (Almaty City, Astana and Shymkent) can be classified as metropolitan areas (metropolitan areas are functional urban areas with a population above 500 000). They accounted for 23.1% of overall population in Kazakhstan in 2009.

Figure 1.5. **Share of population by FUA type**

As a share of population living in FUAs

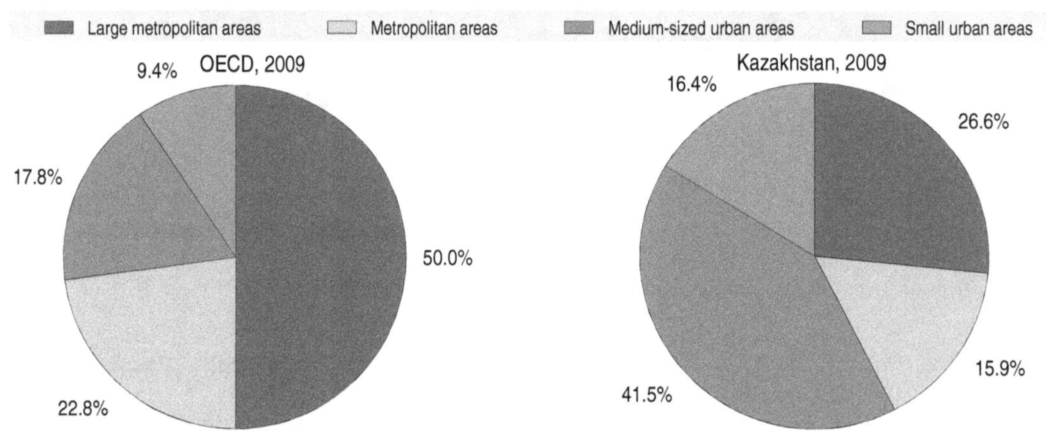

Notes: Metropolitan areas here are decomposed into large metropolitan areas (with an overall population of 1.5 million inhabitants and more) and other metropolitan areas (with a population between 500 000 and 1.5 million inhabitants).

Source: OECD Database (2016), Functional areas by country, data for 2016, http://www.oecd.org/gov/regional-policy/functionalurbanareasbycountry.htm (accessed November 2016).

The population share of metropolitan areas (large urban conurbations) is very low by OECD standards: in the 29 OECD countries with metropolitan areas, their share of overall population was on average 48.6% in 2009. The population share of metropolitan areas was higher than in Kazakhstan in all 29 countries, except in the Slovak Republic, where it was 13.2% (Figure 1.6). The rather low population share of metropolitan areas reflects Kazakhstan's relatively dispersed population structure. As discussed in the OECD Territorial Review of Kazakhstan (2017a, forthcoming), the concentration index of population in Kazakhstan is lower than in most countries of comparable size (i.e. Russia, Canada, China). In Kazakhstan, a large share of population living in FUAs live in medium-sized urban areas (FUAs between 200 000 and 500 000 inhabitants) and small urban areas (FUAs with a population between 50 000 and 200 000) compared to OECD countries (Figure 1.5). This high share of population living in small and medium-size cities is a legacy of the territorial planning from Soviet times.

These small and medium-size cities include many single-industry towns built in the vicinity of mining sites for the purpose of natural resources extraction. While some "rebalancing" towards economic and population density already happened in the 2000s (OECD, 2017a, forthcoming), the low population share of metropolitan areas suggests that there is still much room for increasing population and economic concentration in large urban centres better connected to domestic, regional and global markets.

Figure 1.6. **Share of population living in metropolitan areas (2009)**

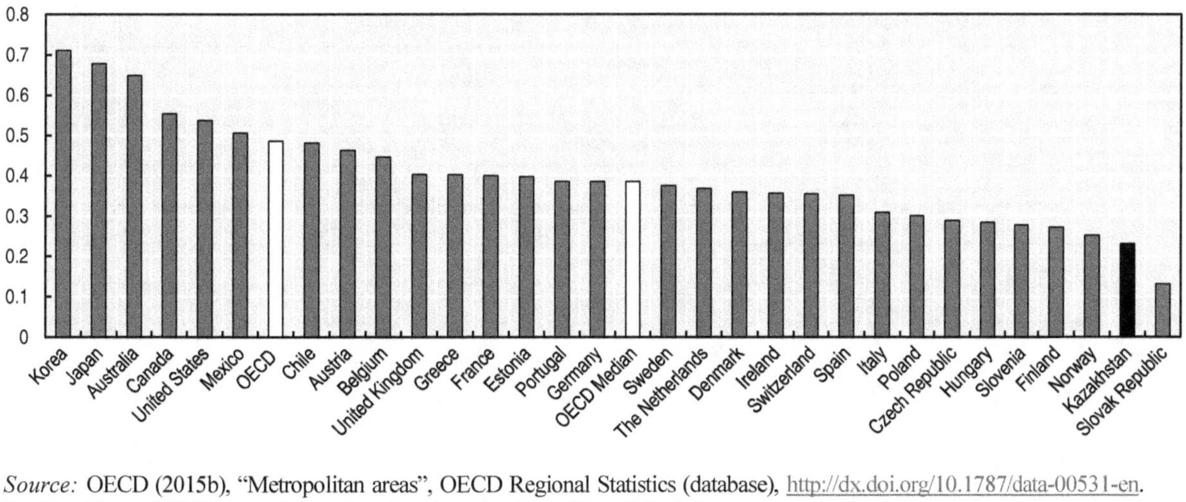

Source: OECD (2015b), "Metropolitan areas", OECD Regional Statistics (database), http://dx.doi.org/10.1787/data-00531-en. For Kazakhstan: OECD research based on data from the Committee of Statistics.

Some basic characteristics of Kazakhstan's FUAs are laid out in Table 1.3. Astana and Shymkent urban agglomerations appear to have relatively small commuting zones, with the population share of the commuting zone below average (19.1%). This is quite surprising in the case of Shymkent, the centre of a first-level urban agglomeration, according to the Regional Development Programme" (RDP). In contrast, the FUA analysis suggests that some medium-size *regional* capitals are significant urban centres with a significant share of population (up to 32% in Uralsk) living in commuting zones, for instance Uralsk, Taraz or Kyzylorda. In

Kazakhstan, commuting zones account for on average 20% of overall FUA population (23.6% in OECD countries). Appendix 1.A2 gives further detail on the FUAs of Almaty City, Astana and Shymkent.

Table 1.3. **Functional urban areas in Kazakhstan (2009)**

City	FUA population (2009)	FUA type	Core City population[2] (2009)	Commuting zone share (%)
Almaty[0]	2 313 498	Polycentric	1 427 226	38.3%
Astana	700 777	Monocentric	613 006	12.5%
Shymkent	679 273	Monocentric	603 499	11.2%
Taraz	465 532	Monocentric	320 634	31.1%
Karaganda	461 564	Monocentric	459 778	0.4%
Aktobe	396 811	Monocentric	345 687	12.9%
Ust Kamenogorsk	378 087	Monocentric	303 720	19.7%
Pavlodar	352 434	Monocentric	317 289	10.0%
Semej	318 981	Monocentric	299 264	6.2%
Uralsk	299 833	Monocentric	202 161	32.6%
Kyzylorda	245 669	Monocentric	188 682	23.2%
Kostanay	232 006	Monocentric	214 961	7.3%
Aktau	234 359	Monocentric	166 962	28.8%
Petropavlovsk	220 082	Monocentric	201 446	8.5%
Atyrau	176 409	Monocentric	165 387	6.2%
Temirtau	169 590	Monocentric	169 590	0.0%
Kokshetau	152 116	Monocentric	135 106	11.2%
Taldykorgan	146 844	Monocentric	123 038	16.2%
Turkestan	145 104	Monocentric	142 899	1.5%
Ekibastuz	142 511	Monocentric	125 012	12.3%
Zhanaozen	114 333	Monocentric	91 332	20.1%
Rudnyj	109 659	Monocentric	109 659	0.0%
Zhezkazgan	87 060	Monocentric	86 227	1.0%
Balhash	68 833	Monocentric	68 833	0.0%
Kentau	58 649	Monocentric	57 121	2.6%
Stepnogorsk	51 404	Monocentric	46 712	9.1%

Notes: 1. The Almaty metropolitan area includes two interrelated cores: Almaty City and the city of Kaskelen. 2. Core City population also covers the population of statutory (administrative) cities.

Source: OECD research based on data from the Committee of Statistics, demographic database (unpublished).

Urbanisation in Kazakhstan

A moderate pace of urbanisation after a decade of urban decline…

Kazakhstan experienced atypical demographic patterns after independence in 1991. During the Soviet era, demographic growth was accompanied by the continuous growth of the urban population and a rising urbanisation rate. However, Kazakhstan's population declined by 9.1% during the 1991-2001 period. The decline of the urban population (-10%) was more pronounced than the fall of rural population (-8.1%), which led to a moderate drop in the official urbanisation rate, from 57.3% in 1991 to 56.6% in 2001. Kazakhstan's cities lost around 930 000 people during this period, mainly because of the emigration of urban Russian and German residents to their areas of origin and low natural population growth. This migratory outflow from Kazakhstan reached its peak in 1994 (when 400 000 people, or 2.5% of the entire population, emigrated from Kazakhstan) and essentially ended in 2003-2004.

After years of demographic decline, the urban population started rising again in 2001, and the overall population began to grow in 2002. In 2011, the overall population rose past its 1991 level (16.3 million); demographic growth stabilised around 1.4%-1.5% annually after 2010. Since 2002, the urban population has expanded at a faster pace than the rural population. The official urbanisation rate has thus been gradually increasing, reaching 57% as of 1 January, 2016. However, several large-scale administrative and territorial changes have affected official urban and rural population figures since 2002 (Figure 1.7).[6]

Figure 1.7. **Official urbanisation rate, 1991-2016**

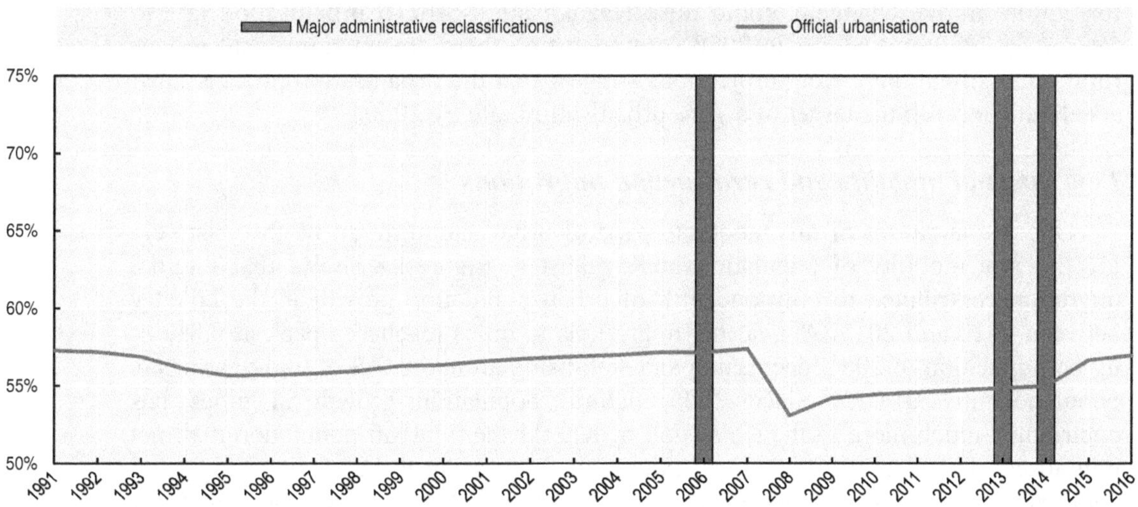

Source: Committee on Statistics of the Republic of Kazakhstan (2016b), Demographic database, available (in Russian) at: www.stat.gov.kz/faces/wcnav_externalId/homeNumbersPopulation?_adf.ctrlstate=u5ioriyfd_4&_afrLoop=1653212230005672.

Zhumasultanov (2011) provides estimates of Kazakhstan's recent urbanisation rate, corrected for the 2007 reclassification, which increased the number of rural inhabitants. According to his estimates, the urbanisation rate was broadly stable between 1991 (54.8%) and 2011 (54.5%) and fell to its lowest level at the beginning of 2001 (50.3%) before increasing again during the 2001-2011 period. To complement Zhumasultanov's estimates for the recent period, Table 1.4 provides a corrected urbanisation rate that neutralises the effect of Shymkent and Almaty City's territorial expansions in 2013 and 2014. The main conclusion is that without this large reclassification of rural inhabitants to urban status, the urbanisation rate would have grown at a much slower pace, reaching an estimated 55.6% at the beginning of 2016 (while the official urbanisation rate was 57%).

Table 1.4. **Estimated urbanisation rate, corrected for administrative-territorial changes**

1991	2001	2006	2011	2015*	2016*
54.8%	50.3%	51.2%	54.6%	55.3%	55.6%

Notes: * OECD estimate. In 2015 and 2016, the new urban residents in Shymkent and Almaty City were subtracted from urban population. The demographic growth rate of their respective districts before the reclassification (i.e. in 2013 and 2014) was used to simulate 2016 new urban residents.

Source: OECD research based on T. Zhumasultanov, "Rasselenie naselenija strany po gorodskoj i sel'skoj mestnostjam", available (in Russian) at: www.stat.gov.kz/getImg?id=WC16200033665.

In 2010-15, the urban population grew by 1.8% annually (corrected for major administrative-territorial changes, see OECD estimates above), compared to 3% in China, 2% in Turkey and during the same period (United Nations, 2014). Kazakhstan's government has a goal of a 70% urbanisation rate by 2050.[7] According to UN Projections, the urban population is expected to reach 13 million people by 2050, with an urbanisation rate of 64.6%. A linear progression of observed urban and rural population growth rates in the 2010-16 period (corrected for administrative changes), could raise Kazakhstan's official urbanisation rate to 59.6%[8] in 2030 and 63.3% in 2050 (provided that there are no significant urban-rural reclassifications). Both projections suggest that the urbanisation process must accelerate to reach the target of a 70% urbanisation rate by 2050.

Low internal mobility and rural-urban migrations

One of the causes of this moderate pace of urbanisation might be the relatively low internal mobility of population in Kazakhstan. Figure 1.8 shows that internal migration contributed to only one-fifth of urban population growth in the country between 2010 and 2015. Annual net migrations to cities reached a peak at 0.8% of urban population in 2006, decreasing and stabilising around 0.5% of mid-year urban population in 2014-15. Since 2006, natural population growth in cities has contributed much more to the expansion of Kazakhstan's urban population than net migrations. The size of interregional migration flows seem to be close to migration patterns observed in Russia, but much lower than those of the United States, Japan or Canada (Aldashev and Dietz, 2014). Internal migration in Kazakhstan is certainly lower than in China, where large-scale rural-urban migration is the main driver of urban growth (OECD, 2015a). Kazakhstan's Economic Research Institute (ERI) came to the same conclusion in a recent study on migrations (Economic Research Institute, 2014). Several obstacles may explain the relatively low level of internal migrations (and, in particular, rural-urban migrations). They include underdeveloped and shallow housing rental markets, the burdensome process of citizen registration (which prevents some internal migrants from accessing public services) and high real estate prices in large cities. Still, rural-urban migrations have been underestimated by official migration statistics – the basis for all estimates in this paragraph – to an unknown extent.

Figure 1.8. **Urban population growth in Kazakhstan**

Left: Contributions to urban growth (2010-15); right: percentage of mid-year population

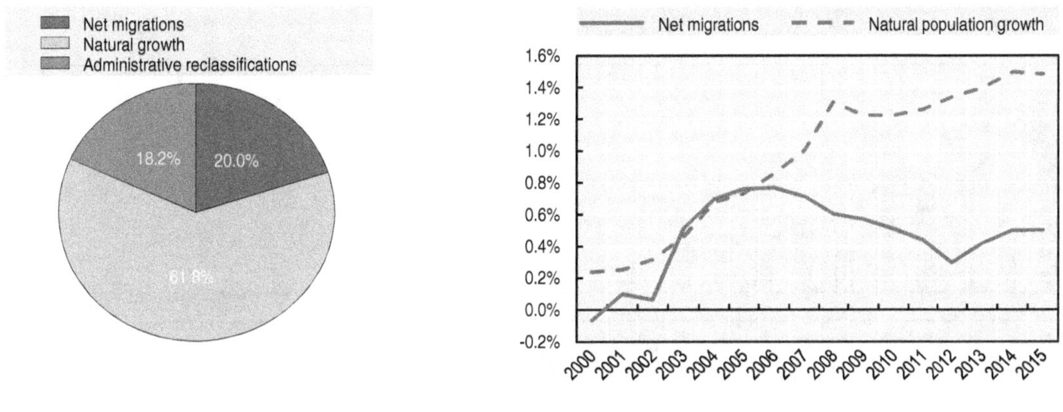

Source: OECD research based on data from Committee on statistics of the Republic of Kazakhstan (2016b), Demographic database, available (in Russian) at: www.stat.gov.kz/faces/wcnav_externalId/homeNumbersPopulation?_adf.ctrlstate=u5ioriyfd_4&_afrLoop=1653212230005672.

Kazakhstan's largest cities are driving urban growth, with evidence of peri-urbanisation

Astana and the two other metropolitan areas (Almaty City and Shymkent) are growing at a faster pace than the 23 other FUAs in Kazakhstan (Figure 1.9). Their share of overall population grew from 18.2% in 1999 to 23.1% in 2009. Their population increased, on average, by 3.1% a year between 1999 and 2009. This was much higher than the average growth rate of metropolitan areas in OECD countries (0.86%) during the same period. In contrast, the average annual growth rate of population in medium-size and small FUAs was only slightly higher than in OECD countries during the same period. Between 2009 and 2014, data for city cores[9] display the same patterns, with city cores of metropolitan areas expanding at an annual rate of 3.2%, versus 1.6% for medium-size cores and 1.8% for city cores of small urban areas.

Figure 1.9. **Annual average population growth by FUA size (1999-2009)**

Kazakhstan OECD countries[1]

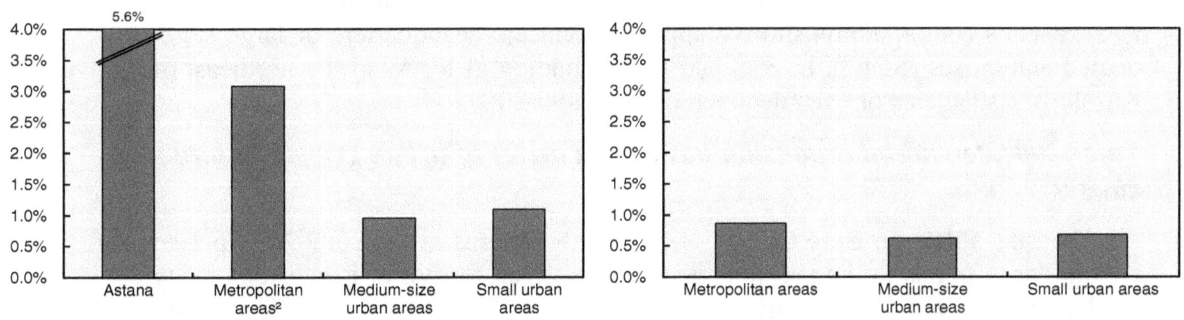

Notes: 1. Denmark omitted (no data available). 2. Astana, Almaty City and Shymkent.

Source: OECD (2015b), "Metropolitan areas", OECD Regional Statistics (database), http://dx.doi.org/10.1787/data-00531-en.

Figure 1.10. **Growth of Kazakhstan's FUAs (1999-2009)**

Share of core and commuting zones in overall population growth

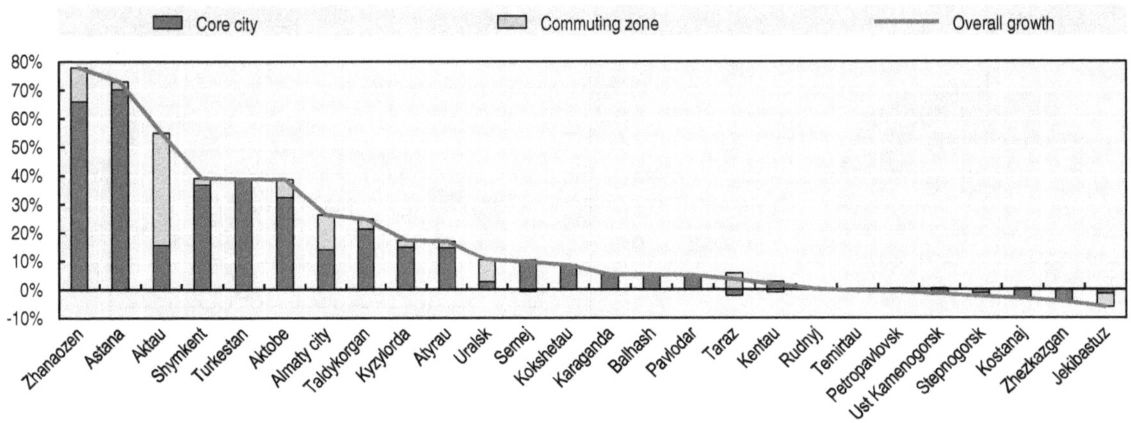

Source: OECD research based on data from Committee on Statistics of the Republic of Kazakhstan (2016b), Demographic database, available (in Russian) at: www.stat.gov.kz/faces/wcnav_externalId/homeNumbersPopulation?_adf.ctrlstate=u5ioriyfd_4&_afrLoop=1653212230005672.

Between 1999 and 2009, population has been growing faster in commuting zones than in city cores. Almaty City, in particular, has been experiencing suburbanisation: the commuting zone of its agglomeration recorded higher population growth between 1999 and 2009 (33.8%) than the two city cores of Almaty City and Kaskelen (22%). This is also the case of several mid-sized FUAs (Taraz, Uralsk, Atyrau, Aktau and Aktobe).[10] In contrast, in the other two metropolitan areas of Kazakhstan (Astana and Shymkent), the city cores grew more rapidly than the commuting zone between 1999 and 2009. In OECD countries, suburbanisation has been particularly strong in large metropolitan areas (of more than 1.5 million people). Figure 1.10 shows the contributions of commuting zones and city cores to overall FUA growth during the 1999-2009 period.

Existing geographic and demographic imbalances affected urban growth patterns in Kazakhstan in the period from 1999 to 2009. Beyond Astana, the fastest-growing cities are in the southern and western areas of the country. In the western areas of Kazakhstan, the rapid growth of Zhanaozen, Aktau is connected to the strong dynamics of natural resource extraction (i.e. hydrocarbons). Astana's impressive population growth during the period corresponds to the relocation of Kazakhstan's central administrative apparatus and the headquarters of large state-owned enterprises (SOEs). In contrast, the population of FUAs in the northeast of Kazakhstan stagnated or even declined during 1999-2009.

Since 2009, territorial expansion has been a driver of urban growth in large cities

Focusing solely on Core Cities,[11] city growth patterns in the 2009-2014 period are similar to trends in the previous decade. However, territorial expansion of city borders was a very significant factor of city population growth in Shymkent, Almaty City and Atyrau (Figure 1.10). While natural growth is usually the main factor of city population growth, positive net migrations play a dominant role in Astana (they account for 60% of population growth) and a significant role in

Almaty City and Uralsk. In contrast, four cities experienced significant net out-migration. Overall, while there were seven cities with a shrinking population in the 1999-2009 period, all FUA cores but one, Zhezkazgan, experienced demographic growth from 2009 to 2014 (Figure 1.11). Even within the four regions experiencing population decline,[12] large cities have been growing and benefit from some intraregional rural-urban migration.

Figure 1.11. **Contributions to city population growth (2009-2014)**

Administrative change (estimates) correspond to the expansion of city borders

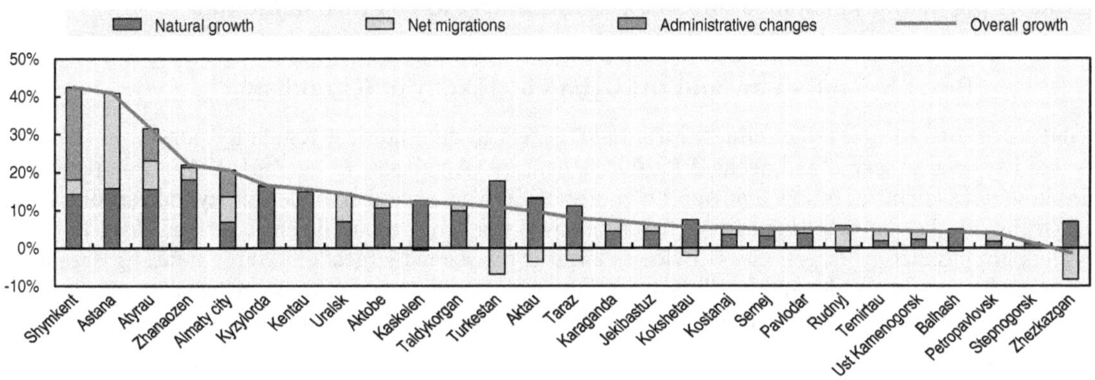

Source: OECD research based on data from Committee on Statistics of the Republic of Kazakhstan (2016b), Demographic database, available (in Russian) at: www.stat.gov.kz/faces/wcnav_externalId/homeNumbersPopulation?_adf.ctrlstate=u5ioriyfd_4&_afrLoop=1653212230005672.

Administrative expansion of large cities is a common practice in Kazakhstan.[13] Since 2009, four cities expanded their administrative borders, sometimes resulting in significant population increases. In some cases, the absorption of neighbouring municipalities seems also to be a way to cope with infrastructure developments and land scarcity in a context of growing population. For instance, according to local authorities, the expansion of city borders in Kyzylorda was indispensable in distributing individual land plots for construction purposes.

The largest territorial expansion took place in Almaty and in Shymkent: In Almaty City, the city territory almost doubled (94%), and population increased by 92 604 people (6%), while in Shymkent there was a threefold increase in city territory, which led to a 20% increase of population. In both Almaty City and Shymkent, according to local authorities, such expansion was necessary to improve transport infrastructure (suburban road network, new railway tracks, car parks and bus stations), build new social objects (schools, hospitals) and develop new housing projects (in Shymkent only). Shymkent has now the largest territory among Kazakh cities (1 170 km^2).

The urban hierarchy is evolving gradually thanks to the rapid development of large cities

The FUAs for Kazakhstan can be used to test the expected relationship between city size (population) and rank, as described by "Zipf's Law" (Box 1.8). Zipf's Law is an empirical regularity, rather than the urban ideal for a nation. However, looking at the current rank-population size relationship and its recent evolution can provide useful insights about where the urban hierarchy of Kazakhstan is likely to be evolving. Using the FUAs' city size distribution, Kazakhstan's cities conform to a large extent to the expected distribution under Zipf's Law. As Figure 1.12 shows, Astana, Shymkent and Taraz (the three largest FUAs after Almaty City) are smaller than their expected size relative to Almaty City. In contrast, the data suggests that many medium-size cities (such as Petropavlovsk and Uralsk) are larger than expected relative to the size of the largest city (i.e. Almaty). This is consistent with the finding that in Kazakhstan medium-size and small FUAs account for a larger share of overall population than in OECD countries. This suggests that the current trend of metropolitan areas (Almaty City, Astana and Shymkent) growing faster (in terms of population) than medium-size FUAs is likely to continue in the future.[14]

Box 1.8. **Zipf's Law and the urban hierarchy in Kazakhstan**

In the context of urban studies, the term "Zipf's Law" refers to an empirical regularity concerning city-size distributions that has been observed and debated for over a century (Auerbach, 1913; Zipf, 1949). The population ranks of cities in various countries follow a power law of a specific type, such that, under the hypothesis of a Pareto probability distribution, the log(rank)-log(size) relationship is linear, with a coefficient equal or close to -1. Put more simply, this implies that the largest city is twice as large as the second-largest city, three times as large as the third and so on along the urban hierarchy. While the relationship tends to break down at small scales, it holds remarkably well for many countries across a very wide range of city sizes (Gabaix and Ioannides, 2004).

The relevance of Zipf's Law in the context of city-size distribution is twofold: First, it relates to efforts to understand the distribution of population and human activity across space; Krugman (1996:40) has argued that such regularity is "spooky" and that there should be a theoretical explanation for it. There is also the question of whether Zipf's Law implies some constraints in the pattern of urban growth, i.e. that the growth trajectories of individual cities could not change the overall city-size distribution (Duranton, 2007). Others raise the question of whether there are different levels of economic efficiency for different urban forms (numbers of cities and their sizes) (Storper, 2013).

In Kazakhstan, the city size distribution has shifted towards a Zipf's Law pattern, because Almaty, Astana (the second-largest FUA) and Shymkent (the third-largest FUA) have been growing faster than medium-sized cities from 1999 to 2009.

Using statutory city size, Linn (2014) finds that Kazakhstan does not conform to the Zipf's Law city size distribution, because medium-size cities are larger than expected compared to the size of Almaty City. However, using FUAs instead of administrative data suggests that, while medium-size cites are indeed larger than expected, Almaty's size is not lower than it should be under Zipf's Law. Almaty's FUA is indeed much larger than the population of Almaty City alone (see Table 1.3). Overall, the city size distribution of Kazakhstan's FUAs conforms better to Zipf's Law than statutory cities, both in 1999 and in 2009. This is consistent with other work suggesting that functionally defined urban systems approximate better the rank-size rule than administratively defined systems (Veneri, 2013).

Sources: Auerbach, F. (1913), "*Das Gesetz der Bevölkerungskonzentration", Petermanns Geographische Mitteilungen*, No. 59, pp. 74-76; Duranton, G. (2007), "Urban evolutions: The fast, the slow, and the still", American Economic Review, Vol. 97/1, pp. 197-221; Krugman, P. (1996), *The Self-Organizing Economy*, Blackwell, Cambridge, Massachusetts; Storper, M. (2013), *Keys to the City. How Economics, Institutions, Social Interaction, and Politics Shape Development*, Princeton University Press, Oxford; Zipf, G. (1949), *Human Behavior and the Principle of Least Effort*, Addison-Wesley, Cambridge, Massachusetts; Gabaix X. and Y.M. Ioannides (2004), "The Evolution of City Distributions", in J.V. Henderson and J.F.Thisse (eds.), *Handbook of Regional and Urban Economics*, Ch.53, North Holland, Amsterdam, pp. 2 341-2 378. This box has been adapted from OECD (2015a), *OECD Urban Policy Reviews: China 2015*, OECD Publishing, Paris, http://dx.doi.org/10.1787/9789264230040-en; Veneri, P. (2013), "On City Size Distribution: Evidence from OECD Functional Urban Areas", *OECD Regional Development Working Papers*, No. 2013/27, OECD Publishing, Paris, http://dx.doi.org/10.1787/5k3tt100wf7j-en.

Figure 1.12. **Zipf's Law for Kazakhstan's functional urban areas (2009)**

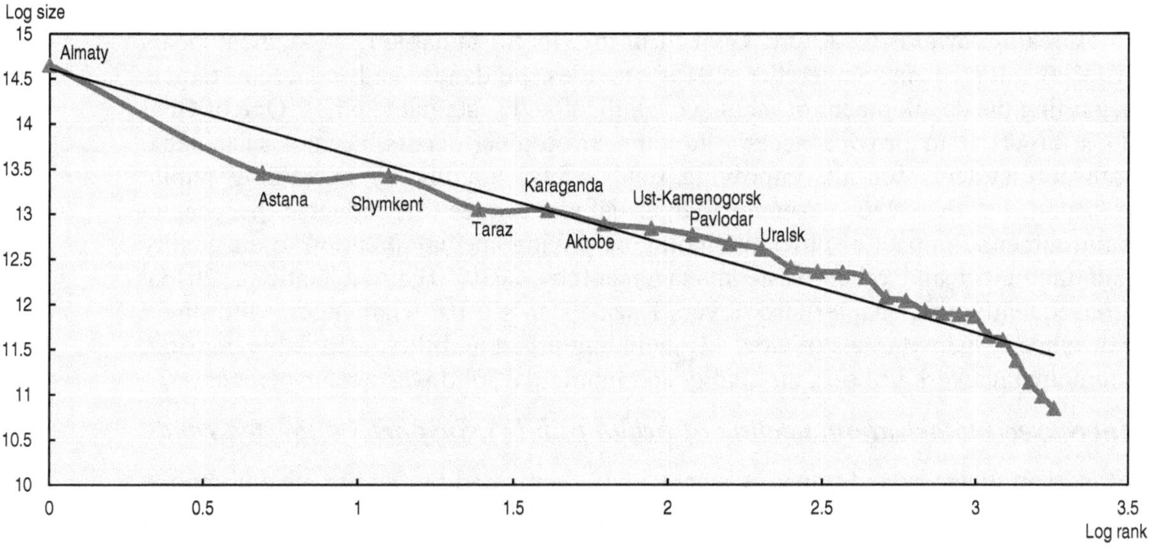

Note: The fitted line of the rank size distribution is y = -0.9744 x + 14.61; $R^2 = 0.9186$.

Source: OECD research based on data provided by the Committee on Statistics of the Republic of Kazakhstan.

Between 1999 and 2009, Kazakhstan's urban structure (based on FUAs) already demonstrated a shift towards the Zipf's Law pattern, mainly due to the strong demographic growth of Astana and Shymkent. Since population in medium and small-sized cities stagnated or grew much at a much slower pace, their relative size is now closer to the Zipf's Law pattern (on Figure 1.13, the 2009 curve is closer to the Zipf's Law line than the 1999 curve).

Figure 1.13. **Zipf's Law for FUAs in 1999 and 2009 (Kazakhstan)**

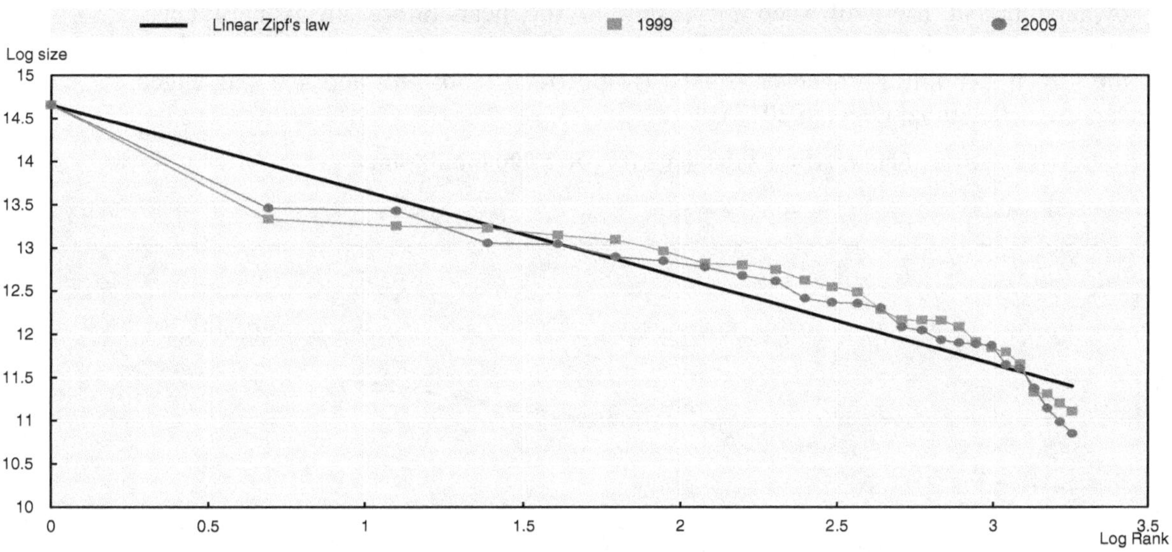

Notes: The linear line is the pure Zipf Law distribution of city size based on Almaty City's size in 2009 (since Almaty is the largest city). The second-largest city is half Almaty's size, the third-largest city a third of Almaty's size, and so on down the city ranks. The 2009 curve is the real city size distribution of FUAs, while the 1999 curve reflects the deviation of 1999 city size distribution from Zipf's Law in 1999. Almaty City is given its 2009 size in the 1999 curve.

Source: OECD research based on data provided by the Committee on Statistics of the Republic of Kazakhstan.

Kazakhstan's urban challenges

Looking towards the future, Goal 11 of the UN Sustainable Development Goals (SDGs) adopted in September 2015 provides guidance and concrete targets regarding the development of inclusive, resilient and sustainable cities. One of Goal 11's targets is to provide access "to safe, affordable, accessible and sustainable transport systems for all, improving road safety, notably by expanding public transport … by 2030". Another target is to "reduce the adverse per capita environmental impact of cities, including by paying special attention to air quality and municipal and other waste management by 2030" (United Nations, 2015). Consequently, this chapter also covers Kazakhstan's urban challenges, with direct relevance to many targets of Goal 11, including urban mobility, affordable housing, municipal network utilities, air quality and municipal solid waste management.

Increased motorisation, decline of urban public transport, congested roads

Urban transport and transit is increasingly dominated by the private automobile in Kazakhstan. The country inherited a legacy of low car ownership and extensive (but not always cost-efficient) urban public transport from Soviet times (Coulibaly et al., 2013). However, car ownership has risen very quickly since the 2000s (see Figure 1.14), with the highest motorisation rate observed in Almaty City (428 per 1 000 inhabitants in 2015) and Astana (385 per 1 000 inhabitants in 2015) (Committee on Statistics of the Republic of Kazakhstan, 2016c). This is in line with global trends in developing and post-Soviet countries, and a consequence of economic growth and higher per capita income. Motorisation rates in Kazakhstan are still lower than in most OECD countries (for instance, Canada and Poland had 594 and 486 passenger cars respectively per 1 000 inhabitants in 2012).[15] High income elasticity of the demand for private automobiles, moderate gasoline prices and road extensions and improvements in and around big cities indicate that car ownership and use will keep increasing in the near future. In Almaty City, motorisation is already equal or close to the level of some OECD countries, such as the Czech Republic, France or Ireland (respectively 450, 489 and 431 passenger cars per 1 000 inhabitants in 2012).

Figure 1.14. **Passenger cars per 1 000 inhabitants**

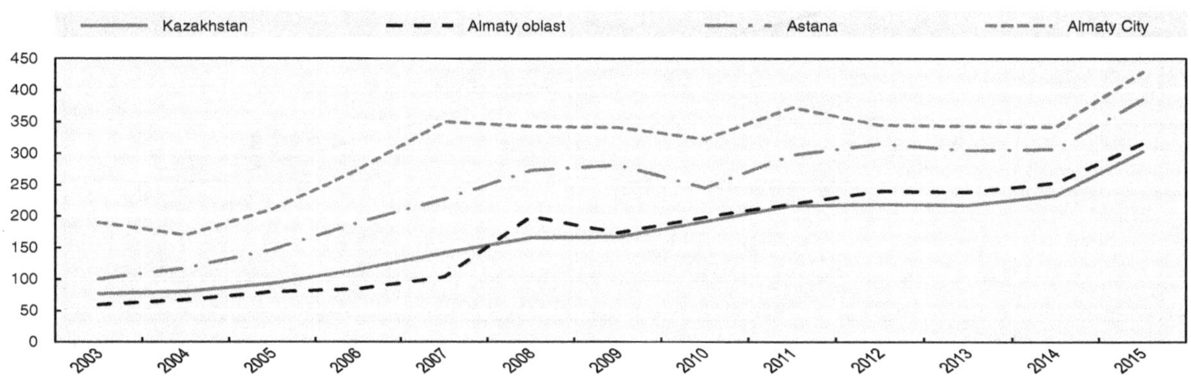

Note: To ensure data comparability over time, this figure uses the time series of registered and unregistered (Russian *snjatyh s ucheta*) passenger cars.

Source: OECD research based on data from Committee on Statistics of the Republic of Kazakhstan (2016c), Transport databases, available (in Russian) at: www.stat.gov.kz/faces/wcnav_externalId/homeNumbersTransport?_afrLoop=2881198183833380#%40%3F_afrLoop%3D2881198183833380%26_adf.ctrl-state%3Dm213q9ir5_110.

The modal share of private cars is relatively high in Kazakhstan's large urban agglomerations. In Almaty, Astana and Aktobe, it was estimated at around 70% in 2010 (ADB, 2012a). In contrast, the share of public transport in Almaty City is estimated around 25% to 30%, which is low compared to many European cities (City of Almaty and UNDP/CAST, 2013). In Almaty City, Astana and Aktobe, the overreliance on the use of cars for urban transit is comparable to the United States' (Linn, 2014). As a result, Kazakhstan's large urban agglomerations, such as Astana and in particular Almaty, suffer from increasing road congestion: in Almaty, current traffic speed for individual cars is as low as 19 km/h (City of Almaty and UNDP/CAST, 2013).

The low modal share of public transport is due to the low quality of public transport services, and the lack of intermodal connections between public and private transport (i.e. parking facilities) and between different types of public transport. Buses are the dominant public transport mode in Kazakhstan's large cities, and increasing road congestion affects their efficiency: in Almaty City, the average bus speed is close to 14 km/h and in many cases, even lower. Inefficient and slow public transport affects mostly lower and middle-income citizens and the elderly, who form the bulk of public transport users (for Almaty, see City of Almaty and UNDP/CAST, 2013).

Urban public transport modes inherited from the Soviet era, i.e. mainly trolleybuses and tramways, have undergone a marked decline, while urban public transport has been increasingly dominated by buses (Figure 1.15), in many cases operated by individual entrepreneurs or private bus companies. Of 87 cities, only three still have operating tramways, and their usage has been declining in recent years.[16] Indeed, there has been little modernisation of ageing rolling stock (except in Pavlodar City).[17] Together with high maintenance costs, this has resulted in poor service, decreasing passenger traffic and the decommission of most tramway and trolleybus lines. Almaty City decommissioned its last two tramway lines in 2015. This contrasts with the trend in many OECD countries (especially in Europe), where light-rail transport is increasingly popular for urban mobility.

Figure 1.15. **Index of passenger-kilometres since 2003**

2003 = 100

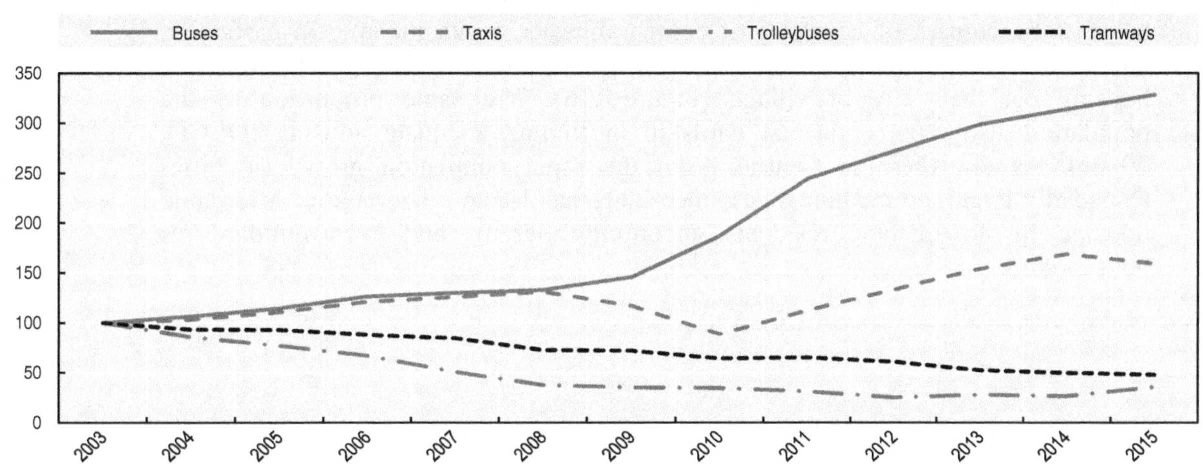

Source: Committee on Statistics of the Republic of Kazakhstan (2016c), Transport database, available (in Russian) at: www.stat.gov.kz/faces/wcnav_externalId/homeNumbersTransport?_adf.ctrlstate=b6lrkbqi2_50&_afrLoop=2947648817962669#%40%3F_afrLoop%3D2947648817962669%26_adf.ctrl-state%3Dudk4hhsnm_17.

Air pollution and a high rate of traffic accidents and fatalities are other by-products of the overreliance on cars for urban and suburban transit. In Almaty City, motor transport accounts for 80% of air pollution emissions, with negative consequences on health, including high respiratory disease. Almaty is also has the highest rate of car accidents per 100 000 inhabitants (345 versus a national average of 118).[18] The fatality rate from traffic accidents in Kazakhstan is higher than in all OECD countries. In 2014, 15 fatalities per 100 000 inhabitants were recorded, while the median for OECD countries was 5.[19]

Astana and Almaty have developed policies to encourage the modal shift from private cars to public transport and improve service quality. The inauguration of Almaty City subway system in 2011 was a landmark event, ad its first line is currently being extended. In 2015, the daily number of commuters of the subway system rose to 40 000.[20] Both Almaty and Astana have plans to develop modern light-rail transit systems (LRT) in the next few years. In the meantime, both cities are renewing their municipal bus fleet and introducing integrated electronic ticketing systems.

Eurasian roads were designed with single-axle load limits well below the international standards in Europe. As in other post-Soviet countries, road traffic has grown rapidly in Kazakhstan since 2000. The rapid shift of goods shipment from the railway to the road network and the high level of road shipments per capita led to a rapid deterioration of roads, raising the demand for funding for repairs and maintenance (Coulibaly et al., 2013; ADB, 2012a). Although repair and reconstruction of major highways is a government priority under Kazakhstan's *Nurly Zhol* infrastructure programme, the poor state of the secondary road network is an economic challenge for many medium-size and small cities that are not located on a major highway.[21] It also contributes to the high level of fatal accidents on Kazakhstani roads.

Despite the growing housing stock, satisfaction with housing conditions is relatively low

Applying the OECD well-being framework to Kazakhstan, OECD (2016a) finds that the country has achieved quasi-universal access to basic sanitary facilities (e.g. indoor bathrooms), but that satisfaction with housing conditions is low and below a benchmark of countries of comparable per capita income. In particular, one-third of the population is unsatisfied with the availability of "good, affordable housing" in their city or village (Figure 1.16). The same proportion of the population also report financial hardship in finding adequate housing (OECD, 2016e). As elsewhere in Central Asia, the rapid population growth in cities (especially large and medium-size) since 2001 has led to a shortage of affordable housing for low-income residents, incoming migrants and even middle-class households.

Figure 1.16. **Level of satisfaction with housing availability**

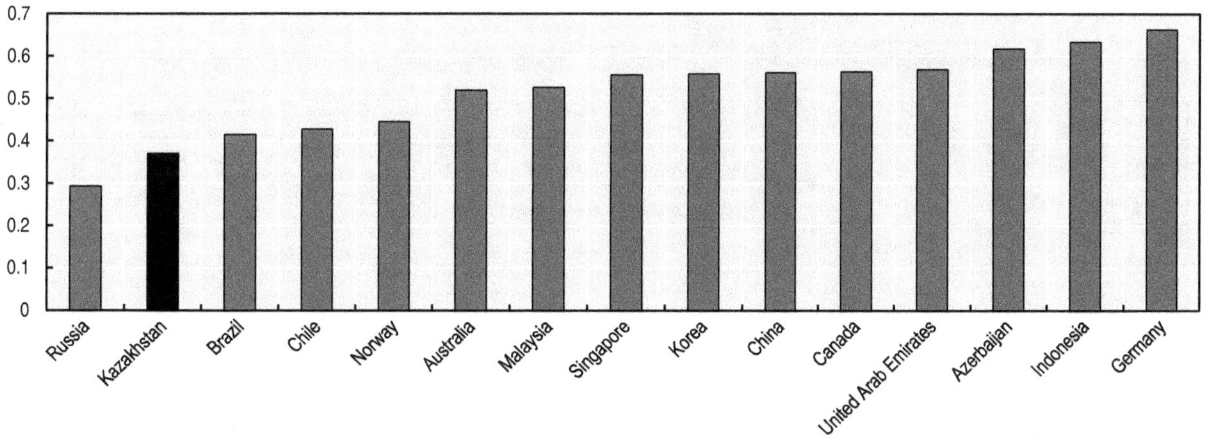

Note: Data for the "levels of satisfaction" graph are for 2014, with the exception of Chile, China, Malaysia and the United Arab Emirates (2013). It shows the percentage of people replying "satisfied" to the question: "In the city or area where you live, are you satisfied or dissatisfied with the availability of good, affordable housing?"

Sources: OECD (2016a), *Multi-dimensional Review of Kazakhstan: Volume 1. Initial Assessment,* Chapter 2, http://dx.doi.org/10.1787/9789264246768-en, OECD Publishing, Paris; data from Gallup (2014), Gallup World Poll (database).

The housing stock has increased considerably since 2000 (Figure 1.17) and Kazakhstan is one of the countries in Eurasia that has seen the largest growth since 2000 (UNECE, 2016), a necessary development given the relatively rapid population growth. The housing stock increased more than twofold in Astana and Almaty, and also expanded rapidly in regions with strong economic and demographic growth, such as Atyrau, Kyzylorda and Mangystau. The average housing area per person increased throughout Kazakhstan. However, there are spatial inequalities: the residents of Astana and Almaty City have more housing space per person than the national average, and Astana is now well above the national average (with 28.5 square metres per capita, compared to the national average of 23.8 square metres). By contrast, residents of poorer cities such as Taraz, or in cities experiencing rapid population growth, such as Zhanaojen, have on average less housing space per capita (18.9 and 16.4 square metres per capita respectively) than the national average.

After independence, as elsewhere in the former Soviet Union, Kazakhstan's authorities undertook a massive privatisation of housing, selling individual housing units at low prices to the sitting tenants (UNECE, 2016). As result, the vast majority of the urban housing stock is now in private hands: in 2014, only 3.2% of the housing stock was in public ownership.[22] Moreover, while the public housing stock has been fairly stable since 2004, the private sector accounted for almost all the growth in the urban housing stock between 2004 and 2014 (an increase of 38%). The public housing stock accounts for less than 4% of the overall housing stock in almost all large cities, including Astana and Almaty City, except in Rudnij and Pavlodar.

Figure 1.17. **Housing stock in Kazakhstan (2001-2015)**

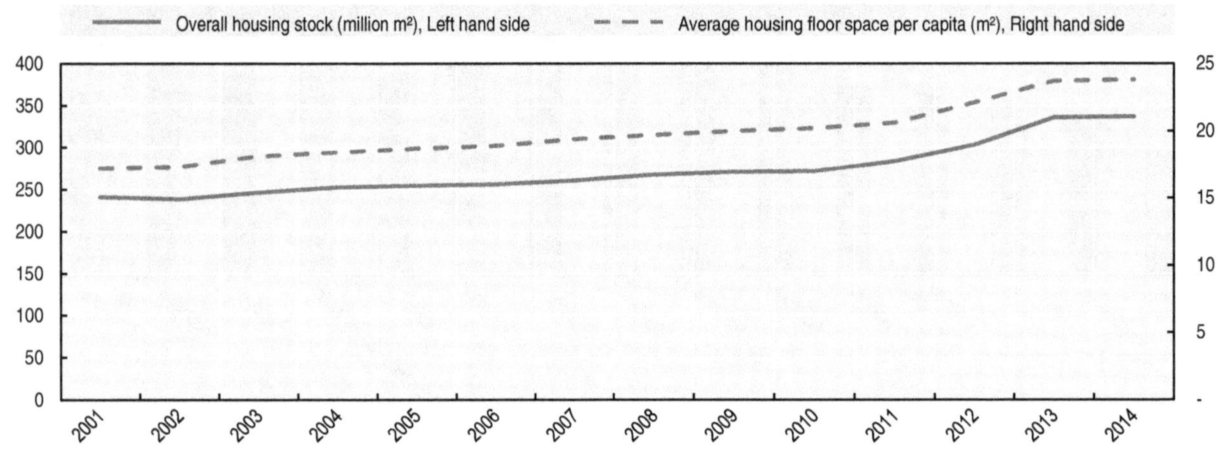

Source: Committee on statistics of the Republic of Kazakhstan (2016d), Housing database, available (in Russian) at: www.stat.gov.kz/faces/wcnav_externalId/publicationsCompilations?_afrLoop=3991147878468215#%40%3F_afrLoop%3D3991147878468215%26_adf.ctrl-state%3D44m4aly8u_55 (accessed 3 September 2016).

A characteristic feature of Kazakhstan's housing sector is the prevalence of detached family homes: they accounted for 56% of newly built housing surface during the 2010-15 period. According to Kazakhstan's law on individual housing construction and the Land Code,[23] every citizen has the right to receive a land plot for individual construction purposes. Citizens can address such requests to local authorities, who must also finance infrastructure development on the land plots assigned to individual construction. While detached family homes accounted for a marginal (5%) share of newly built dwellings in Astana during the 2010-15 period, they represent almost a third of newly built dwellings in Almaty City and Shymkent, and 36% in Aktobe. What is more, detached family homes account for a majority of newly built dwellings in most other cities (Figure 1.18) in the same period. The rapid emergence of detached family homes in peripheral areas is a common feature of Eurasian cities, and corresponds to economic incentives (free allocation of land plots to households, high real estate prices and rents in city centre multifamily dwellings) and to cultural preferences among many Kazakh households. The risk is that it leads to uncoordinated urban sprawl around city centres, with local authorities struggling to provide adequate transport, public utility and social infrastructures in these new low-density settlements. Shymkent, where many single-family homes are not yet connected to the sewage system,[24] offers a good example. The long-term cost of providing urban infrastructure to new districts composed of individually built family homes could be a very heavy financial burden for large cities in the decades to come.

Figure 1.18. **Single-family homes as a share of newly built dwellings (2010-15 average)**

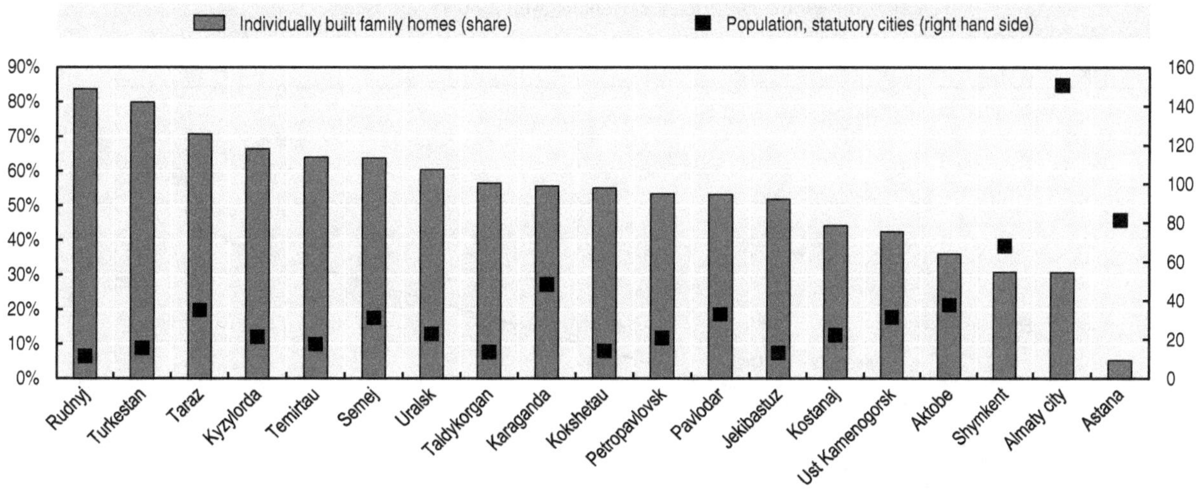

Source: Committee on statistics of the Republic of Kazakhstan (2016d), Housing database, available (in Russian) at: www.stat.gov.kz/faces/wcnav_externalId/publicationsCompilations?_afrLoop=3991147878468215#%40%3F_afrLoop%3D3991147878468215%26_adf.ctrl-state%3D44m4aly8u_55 (accessed 3 September 2016).

While access to water is now quasi-universal among urban households, sewage coverage is still an issue in many cities of Kazakhstan. This has potentially negative consequences on health and the environment. Southern cities in particular have been having difficulty offering urban sewage coverage. Only 60% of the housing stock benefited from sewage coverage in Shymkent in 2014, and less than 38% and 11% in Kyzylorda and Turkestan respectively.[25] Many newly built single-family homes appear not to be connected to the sewage system, because utility companies (whether private or municipal-owned) are struggling to cope with the pace of home construction in peripheral, low-density neighbourhoods. In Kyzylorda (a city with one of the lowest sewage coverage rates), 58.6% of residents lived in single-family homes in 2009,[26] and single-family homes accounted for 66.4% of the area of newly built housing between 2010 and 2015.

Rising housing prices and a shallow rental market

Housing supply seems to be responding to increasing demand, although it may not be sufficient in many fast-growing cities outside Almaty City and Astana. Population growth correlates closely with the number of square metres of new housing space, both at the regional level and in the 38 cities of regional significance (see Figure 1.19). However, some smaller towns, where population is stagnating or falling, are nevertheless seeing significant housing stock growth. In the city of Shu (Karaganda oblast), where population is stagnating, the housing stock has increased by 2.7% every year since 2011. There is also evidence that the housing supply is adequate for commercial premises and vast, expensive housing units, while there is a shortage of affordable, smaller flats. The 2016 economic slowdown has negatively affected the prices and sales volumes of the former, while the demand for modest housing has not slowed down.[27]

Figure 1.19. **Correlation between population growth and housing stock growth (2011-15)**

37 cities of regional significance, Astana, Almaty City and Shu

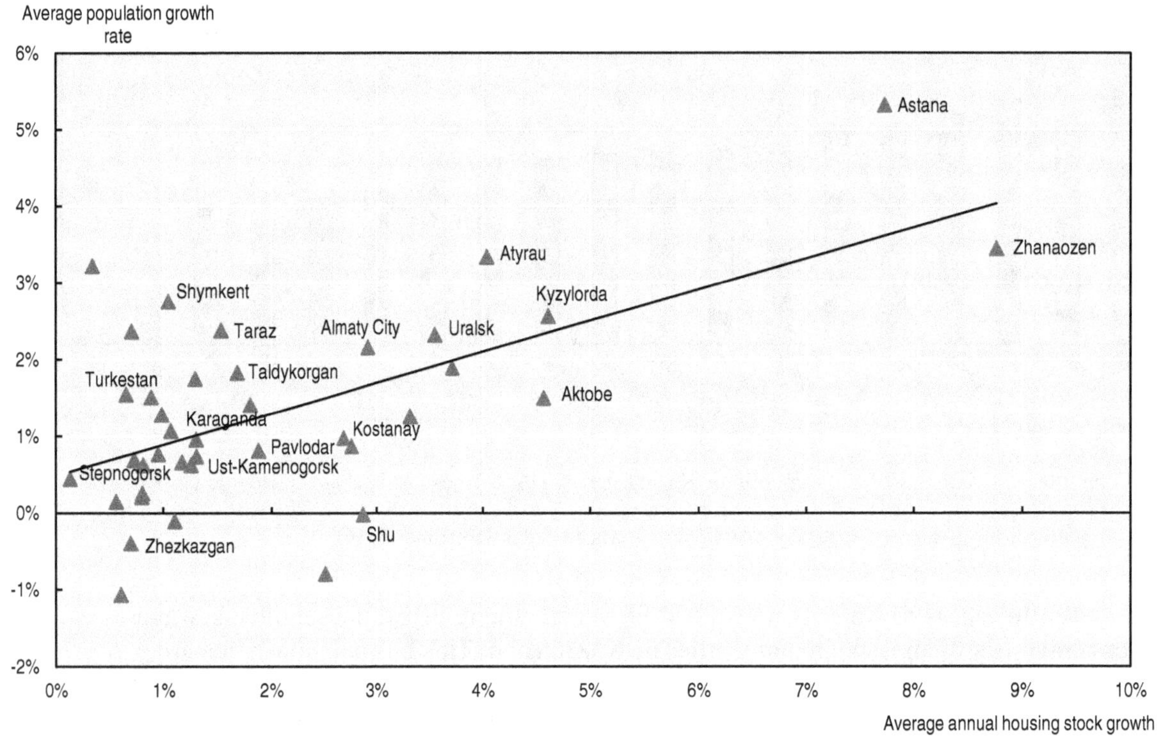

Note: The fitted line is y = 0.4051 x + 0.0048; R^2 = 0.3648. The correlation is not as good when including smaller cities of district significance.

Source: OECD research based on Committee on Statistics, data from the housing database (unpublished).

Between 2001 and 2015, real house prices in Kazakhstan rose almost sixfold, although official statistics only cover large cities and may thus overestimate the growth of housing prices for the country as a whole.[28] Housing prices, both for newly built and for existing dwellings have increased faster than in Russia and in most OECD countries since 2001 (Figure 1.20). Housing prices for existing dwellings declined after the 2007 housing boom, which was fuelled by the introduction of mortgages and led to a banking crisis (OECD, 2016e). Prices resumed their growth after 2011. Housing prices for existing dwellings in Almaty, Astana and Aktau are much higher and more volatile than in the rest of the country, and declined steeply when the real estate bubble ended abruptly in 2008. In contrast, the real estate market in other large cities is less volatile, and the post-2008 correction was much smaller. Since 2001, the growth in overall housing prices was therefore higher in many secondary cities than in Almaty and Astana.

Figure 1.20. **Real house prices indices (2001-2015)**

2001 = 100

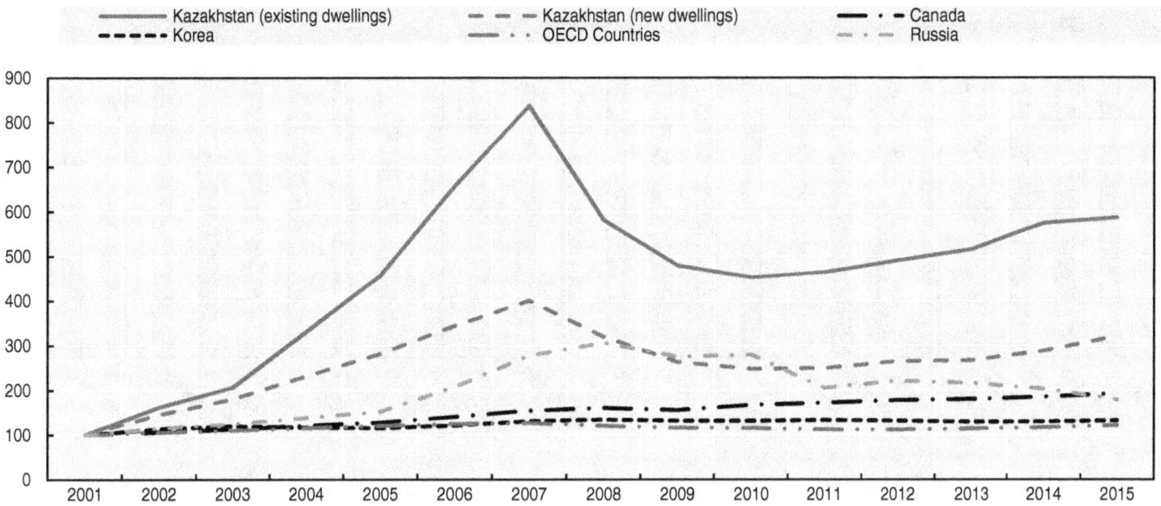

Notes: Nominal house prices deflated using the private consumption deflator from the national account statistics. In countries other than Kazakhstan, prices indices include both existing and new dwellings. Price levels for new dwellings are higher than for existing dwellings in most cities of Kazakhstan.

Source: Committee on statistics of the Republic of Kazakhstan (2016d), Housing database, available (in Russian) at: www.stat.gov.kz/faces/wcnav_externalId/publicationsCompilations?_afrLoop=3991147878468215#%40%3F_afrLoop%3D3991147878468215%26_adf.ctrl-state%3D44m4aly8u_55 (accessed 3 September 2016) and OECD (2016e), "Prices: Analytical house price indicators", Main Economic Indicators (database), http://dx.doi.org/10.1787/cbcc2905-en.

Kazakhstan has one of the world's highest home-ownership rates; 97% of the housing stock was owner-occupied in 2011. This is much higher than both Russia (86%) and EU countries, where owner-occupied housing accounted for 71% of the housing stock (Amann, 2013). Data from the 2009 National Census confirms this: 91% of respondents lived in a housing unit owned by a household member, and only 4.7% rented their current housing. This suggests Kazakhstan's rental market is underdeveloped, and that much renting is informal and undocumented, with no rental contracts and often no registration (*propiska*) of tenants. Among Kazakhstan's large cities (i.e. core cities of the 26 FUAs), only Astana seems to have a significant rental market (26%) (Figure 1.21). In Almaty City, only 8% of residents lived in a rented housing unit in 2009. Weak rental markets are problematic because they impede mobility, which is detrimental to economic productivity. They help explain the relatively low labour mobility across cities and regions in Kazakhstan. Weak rental markets also prevent young people from forming independent households unless they can afford a mortgage. Shallow rental markets usually result in overpriced rents. To attract talented and high-skilled people (from Kazakhstan and from abroad), Kazakhstani cities need to offer more rentals.

Figure 1.21. **Share of population by tenure structure in Kazakhstan's large cities**

Census respondents, 2009

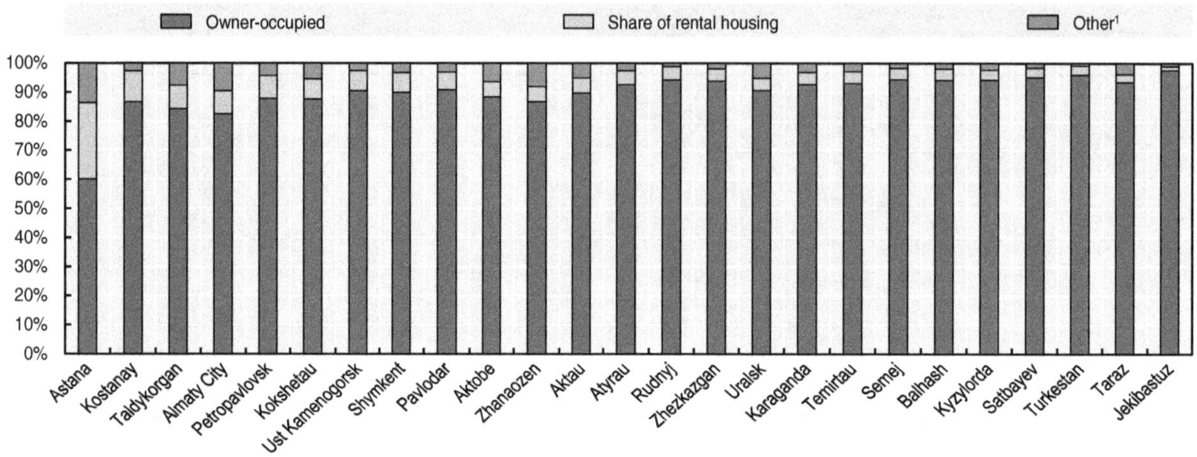

Note: 1. Includes respondents living in a dwelling owned by a third individual (not a household member, but possibly a relative of family member) and not paying rent.

Source: Committee on Statistics of the Republic of Kazakhstan, data from the 2009 National Census (unpublished).

Utility networks need updating, and low utility rates are holding back modernisation of municipal utilities

Kazakhstan's municipal utilities networks (water supply, sewage and district heating) have deteriorated rapidly since independence in 1991. In the Soviet era, these networks were based on inflated demand forecasts, and in single-industry towns (*monotowns*) utility networks were reliant on financial support and technical expertise from the town's dominant industrial facility (ADB, 2012a). During the transition period, little or no investment was made in maintenance and repair of municipal networks. However, this recently changed, and repair and maintenance of municipal utility networks is prominent in the State Programme of Infrastructure Development (*Nurly Zhol*).[29] Through this programme, municipal utility companies can benefit from heavily subsidised loans for which they apply through their local administrations.

The district heating sector is crucial in Kazakhstan's cities: it covers over 50% of the urban heating demand in the country. There are often no alternative heating options for urban households, since there is no natural gas supply infrastructure (except in urban centres in southern Kazakhstan, including Almaty City). Eighty percent of district heating networks are obsolescent, with high distribution heat losses and an elevated number of failures per kilometre of the networks (ADB, 2012b). Heat losses are high in several regions, although Astana and Almaty City seem to perform relatively well (Figure 1.22). Heat losses are particularly significant in cities of south Kazakhstan and Atyrau oblast. Average heat losses in modern, well-maintained European district heating distribution systems are around 5%-10% of the total heat distributed. Strong variations across cities exist, but heat losses can reach up to 50% of the energy produced in some cities (OECD, 2012). Household heating demand is also much higher in Kazakhstan than in European countries, because due to the lack of metering heating bills are not always based on actual consumption. Almost all heating distribution networks are still owned by local *akimats* (ADB, 2012a).

According to the OECD (2012), the modernisation of the residential sector (including district heating and thermal renovation of housing units) represents an opportunity to increase energy efficiency while reducing greenhouse gas emissions. In pilot projects in the cities of Astana and Almaty, potential energy savings from thermal modernisation (including the installation of meters and building-level sub-stations[30] – BLS) were as high as 25% to 30% of total heat distributed. The conversion of local boilers from coal to natural gas significantly reduced CO_2 emissions, energy savings and reduced heating bills for households (OECD, 2012). Modernisation of district heating is thus imperative if Kazakhstan is to reach its greenhouse gas reduction objectives (a reduction of 15% in 2020 compared to the 1990 level, and of 25% by 2050).

Figure 1.22. **Heat loss rates in Kazakhstan's regions**

% of total heat supply, 2010 and 2014

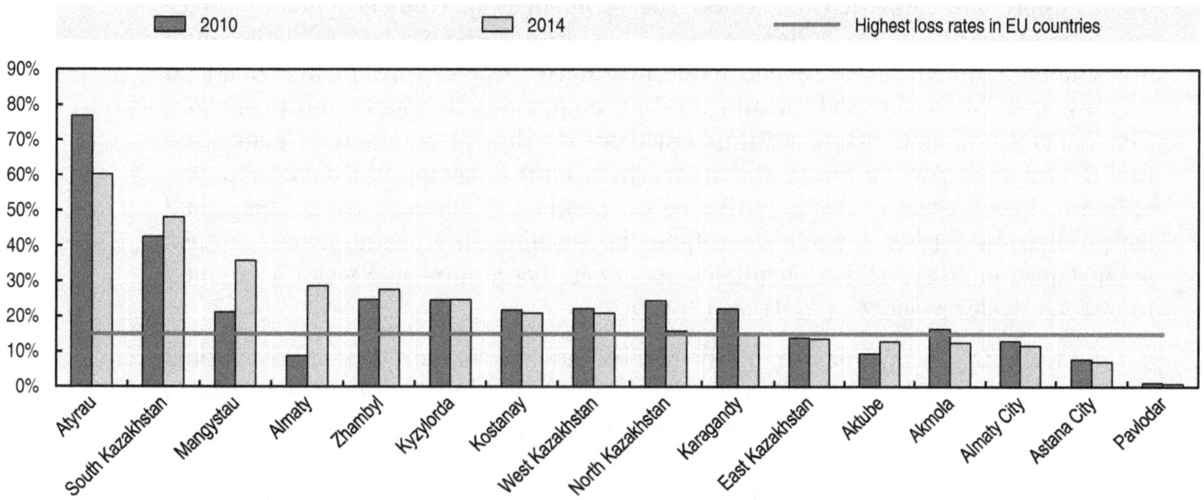

Source: Committee on Statistics of the Republic of Kazakhstan (2015a), Brochure on communal utilities, available (in Russian) at: www.stat.gov.kz/faces/wcnav_externalId/publicationsCompilations2015?_afrLoop=4018574655539556#%40%3F_afrLoop%3D4018574655539556%26_adf.ctrl-state%3D13vgemt9b5_21.

Water and sanitation networks are also in poor condition, and failures are frequent. According to data from the Committee of Statistics, water losses accounted for about one-fifth of total water output in 2014, and more than half of water output in Almaty City. A large industrial city like Karaganda does not provide hot water to residents in the summer. Some water supply networks have very high losses, particularly in Almaty City (Table 1.5) and in Aktobe oblast (where average estimated losses amounted to 30% of overall water supply in 2014). As in the case of district heating, metering is not generalised: 25% of consumers still do not have individual water meters. Most water utilities are owned by local *akimats*, with the notable exception of Shymkent, where it is a majority-owned private business (ADB, 2012a).

Table 1.5. **Estimated water losses (% of overall water supply)**

	2010	2015
Kazakhstan (national)	29.7%	22.6%
Astana	15.4%	24.9%
Almaty City	61.9%	52.7%

Note: Ratio of water losses (Rus. *Uteshka i neuchtennom reshod vodi*) water to total water supply (sewage and water supply systems).

Source: OECD research based on data from Committee on Statistics of the Republic of Kazakhstan (2015a), Brochure on communal services, available (in Russian) at: http://stat.gov.kz/faces/wcnav_externalId/publicationsCompilations2015?_afrLoop=4016293972938445#%40%3F_afrLoop%3D4016293972938445%26_adf.ctrl-state%3Dgyjfif1s9_38.

Significant investments are required to improve the quality of district heating, water supply and sanitation networks. The problem is that tariffs typically cover only operational costs (to various extents) but do not compensate for substantial investments required to renew and modernise networks. As a result, the financial performance of water and heating utility companies is poor: most are not financially sustainable. They are thus not creditworthy for commercial banks and find it hard to borrow on financial markets (long-term financing in local currency is scarce in Kazakhstan, even for profitable companies). Technical losses compound the problem by further degrading the financial sustainability of municipal utilities: for instance, in 2011, ADB Consultants estimated that nonrevenue water accounted for 40% of water produced (ADB, 2012a).

Public utility companies regularly receive ad hoc support from the national government (through local *akimats*): subsidised low interest loans have been gradually replacing direct subsidies. However, these budget transfers are not predictable: the national-level Committee of Construction, Housing and Public Utilities (hereafter, the committee) receives more applications for funding that it can finance. According to the committee, funds are allocated to the most urgent cases, i.e. the most degraded district heating, sewage and water supply networks. However, the efforts of regional authorities to make their case at the national level also seem to play a role in funds allocation, which may lead to suboptimal outcomes. The result is that utility network companies do not have a long-term planning horizon, which leads to underinvestment in municipal utility networks.

Previous research identified insufficient metering and low tariffs as key elements of Kazakhstan's municipal utility challenges. The national government and local *akimats* are promoting the installation of meters. For instance, the installation of heating meters for housing buildings can be financed at subsidised, low interest rates through a government financial vehicle, the Public Utilities Development Fund (*Fund razvitie JKKh*). Differentiated tariffs charging higher fees to consumers without meters are also increasingly common. They provide incentives for homeowners to install meters, but their actual impact on metering coverage varies across regions and subsectors (e.g. district heating, sewage or water supply). In district heating, for instance, one issue is that meters are often installed for buildings as a whole (*Obshedomovoï pribor ushieta*), requiring all homeowners in a building to agree on sharing installation costs.

Another issue related to metering is the lack of ambient temperature control (thermostatic radiator valves) in most buildings. Installing them promotes energy savings and raises household acceptance of metering and consumption-based heating tariffs, since it gives users control over the use of heat. Since 2004, building norms made thermostatic valves on radiators compulsory in new buildings. OECD (2012) recommended that thermostatic radiator valves are installed in old buildings when thermal renovations are conducted. According to the Committee of Construction, Housing and Public Utilities, only 38% of housing units were equipped with thermostatic valves on radiators in 2011 (OECD, 2012).

In Kazakhstan, municipal utility tariffs are regulated by the Committee for Regulation of Natural Monopolies (CREM), which is also Kazakhstan's national competition authority. Municipal utilities (water/sanitation or district heating) fall under the single regulatory framework for natural monopolies. The overriding concern of CREM and local *akimats* seems to be affordability of water, district heating and sanitation services by the population. Maximum tariffs are set for a five-year period, and municipal utilities have to submit all their expenditures and costs to CREM for approval, with indexation based on inflation rates. For instance, their staff expenditures should not rise more than inflation. In case of noncompliance with planned expenditures, municipal utilities must lower their tariff at least for defined periods (tariff compensation). Even though CREM considers that capital expenditures are included in existing tariffs, many experts emphasise that capital expenditure coverage is insufficient to cover rehabilitation and/or replacement of worn-out equipment (ADB, 2012b; OECD, 2012 and 2014b). This is confirmed by field research conducted for this Review. In this context, efforts to attract private investors, including foreign companies, into municipal utilities have failed in most cases. This means that capital expenditures will continue to be (mostly) financed by budget transfers and subsidised loans from the government.

Figure 1.23. **Real growth of selected municipal utility tariffs (indices)**

2000 = 100

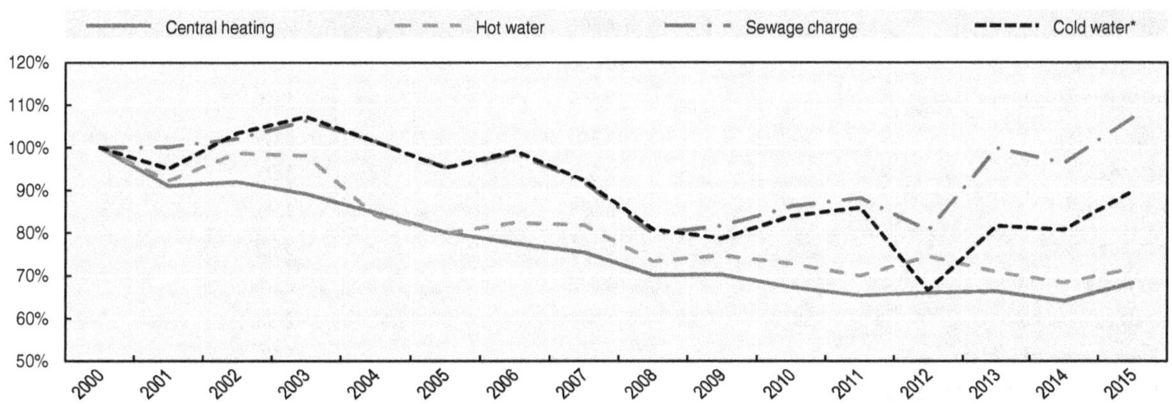

Notes: Series deflated using the Consumer Price Index (CPI) from the Committee on Statistics. *For cold water tariffs up to established norms. In some regions, rates above established norms or for buildings without metering system are higher.

Source: Committee on Statistics of the Republic of Kazakhstan (2015b), "Brochure on communal services", available (in Russian) at: http://stat.gov.kz/faces/wcnav_externalId/publicationsCompilations2015?_afrLoop=4016293972938445#%40%3F_afrLoop%3D4016293972938445%26_adf.ctrl-state%3Dgyjfif1s9_38.

Tariffs on district heating, and hot and cold water, have not increased enough to match inflation since 2000. According to official data, sanitation is the only municipal utility subsector since 2000 where the increase in user tariffs has matched inflation (Figure 1.23). It is worth noting that nationwide tariffs on central district heating have been falling in real terms for almost 15 years. This partly reflects authorities' concern with the social impact of insufficient heating in Kazakhstan's harsh climate. According to the OECD (2014b), rates for district heating in Kazakhstan are lower than in Central and Eastern European countries (Table 1.6). This is largely explained by low fuel price (mainly low coal prices), but also by insufficient or inexistent coverage of capital expenditures in heating tariffs, as noted above. In addition to being a key obstacle to the modernisation of the municipal utility networks, low tariffs on heat and water do not incentivise domestic consumers to save energy and water.

Table 1.6. **Heat prices for residential users in selected cities (2011-12)**

	Kraków (Poland)	**Sofia** (Bulgaria)	**Almaty City*** (Kazakhstan)
Price in EUR/GJ	11.67	12.27	5.93

Notes: GJ = gigajoules. Average exchange rates for 2011-12 (PLN/EUR and BGN/EUR) and for 2012 (KZT/EUR) from ECB and National Bank of Kazakhstan. *: 2012.

Source: For Almaty City, OECD research on Kazakhstan's Committee on Statistics (unpublished data).

Table 1.7. **Heat tariffs affordability in Kazakhstan's regional centres**

	Estimated monthly expenditures on heating (KZT/month), 2011/2012	**Estimated affordability (% of household disposable income spent on heating)**
Astana	4 561	2.2%
Almaty City	6 058	3.3%
Aktau (Mangystau)	2 655	1.8%
Atyrau	4 479	2.6%
Aktobe	2 627	1.5%
Karaganda	3 593	1.9%
Kostanay	5 181	3.7%
Kyzylorda	4 800	3.8%
Kokshetau (Akmola)	4 046	2.3%
Uralsk (West Kazakhstan)	4 360	3.2%
Ust-Kamenogorsk (East Kazakhstan)	2 196	1.5%
Pavlodar	2 514	1.5%
Petropavlovsk (North Kazakhstan)	4 037	2.5%
Taraz (Zhambyl)	3 969	3.8%
Taldykorgan (Almaty region)	6 169	3.7%
Shymkent (South Kazakhstan)	6 307	6.3%

Note: According to international standards defined by the World Bank, the affordability threshold for heating expenditures is 8%.

Source: OECD (2014b), "Energy subsidies and climate change in Kazakhstan", Final Report, OECD, Paris.

Tariffs on district heating vary across regions, reflecting fuel type (gas in Southern Kazakhstan, Taraz and Kyzylorda; less expensive coal in Northern Kazakhstan – including Astana, Karaganda and Pavlodar) and distance to the source of fuel (OECD, 2016a). OECD (2014b) conducted an affordability analysis of district heating prices across Kazakhstan's main cities. The share of household income spent on heating is higher in Shymkent, Taraz and Kyzylorda (Table 1.7 above). In Astana and Almaty, the percentage of income spent on heating appears to be relatively low. The main output of this analysis is that tariffs for district heating could potentially be increased in all regions without reaching an affordability threshold, set at 8% of nominal disposable income, except in Shymkent.[31]

Air pollution is becoming a major health issue in Kazakhstan's large cities

Kazakhstan has high level of CO_2 emissions relative to the size of its economy. Emissions relative to GDP have been fairly stable in recent years. However, Kazakhstan has demonstrated a strong commitment to tackling climate change: in 2009, Kazakhstan ratified the Kyoto Protocol and in the same year announced its voluntary commitment to reduce greenhouse gas emissions by 15% by 2020 from the 1990 base year as part of the UN Framework Convention on Climate change (UNFCC). According to projections based on current policies, CO_2 emissions in 2020 will be comparable to their 1990 level, requiring Kazakhstan to cut emissions by around 15% by 2020 if it is to reach its target (OECD, 2016a). Kazakhstan is also eager to enhance the energy-efficiency of its economy and in developing alternative, renewable energy sources, as demonstrated by the organisation of Expo-2017 in Astana.[32] At the policy level, Kazakhstan adopted the *Concept for transition of the Republic of Kazakhstan to the Green Economy* in 2013.

Figure 1.24. **PM_{10} concentration in cities**

Urban-population* weighted PM_{10} (2011) microgrammes per cubic metre

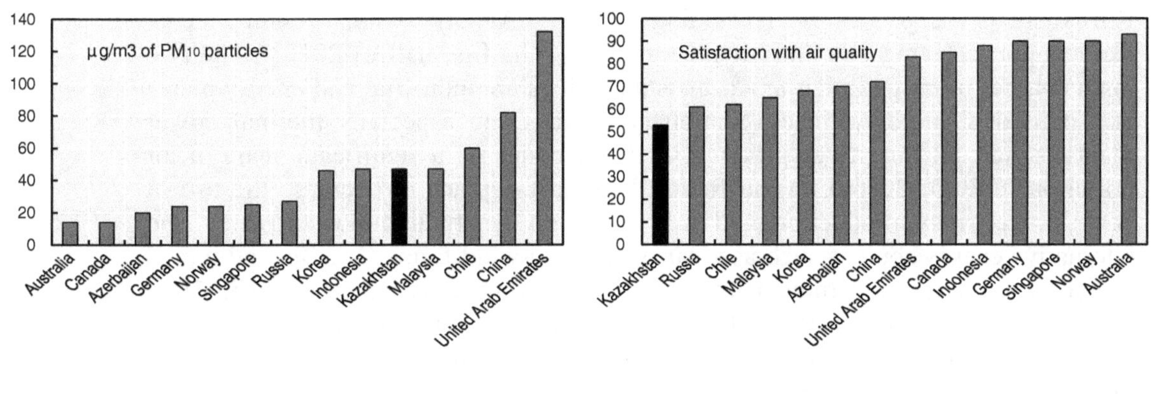

Notes: *: Cities over 100 000 inhabitants.

Sources: OECD, 2016a and World Bank (2016d), World Development Indicators (database), http://data.worldbank.org/data-catalog/world-development-indicators (accessed on 7 October, 2016). For Kazakhstan: OECD estimates (see Table 1.4).

Air pollution is a rising concern in Kazakhstan's large cities. Satisfaction with air quality is lower than in many comparable countries, including China. As Figure 1.24 shows, particle matter concentration (PM_{10}, or particulate matter of less than 10 micrometres) in Kazakhstan's urban areas was above the WHO limit for annual exposures (40 µg/m3) in 2011. Even though particulate matter concentration was lower in 2011 than in other upper-middle income countries, including OECD members (Chile, Turkey), it is expected to rise quickly in Kazakhstan's large cities, given their rapidly increasing motorisation rates and the existing reliance on coal-fired power plants for electricity production in large parts of the country. Moreover, particulate matter concentrations are much higher than the national average in Astana and Almaty City. The estimated health impact of air pollution in Kazakhstan is sizeable: premature mortality attributed to air pollution was estimated at 16 117 deaths for the 2008-2010 period, with the highest mortality estimate due to air pollution in Almaty City (Kenessariyev et al., 2013). This last study also concludes that the impact of air pollution on premature mortality in Kazakhstan is notably higher than in Russia and Ukraine.

In its *Concept for transition of the Republic of Kazakhstan to the Green Economy* (President of Kazakhstan, 2013),[33] Kazakhstan sets targets to reduce emissions of sulphur (SO_2) and nitrogen oxides (NO_2) into the environment to "European levels". However, environmental monitoring systems are not sufficiently funded, and environmental statistics do not always reflect the current pollution load on the environment (World Bank, 2016a). This is relevant for air pollution: even though many items are mandated for monitoring under Kazakhstan's Environment Code, some of the most harmful pollutants (ground-level ozone, small and ultrafine particulate matter, $PM_{2.5}$ and PM_{10}) are not monitored in Kazakhstan (Brown, 2014). This situation makes international comparison of air quality between Kazakhstan's cities and other countries very difficult. Since recent findings suggest that high concentrations of ultrafine particles ($PM_{2.5}$) are especially damaging for human health, experts have recommended that monitoring activities be upgraded to specifically measure the $PM_{2.5}$ component (Carlsen et al., 2013).

According to the Head of *Kazhydromet* (the national environmental monitoring agency), an excessively high level of air pollution was observed in many of Kazakhstan's large cities (including Taraz, Almaty City, Astana, Ust-Kamenogorsk, Karaganda and Shymkent) during the first half of 2015.[34] The two main sources of air pollution in Kazakhstan's cities are industrial and energy plants and individual motor vehicles. Stationary sources and especially thermal power plants using coal for energy production also account for a significant share of air pollution (OECD, 2016a). In the future, Kazakhstan plans to decrease the use of coal in electricity production and rely more on gas-fuelled power plants and alternative energy sources such as solar panels and wind farms.[35] As for individual motor vehicles, the government introduced the Euro-4 emission standard in 2013 (requiring lower emission levels from manufactured and imported cars). This has had a positive impact, helping to reduce harmful emissions (UNDP/GEF, 2015a). One issue is that the majority (57%)[36] of motor vehicles in Kazakhstan have been in service for more than 10 years and therefore do not comply with the new, stricter emission standards. On the other hand, diesel-powered cars account for around 3% of motor vehicles in Kazakhstan, making their emissions less of an issue than in Europe.

Almaty City has a particularly high level of air pollution as a result of the city's geographical position: it is surrounded on one side by mountains and on the other side by factories. Based on a ranking using air quality and other indicators related to health and environment, Almaty was assessed as the ninth most polluted city in the world by Mercer Human Resources Consulting in 2008. Existing research estimating fine particle matter concentration (PM_{10}) from total suspended solids confirms that annual average concentration exceeds 40 µg/m3 (the WHO limit for annual exposures) in most measuring stations of Almaty City, with very high annual average concentrations in the city centre (up to 123 µg/m3). Since motor transport accounts for 80% of air pollution emissions in Almaty, developing alternative forms of transport is paramount for reducing the high level of air pollution in the city.

Municipal waste management is falling behind in coping with rising volumes of solid waste

The current system of municipal solid waste management is not able to cope with rapid urbanisation and economic growth. In Kazakhstan, municipal solid waste collection service does not yet cover the whole population. According to ADB (2012b), the collection rate ranges between 42% to 60%, which is low compared to OECD countries. Statistical reporting on municipal solid waste in Kazakhstan presents deficiencies and inconsistencies, so the findings in this section should be interpreted with caution. Since municipal solid waste collection (and thus statistical reporting) is sparse in rural areas, data for Astana and Almaty were used rather than for Kazakhstan as a whole. Official statistics suggest that generation of solid waste per capita increased rapidly after 2005 (Figure 1.25), with a decreasing trend after 2009. One possible explanation is that rates of waste collection rose rapidly after 2009 in both Astana and Almaty City, prompting households and companies to reduce their solid waste production. Compared to OECD countries, municipal solid waste generated per capita in Astana and Almaty (around 344 and 451 kg per capita respectively) is in the low range of OECD countries, comparable to Mexico, Japan or Korea (Figure 1.26). Kazakhstan policymakers should keep in mind that, over the long term (from 2010 to 2040), municipal solid waste production will grow by at least 50%, due to rising per capita income and consumption (ADB, 2012a). This has been the case in fast-growing OECD economies such as Mexico, Turkey and Chile.

Figure 1.25. **Municipal solid waste per capita (kg per year)**

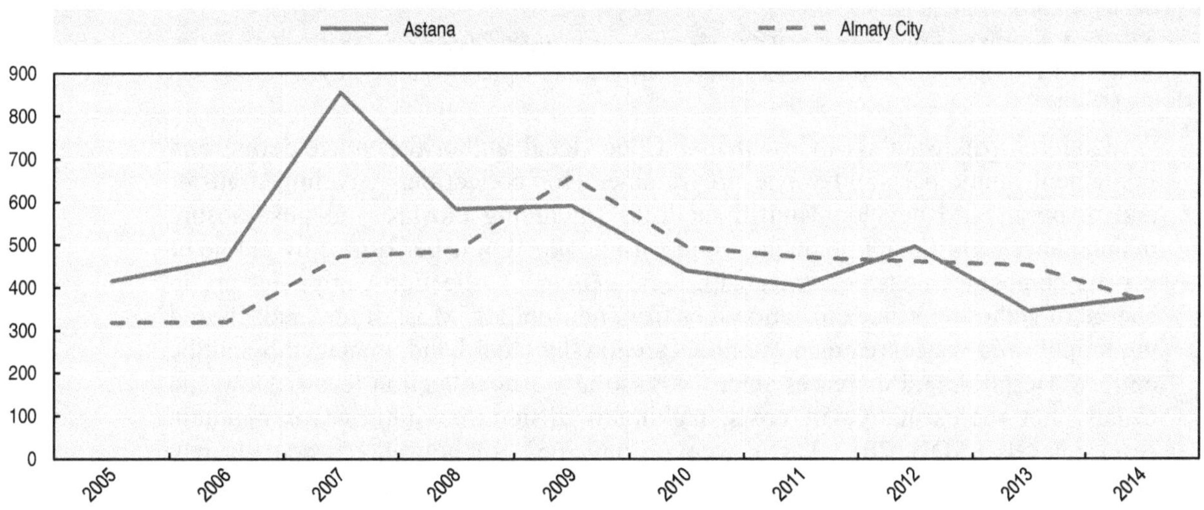

Source: Committee on Statistics of the Republic of Kazakhstan, environment database (unpublished).

According to ADB (2012a), municipal solid waste in Kazakhstan is often dumped into sites that have few, if any, engineered environmental protection systems (open dumps). This presents significant risks for ground water and the environment. In 2013, the government undertook to construct over 150 landfills with adequate environmental protection measures near major cities.[37] Among other forms of treatment, a small share of municipal solid waste is recycled, accounting for 2.2% of total municipal solid waste volumes in 2014.[38] Some large cities have sorting facilities on their landfills (such as Shymkent) or implement sorting practices, a prerequisite for recycling. In Astana, around 8% of overall solid municipal waste was recycled in a dedicated recycling facility in 2014. The unexploited potential for material recovery from solid waste in urban areas is high, whether it is recycling cardboard, paper or organic matter, or use of solid waste as in an input in industrial processes (ADB, 2012a). Indeed, in OECD countries, around a third of municipal solid waste (34% in 2012) on average is subject to material recovery (recycling and composting), which generates marketable outputs and lowers the costs of solid waste treatment.

Figure 1.26. **Municipal solid waste generated in OECD countries, Astana and Almaty City, 2013**

Kg per capita

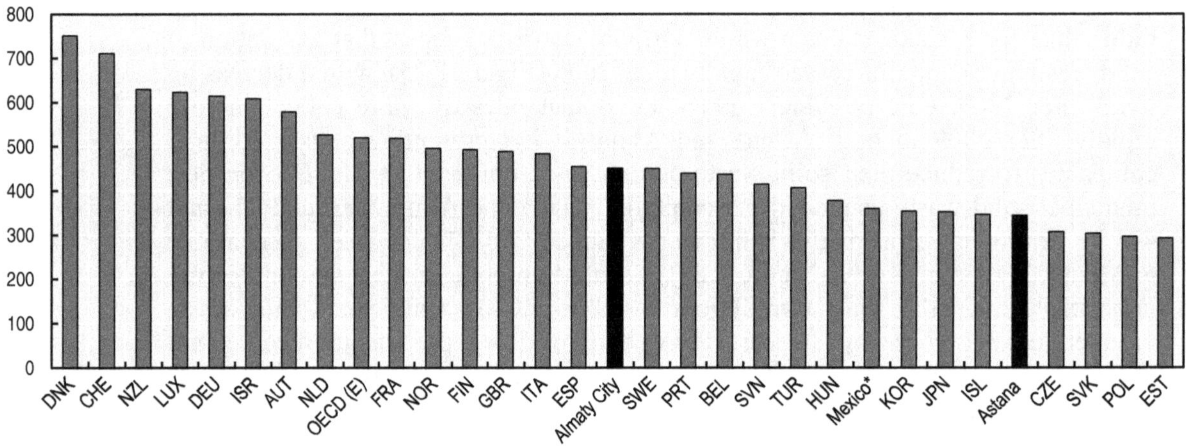

Note: * Data for Mexico are for 2012.

Sources: OECD (2016f), "Municipal waste", *OECD Environment Statistics* (database), http://dx.doi.org/10.1787/data-00601-en (accessed 28 September 2016) and Committee on Statistics of the Republic of Kazakhstan, environment database (unpublished).

Under Kazakhstan's Environmental Code, local authorities must define and implement municipal solid waste programmes (for collection, recycling, transfer and disposal) and develop landfill facilities (including closure and post-closure maintenance activities). In practice, solid waste collection is performed by public or private companies under contract with local *akimats*. Collection companies are in charge of gathering waste collection fees from households. Most of the landfills and municipal solid waste treatment facilities are, on the other hand, managed by public entities. Despite rapid increases since 2009, solid waste collection fees are low and usually not representative of costs, making it difficult to improve or maintain service levels (ADB, 2012a). On average, only 65% of households actually pay waste collection fees to collectors: private waste management companies typically have little enforcement tools to improve payment discipline (court procedures are time-consuming and expensive). Overall, the sector is not attractive for international companies that could help to modernise solid waste management services (UNDP/GEF, 2015b).

Cities, key economic challenges and innovation in Kazakhstan

Urbanisation and economic growth

A country's urbanisation has important implications for its economic development. According to Henderson (2010), while economic development does not happen without urbanisation, urbanisation as such is not a guarantee for economic development. Empirical evidence confirms that no country has achieved high levels of GDP per capita without urbanisation (see the large empty space in the upper left of Figure 1.27). Conversely, some countries have become highly urbanised without much progress with respect to GDP per capita convergence with the United States. This is the case of many countries in Latin America, such as Brazil. In contrast, Korea and China managed to substantially reduce the GDP per capita gap with the United States while experiencing rapid urbanisation (most of Korea's urbanisation happened before 1990, and is thus not displayed on Figure 1.27). Kazakhstan displays an atypical pattern: because of high emigration of city dwellers, the urbanisation rate fell during the economic recession of the 1990s, which widened the gap between Kazakhstan's GDP per capita with the United States'. From 2001 onwards, the country benefitted from a long period of high economic growth, and the urbanisation rate rose moderately.

Figure 1.27. **Economic convergence and urbanisation (1990-2015)**

Kazakhstan's urbanisation rate, based on OECD estimates (see Table 1.4)

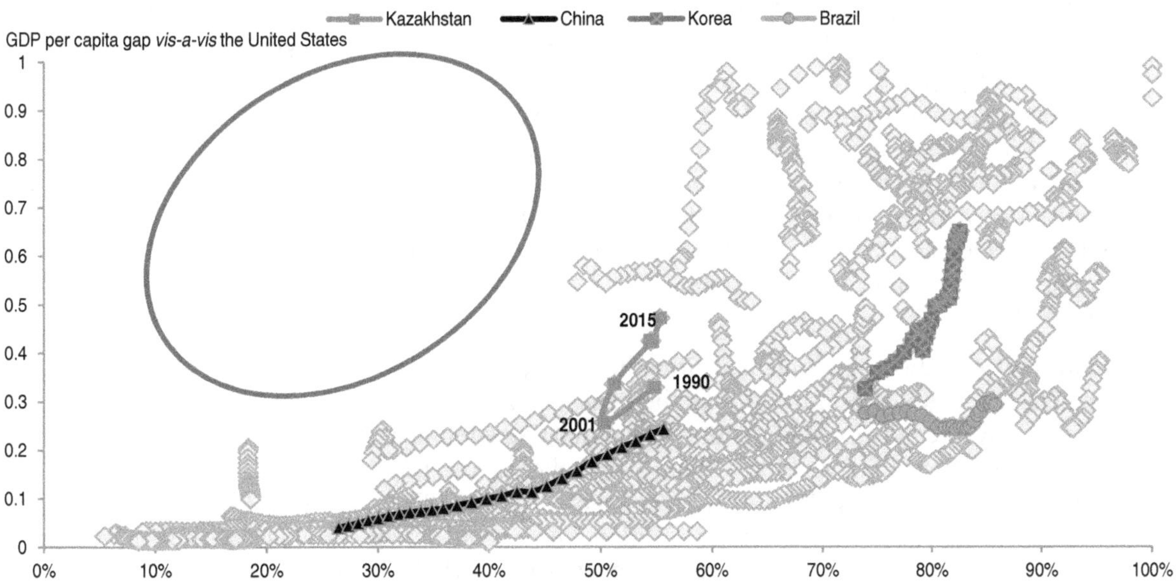

Note: Data cover 91 countries for the period 1990-2015, GDP per capita gap in relation to the United States is based upon PPP GDP per capita in constant 2011 international USD.

Source: World Bank (2016d), *World Development Indicators* (database), http://data.worldbank.org/data-catalog/world-development-indicators. For Kazakhstan: OECD estimates (see Table 1.4).

Typically, the urbanisation process begins with improvements in productivity of the rural sector of the economy due to improved technology or economic reforms (such as the adoption of the household responsibility system in China during the late 1970s) (OECD, 2015a, Chapter 2). This releases labour that shifts from agriculture to more productive employment in the manufacturing and service sectors. Since these sectors benefit from agglomeration economies, production should be increasingly located in high-density locations (Henderson, 2010). In the case of Kazakhstan, however, two important points are relevant when considering the classic urbanisation/economic development nexus. First, extractive industries, especially the oil and gas sector, played a crucial role in the period of high growth from 2001 onwards (OECD, 2016a).

A second consideration is that Kazakhstan's urban system is in large part a legacy of Soviet-era planning. Most of the country's urbanisation took place between 1926 and 1989. Production was organised spatially to consolidate the Soviet Union. In most cases, cities were built around a factory or developed as centres of production. Soviet planners pushed urban growth towards low-density zones, in an effort to exploit natural resources and populate the country's vast territory. This resulted in an excessive dispersion of population and cities across the country, and a smaller share of large cities compared to developed countries (Coulibaly et al., 2013).[39] Many cities were poorly connected to other urban centres. In Kazakhstan, domestic inter-city connectivity is inadequate, partly because much of the transport network was planned in the Soviet era and oriented towards Russia (ADB, 2012a).

As demonstrated in OECD (2017a, forthcoming), the territorial concentration of population and GDP in Kazakhstan has increased more rapidly than in most OECD countries during the 1998-2010 period. The rapid growth of Kazakhstan's metropolitan areas in the 2000s, as documented in this chapter, suggests that this economic and population concentration is still in play. GDP data available for the wealthiest metropolitan areas in Kazakhstan confirm this. Almaty City accounted for 21.9% of Kazakhstan's GDP in 2015, while only 9.5% of the overall population lives in Almaty City. That year, Astana accounted for 11.4% of Kazakhstan's GDP but only 5% of the country's population. The GDP share of Astana and Almaty City (as a percentage of national GDP) has been growing during the last five years, meaning that high value added activities have been increasingly concentrated in the two cities.[40]

This concentration of people and firms in a few high-density "economic growth centres" is key if Kazakhstan is to reap the benefits of agglomeration economies, as recognised by the government in the "Regional Development Programme Until 2020" (hereafter, RDP) and the "Forecast Scheme of Territorial and Spatial Development of the Republic of Kazakhstan Until 2020" (hereafter, Forecast Scheme until 2020). This concentration alone is not sufficient: OECD research suggests that only well-managed, well-connected cities (both internally and with their commuting zone and neighbouring urban centres) support economic growth, by allowing countries to enjoy agglomeration economies while mitigating agglomeration costs (Box 1.9).

Box 1.9. **Agglomeration economies: costs and benefits**

Metropolitan areas and dynamic medium-sized cities have enormous potential for job creation and innovation, as they are hubs and gateways for global networks such as trade or transport. In many OECD countries, labour productivity measured in terms of GDP per worker and wages is seen to increase with city size.

Stronger productivity levels are a reflection of the bonus intrinsic to being in a city, known as the agglomeration benefit. On average, a worker's wage increases with the size of the city where he/she works, even after controlling for worker attributes such as education level. OECD estimates suggest that the agglomeration benefit in the form of a wage premium rises by 2%-5% for a doubling of population size (Ahrend et al., 2014), which is in line with comparable studies for individual countries (Combes et al., 2012). However, agglomeration benefits do not accrue homogeneously across cities, and they show sizeable variations within countries.

Higher productivity is due in part to the quality of the workforce and the industrial mix. Larger cities on average have a more educated population, with the shares of both very high-skilled and low-skilled workers increasing with city size. A 10 percentage-point increase in the share of university-educated workers in a city raises the productivity of other workers in that city by 3%-4% (Ahrend et al., 2014). Larger cities typically have a higher proportion of sectors with higher productivity, such as consulting, legal or financial services, etc. They are also more likely to be hubs or service centres through which trade flows and financial and other flows are channelled. These flows typically require the provision of high value-added services.

Agglomeration costs and benefits

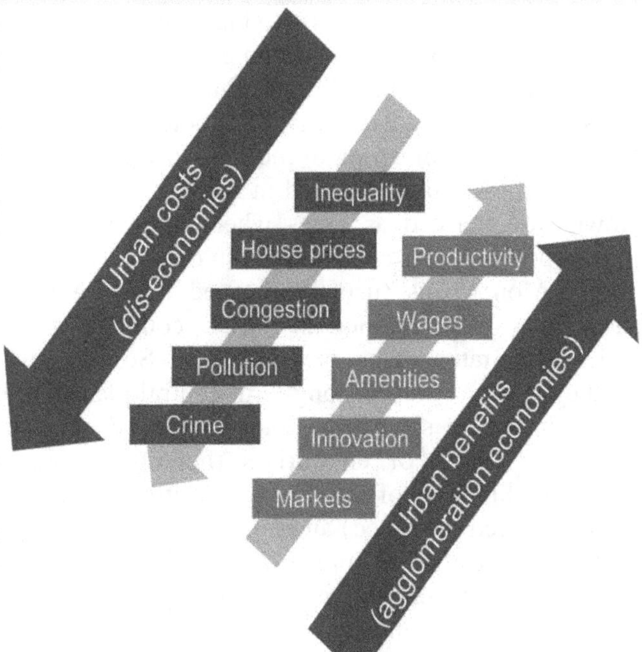

Living in large cities does provide benefits, but it also has disadvantages (see figure above). While productivity, wages and the availability of many amenities generally increase with city size, so do what are generally referred to as agglomeration costs. Some agglomeration costs are financial: for example, housing prices/rents and, more generally, price levels, are typically higher in larger cities. In addition, a number of non-pecuniary costs, such as pollution, congestion, inequality and crime, typically also increase with city size, while trust and similar measures of social capital often decline. Survey data from European cities confirm that citizens in larger cities – despite valuing the increased amenities – are generally less satisfied with the other aspects mentioned, notably air pollution.

Box 1.9. **Agglomeration economies: costs and benefits** (*cont.*)

To some extent, city size is the outcome of a trade-off between these benefits and costs. Mobility across and within cities implies that – at least in the medium to long term – wage levels, commuting costs and other urban (dis)amenities are reflected in land prices, and more generally in a city's cost of living. This is supported by findings suggesting that for increasing population size, these agglomeration benefits and costs go up at a broadly comparable pace [see Combes et al. (2012), for evidence on France, and Gibbons et al. (2011), for the United Kingdom]. A similar picture emerges when looking directly at cities' productivity and price levels. Evidence from Germany shows that, on average, increases in a city's productivity, and hence wages, are matched by similar increases in local price levels.

Sources: OECD (2014a), *OECD Regional Outlook 2014: Regions and Cities: Where Policies and People Meet*, OECD Publishing, Paris, http://dx.doi.org/10.1787/9789264201415-en; Ahrend, R. et al. (2014), "What make cities more productive? Evidence on the role of urban governance from five OECD countries", *OECD Regional Development Working Papers*, No. 2014/05, OECD Publishing, Paris, http://dx.doi.org/10.1787/5jz432cf2d8p-en; Combes, P.-P., G. Duranton and L. Gobillon (2012), "The costs of agglomeration: Land prices in French cities", *CEPR Discussion Papers*, No. 9 240, Centre for Economic Policy Research, London; Gibbons, S. and H.G. Overman and G. Resende (2011), "Real earnings disparities in Britain", *Spatial Economics Research Centre Discussion Papers*, No. 0065, London School of Economics and Political Science, London.

Kazakhstan has developed a policy to tackle the challenges of monotowns

In single-industry towns (or monotowns) a single industry or often a single company (hereafter, core company) account for the bulk of economic activity. This makes monotowns economically vulnerable in times of crisis and economic decline, and increases social vulnerability. Monotowns were particularly widespread in the Soviet Union, a reflection of the size, low population density, and significant deposits of natural resources located in remote, inhospitable regions. In Kazakhstan, monotowns are defined as cities where at least 20% of industrial output and the employed population is concentrated in one or a few core enterprises of the same industry.[41] Monotowns (usually focused on mining or sometimes fishing activities) have also been common in OECD countries such as Canada, Australia and the United States. The specificity of Soviet and post-Soviet monotowns is that i) they are the result of long-term central planning; ii) they were based on supply chains based on substantial transport and energy subsidies, and iii) the main enterprise or group of enterprises (hereafter, core company or companies) acted as the supplier of municipal utilities (water, sewage and sometimes district heating when it existed) and housing for its employees (BISAM Central Asia, 2012). The privatisation of core companies in the 1990s often resulted in a lack of maintenance and renovation of municipal utility networks and degradation of the housing stock. Municipal utility networks are still on the balance sheets of core companies in some of Kazakhstan's monotowns, such as Khromtau (World Bank JERP, 2015).

Among heterogeneous monotowns, a significant share has low economic potential...

Recent trends provide clear evidence that monotowns are increasingly heterogeneous. Not all of them are depressed economically, with substandard living conditions and income levels. They include oil and gas towns such as Zhanaozen, Kulsariy or Aksaï, iron and metal mining towns where metal reserves will soon be exhausted (such as Arkalyk), manufacturing centres for steel and chemical industries and even towns where the core mining activity no longer exists, such as Kentau. Obsolete municipal utility networks are an issue almost everywhere. However, in many monotowns, average monthly wages are well above the regional (*oblast*) average or even higher than in Astana and Almaty City (in the case of oil and gas outposts).

However, recent economic and demographic trends in monotowns suggest that of the 27 monotowns, more than two have "low potential". Around ten small or medium-size monotowns have weak or negative real wage growth and have wages that sometimes lag far behind the regional average (Figure 1.28), a low percentage of residents with tertiary education (Figure 1.29), high self-employment (Figure 1.30) and do not benefit from positive net migration (Figure 1.31), even from rural areas. Geographic location and transport connectivity (which factor into RDP's assessment criteria of economic potential) are also paramount. The sheer remoteness and poor road and railway connectivity to large urban centres typical of many monotowns is a powerful obstacle to economic diversification, especially toward manufacturing activities. Indeed, since transport costs for raw materials tend to be lower than those for manufactured goods, high transport costs tend to reinforce the specialisation in raw commodities and constitute yet another barrier that producers of higher-value manufactures must overcome in order to compete (OECD, 2015c).

In the 2010-15 period, real wage growth in monotowns has fallen been below the national level (3.5% every year on average). In 10 monotowns, real wage growth has been negative (Figure 1.28). This may reflect a variety of factors, including monopsony power[42] of the core company in a small labour market and sector-specific trends (e.g. declining global steel and metal prices). Fourteen monotowns have average wage levels below the regional (*oblast*) average, which is also a size effect (average wages tend to be higher in large cities, particularly oblast centres). The population in monotowns cumulating low average wage (as compared to the regional average) and negative or very weak real income growth (in the lower left corner of Figure 1.28) are likely to face substantial economic challenges, with earnings essentially lower than the regional average and stagnating or decreasing real wages in the recent period. According to the monotown programme, salaries account for around 50%-60% of overall household income in monotowns.

Figure 1.28. **Average wage and real wage growth in monotowns**

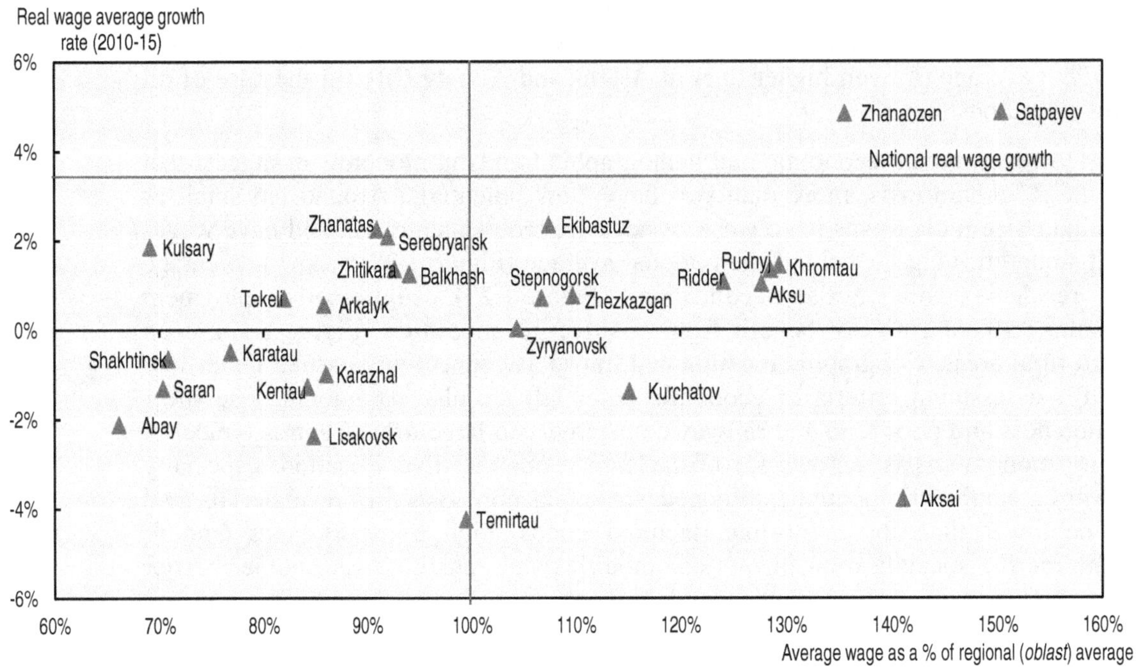

Note: Average wage as a percentage of oblast average (2013-15).

Source: OECD research on Committee on Statistics of the Republic of Kazakhstan, labour database (unpublished).

Figure 1.29. **Share of residents with tertiary education, 2009**

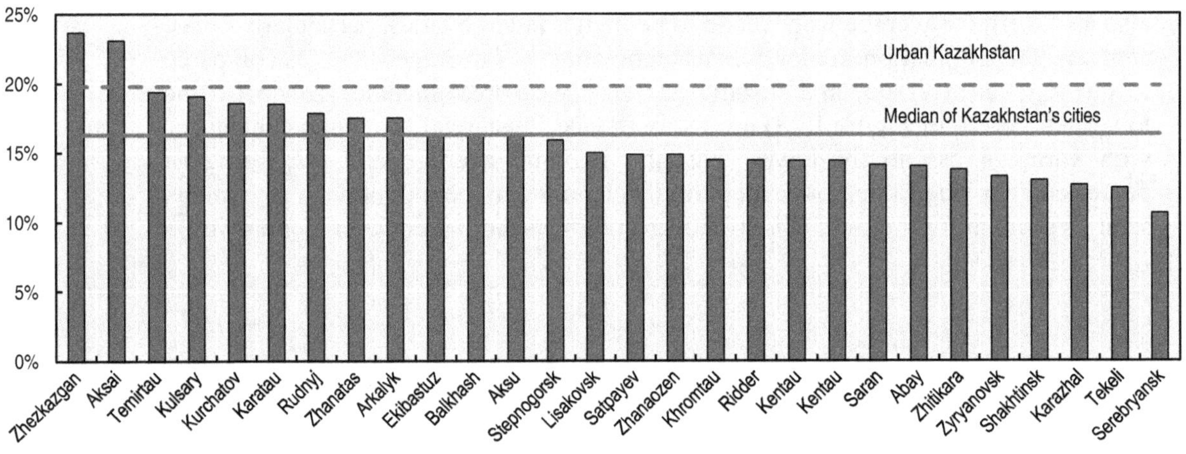

Source: Committee on Statistics of the Republic of Kazakhstan, data from the 2009 national census (unpublished).

Monotowns often have a low share of residents with higher education. In 2009, a few had a substantially lower share of tertiary-educated residents than the average for urban areas (20%) and the median percentage for Kazakhstan's 87 towns (see Figure 1.29 above). A low share of tertiary educated residents is common for mining or factory town populations. However, this lack of human capital can preclude monotowns with a declining core industry from diversifying into new sectors, particularly manufacturing, and from becoming significant service centres for surrounding rural areas.

Ten monotowns have a substantially higher self-employment rate than the level of Kazakhstan's urban areas (Figure 1.30). Self-employment offers an alternative source of income for households after the downsizing or closure of core industries in a town. However, in Kazakhstan, it is closely associated with poverty and lower income levels (World Bank, 2016b). While unemployment rates are relatively low and do not vary much across Kazakhstan's monotowns, self-employment may be a more appropriate indicator for identifying monotowns with a depressed labour market.[43] A high level of self-employment is highly correlated with lower average wages across Kazakhstan's monotowns[44] and urban areas as a whole.

Figure 1.30. **Self-employment across Kazakhstan's monotowns in 2015**

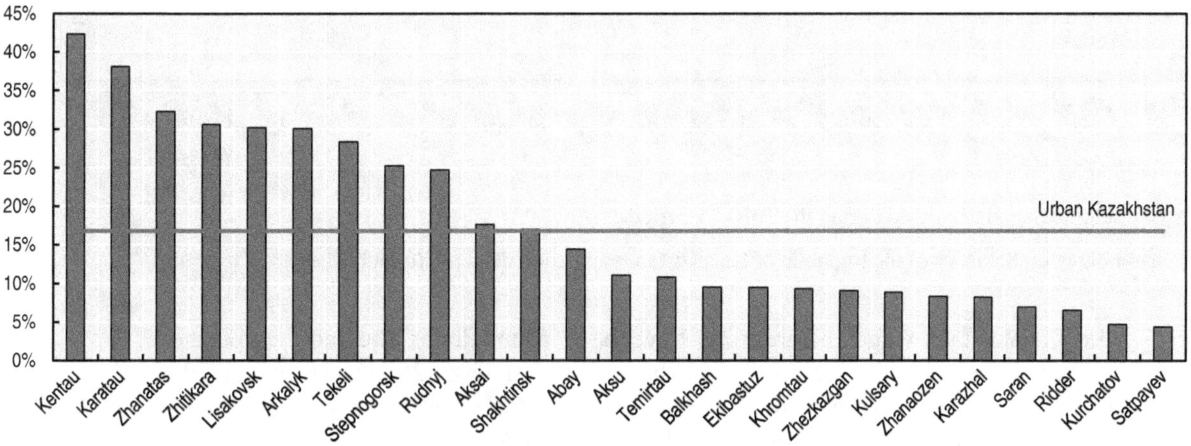

Note: The monotowns Zyryanovsk and Serebryansk are missing.

Source: OECD research based on data from the Committee on Statistics of the Republic of Kazakhstan (2016e), Labour database, main labour market indicators at the district level, available (in Russian) at: www.stat.gov.kz/faces/wcnav_externalId/homeNumbersLabor?_afrLoop=6672220744050857#%40%3F_afrLoop%3D6672220744050857%26_adf.ctrl-state%3Dlhdr4xyv6_47.

Outward migrations from some monotowns may be constrained by poverty ("liquidity constraint")

Kazakhstan's monotowns have experienced relative demographic decline. The 27 monotowns accounted for 14% of Kazakhstan's urban population at the beginning of 2016, but almost 19% of the urban population in 1999. However, since 2009, the population of most monotowns has risen (if usually at a slower pace than in urban Kazakhstan as a whole), as opposed to the steep demographic decline in the previous decade. Population declined in only 8 of the 27 monotowns in the 2009-2016 period, most dramatically in Serebryansk (which has experienced rapid out-migration) and Zyrianovsk. In the same period, around half of monotowns experienced negative net migrations (i.e. net migration outflows, see Figure 1.31). Population outflow from monotowns is a concern because a qualified personnel is overrepresented among emigrants: monotowns therefore lose valuable human capital, which is already in short supply. When emigration leads to a shrinking population and population ageing, local administration end up maintaining an oversized urban infrastructure, which is a burden to local and national public finances.

Figure 1.31. **Yearly net migration, 2010-15**

Share of resident population

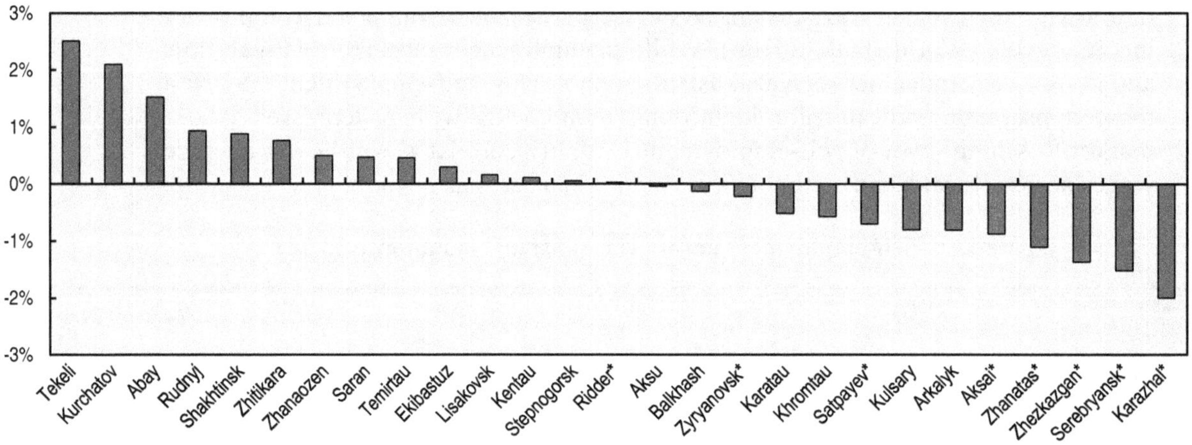

Note: * Overall population decreased during the 2010-15 period.

Source: Committee on Statistics of the Republic of Kazakhstan, population database (unpublished).

In Kazakhstan, wage differentials have been found to be the most important driver of interregional migrations (Aldashev and Dietz, 2014). However, the correlation between average monthly wage and net migrations appears to be *inexistent or even negative* (meaning that higher wages would be correlated to negative net migrations, i.e. net outflows) as regards monotowns.[45] Size does not seem to matter much either, expect for the four monotowns with population higher than 100 000 inhabitants (they all have positive net migrations over 2010-15). Negative net migration is observed both from relatively small and low-income monotowns such as Serebryansk and Karazhal, and from larger, relatively prosperous monotowns such as Zhezkazgan and Khromatau (Figure 1.31).

This suggests that several competing factors play a role in determining migrations flows from and to monotowns in Kazakhstan. In the case of Russia, Andrianko and Guriev (2004) found that there is a liquidity constraint affecting poorer regions: the population cannot leave simply because they cannot finance relocation costs. This counteracts an opposite trend: in the absence of financial constraints, higher wages should reduce, rather than increase, migration outflows. Andrianko and Guriev (2004) estimated that a third of the Russian population in 2004 was locked in a poverty trap because of liquidity constraints on emigration. Our preliminary analysis suggests that such a liquidity constraint on outward migration could affect the population of Kazakhstan's poorest monotowns. Indeed, as in the Russian Federation, interregional labour mobility is relatively low due to obstacles to interregional labour mobility (an under-developed rental market for housing, large distances and high interregional real estate price differentials). Relocation costs are substantial and must be paid by migrants themselves.

Net migrations from and to Kazakhstan's monotowns are thus subject to geographic distance, wage differentials with other cities and liquidity constraints, in the case of the poorest monotowns. This could explain why there is no or even negative correlation between average monthly wages and net migrations. For instance, some monotowns with stable employment and average income levels, such as Zhezkazgan, still experience net population outflows (see Figure 1.31). Indeed, when liquidity constraints are less significant, the wage differential with Kazakhstan's largest cities (for instance, the nearby oblast centre) is a significant driver of population outflows. The data also suggest that a higher percentage of tertiary-educated residents (as in Zhezkazgan) is correlated with higher migration outflows. Residents of monotowns with higher education may be more eager to move out because the premium of higher education (the wage differential with workers without tertiary education) would be higher in larger cities.

Further research could shed more light on migration dynamics in Kazakhstan's monotowns and small towns. However, research carried out for this Review suggests that increasing employment opportunities and income levels in Kazakhstan's monotowns may not automatically prevent net migration outflows (especially of qualified personnel) or population decline. This means that, in some monotowns at least, the medium-term perspective is an efficient downsizing of the network of municipal facilities and staffs (hospitals, schools) as the population gradually declines. If spatial and economic plans fail to take into account the reality of a declining city, disproportionately large education and health facilities will put a heavy burden on municipal and regional public finances.

Monotown policy: a comprehensive plan designed in 2012, that has been partially implemented

Kazakhstan adopted a dedicated state programme on the "Development of Monotowns" (hereafter, monotown programme) on May 2012.[46] It defined 27 monotowns in Kazakhstan, ranging from medium-size cities of oblast significance, such as Temirtau (178 000 inhabitants) or Ekibastuz (130 000 inhabitants) to small towns with a population of around 20 000. The programme has a comprehensive approach of monotown development. It has three major goals: i) developing and improving urban infrastructure (roads, municipal utility networks) and the housing stock, ii) economic diversification and SME development to increase employment, and iii) increasing labour mobility to stimulate voluntary movement to areas with higher social and economic development potential.

The programme also launched a comprehensive diagnosis process of all monotowns, covering all the issues mentioned above (urban infrastructure, housing, entrepreneurship and economic diversification). Based on a national methodology, oblast *akimats* classified monotowns into high, medium and low categories based on their economic potential (Box 1.10). Each monotown also prepared a "Comprehensive Development Plan" (hereafter, CDP, or *Compleksnie programmi razvitia*, in Russian) that details capital investments required to upgrade urban infrastructure (roads, municipal utility networks and housing) and investment projects that could contribute to diversifying the town's economic structure. Most CDPs have the same target indicators: unemployment rate, number of SMEs with a real business activity, investments in fixed assets by companies, rate of degraded municipal utility (water, sewage, district heating) and electricity distribution networks. Sometimes industrial output (in volume) or population numbers are also target indicators.

Box 1.10. **Assessing the economic potential of monotowns**

Monotowns are categorised into high, medium and low economic potential based on several parameters. Here are the parameters that define low economic potential:

- The core industry company has substantially reduced its industrial production in the last ten years and is not profitable.
- The mineral base will be exhausted within the next ten years (for mining monotowns).
- Population is declining; the net migration rate has been negative for the past ten years, and emigration is high among qualified employees.
- Degraded municipal utility and electricity distribution network, with housing stock that includes many substandard housing units.
- Environmental issues, air and water pollution levels are higher than environmental norms.
- Average wages in the town are lower than the oblast (regional) average.
- Poor transport connectivity (including roads in poor condition) and remote location, more than an hour's drive or 75 kilometres from the main cities and transport corridors.

The Regional Development Programme until 2020 does not provide details of the exact methodology or the weight of different criteria. However, of 27 monotowns, only two (Janatass and Arkalik) are classified as having low economic potential. Other monotowns have high or medium economic potential. As highlighted by Linn (2014), the government appears optimistic about its ability to support economic diversification of a vast majority of monotowns.

Sources: Government of Kazakhstan (2014), *Regional Development programme until 2020*; Linn, J. (2014), "Urbanization, Regional Development, and Decentralization", in A. Aitzhanova et al. (eds.) (2014), *Kazakhstan 2050: Toward a Modern Society for All*, Nazarbayev University, National Analytical Centre, Oxford University Press, Group Centennial International, Astana, pp.187-223.

CDPs are the basis for defining the volume of financial support to monotowns from the national and *oblast* budgets. However, even though the methodology and structure allows CDPs to reflect each monotown's specific priorities, the same target indicators were imposed from the national monotown programme. According to BISAM Central Asia (2012), they often do not reflect the specifics of each monotown, and are sometimes overly optimistic and unachievable (especially as regards SME indicators). Employment and population forecasts in CDPs tend to be optimistic as compared to actual figures. For instance, Stepnogorsk CDP's forecast (made in 2014) overestimated employment in 2015 by almost 2000 (or 5%).[47] Over-optimistic forecasts may signal that monotowns' *akimats* do not adequately reflect population decline or stagnation in urban and economic planning. This can result in inefficient public spending because of "oversized" city infrastructures.

Prominent or "anchor" investment projects (usually in the chemicals industry, oil and gas, mining and metallurgy) detailed in each CDP are supposed to be the main driver of economic diversification. The Regional Development programme until 2020 and individual CDPs highlight three other options to revive the economic potential of monotowns: i) investment projects by Kazakhstan's SOEs and state-owned development banks (affiliates of Samruk Kazyna and Baïterek holdings); ii) investment in vertically integrated production units and outsourcing to local businesses by the core industrial company in each monotowns; iii) strengthening the existing industrial specialisation, through modernisation of existing assets or exploration of new mineral deposits or oilfields. Although there is no budget line in the national budget dedicated to these investment projects in monotowns, some of these projects benefitted from low-interest rate loans through state interest rate subsidies.

The monotown programme also places strong emphasis on development of entrepreneurship and SMEs in monotowns. The 2015 national budget contained both subsidised budget credits to support entrepreneurship (amounting to KZT 1.6 billion, or around USD 7.21 million), on top of regular budget transfers earmarked for monotowns. Support for entrepreneurship takes the form of subsidised credits for investment projects and microfinance organisations in monotowns and the operations of entrepreneur support centres, where new entrepreneurs can receive individual consulting and business trainings. Grants from KZT 1.5 million to 3 million (around USD 6 700 to 13 529) are also distributed through city *akimats* of monotowns for new business projects.

The implementation of the initial monotown programme stalled because of budget constraints and initial flaws in the design of the programme. In 2014, the state programme on the "Development of Monotowns" was merged into a unified "Regional Development Programme Until 2020", covering all of Kazakhstan's 87 cities.[48] However, budget constraints have severely limited the scope of the programme. Support for entrepreneurship in monotowns has a dedicated budget line, but a freeze was declared on new projects requiring budget financing in 2015. On the whole, the maintenance and renewal of municipal utility and electricity distribution networks, city roads and other municipal infrastructure items account for the bulk of the monotown programme budget spending in monotowns. This has improved municipal utility networks, roads and electricity networks in monotowns, but in many of them, the lack of (formal) employment opportunities remains a pressing issue.

"Anchor" investment projects are often pre-existing expansion projects by established core monotown companies in their dominant mining or manufacturing branch. The central criterion for assessing "anchor" projects is the forecast number of new jobs. As a result, "anchor" investment projects do not always result in economic diversification. Few monotowns attracted new investment projects from SOEs, except in Stepnogorsk (where an SOE, the core manufacturing company, has been expanding production). As reported by BISAM Central Asia (2012), outsourcing to local monotown businesses is not always advantageous to core monotown companies, given their vertically integrated structure or the insufficient quality of local production. All in all, according to discussions in Kazakhstan's parliament in November 2015, less than half of the 48 selected "anchor" projects have been realised. In almost half of new production units from "anchor" projects, production accounts for 50% or less of installed industrial capacity.[49]

The policy package for monotowns is supposed to be tailored to each town's economic potential (low, medium or high). Most importantly, people in monotowns of low potential are eligible for grants to help them move out and find a job elsewhere, as long as they resettle in the same oblast. However, because only two out of 27 monotowns are considered as having "low economic potential", the implementation of such measures to stimulate labour mobility has been very limited. The assessment of the economic potential of monotowns (and small towns) thus needs to be reconsidered. The following section offers insights that might be useful in this respect.

Kazakhstan's monotown policy should be reformed, decentralised and based on realistic long-term planning

This section provides policy recommendations for the future of Kazakhstan's monotown support programmes, based on experiences from OECD countries and the Russian Federation, whose monotowns face economic challenges comparable to Kazakhstan's. Experience of Russia's monotown support programme suggests that a centralised, one-size-fits-all approach to monotown development (including to the drafting of comprehensive development plans) is counterproductive. In Russia, the federal government set up a specific policy package to support monotowns in 2009: the monotowns prepared comprehensive investment plans and submitted applications for federal co-financing of various investment projects, ranging from infrastructure to capital stock modernisation. Similar to Kazakhstan's CDPs, Russian "Comprehensive Investment Plans" were based on a single methodology developed at the central level with a unified list of target indicators for all monotowns. As a result, only a few investment projects described in the Comprehensive Investment Plans have actually been implemented. Many were unrealistic in design and did not take into account market realities and the priority of local and national businesses or monotowns' core companies (BISAM Central Asia, 2012).

- While a national policy framework (preferably as part of Kazakhstan's urban strategy) is necessary, more power should be delegated to monotown and oblast local administrations in exploring local development opportunities and setting at least some of the "target" indicators in monotown development plans. The business community (especially local monotown businesses and core companies) should be involved in the drafting process.

Both Russia and Kazakhstan's monotown policies are not sufficiently anchored in the long term and suffer from contradictions between policy design at the central level and their implementation. In the Russian Federation, only 50 monotowns (of about 400) received (limited) direct financial support from the federal government under the monotown programme, mostly for the development of municipal infrastructure (municipal utilities, roads, electricity networks). In contrast, most investment projects supposed to create new jobs and encourage economic diversification were not carried out. Monotown development was no longer a top priority of the central government in the Russian Federation after 2011 (BISAM Central Asia, 2012). Similarly, in Kazakhstan the development of municipal infrastructure accounted for most investment projects implemented, and financing of the programme was "frozen" after 2014.

- A long-term perspective, aligned with near-term budget constraints, is essential to the effective implementation of monotown support programmes. It might be useful to focus more on realistic, small-scale market-based investment projects and less on infrastructure investment in the implementation of the programme.

The assessment methodology of the economic potential of monotowns should be revised

The assessment methodology of the economic potential of monotowns rightly takes into account geographic variables (distance from large urban centres, and road and railway connectivity). Experience from selected OECD countries (Australia, Canada and the United States) on local economic development of single-industry towns (most often mining towns) also suggests that the size of monotowns also matters. Larger monotowns benefit from agglomeration economies and are more likely to be able to weather economic downturns in their core industry. In their review of shrinking mining cities, Martinez-Fernandez et al. (2012) found that the most successful revitalisation strategy took place in Sudbury (Canada, Ontario), a mining city of 157 000 inhabitants (corresponding to the largest of Kazakhstan's monotowns), located around 400 kilometres from the Greater Toronto (Canada's largest urban centre).

Indeed, the assessment methodology of the economic potential of monotowns could be revamped to make it more realistic. This would mean identifying the real number of "low potential" monotowns (which is probably higher than 2 out of 27 monotowns). The government might consider small or medium-size monotowns with weak or negative real wage growth and wages substantially lower than the regional average (Figure 1.28), a low share of residents with tertiary education (Figure 1.29), high self-employment (Figure 1.30) and without positive migration inflows (Figure 1.31) as candidates for the "low-potential" category.

More emphasis should be placed on stimulating labour mobility from low-potential monotowns. Efforts to maintain or stimulate economic activity in former mining towns have not always been successful in OECD countries, and indeed, have resulted in many failures. In many cases, revitalisation strategies based on attracting high technology/services and tourism failed to bring about substantial changes (Martinez-Fernandez et al., 2012). It might be more efficient to encourage labour mobility from monotowns of low potential to places with better economic prospects, such as larger cities and urban agglomerations.

In Kazakhstan, significant obstacles (such as under-developed rental markets, large distances, high interregional real estate price differentials and registration procedures) increase the cost of labour mobility. The preliminary evidence suggests the less prosperous (usually smallest) monotowns are poverty traps whose inhabitants cannot afford to relocate. Measures to support labour mobility (including, for instance, relocation grants) from "low potential" monotowns and small towns to larger cities should be introduced Reducing barriers for labour mobility could result in higher spontaneous migration from "low potential" monotowns. Relocations of this kind could improve productivity over the long term, thanks to agglomeration benefits.

Improving the transport network linking monotowns to larger cities is essential

As noted in the "RDP Until 2020" plan, many monotowns suffer from poor connectivity, thanks to degraded roads and poor or no railway connections. Transport connections are as important as the location in determining transport accessibility. For instance, Kentau (South Kazakhstan) is relatively close to larger cities such as Turkestan and even Shymkent, but suffers from poor road and railway connection to national highways and railways. Good transport is especially important for manufacturers, since relatively high transport costs tend to penalise them more than commodity producers (OECD, 2015c).

Investments to upgrade transport infrastructure and connectivity (focusing on the secondary road network) would make other support measures for monotowns more efficient. Such investments could be prioritised for monotowns with manufacturing activities (a key element of diversification in former mining towns) and reasonable economic prospects in the near future (excluding "low potential" monotowns).

While support to SME and entrepreneurship in monotowns is useful…

OECD experience suggests that support for entrepreneurship and SMEs can help diversify the economy of single-industry towns. In Australia, mining towns with a stronger base of non-mining businesses (providing more shopping opportunities for residents or having small-scale businesses connected with surrounding areas, such as in the agrifood-sector) have been more successful in retaining population after mining closure or downsizing (Regional Australia Institute, 2013). Some former mining towns have successfully diversified their economy by developing tourism. For instance, as emphasised in BISAM Central Asia (2012), the small town of Big Stone Gap in the Appalachian Mountains (Virginia, United States) was successful at developing ecotourism and outdoor sports, through support to tourism-oriented entrepreneurship (for example, bed and breakfasts, and kayak and rafting activities).

This suggests that support for non-mining, small-scale entrepreneurship is a viable way to alleviate the inevitable economic and demographic decline in shrinking mining towns. Earmarked support to SMEs and entrepreneurship (business training, grants for start-ups) in monotowns can encourage exploration of alternative economic specialisations (such as niche tourism) by the private sector. OECD field research suggests that current grants for new start-ups in Kazakhstan's monotowns (up to KZT 3 million or around USD 13 529) is too small: their amount could be increased.

Another form of small and medium enterprises (SME) support is to help SMEs in monotowns to band together to conclude contracts with the larger (mining or manufacturing) companies on a competitive basis. Local monotown SMEs are often too small to bid for contracts with large companies (mining or manufacturing), including core industries of the monotown itself. They are also often unaware of their specific requirements in for example, quality and product design. In British Colombia (Canada), this approach helped to increase the economic returns from mining activities in mining towns, while creating opportunities for local SMEs. To be more precise, the Northern Development Initiative Trust (NDIT) created a dedicated website (the supply chain connector, www.supplychainconnector.ca/) to bring together small businesses in the region and help them bid for contracts. In addition, a Contractor/Supplier Boot Camp helps to link SMEs and the major industrial companies by providing them with training on what the major companies need and want, and what their requirements are (Federation of Canadian Municipalities, 2015).

… support for established monotown industries should be limited and carefully assessed

Experience from Russia suggests that sustained public support to established core industries in single-company towns (especially prolonged subsidies to otherwise unprofitable companies) can have negative long-term consequences, impeding economic restructuring and modernisation of manufacturing. There is convincing evidence that labour productivity in Russian monotowns is substantially lower than average. Commander, Nikoloski and Plekhanov (2011) found that the output of enterprises in one-company towns is 70% lower than their peers, after controlling for other factors. Single-company town in Russia have significantly lower marginal products of labour (and higher marginal products of capital), suggesting significant labour hoarding. This means that monotown enterprises typically employ more workers and are less productive than their peers, all other things being equal. Some core industries in Russian single-company towns benefit from many explicit and implicit subsidies from the government (for instance, in the machine building sector through public defence procurement). The risk is that sustained public subsidies and support for weak or unprofitable monotown enterprises lock in a pattern of sub-optimal resource allocation in the long run (Commander, Nikoloski and Plekhanov, 2011).

This risk also exists in Kazakhstan, and the policy package to support monotown companies should take this into account. Low interest-rate credits to core companies in monotowns could end up subsidising investments that they would have undertaken anyway. Subsidies and public support in any form to industries in single-company towns should thus always be temporary and aim to encourage new, self-sustaining profitable activities genuinely contributing to economic diversification.

Municipal utility networks should be separated from core monotown companies

There are a few cases where core monotown companies still manage municipal utility networks (water supply, heating, hot water supply and sewage), including operations and management (O&M) and billing to the population. This is the case in the monotown of Chromtau (Aktobe oblast), where the mining company, focused on chrome-ore extraction, owns these assets. The company prefers to transfer the assets, their O&M and the billing to local authorities. However, the city administration insists that the assets should be repaired before any transfer. These discussions have been going on for years between the two parties (World Bank JERP, 2015).

Transfer of municipal utility networks to local administrations open the door to management of municipal utilities by specialised private sector operators or by a municipal company. Core companies are not necessarily the best managers of these municipal utility networks and may not invest adequately in repair and maintenance, given low utility rates and the anticipated asset transfer to local administrations. The central government could consider designing a specific framework to speed up such asset transfers in monotowns where core companies still own municipal utility networks. The central government could co-finance municipal network repair along with the core company, on condition that municipal utility networks are transferred to the local administration.

Improving the business environment and leveraging foreign investments at the subnational level

A subnational assessment of the business environment is necessary…

Kazakhstan has made improving the business environment for firms one of its priorities for fostering economic growth. It was ranked among the top 10 economies, of 190 economies surveyed, that showed the most improvement in the 2017 *Doing Business* report (World Bank, 2016). According to the survey, the country ranked 35th in *Ease of Doing Business* (out of 190 countries), rising 16 places towards best performers since 2015/2016. The average distance to frontier (i.e. the absolute distance from the best regulatory practices) across all indicators has been constantly improving since 2012 (World Bank, 2015). However, corruption remains a persistent national problem in Kazakhstan, despite recognised progress in the country's anti-corruption efforts. Demands of graft from officials have reportedly most affected medium-sized companies. The government identified control of corruption as one of the key priorities in its "Kazakhstan 2050" strategy and adopted an "Anti-Corruption Strategy of the Republic of Kazakhstan for 2015-2025",[50] while pursuing efforts to increase integrity in the public service (OECD, 2017b, forthcoming).

Many business regulations in Kazakhstan, while based on national-level rules and regulations, are implemented at the local level either by *oblasts* (regions), cities of oblast significance and districts (*rayons*) or by territorial organs of national ministries and government agencies. This includes land-use regulations, building safety and fire inspection, business licenses and construction permits. Therefore, as Linn (2014) emphasises, improvements in the way these rules and regulations are implemented at city level will be paramount in ensuring a business environment supportive of entrepreneurship and conducive to new investments.

The experience of OECD countries suggests that there are often significant differences in the business environment and the implementation of national-level rules and regulations across regions and cities. A recent study on 32 Mexican cities (World Bank, 2016c) measured the ease of *Doing Business* based on four criteria: starting a business, dealing with construction permits, registering property and enforcing contracts,[51] showed substantial differences across cities, with at least one of them performing better than high-income OECD members. The conclusion for Kazakhstan is that an assessment of subnational differences in the business climate would provide a clearer understanding of the differences across regions and cities to incentivise business and investment, and place government in a better position to design and implement policy.

Table 1.8. **Perceptions of obstacles to doing business by oblast**

The darker the shading, the more severe the perception of obstacles to doing business

Region	Skills	Business inspections	Access to finance	Electricity	Corruption	Crime	Transport	Tax administration	Access to land	Business licencing	Courts	Informal sector	Customs & Trade	Compulsory certificates
Kazakhstan														
Akmola														
Aktobe														
Almaty														
Almaty City														
Astana														
Atyrau														
East														
Karaganda														
Kostanay														
Pavlodar														
South														
West														

Source: Berglof, E. (2013), "Transition without an outside anchor: The experience of Caucasus and Central Asia", European Bank for Reconstruction and Development, presentation on 20 May 2013, available at: www.imf.org/external/np/seminars/eng/2013/cca/pdf/eb.pdf.

Kazakhstan also displays substantial differences in the business environment and corruption perception across regions and cities. OECD (2014c) notes that licences delivered by oblast administrations can be a significant administrative burden on firms, and interpretation of national laws and regulations can vary, sometimes significantly, across regions. The fifth wave of the Business Environment and Enterprise Performance Survey (BEEPS), provides insight into the variations of the perception of firms on the business environment across the country. For instance, insufficient education in the workforce is more often reported as the main obstacle to doing business in medium-size cities than in Almaty City or Astana (Table 1.8 above).

In 2016, the central government started a project to implement the *Doing Business* rating in eight large and medium size-cities in Kazakhstan.[52] This rating will provide an assessment of four criteria of the business environment: starting a business, dealing with construction permits, registering property and enforcing contracts. This is a positive step towards monitoring the results of Kazakhstan's recent efforts to improve the business environment for firms and tracking city-level differences and progress towards the implementation of reforms.

…and the capacity and capability of the regional Investment Service Centres (ISCs) need to be upgraded.

In Kazakhstan, *Kaznex Invest* is the investment promotion agency (IPA) under the Ministry of Investment and Development (MID). It is in charge of searching for investors and attracting FDIs into priority sectors; trouble-shooting and support for foreign investors; the promotion of Kazakhstan's image abroad; and, the management of the Special Economic Zones (SEZs). According to the forthcoming 2017 Investment Policy Review of Kazakhstan (hereafter, OECD, 2017b, forthcoming), national and subnational investment promotion agencies play an important role in facilitating foreign investments, and helping the government mobilise FDI into priority sectors (on this topic, see also Harding and Javorcik, 2007). This forthcoming Review covers in detail Kazakhstan's investment policy, including investment promotion policy. In particular, it highlights the challenge due to the fragmentation of Kazakhstan's investment promotion activities and the resulting lack of transparency. Indeed, other governmental institutions in Kazakhstan have similar, if not overlapping, functions as *Kaznex Invest*. They include the Ministry of Foreign Affairs and a special Government Council charged with the co-ordination of major investment projects, which appears to have a large network abroad. While the co-ordinating role of the MID on investment promotion is progressing, the Investment Policy Review also highlights the need for increased co-operation between various institutions to increase the impact of investment promotion and reduce costs.

Kaznext Invest is a relatively young IPA that faces a number of issues, including: unclear core mandate and strategy; inadequate institutional structure; and weak staffing policy and operations. A recent review of *Kaznex Invest* operations conducted by the Eurasia Competitiveness Programme (hereafter, OECD, 2015d) found that the agency's performance was relatively poor compared to selected benchmarks (investment promotion agencies from Turkey, the Czech Republic, Hong Kong and Nicaragua that performed well). It also found that the agency remains primarily oriented towards servicing the needs of the MID, for example, through the preparation of reports on FDI trends, investment climate indicators, rather than dealing with investors, assisting them, and addressing their concerns (OECD, 2017b, forthcoming). The strengthening of *Kaznext Invest*'s performance in dealing with foreign investors and a better co-ordination of investment promotion efforts of the central government is a key element in attracting foreign investors to Kazakhstan's cities and regions. *Kaznext Invest* could improve its investment promotion activities by boosting its sectoral teams and focusing on direct support to foreign investors (OECD, 2015d).

Box 1.11. **Investment Promotion Agency of Kazakhstan: how well is it doing?**

Kaznex Invest was created in 2008 as Kazakhstan's export promotion agency, in an effort to support economic diversification. In April 2010, besides its export promotion function, the agency became the sole Investment Promotion Agency (IPA). Since then, it has performed both these functions and is the sole co-ordinator of Special Economic Zones (SEZ) in Kazakhstan. It also hosts a database on investment projects and foreign investors in the country, and in co-operation with Investor Support Centres (ISC) supports investment promotion in the regions.

The agency is set up as a joint stock company in which the Investment Committee of the Ministry of Investment and Development (MID) owns 51% of shares, with the other 49% owned by the National Chamber of Entrepreneurs of the Republic of Kazakhstan, Atameken. It joined the World Association of Investment Promotion Agencies (WAIPA) in 2011. To boost Kaznex Invest's effectiveness in attracting investors to the key strategic sectors, the government of Kazakhstan requested a review of Kaznex Invest operations from the OECD and a benchmarking in relation to best practices in other agencies, with a view to making adjustments in its mandate, structure, or operations (OECD, 2015d).

Box 1.11. **Investment Promotion Agency of Kazakhstan: how well is it doing?** *(continued)*

One of the most salient findings of the OECD review was Kaznex Invest's low efficiency by comparison with the best-performing agencies. Only 5% of total FDI inflows were estimated to have been directly generated by Kaznex Invest in 2013, as compared to 11% in Nicaragua or 33% in Czech Republic. Reasons for this relatively poor performance included, the relatively large mandate of the institution, which resulted in lesser attention given to investment promotion and facilitation; its focus on serving the needs of the ministry rather than of investors; and a lack of clear strategy, well-identified priority sectors and key performance indicators that were outcome- rather than process-oriented and in line with the pre-identified strategy.

Source: OECD (2017b, forthcoming), *OECD Investment Policy Reviews: Kazakhstan*, OECD Publishing, Paris; OECD (2015d), "Kaznex Invest Strategic Review, OECD Eurasia Competitiveness Programme", Internal Kaznex Invest document presented in Astana on 14 December 2015 (unpublished).

At the regional level, *akims* at the oblast level are responsible for attracting foreign investment. They are assisted in this task by Investment Support Centres (ISCs) located in each oblast capital. ISCs are supposed to work in close co-operation with *Kaznext Invest*, promote their respective region as an investment location and assist foreign investors in dealing with the local administration. In practice, ISCs are usually part of regional social-entrepreneurial corporations (*Socialno-Predprinimatelskaïa korporatsia, or* SPK). SPKs are owned by *oblast akimats* and act as local economic development offices and regional development banks. Some SPKs also manage existing industrial parks within the region. The problem is that ISCs are usually a functional subdivision of SPKs, often with fewer than five staff members. They are thus usually overwhelmed by tasks related to SPK's priorities or statistical reporting to *akimats* and do not have resources to generate investment leads and address investors' concerns. In Shymkent and Astana, ISCs operate within the Joint Stock Company (JSC) "Astana Innovation" and "Shymkent Innovation" respectively. Both organisations have a dual mandate, including supporting business innovation and entrepreneurship (with a focus on energy efficiency of city services and "smart city" development in Astana) and assisting investors. In Almaty City, the ISC (within the JSC "Almaty Development Centre") is the only regional ISC with a comprehensive website dedicated to foreign investors in English (http://investinalmaty.com/en).

ISCs need more resources, functional autonomy, and better connections with the local private sector

There is no one-size-fits-all solution for successful investment promotion at the subnational level, even in OECD countries. Subnational investment promotion agencies are usually small, flexible organisations well-connected to both the local administration and business community. In Kazakhstan, ISCs may require additional resources (both financial and human) but also need to be incorporated into the larger set of investment promotion and facilitation activities of *Kaznex Invest*. In addition, their focus should be primarily on servicing investors and administrative burdens, and tasks related to servicing ministries should be minimised. One option would be to involve both the regional *akimat* and the Regional Chambers of Entrepreneurs in the governance of ISCs, to ensure that the voice of the local private sector is taken into account in ISC governance (as is the case for the Hamburg's Business Development Corporation, see Box 1.13). More generally, investors could be consulted throughout the process of setting up and running the ISC in order to ensure its useful functioning and client orientation.

ISCs should be better co-ordinated with Kaznex Invest and clearly visible in the Invest.kz website

ISCs are assessed by the Ministry of Investment and Development and *Kaznext Invest,* but the latter has little influence on their management. Co-ordination between the national agency *Kaznext Invest* and oblast- level ISCs on investment promotion and facilitation is essential, and should be enhanced. This could be done by giving *Kaznext Invest* a reserved seat on the executive board of all ISCs in Kazakhstan or the use of shared staff and/or facilities, for instance. *Kaznext Invest* could also organise an annual forum for ISC staff to share experiences and good practices and provide them with dedicated business training. Many ISCs do not have websites and are thus not easily visible in the main investment portal for foreign investors in Kazakhstan (http://invest.gov.kz/). Online visibility, including from Kazakhstan's main investment promotion website (http://invest.gov.kz/), could help make investors are aware of the services provided by ISCs in the regions.

Almaty City and Almaty oblast could share costs and conduct common investment promotion activities

As demonstrated by the FUA analysis, the metropolitan area of Almaty covers Almaty City and several districts of Almaty oblast. Setting up a common Investor Service Centre would make sense to service investors interested in investing or expanding businesses in Almaty's agglomeration. Its head could be appointed jointly by the *akims* of Almaty City and the Almaty oblast, and financing could be provided through the LLP Regional Centre for the development of Almaty oblast (owned 100% by Almaty oblast) and the JSC Almaty City development Centre (owned 100% by Almaty City).

The new ISC could focus on international activities on location marketing of Almaty City agglomeration. The Hamburg Business Development Corporation (HWF) offers an example of such co-operation. By concluding agreements on shared services with the neighbouring economic development offices, it promotes the entire Hamburg metropolitan region in its international activities on location marketing (see Box 1.13). In the spirit of Hamburg's HWF, it could have dedicated teams for CIS (Commonwealth of Independent States) and non-CIS investors and provide free commercial real estate services for large investors.

Box 1.13. OECD practice: Hamburg Business Development Corporation

The Hamburg Business Development Corporation (HWF) is a private-enterprise consultancy company that acts as the one-stop agency for national and international investment in Hamburg. Its shareholders include the Hamburg Chamber of Skilled Trades, the Hamburg Chamber of Commerce and local authorities. It is closely integrated with other structures in charge of city branding or tourism promotion in the Hamburg economic region, while retaining functional autonomy. It has dedicated teams for servicing international businesses, local businesses and an additional team in charge of marketing Hamburg as business location across the globe.

Its main tasks include attracting international companies to Hamburg, marketing the location, and supporting companies intending to establish facilities or a branch office in the region. In this last case, HWF provides a free comprehensive commercial real estate service ranging from location consulting to investor support.

HWF provides its services free of charge – a particular benefit for small and medium-sized enterprises. Specifically, HWF's Service for SME advocates for such businesses in dealing with government agencies and the public administration. For its clients, HWF is a guide and intermediary representing their interests to the public administration and, in individual instances, political bodies – providing information on all regulatory issues and helping to speed up administrative proceedings.

Source: Hamburg Business Development Corporation's website, www.hamburg-economy.de/about-us/2238592/willkommen/ (accessed on 14 October 2016).

Innovation clusters in Kazakhstan: the urban dimension

Yusuf (2014) highlights the triangle of innovation: knowledge and education (including research universities), firms and cities. OECD (2016b) and the forthcoming *OECD Review of National Policies for Education: Higher Education in Kazakhstan* (OECD, 2017c, forthcoming) review Kazakhstan's innovation, IP and higher education systems in detail. As part of its Innovation Policy for Competitiveness project, OECD Eurasia Competitiveness Programme (OECD ECP) studied the spatial location of Kazakhstan's innovation system (with a focus on commercialisation of innovation). Building on these studies, the present analysis focuses on the urban dimension of innovation, which is gaining in recognition, since successful, well-functioning cities are at the core university-industry linkages and entrepreneurial activities.

Indeed, large cities tend to have a large share of well-educated and therefore productive residents. This concentration of human capital in a few cities is essential to a successful national innovation system. Indeed, the return on human capital is enhanced by urban locations that attract and bring together various elements of the knowledge spectrum.[53] A symbiotic relationship between human capital, creativity and a conducive urban environment with a good quality of life tends to attract and retain the so-called "creative class" (Florida, 2012).[54] The success of a national innovation system thus depends on a few urban local innovation systems, particularly in Kazakhstan, where research activities and knowledge workers tend to be highly concentrated. Developing successful, smart urban agglomerations with good housing conditions, acceptable levels of congestion and innovation "attractors" (high-level universities, venture capitalist funds, developed financial infrastructure) are essential for stimulating innovation. As Yusuf (2014) noted,

Kazakhstan could aim to turn one or maybe two of its cities into "knowledge hubs" of Central Asia.

Kazakhstan is currently far from the global technology frontier. Great distances between cities, low population densities in many parts of the country, large rural areas and many small towns with relatively poor infrastructure are natural obstacles to the development of an innovation-led manufacturing sector. Human capital tends to concentrate in large cities (and Kazakhstan has few), so the low population share of metropolitan areas (see section on FUAs in this chapter for details) is another constraint.[55] Indeed, results from Boulhol et al. (2008) suggest that the effectiveness of private R&D intensity is significantly affected by the degree of urban concentration, but not by the distance to major markets, a result with encouraging implications for Kazakhstan if urbanisation accelerates.

Kazakhstan has made a priority of spurring innovation at the firm level and attractive multinational enterprises intended as "innovation anchors". The "State Programme on Accelerated Industrial-Innovative Development" (SPAIID) for 2015-19 (taking over SPAIID 2010-14) aims to support innovation clusters and diversification by supporting the manufacturing sector. As part of the programme, the National Agency for Technological Development is charged with distributing innovation grants, including for technology transfers from OECD countries and China, and providing support services for start-ups.

Despite recent improvements, however, the outputs of Kazakhstan's R&D and other innovation efforts are not yet commensurate with the inputs. Kazakhstan is ranked significantly lower (90th out of 128 countries) on the "innovation output" sub-index than on the "innovation input" sub-index (65th out of 128 countries) of the Global Innovation Index (OECD, 2016a).[56] Gross R&D spending remains (0.17% of GDP in 2014) significantly lower than in OECD countries (2.5%), upper middle-income countries (1.6% of GDP) and Russia (1.1% of GDP). Evidence from the World Bank Enterprise survey suggest that Kazakh private firms are less innovative than the average Eastern European and Central Asian (ECA) firms: only 2.5% of the firms surveyed invested in R&D, compared with an average of 10.6% for ECA countries in 2013. One key obstacle to business innovation could be relatively underdeveloped knowledge- and information-intensive services. OECD (2016a) highlights the relatively low contribution of business services to production in Kazakhstan, particularly in manufacturing, and emphasises the positive spill-overs on the manufacturing sector of improving productivity in business services. Business services are essentially concentrated in large and medium-sized urban agglomerations.

Both R&D expenditures and R&D personnel, whether in state-owned or in private companies, are concentrated in Almaty City and, to some extent Astana and a few other cities (Figure 1.33). The R&D "ranking" of Kazakhstan's cities is relatively stable: the main development since 2005 has been the rise of Astana (from 9.1% of national R&D expenditures in 2005 to 19.4% in 2015). The science city of Kurshatov (11 670 inhabitants, home of the national nuclear centre and its research institutes) is by far the smallest city with significant R&D spending and personnel. However, both R&D spending and R&D personnel have declined there since 2010. Almaty City and Astana have the highest concentrations of inhabitants with a doctoral degree[57] (0.89% and 0.74% of the population of 15 years old and more, respectively), followed by Aktobe and Karaganda (0.46% and 0.42%).[58]

Even in Astana and Almaty, the positive externalities from innovation (cluster effects) may be weaker than in OECD countries, given the very low overall level of R&D expenditures in Kazakhstan. For instance, in Almaty City, R&D still accounted for only 0.4% of the gross regional product in 2015.

Figure 1.32. **R&D is highly concentrated in Almaty City**

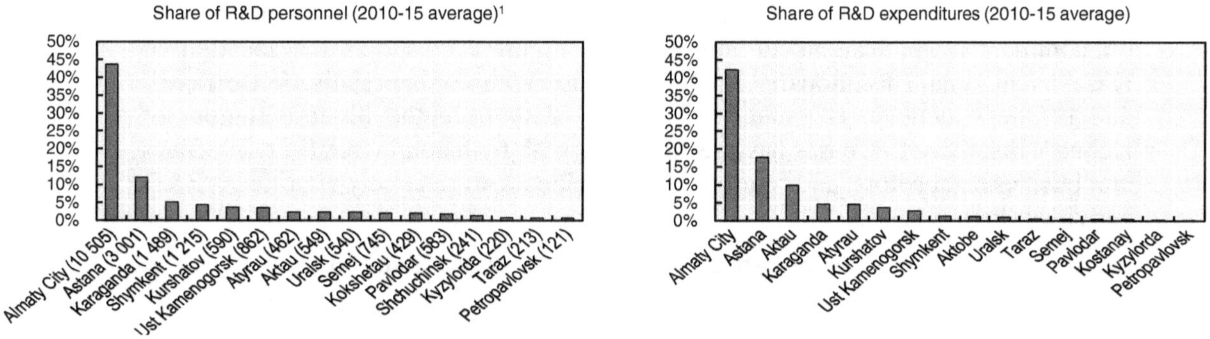

Note: Numbers in parenthesis give R&D personnel per city in 2015. R&D refers to "internal R&D expenditures" and does not include outsourcing.

Source: Committee on Statistics of the Republic of Kazakhstan, Innovation database (unpublished).

Figure 1.33. **Kazakhstan's technoparks**

Including those with commercialisation offices and business incubators

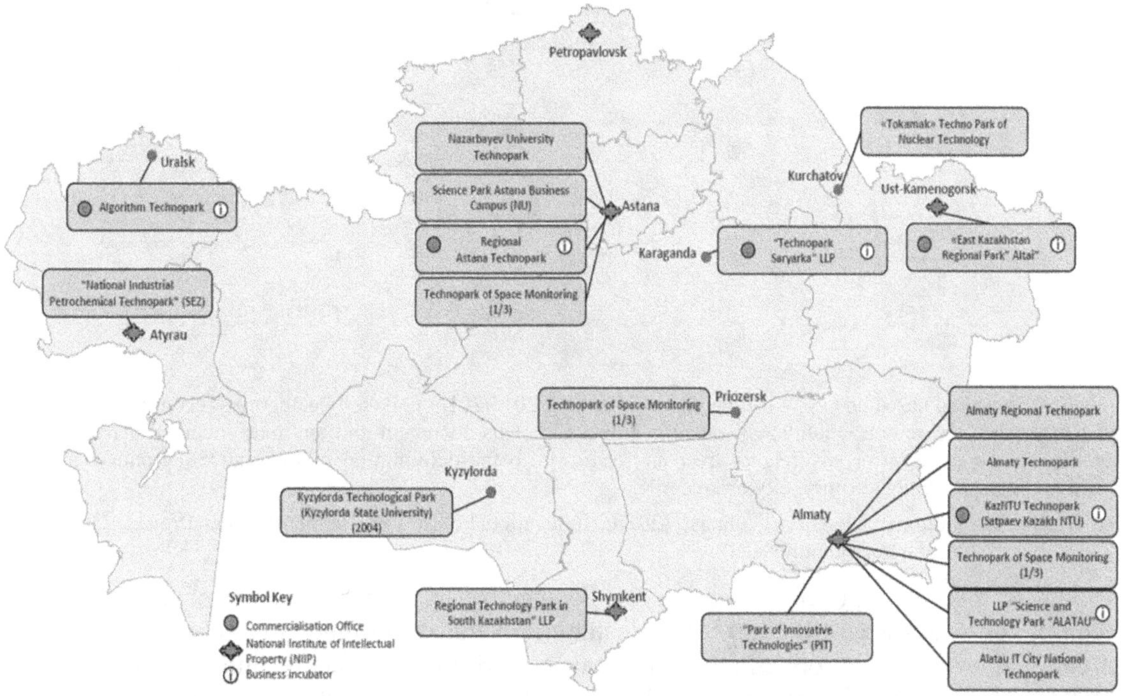

Note: This document and any map included herein are without prejudice to the status of or sovereignty over any territory, to the delimitation of international frontiers and boundaries and to the name of any territory, city or area.

Source: The Kazakhstan Commercialisation Compass (2016), Innovation Policy for Competitiveness project, OECD Eurasia Competitiveness Programme (unpublished).

Institutions creating a favourable environment for innovation and its commercial applications by businesses ("enabling institutions") are also concentred in a few cities. As part of its innovation policy for competitiveness project, the OECD European Comparison Programme analysed the location of key components of Kazakhstan's innovation landscape (e.g. research universities, technoparks, commercialisation offices, business incubators and venture capital). It also recommends that Kazakhstan improves co-ordination and linkages between its numerous institutions and activities of its innovation landscape (including efforts on commercial applications of innovations). Figure 1.33 shows the location of Kazakhstan's main technoparks, including those with commercialisation offices[59] and business incubators. Astana and Almaty City have the highest number of technoparks. Only five cities have technoparks with both commercialisation offices and business incubators, and four of them are cities with relatively significant R&D activities (Figure 1.34).

Figure 1.34. **Kazakhstan's internationally ranked universities**

9 HEI (higher education institutions) appear in QS World University Ranking

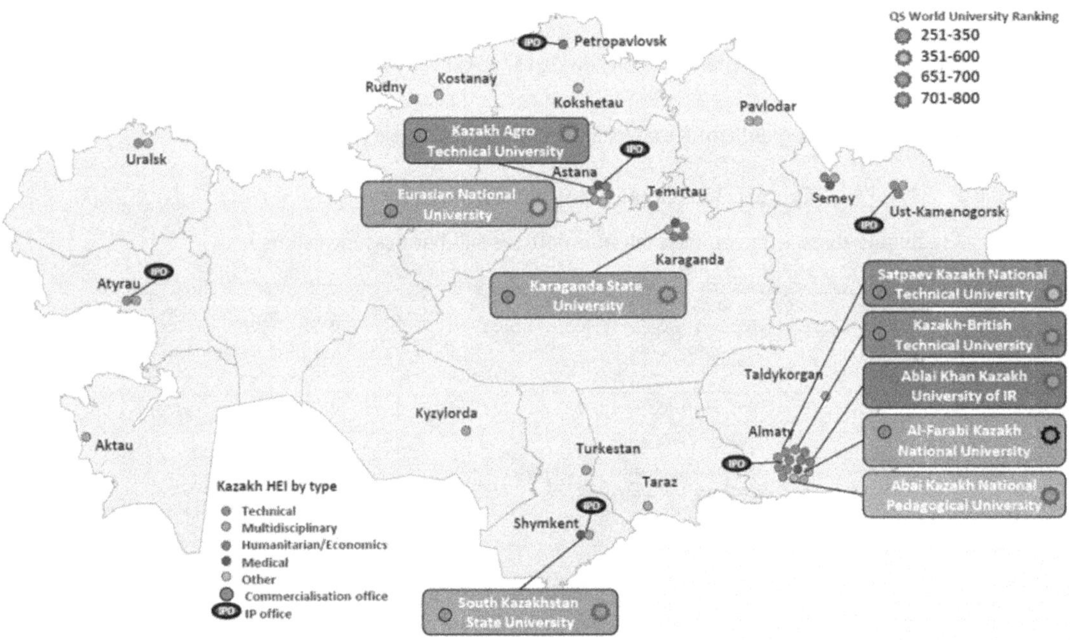

Note: Universities are ranked based on QS World University Ranking 2015/2016; university categories recognised by the Independent Kazakhstan Agency on Quality Assurance in Education. This document and any map included herein are without prejudice to the status of or sovereignty over any territory, to the delimitation of international frontiers and boundaries and to the name of any territory, city or area.

Source: The Kazakhstan Commercialisation Compass (2016), Innovation Policy for Competitiveness Project, OECD Eurasia Competitiveness Programme (unpublished).

Under the Concept of Formation of Perspective National Clusters of the Republic of Kazakhstan till 2020,[60] two leading university and innovation clusters of national level will be formed on the basis of Nazarbayev University (innovation intellectual cluster) in Astana and of the Park of Innovative Technologies (PIT) (*Innovation cluster Almaty tech garden*) in Almaty. While Astana's cluster is entirely hosted at Nazarbayev University, in Almaty City it will build on existing research capacities of the numerous universities and research centres in the city. Research universities are indeed increasingly important in the innovation ecosystems of advanced countries (Yusuf, 2014). In Kazakhstan, a few universities (along with some special research institutes) concentrate most research activities (OECD, 2016b). Figure 1.34 shows the concentration of universities in a few cities (mainly Almaty City, Astana and Karaganda) with a focus on establishments ranked in QS World University Ranking 2015/2016. Most of these universities have commercialisation offices and sometimes their own business parks. Leading research universities such as Nazarbayev University in Astana and Al-Farabi National University in Almaty City can be instrumental in creating university-industry linkages and encouraging commercialisation of innovations.

Figure 1.35. **Fixed broadband Internet access per 100 inhabitants**

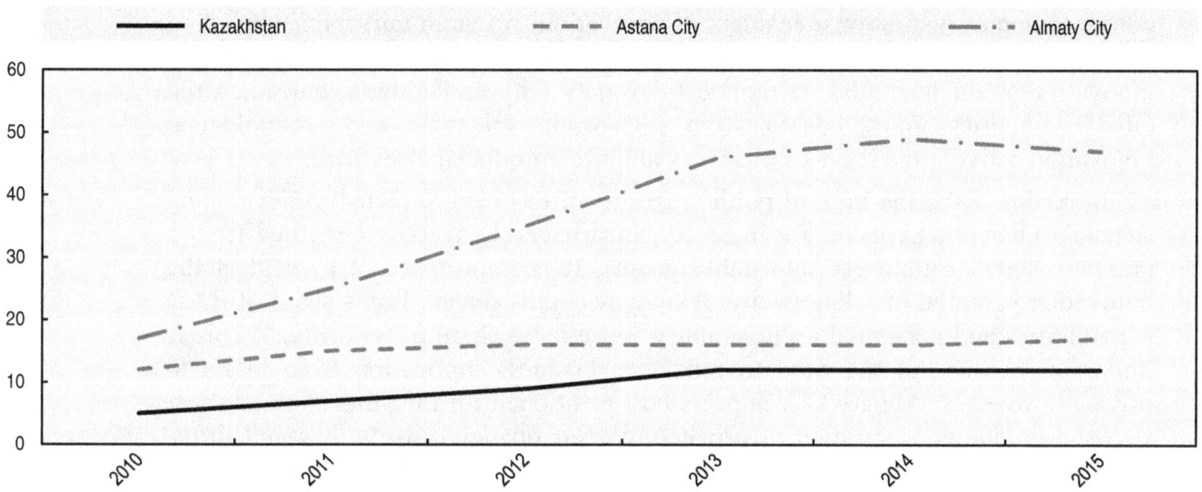

Note: Internet access is much more widespread than fixed broadband connection (in 2015, around two thirds of Kazakhstan's population used the Internet).

Source: Committee on Statistics of the Republic of Kazakhstan, ICT Database (unpublished).

Yusuf (2014) emphasises the key role of easy and cheap access to broadband Internet and advanced telecommunication infrastructure in the development of innovation and software businesses in cities such as Seoul, Copenhagen or Helsinki. Despite recent improvements, Kazakhstan's ICT infrastructure falls short of advanced country levels, and additional improvements are necessary to support the emergence of a modern knowledge-based technology. There is an urban dimension to this, since broadband Internet access has developed much more quickly in Almaty City than in Astana or other regions (Figure 1.35). Improving fixed broadband penetration and making it accessible at reasonable prices in other urban agglomerations should be made a priority, including in Astana, if the vision of Astana as a "smart city" is to be realised.[61]

There is a risk of "policy overload", since Kazakhstan has launched many policy initiatives aiming at encouraging innovation through localised cluster policy. Dispersing scarce public funding over a number of specialised sciences or smart cities, or several innovation clusters based in special economic zones (SEZs), may detract from the success of any one city, including Almaty City. The risk is also that the complex layers of priorities and institutions ultimately exceed the capacity of the national and subnational bureaucracies. OECD (2016b) provides preliminary evidence of this. For instance, 21 technology transfer offices (TTOs) specialised in matching the supply of and demand for technology have been established in the country's most important universities and public research institutes. However, these offices tend to be small and understaffed, and financing from the National Agency for Technological Development ceased in 2014. As a result, the number of applications selected for commercialisation has been limited. OECD (2016b) also notes that the innovative capacity of Kazakhstan's business sector is weak and dominated by SOEs, which poses challenges since stronger innovation performance requires the private sector be at the heart of the activity.

Support for scientific and technological innovation should focus on Almaty City, and Astana to a lesser extent

As Yusuf (2014) recommends, support for scientific and technological innovation should be focused on one or two urban centres and co-ordinated by a high-level body. Almaty and Astana are ideal candidates, given their relatively high concentration of institutional enablers of innovation (research universities, existing technoparks and high human capital). This does not mean that the manufacturing of innovative products should be limited to Almaty City and Astana. Indeed, while OECD countries cities benefit from high-value scientific and technological innovation activity, the fruits of this work are often produced elsewhere.

In recent years, the bulk of public investment has been directed to developing Astana's innovation cluster (for instance, Nazarbayev University benefited from a grant of USD 2 billion for its establishment). It is important not to neglect the innovation potential of Almaty City. Almaty accounts for the lion's share of R&D expenditures and personnel in the country and a large share of its SMEs.[62] This is important because of the need to rebalance business innovation from SOEs to private businesses: Almaty City appears best positioned for this, thanks to its sheer size and unique concentration of privately owned financial institutions and firms. Moreover, the broadband penetration rate (a crucial enabler of research activities) in Almaty City is by far the highest in Kazakhstan. To encourage productive competition between Astana and Almaty City in scientific and technological innovation, excessive concentration of public support on Astana's cluster should be avoided in future.

The spatial dimension of innovation policy and regional development policy should be better aligned

An analysis of key components of Kazakhstan's innovation landscape suggests that Karaganda and Ust-Kamenogorsk may be secondary clusters for innovation and technology transfers in their manufacturing specialities. However, the Regional Development Programme until 2020 emphasises the role of Shymkent and Aktobe as "first-level cities" and "national level economic growth centres". It is worth noting that the innovation and knowledge potential of Aktobe is not commensurate with this role. For instance, Aktobe has no leading university (based on international rankings). It has a regional industrial park, but no functioning technology-transfer or commercialisation office. Aktobe's share of overall R&D expenditures and R&D personnel is lower than Aktau and Atyrau, also located in the Western part of Kazakhstan. Shymkent has more innovation-supporting infrastructures than Aktobe, but lacks the concentration of highly ranked universities and R&D personnel of Karaganda and Ust-Kamenogorsk. On the positive side, Shymkent hosts the main foreign investor in Kazakhstan's pharmaceutical sector (the Polish firm Polpharma), and university-industry linkages could be further explored. Field research suggests that emigration of talented youth with higher education to Almaty City and Astana may be depleting Shymkent's human capital.

Notes

1. Based on OECD calculations based on Zhumasultanov (2011), it attempts to neutralise the largest territorial-administrative changes since 1991.
2. In 2005, the growth rate for both the urban and rural population growth was 1%, while in 2007, the rural population grew faster than the urban because of the reclassification of urban settlements to rural status.
3. This figure for January 2014 takes into account the recent extension of Almaty City's borders.
4. In nine OECD countries, including low-density countries like Canada and Iceland, median municipal size in 2015/2016 was lower than in Kazakhstan in 2009. 2016 figures cannot be computed in Kazakhstan, because municipal population is available only for Census years (last Census: 2009).
5. Definition of urban versus rural areas varies to a considerable extent across countries. Contrarily to the UN World Urbanisation Prospects (based on national statistics), FUA figures are based on a single methodology, and thus allow a meaningful comparison across borders.
6. The largest administrative-territorial change led to the reclassification of 163 settlements (*posiolki*) with a population of over 900 000 people from urban to rural status in 2007 (Zhumasultanov, 2011). Conversely, many rural inhabitants were reclassified as urban due to the territorial expansion of large cities, for instance in the case of Shymkent in 2013 (145 000 people) or Almaty City in 2014 (92 604 people).
7. Forecast Scheme of Territorial and Spatial Development of the Republic of Kazakhstan till 2020, available (in Russian) at: http://adilet.zan.kz/rus/docs/U1100000118.
8. This is higher than the UN 2014 Projections, which forecast an urbanisation rate of 55.8% in 2030. In recent years, both the urban population and the urban share of overall population have grown faster than predicted by UN Projections.
9. Functional urban areas are available only for 2009 and 1999. City cores always match statutory (administrative) cities: administrative data can therefore be used to measure city core's growth after 2009.
10. During this period, three new municipalities have been created in the vicinity of Aktau, to host relocated ethnic Kazakhs (*oralmans*), resulting in a sixfold increase in commuting zone population.
11. Commuting zones are not available after 2009, due to lack of data at the municipal level.
12. The population of the rural *regions* of North Kazakhstan, Kostanay, Akmola and the more industrial East-Kazakhstan have been in decline since 2008.
13. The main territorial expansion in Astana occurred in 2000, but the government expanded the borders of several other large and medium-size cities after 1997.

14. Testing the expected population-rank relationship for 27 statutory cities in 1999, 2009 and 2016 confirms that Kazakhstan's urban system increasingly conforms to Zipf's Law predictions, thanks to the rapid growth of the largest cities.
15. Number of passenger cars per 1 000 inhabitants. All figures for OECD countries in this paragraph are from UNECE Transport database, available at: http://3.unece.org/pxweb2015/pxweb/en/stat/stat__40-trtrans__02-trroadfleet.
16. Source: Committee on Statistics, transport database.
17. Pavlodar Tramway Company is modernising its rolling stock, thanks to an European Bank for Reconstruction and Development (EBRD) loan and subsidies from the regional and the national governments.
18. Source: Committee on Statistics, transport database.
19. For OECD Countries, see ITF IRTAD Database, available at http://data.oecd.org/transport/road-accidents.htm (accessed 13 September 2016).
20. See (in Russian) www.metroalmaty.kz/?q=ru/node/1583.
21. High transport costs increase the cost of goods shipped to these cities and constitute an obstacle to manufacturing exports. They also prevent access to credit, since banks are reluctant to accept as collateral assets in towns that are not connected to major highways.
22. This percentage comprises municipal property and state-owned companies. Source: Committee on Statistics.
23. Law No. 213 adopted on 3 November 1994, as amended, http://adilet.zan.kz/eng/docs/Z940001100; see Land Code (Article 50), http://adilet.zan.kz/eng/docs/K030000442.
24. Source: Head of water utility company TOO "Vodenye Resursi", quoted in the press (available at: http://otyrar.kz/2015/10/zhiteli-desyatkov-tysyach-domov-v-shymkente-zhivut-bez-kanalizacii-i-vody/).
25. Source: Committee on Statistics, housing database (unpublished data).
26. Source: Committee on Statistics, data from the 2009 National Census (unpublished).
27. See *Vlast.kz* business news portal, "Rynok nedvizhimosti Kazahstana: nervy sdajut", available (in Russian) at: https://vlast.kz/jekonomika/19102-rynok-nedvizimosti-kazahstana-nervy-sdaut.html.
28. According to the Committee on Statistics, housing prices are based on different sources (survey of real estate companies and developers, real estate listings) in only 18 cities (Astana, Almaty City, the 14 oblast capitals, Semej and Zhezkazgan.
29. Available (in Russian) at: http://adilet.zan.kz/rus/docs/U1500001030.
30. Building level substations connect the central heating system of each dwelling to the heat network.
31. This threshold is based on an international benchmark used by the World Bank group.
32. Expo-2017 is dedicated to "the future of energy", including renewable energy resources and energy-saving technologies.

33. See "Concept for transition of the Republic of Kazakhstan to the Green Economy", available (in Russian) at: https://strategy2050.kz/ru/news/1211/.

34. See (in Russian) quotes on *Zakon.kz*: www.www.zakon.kz/4762195-v-22-naselennykh-punktakh-kazakhstana.html.

35. See "Concept for transition of the Republic of Kazakhstan to the Green Economy", op. cit. pp. 6-7.

36. Source: Committee on Statistics, Transport database.

37. Weighbridges and other technical measures for emissions reduction.

38. According to data from the Ministry of Energy for 2014.

39. According to Coulibaly et al. (2013), post-Soviet Russia has a much smaller number of large cities (with a population of higher than 500 000 inhabitants) than the United States or Brazil, and a smaller percentage of population living in cities with more than 1 million inhabitants. Similarly, Kazakhstan has a lower percentage of population living in metropolitan areas than almost all OECD countries.

40. This trend also reflects lower oil and gas production (and lower oil prices as of 2014) in the natural resource regions (Atyrau, West Kazakhstan, etc.) after 2010 and the expansion of public institutions and SOE headquarters in Astana.

41. The 2012 monotown programme gave the official definition of monotowns in Kazakhstan. The same definition is now used as part of the Regional Development programme until 2020, available at (in Russian):

    http://adilet.zan.kz/rus/docs/P1400000728.

42. Monopsony is a market structure in which there is only one buyer of a good or service. For workers in an isolated company town, dominated by one employer, that employer is a monopsonist for some kinds of employment. See: http://economics.about.com/od/termsbeginningwithm/g/monopsony.htm.

43. World Bank, 2016 (Section F) also suggest that "self-employment dynamics may more accurately reflect the challenges facing Kazakhstan's labour market than unemployment indicators", p. 17.

44. Across 25 monotowns, the Pearson correlation coefficient between the self-employment rate and average wage per capita was -49% in 2015 (statistically significant at the 95% confidence level).

45. The Pearson correlation coefficient is negative or non-existent using average monthly wage levels, natural logarithm and average monthly wage ratios to the corresponding regional (oblast) average monthly wage. OLS regressions with net migrations, as the independent variable and average monthly wage as one of the dependent variables give the same result.

46. The programme was adopted 25 May 2012, under Government Resolution No. 683.

47. Stepnogorsk's CDP forecast 2015 employment at 38 687 with an increasing trend in time, while actual employment amounted to 36 812. Kentau's CPD forecast 2015 employment at 46 000, while actual employment amounted to 38 440. Employment figures are based on Committee on Statistics' employment data at the district level.

48. RDP also extends the diagnosis process and the urban infrastructure pillar of monotown programme (i.e. developing and improving urban infrastructure) to

Kazakhstan's 41 "small towns". However, it is not clear how many projects have been financed in small towns, given current budget constraints.

49. Source: "Majilis discuss the development of monotowns" [Majilis: o razvitie monogorodov], available (in Russian) at: https://i-news.kz/news/2014/11/18/7812748-mazhilis_o_razvitii_monogorodov.html.

50. The Anti-Corruption Strategy was approved by presidential decree No. 986, dated 26 December 2014.

51. For instance, the quality of land administration index in one Mexican city was among the 25% best performers worldwide (its index was in line with those of Portugal and Ireland), while the worst-performing Mexican city was among the 25% *worst* performers worldwide.

52. Astana, Almaty City, Aktobe, Karaganda, Ust-Kamenogorsk, Pavlodar, Kostanay and Shymkent. See Press release of the Ministry of national economy: http://economy.gov.kz/ru/press-sluzhba/detail.php?ELEMENT_ID=69334&sphrase_id=14282306 for details.

53. On the benefits of attracting highly educated people for cities, see Ahrend, Farchy, Kaplanis and Lembcke (2014).

54. This concept was popularised by the Richard Florida's highly influential book *The Rise of the Creative Class: Revisited* – see references in bibliography.

55. Current trends suggest that the population share of metropolitan areas will increase in the next 20 years.

56. Innovation output measures the results of innovative activities within the economy, while innovation input captures elements of the national economy that enable innovative activities. See Cornell University, INSEAD and WIPO (2015), "The Global Innovation Index 2015: effective Innovation Policies for Development", www.globalinnovationindex.org.

57. Doctoral degrees in Kazakhstan are inherited from the Soviet Union and distinct from the PhD awarded in many countries. Here we take into account both PhDs and Kazakhstani titles (*kandidat nauk* and *doctor nauk*).

58. Source: Committee on Statistics, Data from the 2009 National Census (unpublished).

59. Commercialisation offices are in charge of supporting innovators in turning their innovation into profitable ventures, and provide services such as patentability assessments, market research, and research of funding.

60. Approved by Resolution of the Government No. 1092, dated 11 October 2013.

61. Smart Astana portal provides further details: http://smart.astana.kz/en/about.html.

62. At the end of 2014, Almaty City accounted for 24% of SMEs if individual entrepreneurs and small farming enterprises are excluded. Almaty City had the highest share of SMEs with foreign participation in Kazakhstan. Source: Report on the status of development of small and medium enterprises in Kazakhstan and its regions, DAMU Fund, 2014, available at: www.damu.kz/20664.

References

ADB (2012a), "An Infrastructure Road Map for Kazakhstan", Technical Assistance Consultant's Report, www.adb.org/sites/default/files/project-document/76385/44402-012-reg-tacr-01.pdf (accessed 17 November 2016).

ADB (2012b), "Sector Assessment: (Summary): Multisector (Urban Transport, Water Supply And Sanitation, And Other Municipal Services)", Country partnership strategy: Kazakhstan 2012-16, www.adb.org/sites/default/files/linked-documents/cps-kaz-2012-2016-ssa-03.pdf (accessed 24 October 2016).

Ahrend, R. et al. (2014), "What makes cities more productive? Evidence on the role of urban governance from five OECD countries", *OECD Regional Development Working Papers*, No. 2014/05, OECD Publishing, Paris, http://dx.doi.org/10.1787/5jz432cf2d8p-en.

Aldashev, A. and B. Dietz (2014), "Economic and spatial determinants of interregional migration in Kazakhstan, Economic Systems", Vol. 38, pp. 379-396, https://core.ac.uk/download/pdf/6745673.pdf (accessed 17 November 2016).

Amann, W. (2013), "Housing Review 2013 on 23 countries in the Europe and Central Asia Region", Institute for Real Estate Construction and Housing Ltd, Vienna.

Andrienko, Y. and S. Guriev (2004), "Determinants of Interregional Mobility in Russia", *Economics of Transition*, Vol. 12/1, pp. 1-27, March, SSRN: https://ssrn.com/abstract=513518 (accessed 17 November 2016).

Angel, S. (2012), *Planet of Cities,* Lincoln Institute of Land Policy, Cambridge, Massachusetts.

Auerbach, F. (1913), "*Das Gesetz der Bevölkerungskonzentration*", *Petermanns Geographische Mitteilungen*, No. 59, pp. 74-76.

Berglof, E. (2013), "Transition without an outside anchor: The experience of Caucasus and Central Asia", European Bank for Reconstruction and Development", presentation on 20 May, www.imf.org/external/np/seminars/eng/2013/cca/pdf/eb.pdf.

BISAM Central Asia (2012), "Monotowns of East Kazakhstan: Assessment and possible solutions", UNDP Programme on innovative approaches to regional planning and public service delivery, Almaty, available (in Russian) at: www.kz.undp.org/content/dam/kazakhstan/brochure%20mono-cities%20Semey%20programme.pdf (accessed 24 October 2016).

Boulhol, H., A. de Serres and M. Molnar (2008), "The Contribution of Economic Geography to GDP Per Capita", *OECD Economics Department Working Papers*, No. 602, OECD Publishing, Paris, http://dx.doi.org/10.1787/242216186836.

Brown, W. (2014), "A green growth path", in A. Aitzhanova et al. (eds.) (2014), *Kazakhstan 2050: Toward a Modern Society for All*, Nazarbayev University, National Analytical Centre, Oxford University Press, Group Centennial International, Astana, pp.149-179.

Carlsen, L. et al. (2013), "Assessment of the air quality of Almaty: Focussing on the traffic component", *International Journal of Biology and Chemistry*, Vol. 5/1, pp. 49-69, https://www.researchgate.net/publication/268518356_Assessment_of_the_Air_Quality_of_Almaty_Focussing_on_the_Traffic_Component.

CER, ESCAP, UNDP (2013), "Urbanization in Central Asia: Challenges, Issues and Prospects", Tashkent, www.unescap.org/resources/urbanization-central-asia-challenges-issues-and-prospects.

City of Almaty, UNDP/CAST (2013), "City of Almaty sustainable transport strategy, akimat of Almaty City, Almaty", available (in Russian) at: http://investinalmaty.com/uploaded_files/c29900196aa60326142f236b9a65b73647713c3e.pdf (accessed 24 October 2016).

Combes, P.-P., G. Duranton and L. Gobillon (2012), "The costs of agglomeration: Land prices in French cities", *CEPR Discussion Papers*, No. 9 240, Centre for Economic Policy Research, London.

Commander, S., Z. Nikoloski and A. Plekhanov (2011), "Employment concentration and resource allocation: One-company towns in Russia", *IZA discussion paper*, No. 6034, Bonn, http://ftp.iza.org/dp6034.pdf (accessed 27 October 2016).

Committee on Statistics of the Republic of Kazakhstan (2016a), "National accounts database", available (in Russian) at: www.stat.gov.kz/faces/wcnav_externalId/homeNationalAccountIntegrated (accessed 16 November 2016).

Committee on Statistics of the Republic of Kazakhstan (2016b), Demographic database, available (in Russian) at: www.stat.gov.kz/faces/wcnav_externalId/homeNumbersPopulation?_adf.ctrlstate=u5ioriyfd_4&_afrLoop=1653212230005672.

Committee on Statistics of the Republic of Kazakhstan (2016c), Transport database, available (in Russian) at: www.stat.gov.kz/faces/wcnav_externalId/homeNumbersTransport?_adf.ctrlstate=b6lrkbqi2_50&_afrLoop=2947648817962669#%40%3F_afrLoop%3D2947648817962669%26_adf.ctrl-state%3Dudk4hhsnm_17.

Committee on statistics of the Republic of Kazakhstan (2016d), Housing database, available (in Russian) at: www.stat.gov.kz/faces/wcnav_externalId/publicationsCompilations?_afrLoop=3991147878468215#%40%3F_afrLoop%3D3991147878468215%26_adf.ctrl-state%3D44m4aly8u_55 (accessed 3 September 2016).

Committee on Statistics of the Republic of Kazakhstan (2016f), Labour database, main labour market indicators at the district level, available (in Russian) at: www.stat.gov.kz/faces/wcnav_externalId/homeNumbersLabor?_afrLoop=6672220744050857#%40%3F_afrLoop%3D6672220744050857%26_adf.ctrl-state%3Dlhdr4xyv6_47.

Committee on Statistics of the Republic of Kazakhstan (2015a), Brochure on communal utilities, available (in Russian) at: www.stat.gov.kz/faces/wcnav_externalId/publicationsCompilations2015?_afrLoop=4018574655539556#%40%3F_afrLoop%3D4018574655539556%26_adf.ctrl-state%3D13vgemt9b5_21.

Committee on Statistics of the Republic of Kazakhstan (2015b), Brochure on communal services, available (in Russian) at: http://stat.gov.kz/faces/wcnav_externalId/publicationsCompilations2015?_afrLoop=4016293972938445#%40%3F_afrLoop%3D4016293972938445%26_adf.ctrl-state%3Dgyjfif1s9_38.

Coulibaly, S. et al. (2012), "Eurasian cities: New realities along the Silk Road", World Bank Publications, World Bank, Washington, DC.

Duranton, G. (2007), "Urban evolutions: The fast, the slow, and the still", American Economic Review, Vol. 97/1, pp. 197-221.

Economic Research Institute (2014), "How to improve the migration policy of Kazakhstan?" (Russian: *Sovershenstvovanie* migracionnoj politiki v Respublike Kazahstan) (unpublished presentation).

Federation of Canadian Municipalities (2015), "Canadian municipalities and the mining sector: Insights from British Colombia, Canada", FCM policy brief, www.fcm.ca/Documents/tools/International/Canadian_Municipalities_And_The_Mining_Sector_EN.pdf (accessed 27 October 2016).

Florida, R. (2012), *The Creative Class (Revisited)*, Basic Books, New York.

Gabaix X. and Y.M. Ioannides (2004), "The Evolution of City Distributions", in J.V. Henderson and J.F.Thisse (eds.), *Handbook of Regional and Urban Economics*, Ch.53, North Holland, Amsterdam, pp. 2 341-2 378.

Gibbons, S. H.G. Overman and G. Resende (2011), "Real earnings disparities in Britain", *Spatial Economics Research Centre Discussion Papers*, No. 0065, London School of Economics and Political Science, London.

Government of Kazakhstan (2014), *Regional Development programme until 2020.*

Harding T. and B. Javorcik (2007), "Developing economies and international investors: Do investment promotion agencies bring them together?", *Discussion Papers*, No. 513, September, Statistics Norway, Research Department, www.ssb.no/a/publikasjoner/pdf/dp/dp513.pdf (accessed 18 November 2016).

Henderson. J.V. (2010), "Cities and Development", *Journal of Regional Science*, Vol. 50/1, pp. 515-40.

Kenessariyev, U. et al. (2013), "Human health cost of air pollution in Kazakhstan", *Journal of Environmental Protection*, Vol. 4, pp. 869-876, http://file.scirp.org/pdf/JEP_2013080915494980.pdf (accessed 18 November 2016).

Krugman, P. (1996), *The Self-Organizing Economy*, Blackwell, Cambridge, Massachusetts.

Linn, J. (2014), "Urbanization, regional development, and decentralization", in A. Aitzhanova et al. (eds.), *Kazakhstan 2050: Toward a Modern Society for All*, Nazarbayev University, National Analytical Centre, Oxford University Press, International, Astana, pp.187-223.

Makhmutova, M. (2012), "Internal migration of young people in Kazakhstan: case study of Almaty", Public Policy Research Centre and Soros Foundation, Kazakhstan, http://en.soros.kz/uploads/user_68/2015_06_11__10_35_43__888.pdf (accessed 18 November 2016).

Martinez-Fernandez, C. et al. (2012), "The shrinking mining city: Urban dynamics and contested territory", *International Journal of Urban and Regional Research*, Vol. 36/2, pp. 245-260.

Ministry of National Economy (2014), Order No. 139, available (in Russian) at: http://adilet.zan.kz/rus/docs/V1400010068#z35.

OECD (2017a), *OECD Territorial Reviews: Kazakhstan*, OECD Publishing, Paris, forthcoming.

OECD (2017b), *OECD Investment Policy Reviews: Kazakhstan*, OECD Publishing, Paris, forthcoming.

OECD (2017c), *Reviews of National Policies for Education: Higher Education in Kazakhstan*, OECD Publishing, Paris, forthcoming.

OECD (2016a), *Multi-dimensional Review of Kazakhstan: Volume 1. Initial Assessment*, OECD Publishing, Paris, http://dx.doi.org/10.1787/9789264246768-en.

OECD (2016b), *Boosting Kazakhstan's National Intellectual Property System for Innovation*, OECD Publishing, Paris, http://dx.doi.org/10.1787/9789264260955-en.

OECD (2016c), *OECD Regions at a Glance 2016*, OECD Publishing, Paris, http://dx.doi.org/10.1787/reg_glance-2016-en.

OECD (2016d), "Subnational governments in OECD countries: Key data" (brochure), OECD, Paris, www.oecd.org/regional/regional-policy; for Kazakhstan Committee on Statistics, Administrativno-territorial'nye edinicy Respubliki Kazahstan na nachalo 2016 goda, available (in Russian) at www.stat.gov.kz/faces/wcnav_externalId/homeNumbersPopulation?_afrLoop=1047213434293890#%40%3F_afrLoop%3D1047213434293890%26_adf.ctrl-state%3D2z58uq0bt_94.

OECD (2016e), "Prices: Analytical house price indicators", Main Economic Indicators (database), http://dx.doi.org/10.1787/cbcc2905-en.

OECD (2016f), "Municipal waste", *OECD Environment Statistics* (database), http://dx.doi.org/10.1787/data-00601-en (accessed 28 September 2016); for Kazakhstan Committee on Statistics, environment database (unpublished).

OECD (2015a), *OECD Urban Policy Reviews: China 2015*, OECD Publishing, Paris, http://dx.doi.org/10.1787/9789264230040-en.

OECD (2015b), "Metropolitan areas", OECD Regional Statistics (database), http://dx.doi.org/10.1787/data-00531-en. For Kazakhstan: OECD research based on data from the Committee of Statistics.

OECD (2015c), *The Metropolitan Century: Understanding Urbanisation and its Consequences*, OECD Publishing, Paris, http://dx.doi.org/10.1787/9789264228733-6-en.

OECD (2015d), "Kaznex Invest Strategic Review, OECD Eurasia Competitiveness Programme", Internal Kaznex Invest document presented in Astana on 14 December 2015 (unpublished).

OECD (2015e), *Understanding the Krasnoyarsk Agglomeration in OECD Territorial Reviews: The Krasnoyarsk Agglomeration, Russian Federation*, OECD Publishing, Paris, http://dx.doi.org/10.1787/9789264229372-en.

OECD (2014a), *OECD Regional Outlook 2014: Regions and Cities: Where Policies and People Meet*, OECD Publishing, Paris, http://dx.doi.org/10.1787/9789264201415-en.

OECD (2014b), "Energy Subsidies and Climate Change in Kazakhstan", Final Draft Report, OECD, Paris.

OECD (2014c), *Regulatory Policy in Kazakhstan: Towards Improved Implementation*, OECD Publishing, Paris, http://dx.doi.org/10.1787/9789264214255-en.

OECD (2012), "Promoting energy efficiency in the residential sector in Kazakhstan: Designing a public investment programme", OECD EAP Task Force, OECD, Paris.

OECD Database (2016), Functional areas by country, data for 2016 available at: http://www.oecd.org/gov/regional-policy/functionalurbanareasbycountry.htm.

OECD/UCLG (2016), "Subnational governments around the world: Structure and finance", www.uclg-localfinance.org/sites/default/files/Observatory_web_0.pdf and Committee on Statistics of the Republic of Kazakhstan.

President of Kazakhstan (2013), "Concept for transition of the Republic of Kazakhstan to the Green Economy", Decree No. 577 of the President of Kazakhstan, adopted on 30 May 2013.

President of Kazakhstan (2012), "Conception of development of local self-government in Kazakhstan", Decree No. 438 of the President of Kazakhstan, adopted on 28 November 2012.

Regional Australia Institute (2013), "Rethinking the future of northern Australia's regions", Regional research report, Canberra, www.regionalaustralia.org.au/wp-content/uploads/2013/11/Rethinking-the-future-of-northern-Australias-regions1.pdf.

Storper, M. (2013), *Keys to the City. How Economics, Institutions, Social Interaction, and Politics Shape Development*, Princeton University Press, Oxford.

UNDP/GEF (2015a), *Energy Efficiency in Transport Sector of the Republic of Kazakhstan: Current Measures and Suggestions for Improvement*, Analytical Report, 2015, Almaty, www.eurasia.undp.org/content/dam/rbec/docs/Energy%20Efficiency%20in%20Transport%20Sector%20of%20the%20Republic%20of%20Kazakhstan.pdf?download (accessed 16 November 2016).

UNDP/GEF (2015b), Annex E "Waste Management in Kazakhstan", in "Nationally Appropriate Mitigation Actions for Low-carbon Urban Development", project document (unpublished).

UNDESA (2014), "World Urbanization Prospects: The 2014 Revision", United Nations Department of Economic and Social Affairs, June, https://esa.un.org/unpd/wup/ (accessed September 2016).

UNECE (2016), "CIS Cities: Towards Sustainable Future – The Commonwealth of Independent States Regional Report", UNECE, UN-Habitat, www.unece.org/index.php?id=42438 (accessed 18 November 2016).

UNECE and UNESCAP (2008), "Global Assessment Report of the statistical system of Kazakhstan", January http://www.unece.org/fileadmin/DAM/stats/documents/technical_coop/GA_Kazakhstan_EN.pdf (accessed 23 November 2016).

United Nations (2015), General Assembly Resolution A/RES/70/1, "Transforming our World: The 2030 Agenda for Sustainable Development", 21 October, https://sustainabledevelopment.un.org/content/documents/21252030%20Agenda%20for%20Sustainable%20Development%20web.pdf (accessed 18 November 2016).

Veneri, P. (2013), "On City Size Distribution: Evidence from OECD Functional Urban Areas", *OECD Regional Development Working Papers*, No. 2013/27, OECD Publishing, Paris, http://dx.doi.org/10.1787/5k3tt100wf7j-en.

World Bank (2016a), "World Bank- Kazakhstan Partnership Program Snapshot", World Bank Publications, World Bank, Washington, DC, http://pubdocs.worldbank.org/en/220651460698981308/Kazakhstan-Snapshot-s2016-en.pdf (accessed 5 December 2016).

World Bank (2016b), "Kazakhstan: A Long Road to Recovery", Kazakhstan Economic Update No. 3, World Bank Group, Washington, DC, http://documents.worldbank.org/curated/en/119541468948826131/A-long-road-to-recovery (accessed 5 December 2016).

World Bank (2016c), "Doing Business in Mexico 2016" (Subnational), World Bank Group, Washington, DC, available (in Spanish) at: www.doingbusiness.org/~/media/WBG/DoingBusiness/Documents/Subnational-Reports/DB16-Sub-Mexico.pdf (accessed 9 November 2016).

World Bank (2016d), *World Development Indicators* (database), http://data.worldbank.org/data-catalog/world-development-indicators.

World Bank (2015), "Doing Business Economy Profile 2016: Kazakhstan", World Bank Group, Washington, DC, https://openknowledge.worldbank.org/bitstream/handle/10986/23286/Doing0business0iciency000Kazakhstan.pdf?sequence=1&isAllowed=y (accessed 9 November 2016).

World Bank JERP (2015), "Establishment of policy and institutional roadmap for urban agglomerations in Shymkent and Aktobe", draft diagnosis report (unpublished).

Yusuf, S. (2014), "Knowledge-based economic growth", in Aitzhanova, A. et al. (eds.) (2014), *Kazakhstan 2050: Toward a Modern Society for All*, Nazarbayev University, National Analytical Centre, Oxford University Press, Group Centennial International, Astana, pp.149-179.

Zimovina, E. (2009), "Processy urbanizacii v Kazahstane v postsovetskij period i ih demograficheskaja sostavljajushhaja, Demoskop Weekly, Moscow", available (in Russian) at: http://demoscope.ru/weekly/2009/0363/analit02.php (accessed 9 November 2016).

Zipf, G. (1949), *Human Behavior and the Principle of Least Effort*, Addison-Wesley, Cambridge, Massachusetts.

Appendix 1.A1

Defining OECD functional urban areas

Figure 1.A1.1. **Procedure for defining functional urban areas in OECD countries**

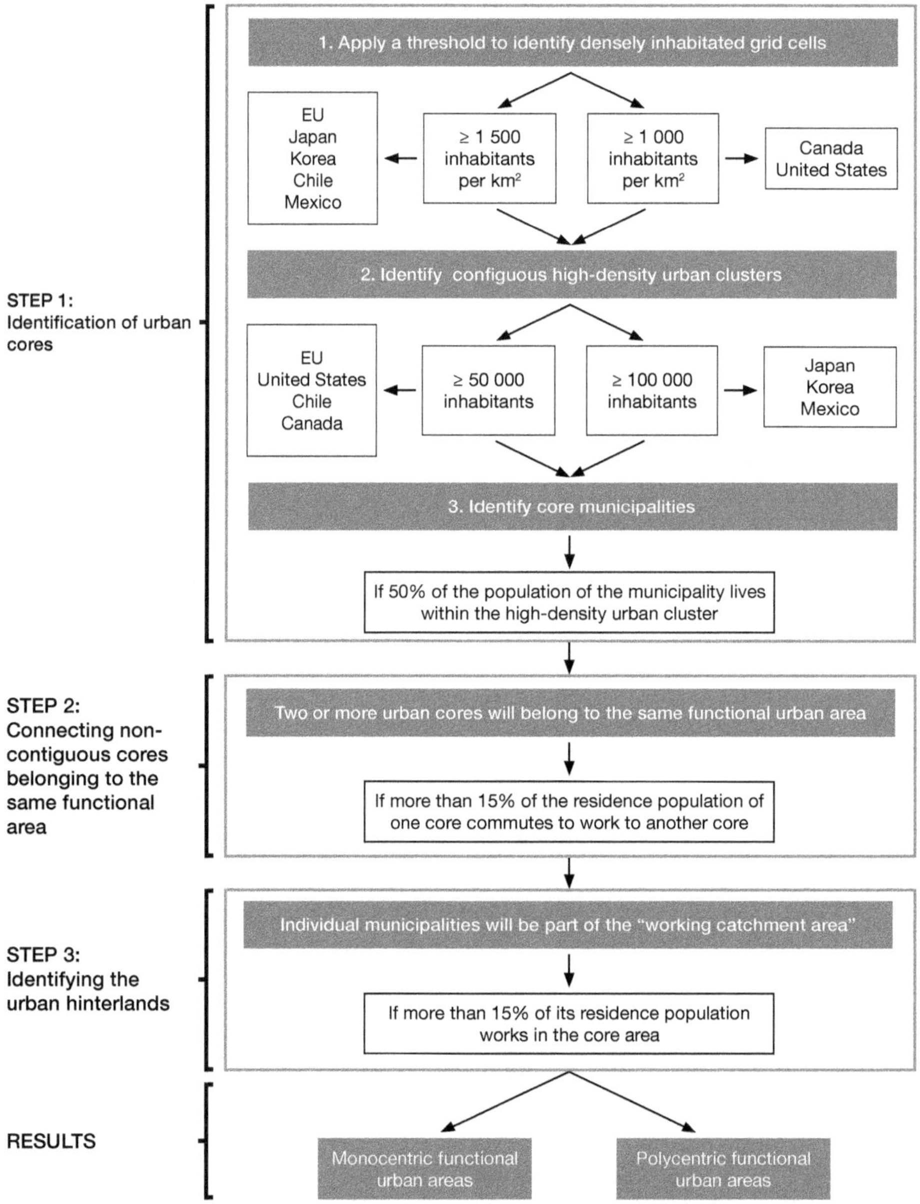

Source: OECD (2016c), *OECD Regions at a Glance 2016*, OECD Publishing, Paris, http://dx.doi.org/10.1787/reg_glance-2016-en.

Appendix 1.A2

Functional urban areas of Almaty City, Astana and Shymkent

Almaty City's FUA

Almaty City is the largest and the only polycentric functional urban area in Kazakhstan, comprising the two interrelated city cores of Kaskelen and Almaty City. Of Kaskelen's employed population, 31% commuted to Almaty City in 2009. The Almaty metropolitan area also includes the cities of Talgar (35% of employed population commuted to Almaty) and Essik (21% of employed population commuted to Almaty City). The share of employed population commuting to Almaty City was even higher in Boraldaï (51%), Otegen Batyr (45%) and Pokrovka (46%). There seems to be very little reverse commuting flow from Almaty City to neighbouring population centres.

Figure 1.A2.1. **Almaty metropolitan area: City cores and commuting zone settlements (2009)**

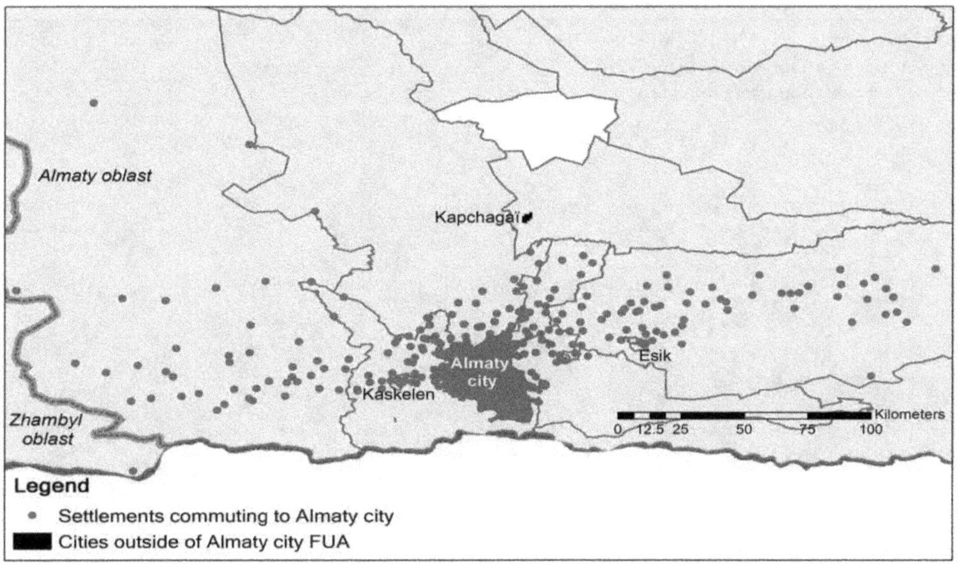

Note: This document and any map included herein are without prejudice to the status of or sovereignty over any territory, to the delimitation of international frontiers and boundaries and to the name of any territory, city or area.

Source: OECD research on unpublished 2009 Census data from the Committee on Statistics, background map from Kazakhstan land cadastre, available (in Russian) at: www.aisgzk.kz/aisgzk/ru/content/maps/ (accessed August 2016).

In 2009, the Almaty City commuting zone comprised 80 municipalities (rural districts, cities, *posiolki* administrations), mainly located in Zhambyl, Ile and Enbekshikazakh districts. The last two districts are among the densest rural districts in

Kazakhstan. As Box 1.6 shows, by definition, commuting zone municipalities have more than 15% of their employed population commuting to the City Core, i.e. Almaty City. Of the city of Kapchagaï, only 10% of the employed population commuted to Almaty City, so it was not selected as part of the commuting zone.

Almaty City has considerably expanded its borders since the 2009 National Census, on which the definition of functional urban areas in this Review is based. Many commuting zone settlements that were considered part of Almaty oblast in 2009 are now part of Almaty City proper, such as the micro *rayon* (former village) of Akjar. The extent of travel-to work flows and the high density of rural settlements around Almaty City calls for enhanced co-operation between Almaty City, Almaty oblast and Zhambyl, Ile and Enbekshikazakh districts on metropolitan issues.

Astana's FUA

Astana was Kazakhstan's second-largest FUA (700 700 inhabitants), just ahead of Shymkent in 2009. Its commuting zone accounted for 12.5% of the FUA population (87 700 people). Astana's core city experienced faster population growth than its commuting zone from 1999 to 2009. Astana's commuting zone includes 35 rural districts (selski okruga) and 2 posiolki (rural settlements) scattered around a relatively large territory in the Tselinograd, Arshaly and even Ereymentau districts. Two municipalities (corresponding to three settlements on the map below) in the North of Karaganda region are also part of Astana's commuting zone (see Figure 1.A2.2). It should be noted that neither of the neighbouring cities of Akkol or Ereymentau, nor the city of Stepnogorsk, are part of Astana's FUA.

Figure 1.A2.2. **Astana's commuting zone settlements in 2009**

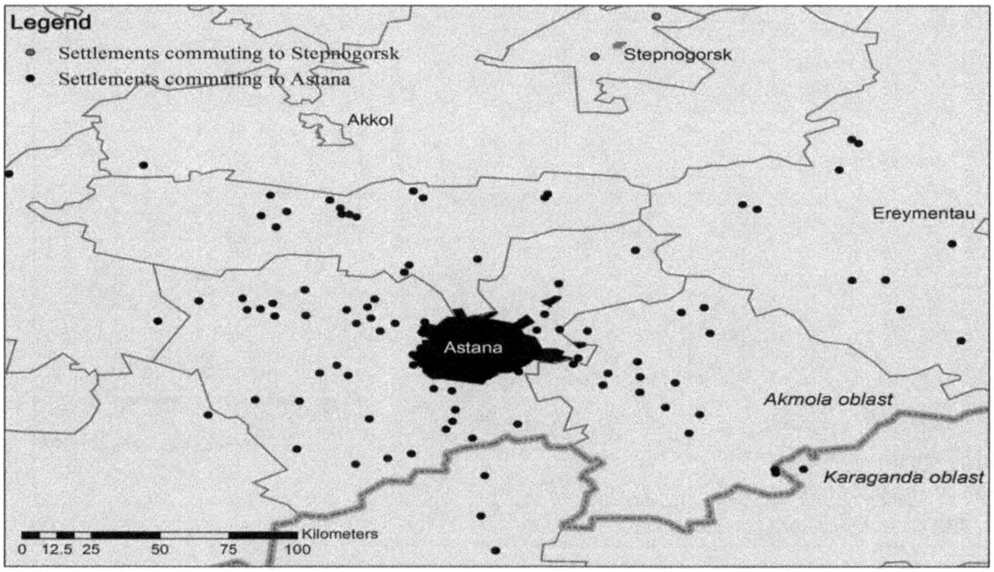

Note: This document and any map included herein are without prejudice to the status of or sovereignty over any territory, to the delimitation of international frontiers and boundaries and to the name of any territory, city or area.

Source: OECD research on unpublished 2009 Census data from the Committee on Statistics, background map from Kazakhstan land cadastre, available (in Russian) at: www.aisgzk.kz/aisgzk/ru/content/maps/ (accessed August 2016).

With the increasing demographic and economic weight of Astana, commuting is likely to grow significantly in the near future. Since 2009, it has provided progressively more employment opportunities: its employed population expanded by 27% between

2010 and 2015, compared to only 6.3% at the national level. Transport policy planning and co-ordination between Astana city and Akmola oblast should tackle the issue of adjusting public transport schedules to increasing commuting flows. The current congestion on Astana's roads (now limited to peak hours during working days) could otherwise deteriorate even further.

Shymkent's FUA

Shymkent, the third-largest metropolitan area of Kazakhstan in 2009 (679 000 inhabitants), had a commuting zone accounting for 11.2% of the FUA population (75 700 people). The largest commuting zone settlements were the city of Lenger (around 18% of whose employed population works in Shymkent) and the village of Koksaek. Shymkent's commuting zone was concentrated in the south and southeast of the city, largely in Tole Bi district (see map).

Figure 1.A2.3. **The FUAs of Shymkent and Taraz in 2009**

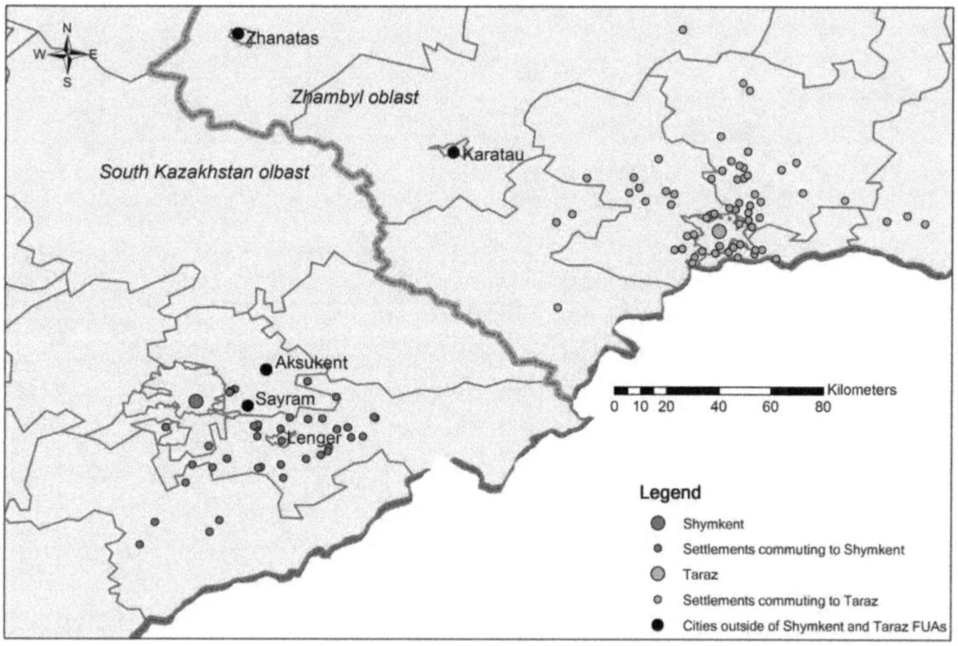

Note: This document and any map included herein are without prejudice to the status of or sovereignty over any territory, to the delimitation of international frontiers and boundaries and to the name of any territory, city or area.

Source: OECD research on unpublished 2009 Census data from the Committee on Statistics, background map from Kazakhstan land cadastre, available (in Russian) at: www.aisgzk.kz/aisgzk/ru/content/maps/ (accessed August 2016).

By contrast, the large population centres of Sayram and Aksukent (east of Shymkent city proper) do not have significant travel-to-work commuting flows to Shymkent. According to data from 2009 National Census, less than one per cent of Sayram's population commuted to Shymkent. Sayram became part of Shymkent city after the expansion of the city's territory in 2014, which means that the new territory of Shymkent has relatively fragmented labour markets.

Taraz (see map) was the fourth-largest FUA in Kazakhstan in 2009 (465 000 inhabitants). The Taraz FUA has a large commuting zone (31% of the FUA's population, or 144 000 people) comprising 29 rural districts (*selski okruga*), mainly located in the Zhambyl and Bayzak districts.

Chapter 2

Towards effective and sustainable urbanisation in Kazakhstan

This chapter looks at the major elements of urbanisation in Kazakhstan. It begins with an exploration of the origins of cities providing an understanding of the main focus of urban policies. This is followed by an examination of urban planning challenges and possible ways to improve urban planning practice in the country. The largest section of this chapter focuses on possible responses to urban development challenges. It explores alternatives to improve the land use planning system; analyses options to bridge the housing affordability gap; examines the need and ways to link land-use, transport and investment; assesses the different alternatives to improve the management of public utilities; and explores practical options to facilitate the free movement of people across urban centres.

The statistical data for Israel are supplied by and under the responsibility of the relevant Israeli authorities. The use of such data by the OECD is without prejudice to the status of the Golan Heights, East Jerusalem and Israeli settlements in the West Bank under the terms of international law.

Kazakhstan's strategic development vision is to become one of the 30 most developed countries in the world by 2050. To achieve this goal, the national government has put in place five major reforms as the country's answer to internal challenges and global threats. This reform package includes the formation of an effective state apparatus, ensuring the rule of law, facilitating industrialisation and economic growth, developing national identity and unity, and enhancing government accountability. However, Kazakhstan cannot enjoy its full economic and social development if the strategy does not acknowledge and enhance the role of urban centres. The experience of OECD countries shows that no country has become rich and developed without successful cities (OECD, 2015a). Cities are the engine of economic development, and their productivity and sustainability is at the core of their success. Kazakhstan will have to invest in urban development to raise standards of well-being and improve the skills of its population if it is to attract foreign and national investment.

Understanding urbanisation in Kazakhstan

The development of cities in Kazakhstan has gone through two phases. The first involved a sharp decline in urban socio-economic development after independence. In the second phase, at the beginning of the 21st century, high prices for raw materials have driven economic growth, allowing government to provide considerable support to large cities and small towns through budget transfers.

Most of the cities were built during the Soviet era

Kazakhstan is the most urbanised country in Central Asia. However, as for other countries in the region, urbanisation now poses certain challenges. Cities are contributing to economic growth and generating business opportunities for people, but they are failing to keep pace with demand for urban infrastructure, housing and transport. The result is a deterioration of living conditions, environmental degradation and poor quality of public services in urban spaces. Part of the problem has its origins in the role cities played in the economy of the former Soviet Union. Most of Kazakhstan's cities were built in the Soviet era and were based on a centralised, planned economy. Each city played its part in massive continent-wide economic chains (Coulibaly et al., 2012). Soviet industrial policy led to significant economic and demographic changes, including the rapid creation of new cities and urban population growth. In Soviet Kazakhstan, rich in natural resources, cities mainly served as the base for the mining of natural resources.

When the Soviet Union broke up in 1991, the countries of Central Asia (Kazakhstan, Kyrgyzstan, Tajikistan, Turkmenistan and Uzbekistan) had mostly agrarian-industrial economies, with a predominantly rural population (CER, ESCAP, UNDP, 2013). None of the Soviet cities was planned to be economically self-sufficient. Each city or town was directly dependent on another city or town, often located in the territory of the other Soviet Republic. During independence, cities played a key role in the country's transition to a market economy (CER, ESCAP, UNDP, 2013). The modernistic and technocratic approaches to planning of urban development dominated the policy arenas (Alexander, 2007). However, most of the cities are struggling to develop, because they are still subordinate to national rules and regional institutions.

In the past 20 years, Kazakhstan's urban development has followed two basic trajectories. The first is the development of two large leader-cities (Astana and Almaty) that led the nation and will soon function as major hubs at the Central Asian level. They are now expected to become important hubs in the Eurasian system of trade, financial, technological and cultural exchanges. The second one is the development of backbone national and regional cities in which local economic activity is concentrated. During the same period, central government's attention to cities has been incremental. The first country development strategy "Kazakhstan 2030: Prosperity, Security and Ever Growing Welfare for all Kazakhstanis", adopted in 1997, focused exclusively on Almaty City, the former capital, and Astana, the new capital city. This strategy helped transform Astana from a small town to one of the largest cities in Kazakhstan in only 20 years.[1] As a result, by 2015, almost a third of national gross regional product (32.3%) was produced in Almaty and Astana, up from only 21% of the total 15 years earlier, in 2000.

The current focus is on urban agglomerations

The new development strategy, "Kazakhstan 2050: New Political Course of the Established State" extends development opportunities for more cities to become centres of economic growth (Nazarbayev, 2014). The government's focus has now moved on from Astana and Almaty to consider urban agglomerations, monotowns and small towns (Box 2.1). Cities located along the international transit corridors or border cities have also started to be acknowledged as drivers of the national economy (Presidential Decree No. 118). The national government has recognised the problem of shrinking minor cities and towns, whose economies are exclusively based on the operation of a certain industry (monotowns).[2] Monotowns are the site of much of the country's industrial capacity.

Box 2.1. **Kazakhstan's main strategic urban development documents**

Strategy Kazakhstan-2050: New political course of the established state (Strategy Kazakhstan 2050). Strategy Kazakhstan 2050 was introduced to provide new long-term development principles and to update the previous planning document, Strategy 2030. Strategy 2050 aims to turn Kazakhstan into one of the 30 largest economies (in GDP and level of urbanisation) by 2050. It emphasises the need to focus on economic diversification and puts a distinct emphasis on urban development, pointing to the development of urban agglomerations, monotowns and small towns. It supports decentralisation of power and supplies local governments' financial and human capacities.

Forecast Scheme for Spatial-Territorial Development of Kazakhstan 2020 (Forecast Scheme 2020). The Forecast Scheme proposes grouping all regions into five categories, based mainly on their share in the country's GDP. The developmental opportunities proposed for the regions are based on the assessment of their current economic output, rather than their long-term potential for using existing unique and unused resources. The document restated the need to mobilise country resources in a few urban areas that could serve as engines of growth for the rest of the country, projecting the urban population would grow to about 70% of the total. This document promotes further urbanisation and formation of agglomerations to develop the foundation for innovation-based growth in major cities. The main "axes of growth" connect cities assigned to serve as "growth poles".

Regional Development Programme until 2020 (RDP). The RDP was developed on the basis of the Forecast Scheme, to serve as a first-level translator of the strategies into the implementation policy. The RDP was adjusted several times after it was first announced in 2012, with amendments in 2014 and 2015 and final approval in 2016. It recommends a distinct set of actions on the basis of four types of settlements: agglomerations, cities of secondary importance (centres of oblasts), small towns and monotowns. Most of the proposed actions were intended to revise legislation and create better conditions for urban development. However, they were not fully realised. The RDP was extended by including sectorial programs, and the main implementation focus was switched to construction of infrastructure rather than development of institutional conditions.

Source: Ministry of National Economy (2016), "Sustainable development of the cities through efficient urban planning", presentation for the UN-Habitat Meeting in Prague.

However, the RDP prioritises the development of urban agglomerations in Astana and Almaty City on the basis of co-operative activities among local governments. The co-operation is regulated by contracts signed between the Almaty City and Astana governments and their respective regional governments. The city of Shymkent is left under the same regional oversight as South Kazakhstan oblast, dealing with the same administrative and fiscal constraints that second-tier cities face. Shymkent is the second most populous city in the country and the largest in territorial area, but has a much lower budget than Astana and Almaty (Table 2.1).

Table 2.1. **Core cities of the three largest urban agglomerations in Kazakhstan, 2016**

City	Population	Territory in hectares	No. of akimat staff	Allocated budget expenses for maintenance of roads, in KZT billion	Allocated budget expenses for cleaning of streets, in KZT billion
Astana	867 790	71 000	896	38.5	25.5
Almaty	1 683 048	76 000	1 491	29.7	9.8
Shymkent	877 455	116 280	509	6.6	2.5

Source: Akimat of Shymkent city (2016), "Концепция социально-экономического развития города Шымкент до 2020 года" [Concept of socio-economic development of Shymkent city 2020], Shymkent, http://shymkent.gov.kz/ru/page/69 (accessed 15 July 2016).

Figure 2.1. **Urban categorisation according to the Regional Development Plan until 2020**

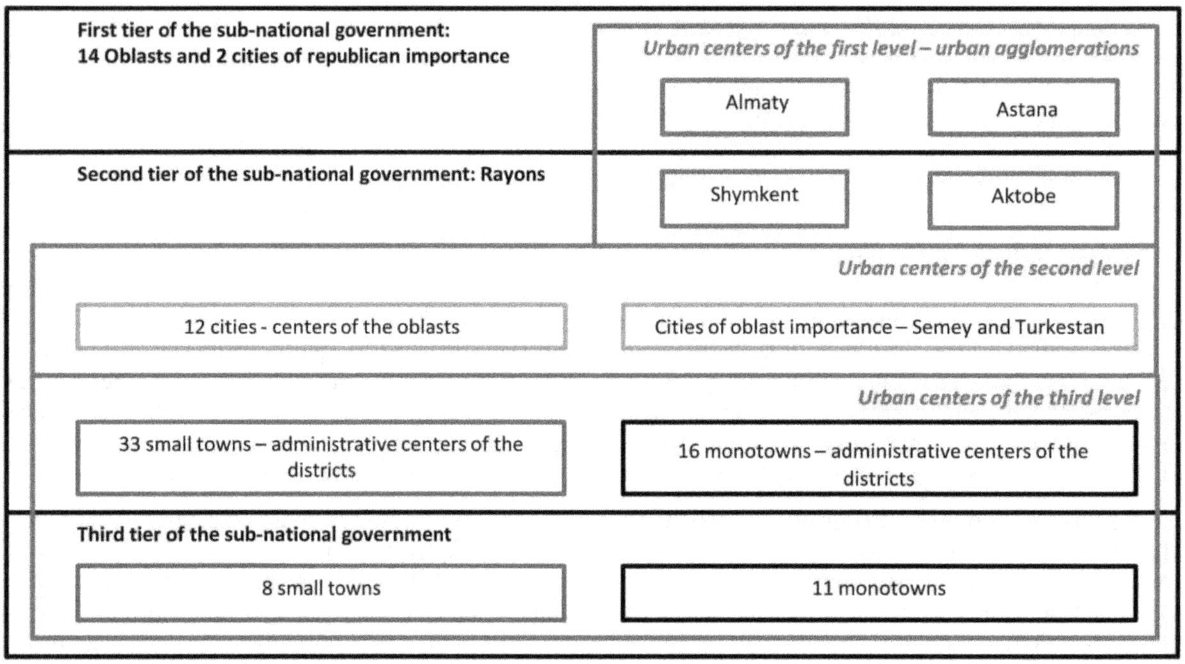

Source: Governmental Decree of the Republic of Kazakhstan No. 728 (2014), Программа развития регионов до 2020 года [Regional Development Programme 2020], dated 28 June 2014, http://online.zakon.kz/Document/?doc_id=31584094#pos=29;-284 (accessed 20 May 2016).

The RDP has not pursued equal opportunities for all urban areas to participate in the country's economy (Figure 2.1 above). Cities such as Shymkent and Aktobe, selected to be cores of the second level urban agglomerations, belong to the second tier of subnational governance and are under the supervision of the South-Kazakhstan and Aktobe oblasts respectively and have similar problems to those of Almaty and Astana, which belong to the first tier. For example, Shymkent has more residents and a larger territory than Almaty and Astana, but a lower number of civil servants and a modest budget (Table 2.1). Turkestan (a tourist and pilgrim destination) and Kentau (a monotown) are defined as urban centres of the third level (Figure 2.1).

In 2016, the central government published the "Interregional Scheme of Territorial Development of Almaty Agglomeration until 2050" (Governmental Decree No.302). This provides a wide range of detailed recommendations on functional zoning of the territory of Almaty agglomeration. "Almaty Agglomeration 2050" includes ambitious objectives such as linking Almaty City and neighbouring towns through the establishment of certain economic clusters (Box 2.2). One of the main drawbacks of the plan is that it was developed without properly involving the main implementing actors: the *akimats* of Almaty City and Almaty oblast among others, which has limited its implementation.

Box 2.2. **The Interregional Scheme of Territorial Development of Almaty Agglomeration until 2050**

The total area of the proposed territory of Almaty agglomeration is 939 500 hectares. The Almaty agglomeration includes 188 settlements of Almaty oblast and Almaty City, such as: City Kaskelen Kapshagay, Talgar, Esik, Uzynagash village, and the village of Zhetygen Otegen Batyr. The population of the proposed Almaty agglomeration was 2.4 million people as of 2014, which accounted for 14% of the total population of Kazakhstan. The urban population was 1.7 million people, or 71% of the total population of the agglomeration, and the rural population 698 700 people, or 29%, in 2014. There are uncontrolled labour migration flows. According to various estimates, in 2016 about 250 000 people come to Almaty City daily to work. Most of the migrants work in low-intensive sectors such as construction and retail trade. Among other suggestions, the agglomeration plan proposes the development of a construction materials cluster in different locations:

- Almaty (Industrial Zone in the Alatau district): production of energy-efficient architectural facades, light steel thin-walled structures, concrete, aerocrete, concrete and commodity fittings, safe, energy-efficient windows, double-glazed windows with photo printing and other glass products, metal structures, overhead cranes, multi-level parking, recycling ash and eco-cement;
- Kapshagay city: production of sandwich panels, paving slabs and curb, gas-blocks;
- Kargaly village (Zhambyl region): extraction and processing of ornamental and building stone, construction sand, as well as the production of bricks, tiles and construction products, in baked clay, ready-mixed concrete production;
- Uzynagash village (Zhambyl region): production of ready-mixed concrete and prefabricated structures, construction of concrete, as well as the extraction and processing of granite;
- Kaskelen city: manufacture of concrete and concrete products and bricks;
- Talgar city: aluminium production for construction, and plastic products (window frames, etc.).

Source: Governmental Decree of the Republic of Kazakhstan (2016), No. 302, "Межрегиональная схема территориального развития Алматинской агломерации" [Interregional Scheme of Territorial Development of Almaty Agglomeration], dated 24 May 2016, https://tengrinews.kz/zakon/pravitelstvo_respubliki_kazahstan_premer_ministr_rk/stroitelstvo_i_arhitektura/id-P1600000302/ (accessed 7 June 2016).

The process of urban policy design should involve the actors in charge of the implementation. Consultation and deliberation with key stakeholders in national governmental decisions is a key element of in success in policy implementation (Robson and Deas, 2008). Continuous production and adaptation of technical projects that are not based on the comprehensive assessment of local needs would not bring any considerable change or help to confront urban development challenges (Leigh and Blakely, 2013). It is not possible to create an urban agglomeration exclusively at the behest of the national government; city and regional governments should have a role in the planning and management. To create new inter-regional policy space, both city and oblast *akimats* have to control territorial development and share some of the managerial responsibilities. Greater attention should be paid to: i) overall co-ordination of the planned activities, ii) distribution of the available resources for their implementation, and iii) co-operation of key actors involved in urban development who have different objectives.

Getting cities right requires new tools and a new vision for development

Kazakhstan is at a decisive moment in its history to adopt the policies to "get cities right". It requires, among other things, holistic and inclusive urban policies that support economic growth. Flexibility and pragmatism in the implementation of those policies will be vital for facilitating adaptation, because opportunities for development are unevenly distributed across the country. Service-intensive cities such as Astana and Almaty face a different set of issues from manufacturing cities like Aktobe. Meanwhile, monotowns in remote locations face the loss of their major employer and shallow labour markets.

Table 2.2. **Getting cities right: the OECD perspective**

Moving from	Towards
An administrative logic, where cities are seen as administrative entities, solving problems within boundaries, even if their impact extends beyond	A functional logic, where cities are seen as functional economic areas, and solutions need to be adapted to the area of impact
Problem-driven, with a focus on issues such as air pollution, congestion, poor economic performance, failing neighbourhoods	Strategic, with a focus on opportunities (e.g. how cities of all sizes can grow and contribute to national policy objectives)
A narrowly defined urban agenda (e.g. national urban policies limited to one or two urban issues, such as infrastructure provision or revitalising distressed neighbourhoods)	A holistic approach (with national government awareness of the full range of policies that can profoundly shape urban development)
A silo approach, with sectoral, fragmented responses to specific challenges (e.g. transport, land use, water, waste, economic development)	Integrated approaches to cross-cutting urban challenges, based on co-ordinated economic, social and environmental policies (e.g. improving the quality of life and citizens' well-being, and green growth strategies)

Source: OECD (2014a), *OECD Regional Outlook 2014: Regions and Cities: Where Policies and People Meet*, OECD Publishing, Paris, www.oecd.org/regional/oecd-regional-outlook-2014-9789264201415-en.htm.

Kazakhstan's cities face common challenges that need to be addressed: i) relatively high natural population growth (i.e. Shymkent) and inward migration to large and medium-size cities; ii) limited water and land resources; iii) environmental degradation, such as air pollution (i.e. Almaty); iv) growing pressure on the urban infrastructure of the Soviet era, which is nearing the end of its service life and requires massive investment to maintain and upgrade; v) isolation from urban networks and overseas markets, which has resulted in high transport and communications costs; vi) limited options for urban transport and mobility; vii) provision of housing to the growing population close, to centres of work and education; and viii) lack of strategic planning capacity to formulate an integrated vision of long-term urban sustainability. These challenges are exacerbated by weak institutional capacity, which is reflected in a lack of financial resources, limited decision-making autonomy and low levels of citizen involvement in urban development affairs.

By getting cities right, Kazakhstan authorities can serve a greater share of the population and economy. The experience of OECD countries shows that cities are an important policy target for national economies. Many economic, social and environmental challenges can be better addressed at the urban level. The OECD perspective to get cities right suggests four changes that Kazakhstan could undertake to enable cities to contribute to growth (Table 2.2).

Kazakhstan could pay particular attention to four possible options:

1. Move from unified and technocratic policies, standards and norms of urban design to *more flexible and locally based practices*. Urban policies are designed with a top-down approach that is not appropriate for balancing public and private development interests in the economic realities of the market. There is a disjuncture between urban planning and development, because citizens and main local market players are excluded from formulating policy.
2. Move from reactive, problem-driven approaches, such as narrow, sectorial policies to *multi-sectorial urban policy packages*. This implies combining land use, housing, public utilities, transport, and green policies for urban development. The current legislative and institutional structure does not allow for approaching urban development issues in an integrated manner. Authorities tend to pay closer attention to quantities of people and square metres rather than to quality of life and well-being. Economic planning and physical planning should be co-ordinated.
3. Move from administratively constrained, short-term subsidising policies to *co-operative, multi-actor-based long-term investment strategies*. This would make it possible to create mobile, resilient and green environments for residential and economic activities, while reducing the costs of development. Nowadays, rural communities adjacent to large cities are excluded from the official procedure of planning and management of urban development. Cities are treated separately from the neighbouring rural and other urban areas. Regional and urban development instruments are not coherent. Decisions should not be based on initial costs, but on a long-term perspective based on the assessment of all the costs and benefits of urbanisation. A balance between urban and rural development could help make better investment decisions that prepare for natural and man-made disasters.
4. View the economic and social realities of the country through the lens of the *right geographic scale, to identify appropriate policy packages*. National policy is typically based on national averages that do not represent any particular region or city. Once the lens is adjusted to the right scale, it will become easier for Kazakhstan to understand the most pressing challenges of each region and how best to address them. While some issues may apply nation-wide, others require complementary policies that vary from place to place. This will require fine-grained data, indicators and policy approaches and require co-ordinating responses with subnational governments.

Towards new urban planning principles

In 2009, the government of Kazakhstan introduced the New Planning System, which delegated economic planning to local governments (Presidential Decree No. 827) (Figure 2.2). The Five-Year Economic Plans serve as the basis for approval of the local budgets planned for three years, including money for implementation of the economic plans. All 14 oblasts and the two cities of republican significance (Almaty and Astana) are now responsible for the "Five-Year Forecast of Socio-Economic Development" (*Прогноз социально-экономического развития/FSCD*) and "Five-Year Programmes of Territorial Development" (*Программа развития территории/PTD*). The Ministry of National Economy (MNE) is the lead co-ordinator, overseeing physical and economic development, and the cities of regional importance must also develop local programmes. The city PTDs can be approved by the *maslikhats* only one month after the approval of the oblast PTD. In 2012, small towns and monotowns also acquired the opportunity to develop their "Comprehensive Development Plan" (*Комплексный план развития/CDP*).

The new planning system could be further improved

Despite recent improvements in the planning framework, urban planning practice is still limited mainly to the production of urban design projects and ambitious economic plans. The CDP has not yet been integrated into the national economic planning system. At least four main critical challenges for the new planning system for economic development remain:

- *Economic plans and general plans are not coherent.* The strict alignment with the MNE methodology makes it difficult to link local economic plans with the general plans, as they follow different technical norms. In many cases, the general plan suggestions are included as part of the subsections of local economic plans, aiming to describe the territorial development actions (Akimat of Almaty City, 2011). The city governments do not have the legal and fiscal capacity to fully integrate these two locally available tools.
- *The economic plans are not always tailored to local budgets.* The city *akimats* include overambitious objectives that do not identify viable financial and institutional resources. Budget execution is constrained by deadlines that make reservation for long-term development projects included in the economic plans almost impossible (Budget Code No. 95-IV). The evaluation of Astana City PTD's implementation shows that even the well-financed *akimat* of the capital city could achieve only some (10%-20%) of the planned objectives (Akimat of Astana City, 2015).
- *Local economic plans in general fail to reflect local needs.* They have to be produced in accordance with performance development indicators defined by the Ministry of National Economy (MNE). A subordinate office in the *akimat* called the Department of Economy and Budget Planning (DEBP) is responsible for developing local economic plans. This is directly subordinate to the local *akim* and represents local government interests to the national government. There is no direct subordination between MNE and DEBP, but DEBP depends on MNE decisions. The DEBPs are involved in the quarterly and annual reporting to the MNE on progress on economic development.

- *Policy formulation still adopts a sectorial approach.* Each sectorial ministry reacts to the sector's specific needs by developing sectorial programmes. The New Planning System simply transferred the old sectorial planning from the centre to local governments.

Figure 2.2. **Planning framework for urban and economic development in Kazakhstan**

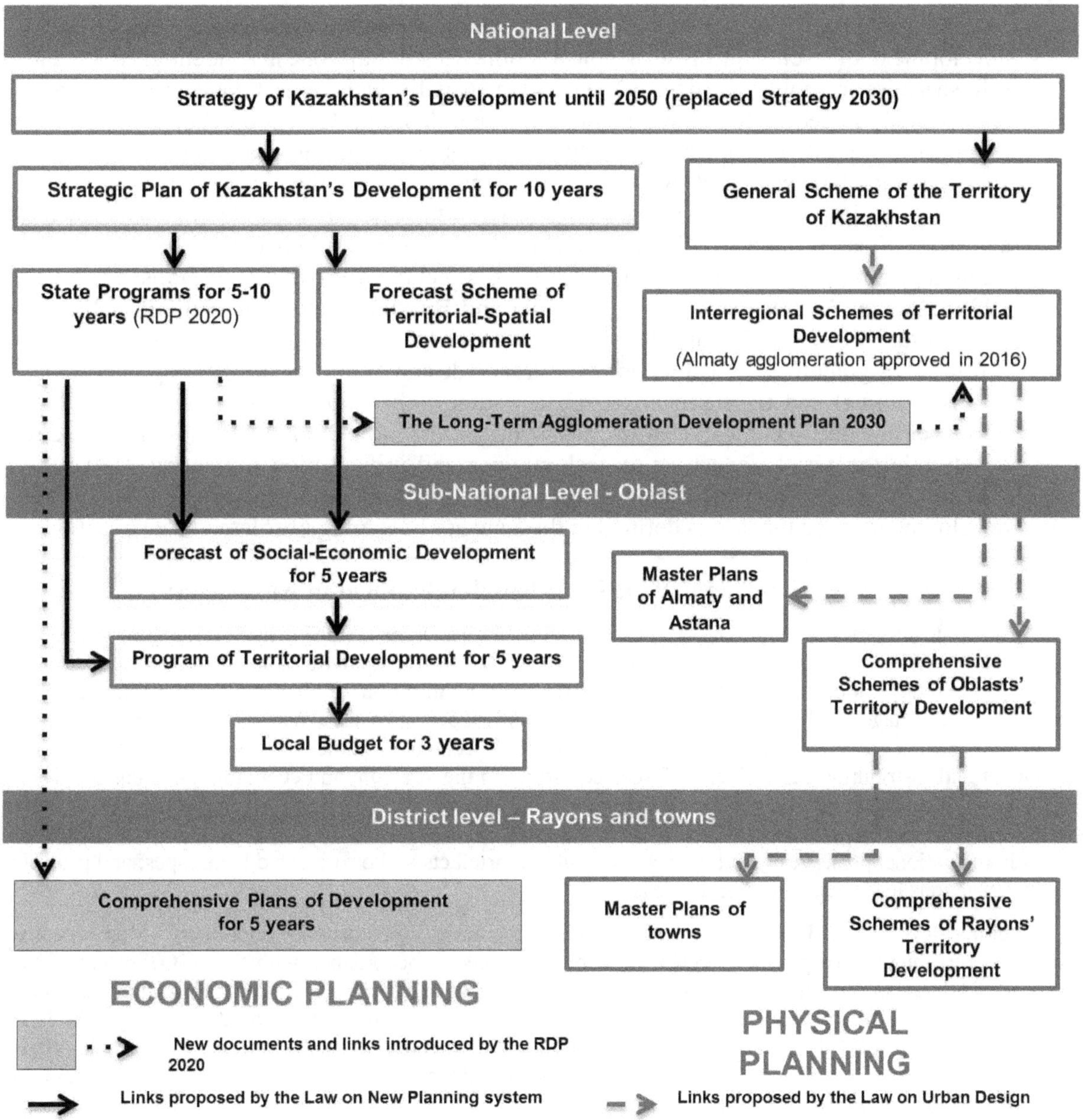

Source: Based on: Law of the Republic of Kazakhstan No. 242-II (2001), "Об архитектурной, градостроительной и строительной деятельности в Республике Казахстан" [The Law on Architectural, Town Planning and Building Activities in the Republic of Kazakhstan], (with additions dated to 07.04.2016); Presidential Decree of the Republic of Kazakhstan No. 827 (2009), "О системе государственного планирования в Республике Казахстан" [On the system of State planning in the Republic of Kazakhstan], dated 18 June 2009, www.economy.kz/sgp/2030/ukaz2.doc (accessed 10 October 2014).

Enhancing urban planning

To further improve Kazakhstan's economic and urban planning system, authorities might wish to consider the following recommendations:

The general plan should be based not only on technical norms but also on a local needs assessment

In Kazakhstan, the general plan is the main document that guides the physical development of a city: priority of construction, functional zones, residential areas and infrastructure for public services. General plans usually include a 30-year projection and are updated as needed. Kazakhstan should manage this long-term projection carefully, as long-term forecasts are not always reliable. A soft approach to planning rather than a strict one may be considered. Apart from the general plans at the national level, there are regional, district, city and local plans (Box 2.3). In the last 20 years, 87 cities and towns, and approximately 88% of villages, developed their general plans (Ministry of National Economy, 2016). These are drawn up under the technical provisions established in the 1996 "Law on Architectural, Town Planning and Building Activities in the Republic of Kazakhstan" (Law on Urban Design). According to the Law, city development must follow the guidelines set out in the urban design projects (*градостроительная документация*) and the national technical norms (*нормативная документация*). The norms define the technical characteristics of architectural and urban design projects, construction materials, construction technologies and urbanisation in general. However, the general plans are no longer effective for planning and management of urban development, since the norms defined in the Law are becoming obsolete.

Box 2.3. **General plans for urban development in Kazakhstan**

National-level general plan. The "General Scheme of the Organisation of the Territory of the Republic of Kazakhstan" (Генеральная схема организации территории Республики Казахстан/GSOT) is an urban design project containing a long-term spatial vision for rational organisation of the territory: utilisation of regional competitive advantages and achievement of sustainable development of the country. It is the main guiding urban design project that serves as the basis for urban design projects at lower levels. It includes: basic principles of settlement and distribution of production forces according to the strategic and economic planning provisions; key provisions of rational environmental management and economic activities; the development of nationwide production, transport, engineering, social and recreational infrastructure; key measures to improve environmental issues in the national preserves with historical and cultural artefacts and/or protected landscapes; and provisions for use or restrictions in especially protected areas.

Regional-level general plans. The "Interregional Schemes of Territorial Development" (Межрегиональные схемы территориального развития/ISTD) must be developed in accordance with the GSOT project. The ISTD defines guidelines for territorial development based on: the pre-established system of settling; social and economic situation; climate; availability of natural resources; and the position of the regions on the territory. The ISTD also aims to serve as a plan for consolidated development of territories of two or more regions. "Comprehensive Schemes of Oblasts' Territory Development" (Комплексные схемы градостроительного планирования территорий областей/CSOT) determine the physical development of oblasts and cities with special status (i.e., Almaty and Astana). The CSOTD must be developed based on the GSOT and ISTD projects.

District-level general plans. The "Comprehensive Schemes of Rayons' Territory Development" (Комплексные схемы градостроительного планирования территорий районов) determine the physical development of *rayons*, rural areas (сельский округ), industrial complexes (территориально-производственных комплексов), suburban areas close to large cities (пригородных зон крупных городов), recreational areas and preserves. These must be developed in accordance with the GSOT, ISTD and CSOTD projects.

Box 2.3. **General plans for urban development in Kazakhstan** (*cont.*)

City general plan. Formally, general plans (Генеральные планы) are used to determine the physical development of cities, towns and villages. The general plan must be developed in accordance with national and regional level projects, as well as with previous versions of the general plan. Plans are developed for a period of 10 to 15 years and are the basis for development of long-term, medium-term and short-term programmes for socio-economic development of cities and other settlements. The general plan is developed based on many different technical norms. Nowadays, general plan proposals are based on demographic forecasts without any serious social and economic assessment. Knowing the estimated number of people, the work of urban designers is limited to spatial distribution of these normative provisions through functional zoning of the city map.

Locality general plan. Detailed local plans (Проект застройки/DLP) must be aligned with the guidelines of the Master Plan and include: the demarcation of the territory into functional zones; red lines and controls for the building line; reserved areas for placement of objects of social, cultural and communal services for the population; state, private and other forms of ownership; property ownership; organisation of the road network and transport services and utilities; streets profiles; landscaping; public facilities, and other requirements.

Source: Law of the Republic of Kazakhstan, No. 242-II, (2001), "Об архитектурной, градостроительной и строительной деятельности в Республике Казахстан" [The Law on Architectural, Town Planning and Building Activities in the Republic of Kazakhstan], (with additions dated to 7 April 2016); SN RK 3.01-00-2011 Инструкция о порядке разработки, согласования и утверждения градостроительных проектов [Instruction on the Development, Co-ordination, Approval and the Design Documentation for Construction].

According to the Law, *akimats* play a key role in the design and co-ordination of the urban design project through the Department of Architecture and Urban Design (DAUP), which is responsible for supervising physical developments in the city. However, in many cases, private urban design companies produce the general plans at the request of the city *akimat*. The costs of producing the general plans do not usually include any deep field assessments or analytical research based on updated and reliable data.

The DAUP usually lacks the capacity to guide the process of development of the general plan. In practice, it is overloaded with daily regulatory activities and does not have the time or expertise to approach a city's development strategically. The DAUP staff has little capacity to supervise urban design processes and usually fails to monitor a city's overall physical development. The DAUP's role is to: write terms of reference and get the final product. *Maslikhats* also rarely take part in the planning process, except at official public hearings that take place on only two occasions: in the initial stages, to choose the main strategy, and at the end, to approve the final project. The urban design process does not include any productive inter-departmental and cross-sectorial interactions. Consultations with public and local authorities take place only if these consultations are initiated by urban designers and supported by the chief architect (the head of the DAUP).

Generally, the general plans are drawn up as technical projects without comprehensive assessment of the local situation. The main emphasis is on demographic forecasts. City *akimats* are more interested in showing positive demographic growth that allows them to apply for social transfers from higher levels of government. An increase in the number of people in a city is an opportunity to increase the budget of the local *akimat*, because public expenses are directly linked with the number of inhabitants registered in the city (Akimat of Pavlodar city, 2007). General plans normally include predetermined quantitative features: such as number of square metres of housing, educational, recreational areas and greenery per person, guided by the technical norms defined and approved at the national level. The current system of normative documents has passed through numerous updates, but the new versions are rewritten or slightly updated. The norms are generalised and unified, making it hard to tailor them to local needs and conditions.

The approval of urban design projects is a complex administrative procedure defined in the Law on Urban Design and includes many submissions to different ministries and state agencies. The length of time for approval may vary from a few months to several years.[3] The process of approval is especially long and complicated at the central level, rather than the local level. In some cases, they need to be updated by the time they are approved. National and local examining authorities assess the general plan only in terms of its compliance with the technical norms, rather than with local needs. Once the urban design project is approved, it can be used to supervise urban development. However, in practice, urban design stops when the general plan is delivered, because it takes place outside the budget planning process and land use.

General plans should be linked to a budget line for implementation

A local budget line is normally defined for the production of a general plan, but no budget is allocated for its implementation and monitoring. Since urban design projects are not subject to careful economic analysis, they can hardly be integrated into budgeting and economic planning cycles. Ideally, the general plan decisions should be further developed during the phase of detailed district general plans. However, city *akimats* usually do not have budget allocations to order district-specific plans (Akimat of Uralsk City, 2015). In many cases, local governments have to attract additional financial resources to implement the plans. The short-term budget provisions diminish the city *akimats*' capacity to forecast and be prepared for the long-term development of the city. The lack of financial resources for the implementation of the general plans leads city *akimats* to use the plans as an instrument to get special-purpose transfers from oblast or central government to develop public infrastructure. Most national policies, including budgets for construction of social housing and public infrastructure, come to the city with separate budget allocations. General plan proposals are also used by the city *akimat* to calculate public expenses needed for construction of public facilities such as schools, hospitals, roads and communal infrastructure. At the same time, in many cases, general plans lack reliable economic indicators of development and are not able to serve as the decision-support tool for long-term adequate investment, such as urban transport projects.

General plans should be connected to environmental objectives

According to the Law of Urban Design, all general plans have to include an Environmental Impact Assessment (EIA). However, an EIA is a *post factum* activity limited to an evaluation of the development decisions of urban designers (UNECE, 2008). The assessment is narrowed down to measuring the negative impact of urban development and designing measures for mitigation of expected ecological outcomes. The EIA includes calculations of emissions, amount of solid waste and other direct effects of urban development. Preventative measures to limit or even avoid the negative effects of urban development are considered, but no implementation plan or budget for their execution is drawn up. The pre-assessment of the environmental situation that is conducted in the early stages of urban design does not have any great impact on the final decision regarding a city's development. As a result, none of the general plans is designed to make the city environmentally friendly and energy efficient. Indicators such as raising levels of air pollution due to the increase in the number of private cars in a city are set aside.

The lack of attention to environmental conditions makes cities vulnerable to natural and man-made disasters. In many cases, the urban design solutions are proposed based on the old maps of geological and environmental conditions. No detailed field research of current environmental pollution levels or geological and hydrological studies is carried out. As a consequence, the new directions for city development sometimes run counter to the logic of environmental safety and sustainability. The city *akimats* consider the results of the EIA only as recommendations, and no serious preventive actions are carried out in practice.

Ensure that the general plans are operational and the legal framework coherent

Making development plans operational is a problematic issue in Kazakhstan (OECD, 2014b). There are at least five aspects that Kazakhstan's authorities may wish to consider in this regard: i) regularly monitor and evaluate progress to allow continuous improvement and adaptation of the general plans to local needs; ii) ensure transparency by communicating the details of the general plans with the wider community, explaining the expected economic returns, for example, and an increase of local revenues to finance urban development projects; iii) during the approval process of the general plans, assess not only the compliance with the technical norms but also the local financial, human and natural resources needed for its implementation; iv) link the preparation and implementation of the general plan to the budget process; and, v) engage the local community, including civil society and the private sector, in the preparation of the general plans, as urban development should not be seen as an exclusive prerogative of the national government or local akimats. The constant improvement of legislation has not yet changed the planning practice or supplied municipal governments with workable tools to manage urban development in a participatory way.

Ensuring coherence in the legal framework is essential, in particular between the Law on Urban Design, the Civil Code and the Land Code. Despite many improvements, the Law on Urban Design is still far from being a powerful legislative instrument that promotes better urban development (Tutubaev, 2010). The Law is still declarative and includes information that conflicts with other legislation regulating urban development. In several cases, an actor who had violated local construction rules could not be fined because his actions were in compliance with higher-level legislation, such as the Civil Code or the Land Code (Tutubaev, 2010). Typically, conflicts regarding private and public interests arise because of the lack of public disclosure about land use and new developments.

General plans should be based on high quality information and citizens' input

Bridging the overall information gap in the sector of urban design and land use management would contribute to transparency and informed public participation. The general plan is disclosed to citizens only occasionally, during specific public hearings. Some city *akimats* hold public sessions of the Urban Design Council (*Градостроительный совет*/UPC).[4] Though some positive changes have occurred as a result of wider professional public hearings on general plans and new developments, city development is not fully communicated, with an emphasis on important local community concerns such as housing and transport. During professionally arranged discussions, members of the general public feel uncomfortable participating, because they cannot read comprehensive maps or understand the terms used in project presentations. Informing citizens and encouraging them to participate in city development requires considerable work to explain the legislation. The Law on Urban Design does not provide any mechanism governing how the local urban development rules are designed and approved,[5] or any guidelines on how to make information accessible to a wide range of actors. On the other hand, private actors such as real estate companies actively participate in all meetings.

Open information systems for public participation need to be developed. The interactive maps showing current land use, new opportunities for the land purchase and general city development direction can be useful to ensure that public authorities, individuals, and other legal entities have reliable information that is necessary for investment and other economic activities in the city. For instance, the Almaty *akimat* has a website (http://almaty.genplan.kz) that presents sets of documented information (not always with maps), including all data about the current and planned development of the city territory: ownership and use of properties and land parcels, planned construction projects, and other necessary information for the implementation of urban development activities. However, the information provided by city *akimats* is not always up to date.[6] Not all city *akimats* have the resources to create open systems or publish information about the city's current land use and development plans through interactive public IT platforms. *Akimats* could also use statistical data from the Statistics Committee or national research institutes, and conduct field surveys to collect information on citizens' views on urban development strategies.

Responding to national urban challenges

To make the vision of "Kazakhstan 2050" a reality, the country has to get urbanisation right. For that, Kazakhstan needs to tackle a number of urban challenges, including: modernisation of the land-use planning system; diversification of the options for accessing housing; upgrading infrastructure for public utilities; ensuring intra-city connectivity; and adopting a strategy for migrants.

Modernise the land-use planning system

Recognising the importance of land use planning in controlling the current urbanisation process of Kazakhstan will be essential to ensure sustainable, productive cities with high levels of well-being.

A lack of control of land use within cities

Most of the key problems facing Kazakhstan's cities are related to a lax land use planning system. Urban sprawl, pollution, deficient delivery public services (utilities), housing gaps and weak intra-city connectivity are all problems that derive from the lack of appropriate land-use planning and the implementation of regulation. The most urgent need is for urban policy packages promoting efficient use of land for proper allocation of real estate development, as well as the provision of efficient public transport (Ryser and Franchini, 2015). The misallocation of land resources is leading to a shortage of land for sustainable development of a city and its adjacent neighbourhoods.

In Kazakhstan, bridging land-use zoning, transport and the adequate use of natural resources at the city level is not an easy task. Part of the problem is the governance of land use.[7] The management of land as well as other natural resources is highly centralised. The main local-level actors responsible are direct representatives of the central government. For example, water basin inspectors responsible for environmental control and use of natural resources supervise *oblast*-level governments. On the other hand, public transport operation is highly privatised and city-specific, with few opportunities for development of cross-administrative transport links.

Furthermore, the absence of effective land-use planning and managerial tools prevents an efficient use of resources for city development and is contributing to urban sprawl. City administrations are constantly seeking land for the implementation of national policies related to housing and construction of new public infrastructure (Akimat of South-Kazakhstan Oblast, 2016). To acquire the land, city *akimats* need to apply for resources to higher-level governments. A considerable amount of time intervenes between application for public funding and the allocation of the resources needed. When the city *akimat* finally receives transfers for the construction of public facilities, territory formerly reserved in the general plan for public use has generally already been purchased by private actors (Akimat of Almaty City, 2016). In many cases, city *akimats* responsible for construction of social housing or communal infrastructure cannot afford to buy the land back from private parties because the cost exceeds the market price.

Box 2.4. **The territorial expansion of Almaty City**

The first considerable expansion of Almaty's administrative borders took place in 1998 during the preparation of the first edition of the Master Plan. The total area of the new territories amounted to 4 700 hectares from the Almaty region. With these additional territories, the city received not only enterprises, but also 28 villages from the Almaty region and additional land for the construction of low-density housing. A mixture of legal and illegal housing appeared on these new city territories within a few years (1998-2005). In 2012, the city limits were expanded even further. The total area of new municipal territories was equal to 11.900 hectares. In 2014, the city limits were again expanded by 23 200 hectares, which included 27 settlements and a population of more than 92 000 people (President of Kazakhstan, 2014).

The city's territorial growth is always justified in different ways. These include such goals as to improve urban and industrial infrastructure, expand entry routes to the city, and develop mountain recreation and sport facilities for the Asian Olympic Games in the National Ile-Alatau Natural Park. The local environmental NGOs raised awareness about the construction of the new sport complex in the territory of the national park (NGO Green Salvation, 2014). In 2014, the city *akimat* used national safety concerns to justify expansion. It argued that the municipality was better prepared to face local extremist groups of neighbouring villages. The extension of the city borders generated expenses to build public facilities (hospitals and schools) and provide communal services (electricity and fresh water) to new residents. That year, the city received additional transfers of KZT 3.3 billion to develop engineering and social infrastructure in the new territories (*Akimat* of Almaty City, 2016). However, the transfer did not cover the cost of full modernisation of the city's infrastructure, or the provision of services to the outer parts of the city. Most of the newly added settlements are located at a considerable distance from energy sources, increasing construction costs. In addition, for some new city residents, the new city rates for communal services were much higher than regional ones.

Source: NGO Green Salvation (2014), *Letter to the President of the International Olympic Committee*, www.greensalvation.org, retrieved in February 2016; Official website of Almaty City *akimat*: http://almaty.gov.kz/, retrieved in March 2015; interviews with NGOs and urban planning companies, February-April, 2016.

Expenses for the provision of public facilities are increasing, mainly because the city is constantly losing free land for development inside the city. In consequence, city *akimats* turn their attention to the expropriation of regional land adjacent to cities. It is easier for a city *akimat* to add rural neighbouring land to a city's territory, because it is generally agricultural area that can be owned only by the state. As a result, many city governments that had been interested in acquiring more public land became interested in the extension of the city's borders. The extension of the city borders has become a key solution in the cities' general plans to ensure availability of new resources, such as land required for further demographic growth. It is an ordinary practice that is perceived by city governments as a solution to most of the city development-related problems, for example in Almaty (Box 2.4.). This is also facilitated by the fact that it is not mandatory to develop a comprehensive feasibility study to approve the need for change of the city boundaries (Law No. 2572-XII). City planning does not consider the resources needed to satisfy the needs of the future inhabitants of the city.

Almost all general plans include positive demographic forecasts and call for the extension of the city's territory. Most of the city administrations sometimes extend their territorial borders to include additional land for urban development.[8] Usually, the extension of city borders is explained by the need to use vacant land for the development of housing and public infrastructure or to solve the problems of suburban areas that demand better public service delivery that cannot be provided by the rural governments (Akimat of South-Kazakhstan, 2016).

Moreover, city governments have little control over land use, which prevents them from locating new developments strategically and in line with city needs. City *akimats* are mainly accountable for the rational use of land, construction permits and the provision of land for different uses in the city. However, in practice, land-use allocation is sometimes separated from their jurisdiction because it is also the responsibility of the territorial branches of the Committee for Land Management under the Ministry of Agriculture. This duplication of tasks by local government and by representatives of the central government presents many difficulties for land-use management. One consequence is that the disposition of individual plots is usually determined without proper consideration of local city development plan proposals or how new development will impact the city's long-term development.

Land and real estate markets are not managed in a co-ordinated manner. The delegation of land use and property taxes to the local level limits the increase of local revenues, because of the lack of appropriate land use management. Local governments were given authority to change the rate of the land use tax, but they do not fully make use of this opportunity to increase city revenues. The proportion of land use taxes collected in self-generated revenue is very low. Similarly, city governments underutilise the property tax, due to the absence of reliable databases covering all the real estate properties in the cities. Institutional changes and legislative adjustments are needed to allow city governments to use locally existing tools for integrated land-use management.

The land registry is only used as a tool to register current uses. The national government supports the introduction and development of local registry systems, such as land use or water cadastres, amongst others but they are developed and managed separately. Moreover, a monopoly for the implementation of the Urban Zoning Registry (*Государственный градостроительный кадастр/UZR*), an integrated system, was granted to the State Republican Enterprise "GosGradCadastr" created by the national government (Box 2.5). At the city level, the *akimat* is responsible for creating and operating the "duty plans". Duty plans are a feature of the UZR that is used to monitor urban development, and includes information about properties and engineering infrastructure. All city *akimats* (and respective departments, such as DAUPs) are responsible for timely updates of duty plans.[9] The UZR has to serve as the main tool for monitoring city development (Government of Kazakhstan, 2009). Legally, land should only be allocated under an approved general plan based on the UZR (Government of Kazakhstan, 2003). In practice, land-use authorities provide a land parcel for private purposes, without referring to zoning suggested by the current general plan, mainly because no UZR has yet been created at the city level. Some cities, such as Astana, Almaty, Kyzylorda, Karaganda, Taldykorgan, Uralsk and Kokshetau have UZR, but on a basic level, including information about properties and infrastructure. These registries are also not well integrated with existing land use registries.

Box 2.5. **Kazakhstan's Urban Zoning Registry**

The Urban Zoning Registry (UZR) is part of the State Registry of Kazakhstan (Государственная информационно-правовая система кадастров) and is formally reunited to contain: i) information about the previous and current state of city territories and buildings; ii) small architectural forms and elements of improvement; iii) information on urban development planning; iv) used and vacant territories; v) facilitate functional uses of different parts of the city; vi) information on environmental, geological, hydrogeological, geotechnical and seismic conditions; and vii) access to the city's communal infrastructure. Legally, the UZR data system should be created based on information extracted from the approved urban design projects, cartographic materials, geological surveys, environmental and statistical data, and other information important for regulation of city development. The UZR must be used not only for implementation of architectural and construction control, but also for property taxation, and development and implementation of urban design projects such as general plans.

Source: SN RK 1.05-01-2011 Государственный градостроительный кадастр [State Urban Design Cadastre of the Republic of Kazakhstan].

Most of the city *akimats* do not use the UZR in their daily activities because they do not have it or lack the capacities to use it properly. Not all city administration can afford to have workable decision support systems. The creation and operation of the UZR is difficult, due to the initial costs of implementing it and the need of qualified staff to run the system. Another problem is that the city governments usually obtain the UZR in a fixed form that cannot be updated in an easy or timely way, due to low capacity of the civil servants responsible for its maintenance. The Law on Urban Design stipulates that the UZR should be a process and supply the municipal government with a decision-making map showing the division of the city territory into different zones, with restrictions on their use (functional and physical parameters). However, the UZR has not yet been used as a tool to initiate new developments, granting of building permits or assessment of investment activities.

Develop a comprehensive land-use planning system

As Kazakhstan's cities grow, effective and early land-use planning is essential to plan for the infrastructure of the city, conduct effective zoning, control the expansion of the city, and become better prepared to satisfy the needs of housing and transport of new inhabitants. The current practices and planning system does not provide for this, since its approach is sectorial. The experience of OECD countries suggests that comprehensive land use planning is an effective instrument for controlling the unregulated conversion of farmland to urban land and urban sprawl (OECD, 2010). A comprehensive plan lays out the future use of land and the development goals of a particular jurisdiction. The aim is to mitigate conflicts between different land uses and to help co-ordinate issues such as transport, housing, public utilities and economic development. Kazakhstan's authorities may wish to analyse the experience of France and the Netherlands (Box 2.6), which have promoted sustainable urban development through comprehensive land use planning. The main features of their system are:

- authority of municipalities over city planning and land-use control;
- detailed, plot-by-plot reviews of land use;
- emphasis on maintaining the status quo; a general prohibition on new development in the suburbs;
- new suburban development must be incorporated into the land-use plan, i.e. new development requires planning approval;
- regional planning at regional levels, beyond the administrative boundaries of a single municipality, with which a city plan prepared by a single municipality should conform;
- planning processes with an emphasis on governance, as a consensus-building mechanism between related levels of government, in addition to strong public involvement in the process (OECD, 2010).

The experience of Japan may also be of relevance for Kazakhstan, since in both countries, the central government plays an important role in functional zoning. However, local governments are gradually becoming more important. In Japan, territorial zoning is governed by five legislative acts that fall under the jurisdiction of three different ministries and are thus often managed by different local government departments. Co-ordination has proven to be an urgent issue. The 1974 National Land Use Planning Act thus integrated the five sets of regulations into a comprehensive land-use plan. Now, districts that need strict land-use regulations, such as environmental conservation areas, are directly designated by the central government. Higher-level local governments (prefectures) designated the Urbanisation Promotion zone, Urbanisation Control zone and Agricultural Promotion zone in co-operation with municipalities.

Box 2.6. **Comprehensive land-use planning in France and the Netherlands**

In **France**, new construction is generally only allowed in built-up areas. Construction in other areas is generally prohibited, based on the *"principe de la constructibilité limitée"* (the principle limiting the possibility of construction) of the national *Code de l'urbanisme* (urban planning code). However, there are cases where construction in green fields is allowed based on the municipality's land-use plan. Municipalities can choose the level of control among several different methods. They have the authority to either formulate a *plan local d'urbanisme* (or PLU, a local urban plan that includes detailed land-use regulations and sets the zones where construction is permitted) or a *carte communale* (the municipality map demarcating areas where construction is permitted), depending on the context of the municipality. PLUs are designed for a 10- to 15-year period and are appropriate mostly for urban municipalities. Construction in green fields is only possible when allowed by the PLU or by the *carte communale*, and municipalities must otherwise comply with the national principle of limiting construction. To set up the PLU and the *carte communale*, municipalities must go through a public hearing and co-operative procedure with the central government. When development does not conform to the plan, it can legally be refused connection to infrastructure such as electricity and water grids.

To co-ordinate policies related to urban planning, housing, economic development, transport and commerce of multiple neighbouring municipalities, *Établissements publics de coopération intercommunale* (EPCI) and associations of EPCI and municipalities can voluntarily formulate and approve a *Schéma de cohérence territoriale* (SCoT) covering the area. A SCoT is not intended to regulate land use, but to set strategic urban

Box 2.6. **Comprehensive land-use planning in France and the Netherlands** (*cont.*)

restructuring policy by formulating items such as housing demand analysis, proposals for alignment and sustainable development (*Plan d'aménagement et de développement durable*, PADD), drafting basic guidelines for carrying out a PADD, maintaining built-up areas, demarcating natural and forest areas and transport projects. The SCoT must be approved by the coalition of municipalities.

In **the Netherlands**, the Spatial Planning Act manages land development at three levels of government: national, state and municipal. The national planning agency issues broad guidelines for land use that provide an outline for the strategy, policy and purpose of land development, based on the ecological and economic environment of the entire nation. Municipalities are required to formulate *Bestemmingplan* (Bm plans) in green fields for the purpose of controlling urban growth and can voluntarily formulate Bm plans in built-up areas, according to the Spatial Planning Act. Bm plans include land-use and building regulations, and can be used for both development and conservation purposes. New development requires updating the Bm plan and should conform to the updated Bm plan unless both the municipal parliament and state authority approve an exemption. The planning process includes state government approval and public involvement. Bm plans should be updated every ten years and generally cover the entire national territory. They differ in the degree of detail, depending on the local context. Built-up areas and newly developed areas tend to have detailed Bm plans, while areas where development pressure is weak do not generally need such detailed regulation. There is a certain level of flexibility in the content of the Bm plans. They are formulated as necessary, so a collection of Bm plans does not show overall land use structure and policy of the entire municipality. Municipalities thus often formulate structure plans to show the consistency of land-use policy in the municipality.

Source: OECD (2010), *Regional Development Policies in OECD Countries*, OECD Publishing, Paris, http://dx.doi.org/10.1787/9789264087255-en.

Based on the experience of OECD countries, Kazakhstan could do well to define clearly the authority and competences for land-use planning across different levels of government, as part of the comprehensive land-use plan system. Land-use planning falls mostly into the jurisdiction of local governments since it is place-based by definition and context-specific (OECD, 2017, forthcoming). Monotowns and cities of oblast significance, for example, face very different problems. Denmark, for example, has strong local planning competencies transferred from the regional level. The national government, however, has formal influence on development and can make detailed spatial plans and directives and veto planning decisions taken at lower tiers. In Finland, on the other hand, spatial planning competencies are shared between the subnational and national governments. Although the Regional Councils act as regional development agencies, local authorities have more powers and independence in land-use planning matters (Silva and Acheampong, 2015). The decentralisation of land-use planning to local governments should be reinforced, as it requires a high level of information of local conditions that central government often lacks. It should be noted that the institutions responsible for spatial planning at the national, regional and local levels derive their power and mandate from legislative instruments in the form of acts, ordinances and decrees.

Update and adopt regulatory instruments for adequate land-use management at the local level

Kazakhstan needs a more comprehensive land use management method that connects planning and implementation of closely related urban policy issues, such as economic development, social well-being, housing, utilities and transport planning. National policies on housing and public utilities should be reviewed through the lens of land use and the creation of better living conditions in Kazakhstan's cities. The current land-use planning system could guide urban development more effectively if the land registry and Urban Zoning Registry were properly integrated (Musabaev, 2013). The UZR should be used as a strategic tool not only for urban planning but for economic development. It should be used not only as a registry, but as a decision-support system in strategic socio-economic planning. The national government could provide assistance to city governments for using the UZR. This can be done through conducting land surveys, such as real estate check-ups for effective taxation strategies.

The experience of OECD countries suggests that establishing a zoning registry or zoning system is only the first part of the job, and that its implementation and dissemination are equally important. Some countries, such as Australia, Canada, Mexico and the United States, require builders to obtain some form of zoning or urban planning approval before building or even before obtaining a construction permit; the aims is to ensure that the proposed building is constructed in the appropriate zone, depending on the city's zoning requirements. In Finland, France, Latvia, the Netherlands and New Zealand, urban planning clearance or a certificate is generally obtained but is not mandatory (Delion et al., 2015).

Box 2.7. **New Zealand's experience in zoning practices**

New Zealand uses two main types of planning documents: regional plans and district plans. Regional plans specify general requirements such as air and water quality and the use of coastal areas. District plans are detailed planning guidelines that outline the specific land-use and design requirements for builders. The district plans are legally binding, cover the entire useable land in a municipality and are periodically reviewed to ensure that they reflect the changing urban needs. Each district plan is approved through a participatory process in which the district council holds public hearings to allow residents to submit suggestions or objections. Once the residents' comments have been processed, the plan becomes "operative" as a statutory document that regulates land development activities for the entire municipality.

All municipalities in New Zealand have a detailed, up-to-date zoning plan that has been approved through meaningful public involvement. The plan provides investors and developers with reliable information to guide them in the design and conceptual stage of a project before they apply for a construction permit. Moreover, it provides municipal authorities with a consistent basis for approving or rejecting construction permits with little discretion involved. Municipalities have official time limits to make a decision: 20 working days for simple cases and four months for more complex cases that involve public hearings.

Source: Delion, M.L. et al. (2015), "Zoning and urban planning: Understanding the benefits", *Doing Business 2015*, www.doingbusiness.org/reports/case-studies/2014/zoning-urban-planning.

It is in the interests of Kazakhstan and its cities to invest in good zoning practices as an instrument for effective land use management. Capacity building among the civil servants responsible for the land use management is a necessary complement to this process. Kazakhstan should avoid issuing restrictive zoning rules and single-use zoning, since they lead to inflexible planning regulations. Zoning should be sufficiently flexible to give private actors leeway to shape development and allow neighbourhoods to change over time. Zoning regulations and planning decisions should target nuisance levels. In general, all uses that create fewer nuisances than the maximum level specified for a zone should be permitted by the *akimat.*[10] Through zoning, city *akimats* can ensure the proper use of land and avoid mixing incompatible land uses. It can be used as a regulatory tool to respond to threats such as flooding, earthquakes and the loss of infrastructure through natural or man-made disasters. Zoning plans can take into account environmental threats, to protect citizens, but can also be used to promote the conservation of energy and natural resources and the protection of the environment. Land-use regulations should also promote competition between businesses. *Akimats* should not permit the use of private covenants on land that aim at stifling competition. A lesson from OECD countries such as Sweden is that the zoning process should not be too complex or restrictive, as it can have an adverse effect on housing supply and prices. Kazakhstan's authorities may wish to emulate the experience of New Zealand, whose zoning practices are comprehensive, predictable and easy to implement. Box 2.7 above illustrates the use of municipal planning and zoning as a tool to facilitate the construction permit process.

Land-use regulations and instruments can be used to control urban sprawl

Given the population growth in some parts of the country, particularly in the south and in the larger cities, Kazakhstan authorities may wish to consider promoting a more intensive use of land within the existing boundaries. This has to be done with caution, as discouraging construction outside the city limits may have a negative impact on housing affordability in central areas, and land use should guarantee affordable new housing as the population grows. Abandoned and underused parts of the cities deserve to be made the priority for development, and any attempts to develop beyond a city's boundaries may need to be restricted. The former or partly used industrial sites occupying considerable areas of the cities will have to be in the redevelopment agenda. In the case of single-industry towns, it can be especially important to reuse post-industrial zones and brownfields. Reducing the regulatory burden and streamlining permits and other administrative procedures can be a relatively inexpensive way to promote the development of brownfield areas. City governments, with the support of oblast and central governments, can promote the redevelopment of brownfields in a number of ways, beginning with a "fast-track" type of streamlined and simplified permitting system for projects on brownfield land, as a minimal intervention approach. However, it is necessary to manage the redevelopment of former industrial zones, because concerns over environmental conditions may emerge. An expedited and simplified review was implemented in Germany due to concerns over urban sprawl in the 1990s. A number of initiatives were instituted to promote a higher intensity of land use, including a simplified set of planning rules for infill development as part of the Research for the Reduction of Land Consumption and for Sustainable Land Management (REFINA) initiative, which began in the mid-2000s.[11] Other options include providing density bonuses or other subsidies in these areas or investing in public infrastructure. These strategies can be particularly effective when targeted at locations near transit, or on transport corridors where redevelopment is more likely to succeed. Government may need to pay special attention to the urban cultural heritage so that it is not affected by the new infill developments.

Kazakhstan's territory is extensive, but letting cities grow indefinitely will have costs in terms of infrastructure for public utilities, mobility and pollution. It is critical to control urban sprawl by integrating housing policy into city development plans, transport policy and better land-use management. The housing policy should be in line with efforts towards more compact cities. Silva and Acheampong (2015) found that in all OECD countries, various zoning policies are implemented to limit sprawl, manage the type and extent of development and maintain agricultural activity and rural landscape in peri-urban areas. *Up-zoning*, *mixed-use zoning* and *minimum density zoning* policies are implemented to encourage higher- density development areas.[12] These are some options that could be explored and even piloted in some cities in Kazakhstan to control urban sprawl before they are applied at the national level. Alternatively, each city may be authorised to apply the instruments that best fit its needs. Some cities, such as Almaty, Shymkent and even Astana, may focus on the compact city even in the context of growing populations. Emphasis should be given to connectivity and mobility to achieve this. Transport investments and land-use planning can give sharper focus to the inner city, providing transport options that support a mix of residential and commercial uses in medium-density inner city. The compact city strategy of Adelaide in South Australia could be a valuable example for cities in Kazakhstan (Box 2.8). The national government may consider revising the policy decision to grant every citizen 1 000 square metres of land for housing construction. This land is normally located in the city suburbs and contributes to urban sprawl and increasing the cost of public service delivery.

Box 2.8. **Adelaide's compact city strategy**

In the next 30 years, Greater Adelaide's population is forecast to grow significantly. Its regional and local authorities are developing a series of initiatives to accommodate a growing population in a more compact city. Three of the main strategies are:

- Relaxing height density and zoning constraints in the city centre, and rezoning corridors and areas in the inner metropolitan area through the inner Metropolitan Growth Project, to facilitate higher density and mixed-use development.
- Redeveloping Bowden from an industrial site into an inner urban "village" as part of an AUS 1 billion urban renewal project to accommodate 3 500 new residents, new retail outlets and offices oriented around Bowden station.
- Undertaking major projects within the Adelaide central business district, as a catalyst for bringing people back into the central city.

City authorities expect that focusing transport planning and investment on these areas is likely to deliver the greatest increase in housing and employment densities.

Source: Government of South Australia (2013), "Building a Stronger South Australia: Integrated Transport and Land Use Plan: [Fact sheets]", Department of Planning, Transport and Infrastructure, http://trove.nla.gov.au/work/186995998?selectedversion=NBD52180140.

Kazakhstan could also consider the convenience of using greenbelts. A greenbelt is a zone of open land dividing a city from its surrounding countryside. In principle, all development activities are prohibited in the areas within the greenbelt. Some cities in OECD countries that have a greenbelt policy are: Vienna, London, Barcelona, Berlin, Tokyo, Toronto, Vancouver, Washington, DC, Chicago, Sydney and Seoul. The experience of these cities and others suggests that in order to ensure that development pressures are shifted away from the designated green areas, strong land-use controls must be enforced through comprehensive land-use plans at the national and subnational levels (Silva and Acheampong, 2015). Government may need to buy land in the designated green areas. A nation-wide policy may be based on the experience of Astana in using a green belt as part of the first general plan of the city.[13] However, it should be noted that the use of greenbelts is not without its drawbacks. Greenbelts are seen as the most restrictive form of urban containment policy. In some cases, it can lead to unsustainable urban expansion, increase land prices, housing shortages in areas within the greenbelt and leap-frog development into areas beyond the greenbelts.

An alternative to greenbelts is the use of urban growth boundaries (UGBs). These delineate land at the periphery of cities where urban-scale development may occur, and keep zoning for land outside this area as rural. UGBs are similar to greenbelts, but differ in that they designate a ring of open space around a city where development is strictly prohibited. These boundaries should not be static and may require revisions regularly in fast-growing cities. If the right amount of land is allotted for projected growth during a specified period, planners can strike a balance between regulated development and urban growth (Aoki, 2005). Over the past 50 years, growth boundaries have become a popular urban growth management tool, but there are some concerns about the risk of unintended negative side effects; primarily the potential to artificially inflate housing prices on the one hand, and on the other, to push development into nearby areas outside the growth boundary, resulting in worse outcomes in terms of urban compactness.[14] Policy makers in Kazakhstan would be well served by examining the experience in measuring spatial planning strategies of urban containment in the United Kingdom and Germany, as these two countries focus on different aspects of the phenomenon; the former measures new dwellings built on brownfield land and the latter monitors the absolute growth (Box 2.9).

Box 2.9. **Urban containment in the United Kingdom and Germany**

The United Kingdom and Germany offer examples of different approaches to measurement and policy efforts to contain urban expansion. The United Kingdom focuses on growth boundaries and preventing urban land use encroaching into rural areas and Germany on reducing the overall area of urbanisation. Wong and Schulze Baing (2010) shows that the U.K. system has been more successful than that of Germany, with more than 60% of new housing being built on previously developed land. He attributes this success to the U.K.'s more centralised planning system, which makes extensive use of greenbelts, and the relatively heterogeneous application of planning controls across Germany.

It should be noted, however, that there are trade-offs to the containment strategy. Germany has not seen the same sharp increases in housing prices as the United Kingdom, where housing affordability is a major public concern. Low housing supply elasticities, due to restrictive land use, have been argued to be one of the major reasons for decreasing affordability of housing, especially in economically vibrant areas of the United Kingdom (White and Allmendinger, 2003). Moreover, there are additional challenges to urban containment strategies. It can be difficult to manage the increased congestion generated by higher density development. Constrained urban areas may also be less economically efficient. They may also generate environmentally undesirable commuting patterns (due to leapfrog development, for example).

Source: Wong, C. and A. Schulze Baing (2010), *Brownfield residential redevelopment in England: what happens to the most deprived neighbourhoods?*, Joseph Rowntree Foundation, https://www.jrf.org.uk/sites/default/files/jrf/migrated/files/brownfield-residential-redevelopment-full.pdf (accessed 17 September 2016) : White, M. and P. Allmendinger (2003), "Land use planning and the housing market: A comparative review of the US and the UK", *Urban Studies*, Vol. 40/5, pp. 953-972.

Cities in Kazakhstan, with the support of oblast and central governments, would be best advised to use a mix of regulatory instruments to management urban growth. No single best solution or tool exists to manage urban growth without negative side-effects. Authorities may not be able to stop urban growth in the context of population growth, but the containment policy should be better focused on directing growth and controlling the timing and extent of development to areas where the city authorities deem it best. Table 2.3 shows a number of development management instruments used by OECD countries that Kazakhstan may wish to use to build a package of instruments suitable to each city.

Table 2.3. **Development management instruments applied in OECD countries**

Regulatory instruments	Incentive-based instruments	Fiscal instruments
Development moratoria	Brownfield redevelopment incentives	Dedications (e.g. infrastructure levies)
Greenbelts	Capital gains tax	Development impact fees
Rate of growth controls	Conservation easements	Land value tax
Urban growth boundaries	Historic rehabilitation tax credits	Linkage fees
Urban services boundaries	Joint development	Property tax
Zoning policies	Location-efficient mortgages	Real estate transfer tax
	Special economic zones	Special assessment tax
	Split property tax	Subdivision exactions
	Tax increment financing	Tap fees
	Transfer of rights development	
	Use-value tax assessment	

Source: Silva, E. and R. Acheampong (2015), "Developing an Inventory and Typology of Land-Use Planning Systems and Policy Instruments in OECD Countries", *OECD Environment Working Papers*, No. 94, OECD Publishing, Paris, http://dx.doi.org/10.1787/5jrp6wgxp09s-en.

Bridge the housing affordability gap

A growing population is creating pressure on local governments to meet the demand for new housing. Providing access to well-located and high-quality affordable housing is one of the main urban challenges of Kazakhstan's cities. National housing policy in Kazakhstan is carried out in the absence of adequate control of urban development and effective land use policies, which usually leads to urban sprawl.

Demand for more, better-quality housing is rising

After the collapse of the Soviet Union, housing construction in Kazakhstan suffered a sharp decline until 2000. The transition to a market economy and large-scale privatisation resulted in the fact that virtually all public housing became private within a short period, at very low prices. According to UNECE (2016), the privatisation process was not supported by clear and forward-looking policies, legislative measures and regulatory methods in the sphere of housing management and maintenance. Despite the growing housing stock, in 2015, the number of citizens applying for public housing programmes increased. In that year, more than 300 000 people were on the waiting lists of public housing programmes: over 100 000 of those were part of the vulnerable population, 124 000 were state employees and civil servants, and 43 000 were orphans (Kuramyssova, 2015). As noted in Chapter 1, there seems to be an adequate stock of houses for commercial purposes, but it is expensive. The problem is exacerbated by the poor quality of the housing stock, with the majority of housing being old, dilapidated and in need of replacement. Kazakhstan has a total of 283 million square metres of housing stock, of which around 82 million square metres was built after 1991 and the remainder was built during the Soviet era and is of poor quality. There are many cases of accidents related to the low quality of housing construction, such as wall cracks, roof leaks and poor drainage systems. City *akimats*, in general, have to pay for the costs of poor construction by providing temporary accommodation to people evacuated from poor-quality housing. The housing stock is also not energy-efficient, as almost 65% of housing in the country consumes two to three times more energy than European homes. The challenge for the national government is thus twofold: to increase the number of affordable housing options and improve the quality of the housing stock.

The limited connection between city planning, land use and housing development has led to an increase in social inequality. Current housing policy does not allow for providing housing where there is real demand. The selection of housing to be subsidised by the government in the framework of social housing programmes is based on the pre-established maximum price per square metre, which differs from city to city. To save on initial construction costs, developers build new housing where land is cheaper (often the periphery of cities), rather than where there is demand. There are no special requirements in terms of location directly impacting the costs and comfort of living. The owners of social housing continue to bear considerable costs related to the poor quality of construction and unsafe and inadequate location. The new project of the Shymkent city *akimat*, "Shymkent City", located on the edge of rural land, without good connections to the rest of the city districts by public transport, is a good illustration of this phenomenon.[15]

Until 2008, Kazakhstani real estate investments had attracted massive capital inflows from the banking sector, resulting in a real estate bubble. Despite the 2008 crisis, people continued to borrow money to buy houses, but only high-income groups are now able to afford them, given the high interest rates on mortgages, of 13%-15% in 2016. This has prevented many citizens from entering the real estate market. As a consequence, a growing percentage of home seekers from middle and low-income groups have registered for social housing.

There are several public housing programmes in Kazakhstan. They are currently regrouped in the Regional Development Programme until 2020, which was merged with the pre-existing "Affordable Housing 2020". As a general rule, access to public housing programmes is reserved for specific population groups, among which are civil servants, military personnel and public sector employees (teachers, health care personnel), young couples of under 30-35 years old and vulnerable population (i.e. disabled people). However, each public housing programme has its own specific conditions for beneficiaries, complicating the application process for social housing programmes. Low-income people are not a target of social housing programmes in Kazakhstan, since no income limits apply for public housing programmes.

Social housing can be directly rented to eligible citizens by local authorities from the municipal housing stock. However, as Chapter 1 shows, the municipal housing stock is usually limited and plays an insignificant role. In 2014, the national government announced the State Programme for Infrastructure Development (*Nurly Zhol*) for 2015-19. *Nurly Zhol* funds are channelled through state-owned development banks,[16] which are expected to acquire up to 29 000 units from private developers, below a predefined maximum price. The housing component of *Nurly Zhol* is focused on Astana, Almaty, Shymkent and Aktobe, which alone account for 60% of the rental units commissioned. Housing units are then sold to eligible households on waiting lists at highly subsidised prices (with various lease purchase mechanisms). Some funding is earmarked for rental housing without lease purchase mechanisms, to develop the rental market. Overall, the national government is investing in a huge burst of housing construction, but the challenge is how to make them affordable and of good quality.

One common feature of social housing programmes in Kazakhstan is the central role of oblast *akimats*, and particularly their Housing Departments. They are in charge of managing waiting lists of eligible households and check their eligibility under various criteria, including their financial capacity. According to Sharipova (2015), this presents obstacles for many eligible public servants and state employees who do not pass the screening because their wages are too low. Sharipova (2015) also finds that a majority of applicants report that the application and selection process is not transparent, especially in Almaty City and Astana. *Akimat* employees seem to enjoy opportunities to favour a specific application over another, with occasional reports of bribery. The national government and local authorities might wish to consider introducing anti-corruption measures in public housing programmes, especially in large cities, to enhance the transparency of the allocation process.

Ensure affordable housing through the planning system

Kazakhstan needs to provide affordable housing options to encourage social inclusion, while promoting sustainable urban development. New development in cities has increased the housing stock, but an increasing number of citizens cannot afford to buy housing, and social housing is extremely limited. One option for Kazakhstan would be to revise the existing land-use regulations to ensure that they do not contribute to increasing property prices. Since the cost-benefit ratio of land-use restrictions falls with increasing housing costs, the continued sustainability of development restrictions should be progressively reassessed if housing costs increase. OECD countries' experience shows that if land-use restrictions limit the growth of housing to a rate of the number of households, housing costs are likely to rise. *Akimats* should ensure that the annual increase in housing units in an urban area are at least as large as the increase in the number of households, which would require them to collect better data on migrants, for example. To reduce housing costs effectively, *akimats* need to ensure that the number of newly constructed housing units is higher than the number of new households. New housing development should be compact and transport-oriented, using a mix of densification and brownfield development to control sprawl (OECD, 2017, forthcoming).

The experience of OECD countries such as Canada, France, Ireland, Spain, the United Kingdom and the United States suggests that another way of approaching the housing affordability gap is by adopting an inclusionary approach. It is a means of using the planning system to create affordable housing. Inclusionary housing refers to a programme, regulation or law that requires or provides incentives to private developers to incorporate affordable or social housing as part of market-driven developments, either by incorporating the affordable housing into the same development, building it elsewhere, or contributing money or land for affordable housing (Calavita and Mallach, 2010). This approach would allow government to focus on housing for all kinds of people and not just on particular groups. This is a viable way of dealing with spatial segregation produced by rural-to-city migration. But the scheme has to be designed by the national government in an intense dialogue with subnational governments and local communities. At the same time, central government has to formulate an explicit policy on how to value the diversity of people of different socio-economic backgrounds in neighbourhoods.

Under this approach, Kazakhstani authorities may request developers, either as a condition of approval or in return for incentives such as density bonuses, to set aside for affordable housing a percentage of units in a development, selling or renting them to households whose income fall below specified income ceilings at prices or rents they can afford. This could encourage social inclusion in new developments by ensuring that such new projects contain economically diverse populations, as well as mixes of tenure types, e.g. rental housing and owner-occupied dwellings (Calavita and Mallach, 2010). However, for this to produce acceptable results, it is necessary that housing provision and land use planning be linked. The land-use plans should designate the amount of land to be dedicated to housing development and lay out the ground rules for that development. Plans should not be too rigid, because in a context of changing circumstances, they could contribute to a scarcity of land for development and push up housing costs.

One of the areas that could be problematic for Kazakhstan, as it has been in OECD countries, is that developers may argue that the amount of affordable housing requested by authorities is too high. The United Kingdom's experience shows that negotiations with developers over viability require a sound understanding of development economics (Burges and Monk, 2008). In a majority of cities in Kazakhstan, developers and local authorities would not be operating on an equal playing field in terms of the skills and resources needed to assess viability, as subnational government lack professional staff. In Kazakhstan, the national government could provide a mandate for local governments to adopt an inclusionary housing approach. France's national government passed the Law on Solidarity and Urban Renewal (*Solidarité et renouvellement urbains*), explicitly mandating that every metropolitan commune above a certain population size designate at least 20% of its total housing stock as social housing. While the act does not require inclusionary housing, it gave individual communes a tool for imposing inclusionary requirements on private developers (Calavita and Mallach, 2010). In Kazakhstan, a similar practice would give local governments a mandate and freedom for negotiation if private developers question the viability. City *akimats*, as the leading authority, could issue a "shopping list" of features that should be expected in a development. In addition to affordable housing, this could include the provision of community facilities, contributions to community forests, landscape improvements, local labour and training facilities, park-and- ride areas, public transport improvements and provision of public art. Local authorities could indicate what their priorities are among the various planning obligations, if viability is an issue for developers (Burges and Monk, 2008).

The lack of urban development control and demand for single-family dwellings has resulted in the mass-production of houses around the cities on inexpensive, peri-urban land. With an inclusionary approach, affordable housing should be provided through the land-use planning system. In the United Kingdom, the affordable housing policy, through the planning system, aims to: provide quality homes in mixed sustainable communities for those in need; widen the opportunities for home ownership; and offer greater quality, flexibility and choice to those who rent (UK Government, 2006).

The pressing question for Kazakhstan is to determine which type of social housing system it needs, and the allocation of the houses reserved for inclusionary purposes. In the broad-base system, social housing is open to all citizens without necessarily applying any priority criterion in the allocation of dwellings. In targeted systems, social housing operates apart from the private rental market, and only households for which the market is deemed unable to deliver housing will benefit from it. Income thresholds or vulnerable groups could be criteria for eligibility in this system. Table 2.4 shows a comparison of types of social housing systems across OECD countries that may lead Kazakhstan's leadership in its debate to define the best system for the country. It must be noted that in several OECD countries, as in Kazakhstan, the number of applicants for social housing has risen, possibly due to the declines in housing affordability associated with increases in real house prices, while at the same time, the relative share of social housing in the overall housing stock has fallen. Kazakhstan needs to consider that this tightening in the social sector could put pressure in the effectiveness of the allocation process as queues are likely to build up. A frequent reassessment of eligibility could help free up social housing for needier households (Andres et al., 2011).

Table 2.4. **Types of social housing systems**

Based on eligibility and allocation criteria

Size: Percentage of social housing in the total dwelling stock	Broad-based system	Targeted system	
	No income limit: waiting list	Income limits: waiting list with some combination of priority groups	Income limits: needs/priority based allocation
0%– 5%	Luxembourg	Estonia, Korea, Mexico, Norway, Slovak Republic, Switzerland, United States	Australia, Italy, Portugal, Hungary, Greece, Slovenia
6%-10%		Belgium, New Zealand, Ireland	Canada, Germany, Israel
11%-20%	Sweden	Poland, Spain	Czech Republic, Finland, France, United Kingdom
More than 20%	Denmark, Netherlands	Austria	

Source: Andres, D., A. Caldera Sánchez and A. Johansson (2011), "Housing Markets and Structural Policies in OECD Countries", *OECD Economics Department Working Papers*, No. 836, OECD Publishing, Paris, http://dx.doi.org/10.1787/5kgk8t2k9vf3-en.

Stimulate the local rental housing market

In Kazakhstan, the rental housing market remains underdeveloped and unexploited, and is mostly informal. Housing policy has exclusively focused on home ownership and has not explored other possibilities for increasing citizens' access to housing. The bias toward home ownership is hardly unique to Kazakhstan, and in OECD countries as diverse as Mexico and the United States, most of the housing assistance supports home ownership (OECD, 2015b). Despite the shortage of housing in the country, the real estate market is full of housing for sale and rent that remain vacant. Interviews conducted for this review suggest that the population is generally unwilling to rent housing because of the unregulated market, high price of rentals, lack of legal certainty and for cultural reasons. According to the JSC Real Estate Fund Samruk-Kazyna (*Фонд недвижимости/REF*), demand is lower for rentals than homeownership.[17]

Tenants' rights are not well protected. Landlords have the prerogative, when short-term agreements expire, of changing the rental conditions, price, rental term and other elements at their own discretion and still remain legal. The landlords violate the national legislation by providing houses for rent without registering them as business activity. A considerable number of homeowners in Almaty City, for example, live off renting out residential premises. The homeowners do not wish to become formal self-employed entrepreneurs because of the tax liabilities involved. The state thus loses a fair amount of revenue that could be used to provide public services. Furthermore, people have started providing rental services in social housing settings to earn money. The government's reaction was to introduce special fines in 2016, in case the housing granted by the state and that is used for commercial purposes such as renting. When renting a house in the informal market, tenants can be denied access to public services such as health and education, which is particularly damaging to migrants.

To stimulate the rental housing market and help to bridge the housing gap, Kazakhstan's authorities may wish to consider the following measures:

- *Design a national rental housing policy*. While a number of possible strategies to boost the rental housing market could be proposed, it will be important for Kazakhstan to begin with broad measures targeting the fiscal, regulatory and legal framework, to ensure a more balanced treatment between rental housing and home ownership. These efforts should be prioritised in a coherent national policy for rental housing. Authorities should proceed with caution. Peppercorn and Taffin (2013) suggest that the introduction of a more robust rental policy component to housing policy should be properly sequenced: first, assessment; second, legal; third, tax; fourth, finance; and fifth, subsidies. Kazakhstan needs to define a rental housing policy approach. For example, consideration could be given to a broad-based system or a targeted system, which are both compatible with social housing, as explained above.

- *Review the regulatory framework to balance treatment for property owners and tenants*. This will help not only to change the market but encourage people to rent. Rental housing supply is influenced by a range of regulations covering rents and tenant-landlord relationships that the government can use to address market irregularities. In OECD countries with a relatively large rental sector, regulation appears to be comparatively strict. In Finland, New Zealand and Slovenia, rent control is lax. Rent control in social housing is generally stricter, as it is in Kazakhstan, than in the private sector, consistent with the idea that key function of social housing is to provide affordable housing (Andres et al., 2011). The experience of OECD countries suggests that rent control that is stricter in social housing than for the private sector may unintentionally undermine mobility among social tenants. Mobility is important to maintain support to the labour market. Kazakhstan, like most OECD countries, may wish to focus on regulating contractual aspects of tenant-landlord relations. The main motivation for restricting freedom of contract is that bargaining between landlord and tenants is often unequal, either the risk that landlords exploit their market power or that tenants hold up landlords' property (if no sanctions for unpaid rents are provided for, for example). Box 2.10 provides a summary of the rental market regulation in across OECD countries, which cover two key areas of rental markets: rent control and tenant-landlord relations.

Box 2.10. **Indicators of rental market regulation**

Rent control indicator:

- *Control of rent levels*: Stipulates whether initial rent levels can be freely negotiated between the landlord and the tenant, the coverage (e.g. sitting tenants, new tenants, new construction) of the controls on initial rent levels and the criteria for setting them.

- *Control of rent increases*: Stipulates whether rent increases within a tenancy contract can be freely agreed upon, establishes how rent increases are to be applied, by indexation to some cost/price index, caps on rents or by negotiation or administrative procedure), and the extent to which landlords can pass on cost increases to renters.

Box 2.10. **Indicators of rental market regulation** *(cont.)*

Tenant-landlord relations indicators:

- *Ease of tenant eviction*: Includes information on valid reasons to evict a tenant beyond failing to pay the rent or breach of contract, time periods when eviction is not permitted, how a tenant-landlord eviction dispute is settled (regular court system or arbitration/specialised court).
- *Tenure security*: Includes information on whether contract duration can be freely agreed upon between parties, average contract length and required notice period by landlords in case of contract termination.
- *Deposit requirements*: Includes information on whether the landlord can collect a security deposit, and if so the amount.

Source: Andres, D., A. Caldera Sánchez and A. Johansson (2011), "Housing Markets and Structural Policies in OECD Countries", *OECD Economics Department Working Papers*, No. 836, OECD Publishing, Paris, http://dx.doi.org/10.1787/5kgk8t2k9vf3-en.

- *Analyse some tax incentives for rental properties.* As part of national policy, Kazakhstan may use taxation as a tool to encourage investment in rental housing. Property taxes are one option subnational governments can use to raise the revenue they need to provide public services; taxes on rental housing could be used in the same fashion. Across OECD countries, owner-occupied main residences often receive benefits and tax subsidies that are higher than those for rental housing, normally because the aim is to encourage home ownership. Few countries, like Switzerland, are tenure-neutral. Peppercorn and Taffin (2013) found that policies providing more favourable treatment for home ownership than for rental are more common, but often discourage ownership of rental housing. Kazakhstan could assess the extent to which taxation of rental housing is an obstacle to investment. One first action would be to measure the effect of each tax on the rate of return. This might be technically difficult, but the ministries of finance and national economy could develop models to measure this. Another option would be to estimate the effect of tax evasion. Finally, taxation of rental housing should be compared with taxation of alternative investment supports, financial products and non-residential real estate, as well as owner-occupied residences (Peppercorn and Taffin, 2013). Kazakhstan may also analyse the convenience of using tax credits, as they offer a more direct, controllable and progressive method for affecting household and business behaviour. Blanco et al. (2014) suggest that tax on rental properties should be imposed only on net income, allowing deductions for operating expenses, depreciation of assets, losses and so on. Germany's fiscal framework, which is considered much more favourable toward rental property and small-scale owners of rental property, could offer one model.

Regulate housing construction to ensure safety

Quality, rather than quantity, of housing should be emphasised. Housing quality can be improved and maintenance costs decreased by strategic investment when preparing the site for new development (on such features as drainage systems, transport links and communal infrastructure), promoting energy- efficient design of the building, and using durable and reliable construction materials. The quality of housing can be increased by consulting with potential occupants about their expectations concerning the location and design of the living space provided. Saving on initial costs of construction may negatively impact the quality of new housing.

Housing projects should make safety considerations a priority. Despite legal restrictions on construction in some areas, new housing developments are nevertheless built in hazardous areas. Most of Kazakhstan's cities located on the rivers face risks of flooding. Cities in the southern and eastern regions, close to mountains, are in constant danger of earthquakes and mudslides. Since most of the urban population live in areas at high risk of natural and manmade hazards, locating housing in safer areas requires the attention of the national government.

Several legislative documents, such as the Environmental Code and the Land Use Code, designate urban development limitations in risk zones and no-construction zones. These legal acts are complemented by technical norms, such as construction standards for sanitary conditions and earthquake safety. National and local state officials, including *akimats*, are responsible for controlling and regulating development in these natural-hazard risk zones. However, many building-code violations remain. Enforcing regulations is problematic thanks to the lack of information and management tools, as well as capacities, at the subnational level. There is a general lack of co-operation and co-ordination between the local administrators responsible for land use (Land Use Committee), environmental protection (Watershed Inspections) and use of natural resources (Environmental Department of *akimats*). Interviews with city *akimats* suggest that administrators do not have the qualified staff or funds for information databases, monitoring tools and on-site measuring equipment to adequately control urban development.

On-site informational tables or campaigns for the local community and developers are not available to indicate what is allowed in risky locations such as riverbeds. The land registry is not integrated with the urban registry or environmental registry systems. Plots for some developments are allocated without considering the potential impact on the environment. The environmental impact can be identified at the design stage, when a new development project's environmental impact assessment (EIA) has to pass state approval. However, not all constructions (e.g. individual housing units) have projects and EIA to be submitted for state examination. Criteria for obtaining financial support by private contractors need to include an assessment of the location of new development and its environmental impact.

Link land use, transport, tax policy and investment

How best to integrate housing and transport policies with other urban improvements is one of the key challenges for urban development authorities in developed and developing nations alike. Attracting investment for urban development is difficult if the city cannot supply a reliable transport system.

Inadequate public transport policies affect urban quality of life

Ensuring sustainable, accessible modes of urban transport is a challenge for Kazakhstan's cities. Part of the problem originates in the lack of a strategic approach to planning and managing urban transport. The major cities are becoming increasingly congested and are now trying to minimise traffic, reduce the environmental impact and increase cities' economic competitiveness. Poor intra-city connectivity has increased the number of private vehicles, since public transport service does not guarantee safety, quality speed and comfort. Table 2.5 shows how the number of private vehicles has doubled in Almaty City, whereas the public transport fleet has barely risen. Some reasons for this are:

Table 2.5. **Public and private transport in Almaty City, 2001 and 2011**

Parameter	2001	2011
Almaty population (in million)	1.13 million	1.4 million
Number of private vehicles	201 527	459 686
Number of public transport vehicles exploited daily on routes	1 120	1 550
Passenger traffic on the public transport system	695	1 377

Source: LLP NII TK, Research Institute of Transport and Communications, Almaty City, 2016.

- *The predominance of a sectoral policy approach to urban development.* This has created imbalances in the distribution of transport, housing and employment in most of Kazakhstan's cities, which prevents access to basic public services such as culture, mobility, education and leisure. Astana's Master Plan Until 2030 is composed of different sections: housing, transport, utilities and health care, but there is no cross-cutting analysis of the main urban priorities of the city and how each sector is going to help achieve them.
- *Blurred lines of authority of city* akimats *on public transport planning.* The city *akimats* do not have the authority, resources and expertise for long-term strategic urban transport planning. Their role is limited to identifying the main routes for public transport, construction of additional highways, and minor adaptations of the existing public transport network to accommodate emerging popular passenger routes. Generally, *akimats* are only able to optimise traffic flows as a way to improve transport, because the relevant decision-making power for transport planning has not yet been delegated to any of the city authorities. Moreover, private operators are mostly interested in serving transport lines or routes that have high passenger demand.
- *Lack of professional personnel specialised in urban transport.* In general, city *akimats* seem to suffer from an acute lack of capacity to plan and manage a fully functioning system of urban public transport. Technical transport specialists are needed in the main urban centres. This is an obstacle to the formation and development of a transport strategy, in line with housing policies and the development or adoption of effective management tools for urban transport.
- *Cities do not offer alternatives to public transport, encouraging a car-oriented transport system.* Public transport is mostly provided on buses, the majority of which are old, unsafe, inadequate and a source of pollution. Only Almaty City has a metro line, with plans to build a tramline. Many cities depend on taxis, most of them informal (but cheaper) private cars operating as taxis, which increases traffic in some cities. Low fuel prices and parking space for cars provide further incentives for private vehicle use and limit cities' income for public transport improvements. Moreover, transport routes do not cover the entire urban territory, and the frequency of service is unreliable. Since origin and destination surveys are not carried out, and no ticketing system has been established, planning is not

based on demand. As a result, new routes overlap by more than 30% with existing ones.

- *Funding for public transport is limited and focused on road maintenance.* Transfers from the national budget to finance urban transport are insufficient. The city budget is composed mostly of transfers for the construction of new roads and road structures (multilevel intersections, pedestrian under- and over-ground crossings, etc.). Public funding for developing the passenger transport system is an exception. The fares for public transport do not cover operating expenditure, and investing in new vehicles is even less likely. The low level of purchasing power of transport users does not allow companies to charge high travel fares. Usually, an established ceiling for the travel price is set. Private transport companies are small- and medium-sized businesses (limited enterprises and individual entrepreneurs) with limited financial resources and physical facilities. Their imperative is thus to try to save on the quantity and quality of hired personnel, the condition of vehicles and the establishments they use to service the vehicles.
- *Land use, transport and housing are not linked to environmental protection.* There is little evidence that the 2013 Concept of Green Economy links urban development challenges and policies (such as transport, housing and land-use) to green growth objectives. Its main focus is how to deal with agricultural land, while clean-up of the most heavily polluted urban brownfields, which occupy large areas of urban land, is not considered.

Clarify the role of cities in transport and housing planning and reinforce technical capacity

As in OECD countries, Kazakhstan's different levels of government have distinct, often un-co-ordinated, roles in urban transport provision, housing planning and land use. The national government could achieve greater clarification and co-ordination in investment decisions for urban mobility by more clearly delineating responsibility for urban transport, housing and land use. One option would be for the central government to consider providing funding and infrastructure and enforcing regulations, while oblast-level governments were responsible for the planning, design, operation and control of inter-regional transport systems. Cities of *oblast* significance could focus on intra-connectivity, traffic control, public security and maintenance of the local road network. These cities could also participate in the planning of urban transport under the guidance of the *oblast* government. Almaty and Astana, as cities of *oblast* level, should be empowered to act in both inter and intra-connectivity projects. The national government can play a key role in the establishment of institutional and legal conditions for integrated planning and management of urban transport. The local governments should be supplied with a legal framework, decision-making autonomy and capacity to operate a workable integrated management system for a public transport system currently dominated by private carriers.

When conducting land use and new housing planning, cities should be required to consider the mobility and accessibility needs of new inhabitants, and the impact of housing development on mobility in the city as a whole. As Linn (2014) argues, land-use planning needs to make adequate provision for public rights of way, if congestion is to be kept to acceptable levels. Two issues are critical: first, that the national government and even oblast governments reinforce technical and managerial skills of city *akimats* in public transport planning. Urban transport and housing officials should understand that urban transport and management is complex and multidimensional, that strategies should be comprehensive and multimodal, and encompass both supply and demand measures. A transport strategy should not be limited to adding more capacity and should reflect linkages between transport, land use and human behaviour. The priorities for governments at all levels should include recruiting experts, and training and retraining officials in a wide range of skills. This would make it possible to develop holistic and multisectoral approaches, integrating economic, political, communications and environmental issues in urban design. Training should be provided not only for technical level staff but for officials in management-level positions. Secondly, co-ordination and collaboration should be promoted across departments within the city *akimats*, as well as co-operation with other levels of government. Kazakhstan might also consider the use of information and communication technologies (ICTs) to improve accessibility in cities, moving away from a focus on mobility.

A wide package of financing options for urban transport

Linn (2014) suggests that Kazakhstan needs to limit the growth of car use and ownership, given the current rates of pollution and congestion. A more practical course might in fact be to focus on providing alternative means of transport at affordable tariffs, with the emphasis on offering optimal mobility and accessibility. Without reliable public transport, residents will continue to use their cars. Another crucial step would be to ensure sound financial mechanisms to help to invest in modernisation and expansion of the fleet, and exploring new modes of transport. In Astana, Almaty and Shymkent, urban transport policies require an investment strategy involving different levels of government, the private sector, investment banks and private operators. Finding the necessary resources will not be easy, given the current fare model and lack of financial support. The challenge will increase if urbanisation continues to put pressure on resources allocated to public transport.

Kazakhstan's cities need to modernise the public transport business model. This, in addition to its reliance on public budgets, should include earmarking of charges and levies for public transport, the development of partnerships with private investors and the development of a revenue strategy. The experience of Mexico City, for example, suggests that complementary resources are needed to help pay for the overall costs. The national government might allow cities to tax those who benefit most from public transport, such as employers, retailers and the owners of real estate. Charges can also be levied on automobile use, including parking charges and fuel taxes. Linn (2014) proposes that Kazakhstan cover the cost of urban transport and infrastructure investments and subsidies by taxes on automobile ownership.

Public transport can also be financed through public-private partnerships (PPPs). These are complex instruments, and need to be a real partnership that distributes risks and rewards in a way that meets the expectations of all parties. Financial partnerships with long-term investors – banks, urban developers and so on, are another possibility, but the risks must be clearly allocated if such partnerships are to work. Private finance can become a key source of urban policy packages because it can provide finance more efficiently and create a new commercial culture of accountability. Meanwhile, co-investment in partnership with the private sector involves careful preparation to attract and guarantee the security of the investment.

Kazakhstan's cities also need to develop a strong revenue strategy and to take a more commercial approach that helps to cover their operating costs. New sources of income need to be explored by tapping into non-fare revenue streams. The experience of OECD cities such as London, Paris and Mexico City suggests that a regular, systematic and sophisticated fare-review mechanism is necessary to sustain public transport services and enhance quality. Efficient fare regulation will take many factors into account, including affordability for passengers, changes in service production costs, and the resources needed to invest in capacity and service quality (UITP, 2013). Public transport providers could also make better use of secondary revenue streams to capitalise on their assets, including advertising space and retail outlets.

A strategy-driven planning approach for transport, land use, taxation and infrastructure

Kazakhstan could benefit from a closer link between land-use planning and urban infrastructure planning (Linn, 2014). OECD countries' experience suggests that the cross-sectoral nature of transport offers an opportunity to address such issues as climate change, marginalisation and economic development. Kazàkhstan's predominantly sectorial approach is ill-equipped to combat global issues such as climate change and urban challenges like air pollution, provision of water and the growing urban population. Shifting from the sectorial approach will make it difficult to integrate policy making, given the existing regulations, division of responsibilities across levels of government, the rigid budgeting system, and the differences between the scales of land-use development, transport networks and administrative boundaries. The central government should focus on helping cities to realise the connection between cross-sectoral information sharing and planning of sustainable regional transport solutions.

Arts et al. (2014) suggest that dealing with typical urban challenges such as increased traffic, pollution, long commuting times and so on, requires a shift from the current small-scale ad hoc, *technical solution-driven* planning approach towards a broad, network-scoped *strategy drive* approach. Integrating land-use and infrastructure planning can promote an adaptable, sustainable and robust transport network, offering users better connections between the different transport networks via multimodal hubs, with close co-ordination of infrastructure and spatial development. Arts et al. (2014) propose a basic framework to conduct more integrated strategy-oriented planning; the framework covers six dimensions: i) spatial concepts with synergetic effects on accessibility (the spatial dimension); ii) multimodal network optimisation at various spatial scales (the network dimension); iii) life-cycle issues (the time dimension); iv) combined value creation and capturing (the value dimension); v) organisational empowerment for integrated planning (the institutional dimension); and vi) implementation drivers for integrated planning (the dimension of implementation). Utrecht, in the Netherlands, is one instance that shows how a traditional sectorial and project-driven approach to road infrastructure failed, since it did not consider the effect on the investment climate and spatial quality of the areas around the infrastructure (Box 2.11). Kazakhstan may also wish to use transport taxes to encourage more compact urban development, especially in larger cities. Taxing transport and especially car use more heavily to reflect its true costs (including externalities from driving such as air pollution, congestion and noise) could promote more compact patterns of urban development.

Box 2.11. **Ringway Utrecht: an integrated approach for transport and land-use planning**

Utrecht, in the heart of the Netherlands, is centrally situated in its road and rail network, surrounded by national landscapes. The Ringway project began at the end of the 1990s, with a traditional project focusing on traffic congestion on the Highway Ring, where three important highways intersect. In the 1980s, public resistance to the construction of the A27 arose because the highway crossed the Amelisweerd estate, an area of high natural and cultural value. In 2007, a decision to solve the problems of the Ringway by expanding the A27, again provoked strong resistance, on the grounds that another part of the Amelisweerd would be compromised, and the barrier between the University campus and the city would increase, given that the project had a rather isolated scope on the highway. The Dutch government infrastructure advisor recommended setting up a "Quality Team" for independent advice on the spatial characteristics of the project and to add spatial research to the technical and mobility research typically conducted for such large-scale infrastructure projects. The study led to a broader understanding of the project.

After analysing the relevant policy documents from national, provincial and municipal governments, the Quality Team concluded that the project's scope should not be limited to the highway. Instead, it recommended that it include: the long-term multimodal functioning of the mobility network (the Ringway carries 35% of local traffic; and a relatively small shift to the local network or other modalities could solve the congestion at the national highway system near Utrecht); the investment climate of the eastern part of Utrecht including the campus; and the connectivity between Utrecht and the surrounding rural landscape. This favoured a shift from a defensive discussion about the highway project into an opportunity and quality-driven discussion, in which infrastructure was only one element. Gains of the shift towards a more integrated approach included:

- *Long-term investment climate*. Spatial-economic development models for the university campus, together with the A27 Highway and redevelopment of the adjacent Rijnsweerd business park.
- *Long-term network availability*. Due to the limited space available around the highway, a multimodal network development near the A27 and the campus is being formulated to expand capacity. This was not included in the initial project.
- *Liveability*. The A27 constitutes a major barrier blocking the inhabitants of Eastern Utrecht from reaching recreational areas around the city, especially by bicycle. Recent proposals suggest that the project be combined with better bicycle connectivity with nature and rural areas. This should increase liveability and reduce noise and air pollution.
- *Project communication*. This integrated approach led to better stakeholder communication on mobility and infrastructure.
- *Financial opportunities and spatial planning*. The early adaptation of spatial interest in the area surrounding the project created some integrated mobility solutions that made for significant cost savings, and higher spatial quality for the neighbourhoods surrounding the project.

Source: Arts, J., T. Hanekamp and A. Dijkstra (2014), "Integrating land-use and transport infrastructure planning: Towards adaptive and sustainable transport infrastructure", Transport Research Arena, Paris, https://trid.trb.org/view.aspx?id=1316947.

The main lesson of the Utrecht case is that most urban highway infrastructure deals with a significant percentage of urban mobility, but a shift towards other modalities may solve congestion and offer cost-effective, sustainable and resilient alternatives. Research indicates that urban regions have the highest opportunities (network availability and density) for a shift towards an integrated multimodal land-use strategy (Arts et al. 2014). Similarly, the government of Adelaide, in the South Australia region, in its quest to build a more compact city by enhancing public transport, has found that trams are introduced alongside initiatives that aim to: i) enhance the population's access to employment, services shops, education, entertainment and leisure opportunities, particularly if these opportunities are in the inner and middle city; ii) improve the connectivity of urban areas by offering convenient modes of transport; and iii) reduce car dependency, since those who live and working along tram routes tend to have lower rates of car ownership (Government of South Australia, 2013).

Promote and improve the capacity for cross-sectoral planning

Kazakhstan's institutional structure does not favour cross-sectoral planning. Land use, transport and housing have important implications for the environment, but they are approached in silos. Stead and Geerlings (2005) suggest that to integrate land-use, environment, transport and housing, joint teams working on strategic planning could help save costs and improve policy co-ordination. Clear guidelines, rules and procedures for policy integration set out by the national government are an important part of this process. Kazakhstan could promote the use of joint teams working on strategic planning to maximise the accumulated experience in government. Those with cross-disciplinary experience of working in different parts of the organisation or public administration are better equipped to promote policy integration (Stead and Geerlings, 2005). Land-use, transport, housing, environment, infrastructure investment planning is interdisciplinary and requires a wide range of skills and competencies.

Another way of promoting cross-sectoral planning is the creation of urban planning institutes. In some countries, these are created at the municipal level, where capacity is really needed, for instance in Mexico (OECD, 2015b). In some cases, these institutes have a metropolitan character, with a larger geographical scope and function. The Metropolitan Planning Institute of Guadalajara in Mexico, for example, is decentralised and inter-municipal, and has technical autonomy, and other such institutes exist in Brazil, Canada, France and the United States. These can be both public and private specialised institutions that provide intermediation services between the knowledge and information generated by academic institutions, urban observatories, national and international good practices banks, and the local authorities (Figure 2.3). They analyse data for policy and programme decision-making, gather knowledge from academic sources and use it to support policy design and evaluation and to train personnel of the urban authorities. They could also adapt international experience to local needs.

Figure 2.3. **The role of urban institutes in urban management**

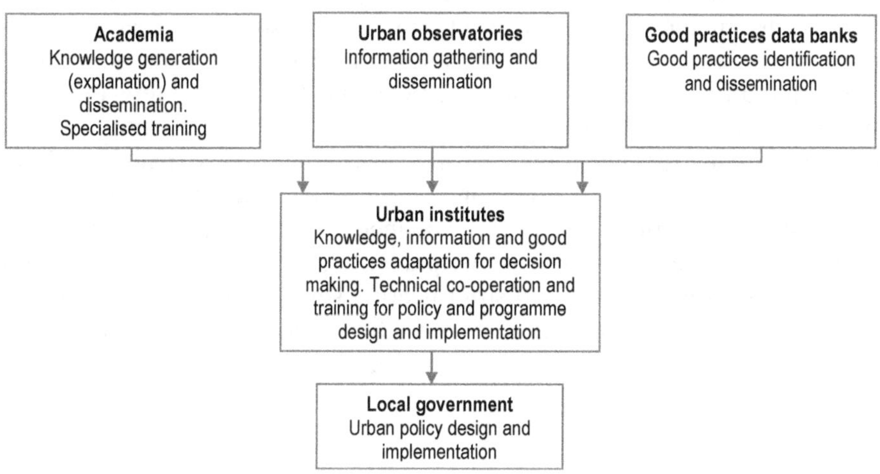

Source: Rojas, E. (2012), "The Contribution of Urban Institutes to the Governance of Urban Areas: challenges and opportunities in Antofagasta, Chile", report prepared for the OECD Territorial Review of Antofagasta, Chile (unpublished paper).

The key aspects are the ownership of the institute and the sources of funding. Urban institutes can be owned by national/central, state, or municipal governments, associations of governments or by private entities.[18] The potential sources of funding include the sale of services, transfers from parent institutions or proceed from endowments specially established to finance the institution, or a combination of these sources. These institutes work on a wide variety of topics and have multidisciplinary teams. Research on urban challenges (urban land, housing, transport, sanitation, economic development, environment, energy and social issues), provide policy advice, urban planning in trans-sectoral issues (land use, strategic planning, environmental management) or sector development (housing, transport, economic development), project design and provide a forum for debate and analysis of urban problems.

Several urban institutes could prove instructive for Kazakhstan. The Urban Research and Planning Institute of Curitiba in Brazil (IPPUC) helps guide an integrated approach to urban development. The *Institut d'aménagement et d'urbanisme de la région Île-de-France* (IAU) illustrates the benefits of specialisation in a specific territory and on a limited set of problems. IAU has developed in-depth knowledge of the Île-de-France and has world-class capacity in land use, transport, environment and economic development planning (Rojas, 2012).

Improve the infrastructure and management of public utilities

Public utilities pose a major urban and investment challenge in Kazakhstan, as it shifts from the provision of infrastructure funded by central government transfers to a market-based model.

Ageing public utility infrastructure is a common feature of urban centres

In Kazakhstan, large and medium-sized cities have infrastructure for such public utilities as gas, water, sewage, and hot water supply, but such amenities are lacking in other human settlements. Large differences in the quality of service are typical. Kazakhstan has not been able to keep up with the growth of large cities, and infrastructure investment is limited. The infrastructure and public services provided in older neighbourhoods cannot serve the needs of a growing population. Poor infrastructure and obsolete technology also waste energy and resources. Issues faced include: i) deterioration of engineering networks and infrastructure for urban transport, water supply and sanitation, solid waste management and heating; ii) few meters measuring consumption; iii) obsolete technology that wastes energy and resources; and, iv) insufficient funds for maintenance, modernisation and expansion. Better public infrastructure for the delivery of communal services (water, sewage and heat) is vital to sustain inclusive economic growth and enhance economic opportunity. Urban utility companies are often operated by municipal enterprises that rely on ad hoc budget transfers. Low tariffs for water and district heating services do not fully cover operations and maintenance costs, reducing funds for renewing obsolete infrastructure. Modernisation of public utility systems must be made a part of strategic urban policy packages.

Box 2.12. **Public utilities challenges across cities in Kazakhstan**

Kazakhstan has a significant backlog in urban communal services. The growing urban population means that investment in its maintenance and expansion is urgently needed. Some of the main challenges are:

- **Water supply and sanitation**. Approximately 86% of the population has access to drinking water, and 81% to sewage. However, water supply is irregular or on a scheduled basis. Water revenues lost through system losses range from 25% to 60%, although the true figure may be higher due to lack of metering. Drinking water quality does not always comply with regulations, and 75% of the assets need replacement.
- **Solid waste management**. All major cities have inadequate systems unable to cope with rapid urbanisation and economic growth. Progress has been made, but illegal dumping is common in urban centres. An estimated 0.4 to 0.9 kilogrammes per capita of waste is generated, but the collection rate is low, at about 40% to 60%. Waste is disposed of at existing untreated landfill sites.
- **District heating**. This is the main priority for cities around the country. An estimated USD 3 billion for core investments and up to USD 8 billion of investment for an integrated approach is required for district heating rehabilitation and improvement, which covers energy efficiency and housing improvement. The inefficiency and outdated distribution and piping network is producing heat losses, due to leakages, lack of proper thermal insulation and the housing stock's lack of energy-efficient infrastructure.
- **Urban transport**. Kazakhstan has the highest rate of car ownership in Central Asia (154 cars per 1 000 inhabitants). Combined with inadequate traffic and parking management, the increase in car ownership has increased traffic congestion and car accidents. Old trams and trolleybus lines are progressively disconnected because of the poor service and high operation and maintenance costs. In most cities, public transport relies on buses, and the light-rail transit (LRT) networks suffer from serious lack of rationalisation.

Source: ADB (2012) *Sector Assessment – Country Partnership Strategy: Kazakhstan 2012-16.* www.adb.org/sites/default/files/linked-documents/cps-kaz-2012-2016-ssa-03.pdf.

Reforming local public utilities requires a long-term perspective

Kazakhstan needs to establish clear priorities to enhance the rehabilitation of municipal infrastructure, seeking financial modalities that can support the sustainability of the sector and bridge the infrastructure gap (ADB, 2012). Delegation of communal services to the private sector will work only if the national government helps city governments modernise communal infrastructure. However, city *akimats* need to be more pro-active in finding ways to refurbish urban infrastructure. Reactive approaches are not enough, since the problems multiply under the pressure of new developments and time. Partial renovation and construction of public utilities, driven by a need for new housing, may not be the ideal solution. The modernisation of the public utility systems has to be part of a strategic urban policy package. Investment in the communal infrastructure can be a generic part of the National Green Growth Strategy, allowing the city *akimats* to establish their own local funds for long-term infrastructure projects.

The national government recently began to provide low-interest loans to city governments to renew public utilities infrastructure. This strategy could be reinforced by reviewing the experience of some UK municipalities that have started to accumulate financial resources for joint housing and communal infrastructure developments, by creating the Local Growth Fund.[19] However, the national government may wish to consider reform of the local public utilities on the basis that the public sector alone cannot guarantee their effective and efficient production. The reform should help local authorities adopt useful management tools. ADB (2014) suggests that operations and maintenance support contracts could help reduce risks for municipal utilities and make room for co-operation with private sector operators and investors.

A reform to enhance private-sector participation in municipal utilities needs to have two preconditions. First, a tariff reform should gradually bring tariffs closer to cost recovery, to improve the creditworthiness of municipal utilities and their appeal to private investors. The challenge for Kazakhstan lies in creating a regulatory environment that limits opportunities for abuse (e.g. high prices for consumers and poor service standards) but creates sufficient incentives for investment. Second, as part of a strategic urban policy package, the regulation and supervision of municipal utilities need to be more co-ordinated at the national level, with a coherent strategic long-term vision (ADB, 2014). The government may consider drawing on the expertise of development financial institutions in both tariff reform and in improving implementation capacity at the national and local (oblast and city) levels. The critical issue in reforming public utilities should be to achieve a balance between the public sector, which has both to stimulate use and perform strategic control, and the private sector, which must perform investment and management functions (Caruso et al. 2003). The reform should look for innovative, low-cost options that aim at universal, affordable and sustainable provision of utilities. Emphasis should also be placed on cost recovery through improved service provision and delivery, rather than on payment collection (Friedrich Ebert Foundation, 2007).

Caruso et al. (2003) have identified four reference models for the organisation of public utilities companies: i) multi-utility companies (with a single governance centre and local activities); ii) inter-municipal companies (with a single governance centre and extra local activities); iii) an integrated system of companies (with multiple governance centres and mainly local activities); and iv) independent entrepreneurial poles (multiple governance centres and extra local activities). In Kazakhstan, the first two models seem best suited to the structures already in place. The multi-utility company model could be adopted where infrastructure and market synergies can be exploited, while the difficulties are related to a higher management complexity, due to the specific needs of the different public utilities. One example of a multi-utility company is the *Azienda Risorse Idriche di Napoli S.p.A.*, the first multi-utility company in Italy, in which the public sector is the majority stakeholder. The municipality's role was to guide and supervise, while the private partner was in charge of the management of the service (Caruso et al., 2003). An inter-municipal company model may be desirable in areas of the country with lower density and similar needs. Kazakhstan may also consider the OECD recommendations on how to improve the regulations for competitiveness, applying them to the public utilities sector (OECD, 2014c).

Encourage energy efficiency in the construction sector

In order to encourage energy efficiency in construction, barriers that discourage developers and citizens from optimising energy efficiency must be removed. Pro-active instruments to give stakeholders reasons to adopt efficient practices are needed, and financial incentives may be required. The high costs of energy-efficient equipment, and the difficulties in mobilising additional financing to cover these costs can deter citizens and developers from such investments. High energy prices, by removing subsidies, or through carbon taxes, can help improve the competitiveness of energy-efficiency investments, as some EU cities that have developed a green building market have found. However, UNDP (2010) has found policies reducing upfront costs more effective, as long as beneficiaries and eligible technologies are well defined and the level of tax credits is high enough. Subsidies can be effective, but entail high administrative costs. Tax incentives generally have lower management costs. In some cases, according to UNDP (2010), it may be more effective to provide low-interest loans for the entire investment cost than a subsidy for a fraction of the cost. The experience of London, Amsterdam, Hamburg and Barcelona show many options for councils to use financial incentives to promote sustainable housing. Reducing permit fees (Building Act), user fees (rates), consent fee waivers, providing financial assistance and capacity building (loans), discounts on particular products and services, among other instruments, can all help promote energy efficiency in construction (Brilhante and Skinner, 2015). At the national level, Mexico has introduced "green mortgages," under which loans made to workers through social housing funds can only be used to buy houses built with green technologies (OECD, 2015b). Kazakhstan could also analyse the experience of the Mexican housing NAMA (Nationally Appropriate Mitigation Actions, NAMA), which is an instrument that allows government to move towards a broad sector–wide implementation of sustainable housing. The Mexican housing NAMA comprises the following objectives: i) improving the capacities of authorities at all levels of government on energy efficient and sustainable housing, as well as introducing building codes and legislative frameworks; ii) supporting the development of a local market for environmentally friendly technologies; iii) improving and disseminating existing promotion and incentive instruments with more ambitious energy efficiency standards at federal and state level; and, iv) fostering the application of more ambitious energy efficiency standards through the provision of investment grants for incremental costs as well as the inclusion of additional eco-technologies.

Table 2.6. **Key requirements for energy-efficiency policies**

Policy instrument	Key requirements
Energy building codes	• Stakeholder participation in elaborating the regulations • Extensive testing • Acceptable costs • Detailed enforcement plan • Supporting tools • Regional exchanges and benchmarking
Utility programmes	• Fair rules that do not distort competition • Appropriate clear and transparent mechanisms for cost recovery and removal of disincentives • Simple, low-cost, well-agreed-upon procedures for measurement and verification • A strong regulator to enforce targets, with incentives for compliance or penalties for noncompliance • Targets that are reasonable, but significantly higher than business as usual
Taxes or tax reductions	• An acceptable global taxation level • A long-term commitment by policy makers • A tax level that is significant enough • Eligibility rules that are restricted to new, low-market-share technologies • Information and communication about the tax, both in general and when it is paid.

Source: UNDP (2010), "Promoting energy efficiency in buildings: Lessons learnt from international experience", Environment and Energy, http://thegef.org/sites/default/files/publications/eebuilding_web_2.pdf (accessed 21 November 2016).

In the case of new buildings, Kazakhstan might introduce an Energy Building Code or establish minimum, mandatory energy-efficiency standards or requirements for building components and equipment. Standards are more useful for renovations of existing buildings, in which upgrades of components and equipment present significant opportunities for improving energy efficiency. Kazakhstan may also wish to introduce utility programmes in some of the larger agglomerations. Table 2.6 above shows some of the features that such programmes should have to achieve the desired effect.

Local authorities could contribute to energy efficiency by offering education, advisory services, technical assistance, in-house advice and education. They can help raise public awareness of energy consumption and the benefits of energy efficiency (both environmental and financial) and how to implement these measures. These campaigns could help citizens by informing them of the possible energy-saving actions and their benefits. In urban areas with a higher level of awareness of such issues, citizens may need more assistance to help choose technical solutions, find companies to do the work, and determine what financial options they have. Like EU municipalities, city *akimats* can also use policy to encourage change by using ratings systems for sustainability features and urban design initiatives; but this would require a reform, as tariffs are established by the national government. If *akimats* want to be more pro-active, they can offer flexibility within local planning provisions, fast-track consents and use regulations to encourage change through byelaws and district plans (Brilhante and Skinner, 2015).

Promote public-private partnerships in the utilities sector

Public-Private Partnerships (PPPs) are another way to encourage private sector participation in the sector. This will not be an easy task, since investing in public utilities infrastructure and service delivery may not be financially viable from a private sector perspective. Nevertheless, Kazakhstan might start to create the underpinnings to establish PPPs, in line with the "Kazakhstan 2050" development strategy, which envisages a guiding role for the private sector in contributing to economic development.

OECD (2005) has found that in developing countries, many governments see private investors simply as a source of financing to be used to supplement dwindling public funds. This fails to recognise the minimum expectations companies have in the business environment. Private utility companies, on the other hand, tend to rely heavily on contracts, neglecting the fact that authorities in developing countries do not have the capacity to underwrite large risks (e.g. macroeconomic shocks and public upheavals, for example). This suggests that the best an emerging country authority, such as Kazakhstan, can do to enhance the success of PPPs is to develop a knowledge of the obstacles, prepare to address them, and inform all levels of the public administration before they set up a PPP. Such obstacles may include: conflicting objectives; procedures that lack transparency and objective criteria; a weak legal environment; a conflicting public governance scenario; preferential treatment to incumbent service providers; an environment where the rule of law is not firmly entrenched; and governments that do not acknowledge contracts signed by previous administrations (OECD, 2005).

Kazakhstan would need to build the capacity and experience in PPPs in the utilities sector at subnational levels of government. In this sense, the "Kazakhstan Public-Private Partnership Centre" will be seminal in assisting local authorities in their pursuit of PPPs for communal services (Box 2.13). The 2015 PPP Law could help advance the use of PPPs in the country and cities. It aims to: institutionalise PPPs with a view to creating a more extensive legal framework; develop a classification of PPPs and introduce a classification of different types of contractual partnerships, including concessions, trust management, financial lease and life cycle contracts; introduce the concept of government-owned companies acting as public partners; and allow the creditor to be part of the PPP contract.

Box 2.13. **Kazakhstan Public-Private Partnership Centre**

The Kazakhstan Public-Private Partnership Centre is the country's leading centre of research and expertise on the development of Public Private Partnerships. It has a unified team of experts with knowledge and practical experience in the field of PPPs and focuses on research, examination and evaluation of the implementation of investment projects in the field of PPPs and co-operates with legislative and executive bodies, national companies and international and nongovernmental organisations at all levels. Its mission is to create the conditions for successful partnership between government and the private sector, and develop and consolidate their capacity to implement PPP projects and increasing private investment in the national economy.

In 2014, with the JSC National Holding Baiterek, it created the Public-Private Advisory Centre to promote infrastructure development by providing services to structure and maintain infrastructure projects implemented by PPPs. It supports PPP projects by developing documentation (the concession proposal, tender documentation, the draft concession agreement), negotiating with potential investors and concessionaries.

Source: The Kazakhstan Public-Private Partnership Centre, http://pppac.kz/?page_id=1045&lang=en.

The use of PPPs in public utilities in Kazakhstan will require preparatory work on the part of the local authorities, and training of their legal staff. For instance, to attract private capital to invest in the public utilities sector in Pavlodar, local authorities had to: i) select the priorities of the municipal services sector that needed urgent investment; ii) form the requirements package for investor, noting the environmental, social, historical and other peculiarities of the city; iii) work out the legal, economic fundamentals of concession agreements in the municipal services sectors; iv) create the regulatory agency with functions of the Public Private Partnership Centre that could work at the regional level; and v) draw up the integrated database of the municipal services' assets (Bayadina, 2014). These recommendations are based on the experience of the oblast and city of Pavlodar, but they may be equally valuable for other cities, as they present similar problems in the public utilities sector. In the medium term, to increase its capacity and experience with PPPs, Kazakhstan central and local authorities could assess the experience of current PPP projects, such as: the ring road around Almaty (BAKAD); and the Almaty LRT project. Other PPP projects that could benefit from this experience are the Shymkent bypass (a 48-kilometre bypass around the city); Bukhtarma water reservoir bridge (a 1.3-kilometre bridge in eastern Kazakhstan); and Almaty railway bypass project (a 75-kilometre railway line around the city).

To reinforce the national and subnational authorities' work on PPPs, the national government may wish to observe the OECD Principles for Private Sector Participation in Infrastructure (OECD, 2007). Their objective is to assist governments seeking private-sector involvement in infrastructure development, attracting investment, and mobilising private sector resources for the benefit of society. The experience of OECD countries suggests that if PPPs in infrastructure for public utilities are to work, the decision to involve the private sector must be guided by an assessment of the relative long-term costs and benefits and availability of finance. The pricing of risks transferred to the private operators must be taken into account, as well as prudent fiscal treatment of remaining risks in the public domain. It is also necessary that national authorities provide an enabling policy framework for investment. Public acceptance and capacity at all levels of government are also needed to implement the projects that are agreed upon. Moreover, the government's expectations regarding responsible business conduct need to be clearly communicated to their private partners. Kazakhstan could also adhere to the OECD Principles for Public Governance of Public–Private Partnerships (OECD, 2012). This set of principles aim to provide concrete guidance on how to make sure that PPPs represent value for money for the public sector. They focus on three objectives: i) to establish a clear, predictable and legitimate framework supported by competent and well-resourced authorities; ii) to ground the selection of PPPs in value for money; and iii) to use the budgetary process transparently to minimise fiscal risks and ensure the integrity of the procurement process.

Facilitate the free movement of people across urban centres

Internal migration is a spatial phenomenon that contributes to high levels of urban growth and urbanisation. However, the lack of adequate planning for migration results in squatter settlements, slum areas, traffic congestion, urban poor and urban sprawl. Kazakhstan's national and subnational authorities show little evidence that they have taken the necessary steps to absorb newcomers into cities.

Internal migration is contributing to urbanisation and the economy...

In contrast to the Soviet period, when mobility was largely restricted, people in independent Kazakhstan enjoy freedom of movement, although certain restrictions apply. According to the 2009 census, internal migrants represented 14.9% of the total population.[20] The percentage of internal migrants is larger in big cities: in 2009, 72% of Astana's population and 45% of Almaty's population had moved there from other regions of Kazakhstan in the decade from 1999 to 2009. Migrants have been transforming the sociocultural and ethnocultural makeup of Kazakhstan's largest cities (Zabirova, 2004). In the long run, internal migrants are attracted to regions with higher wages and income levels, and a high share of formal (wage) employment (the self-employed tend to be poorer than average in Kazakhstan). Cities are major recipients of intra-regional and interregional migrations, and internal migration is a driving force in Kazakhstan's gradual urbanisation. However, its importance should not be overestimated: in most large cities, natural population growth is higher than net inward migration (see Chapter 1).

Of all regions, Akmola, Aktobe, South Kazakhstan, Zhambyl and East Kazakhstan oblasts experience the highest outflow of people,[21] and migrants are transforming the makeup of the country's largest cities (Zabirova, 2004). Distance plays an important role in determining internal movements in the country, but migration across cities or regions can also be explained by economic incentives, since migrants are attracted by higher wages or incomes. Astana and Almaty, and urban areas of the oil and gas industry-based oblasts of Atyrau and Mangystau, are the main destinations for internal migrants looking for jobs or better prospects. In Astana, the number of citizens increased from 289 700 to 814 400 between 1996 and 2013.[22] The share of the service sector of Astana's economy increased from 1% in 2000 to 10% in 2013. Astana receives people mostly from the comparatively close regions of Akmola, Karaganda, Kostanay and East Kazakhstan, while Almaty receives most of its immigrants from Almaty oblast, Zhambyl, Kyzylorda, Taraz, South and East Kazakhstan.

Zabirova (2004) found that migrants to Astana are not only of low socio-economic status, unstable employment and poor or no skills, but also well-off, educated and skilled people who are looking for career development and other professional possibilities, some of them from Almaty. The needs of these migrants are diverse, but urban development plans do not seem to accommodate migrants of different backgrounds and needs. Migrants to Almaty City come from neighbouring cities to fill the vacancies left by outgoing migrants. The rural-to-urban migrant group includes individuals who are financially and materially well-off by comparison with a similar group in Astana. The number of seasonal workers in Almaty City is larger, which means that socially disadvantaged groups are often on the move.

... but registration of internal migrants and their access to public services is a major issue

Internal migration is regulated by the Constitution, Law N477-IV on Migration of 2011, and other legislation. According to the Constitution, Kazakhstan's citizens have the right to move and resettle in the country. The 2011 Law on migration aims to guarantee the freedom to resettle, but is also concerned with the optimisation of internal migration flows, sustainable migration and housing of migrants. The optimisation of internal migration flows and ensuring the rational settlement of migrants in the country is of key concern.[23] Under current legislation, Kazakhstani citizens are required to be registered at their place of residence within ten days of their arrival. To obtain registration at a given address within a city, internal migrants must provide evidence of ownership (property title to real estate) or a tenancy agreement and the consent of the real estate owner in written form. In practice, landowners most often do not want to be involved in the formal registration of their tenants (the rental market in Kazakhstan's cities is largely informal). Migrants living in informal housing units (i.e. homes not included in the state real estate registry) are also not able to register because they cannot provide a valid address.

Migrants are thus often not registered in their city of residence. Sometimes they remain registered in their previous place of residence (usually small cities in the countryside). A survey of 1 000 young migrants of 14 to 29 conducted in Almaty City in 2012 showed that 54.2% of the respondents had no registration in the city, while 50.9% were still registered at their previous place of residence (Makhmutova, 2012). This problem also exists in Astana: of 124 internal migrants who had settled there permanently, 24% did not have registration there in 2014 (Tukmadieva, 2015).

Although city registration is not formally required to obtain a job outside one's place of residence, provision of public services in Kazakhstan is tied to registration status and available only to those formally registered in their city of residence. It is not possible to enrol children in kindergarten or public schools without local registration. Access to public health care is also based on local registration status. In Astana, almost 30% of migrants surveyed could not access the public health care system because they had no local registration, and 18% could not enrol their children in kindergarten. Many internal migrants also reported that employers required local registration certificates when hiring new employees, even though this is not a requirement under Kazakhstan's Labour Code (Tukmadieva, 2015).

This situation creates fertile ground for corruption and bribery. According to Makhmutova (2012), many internal migrants with children had to resort to questionable measures, including bribing the kindergarten administration or buying registration certificates, to obtain kindergarten places. Out of 1 000 internal migrants surveyed, around 15% had paid for registration (illegally) or were registered at the addresses of friends. Tukmadieva (2015) found out that in Astana, 22% of internal migrants surveyed had paid for registration (illegally) in 2014. The most common reasons for doing so include enrolling children at school or in kindergarten, accessing medical services and renewing passports or other ID documents. Of internal migrants, 23% reported that employees of citizen service centres (*Tsentri obslujivania naselenia*) and medical personnel, for instance, took advantage of their lack of local registration to ask for a bribe.

The unregistered status of many internal urban migrants compromises the accuracy of population and migration statistics. Internal migration data is tracked by the Agency for Statistics, using information supplied by the Migration Policy Committee and the Public Service Centres that collect registration records. Unreliable figures for registered migrants pose problems in calculating the real number of people living in a given place. Official statistics do not always reflect the number of people for whom public services are needed. City *Akimats* prefer to work with their own statistics rather than with official figures.

The registration issue is only one aspect of the social and spatial marginalisation of many internal migrants. Job-seekers moving to Almaty, for example, often encounter difficulty finding housing and work legally, so they take refuge in micro-districts on the outskirts of the city where they are not officially registered, do not own property and have limited access to public services (Makhmutova, 2012). In the absence of the cities' readiness to accept and accommodate new residents, they join informal economic sectors.[24] By settling in cheaper peripheral areas around large cities, migrants contribute to urban sprawl. Since land and property prices are high, they usually occupy rural land and build individual houses from the cheapest accessible local materials (e.g. clay) with poor amenities (furnace heating and no central sewage system), and are vulnerable to natural disasters such as earthquake and flooding.[25] Migrants living in unauthorised housing such as former *dachas*,[26] have no valid address and thus no official status.

Internal migration should be an integral part of urban planning

Kazakhstan's national authorities would do well to recognise that internal migration contributes to the urban economy. Not all migrants are highly educated, but they are highly motivated and entrepreneurial. They bring a diversity of skills and competencies to the urban economy necessary for development. Guest (1994) argues that countries with low levels of internal migration remain economically weak in their development. Rural-to-urban migration plays an important role in transforming skills and competences that are required by urban sectors, especially in industrial expansion. Internal migration cannot be stopped, but by linking it to urban planning, authorities can prevent negative side-effects and make the most of newcomers' skills. Uncontrolled migration leads to urban poverty, slums, urban sprawl and social segregation. Kazakhstan's cities need to plan for development, taking into account migration inflows and migrants' needs for housing, public services (utilities), education, and health care. A temporary housing system could be considered, at least in the larger centres of migration, Astana and Almaty City. By controlling and stimulating labour mobility, Kazakhstan can avoid losing talented people who relocate abroad.

A comprehensive migration policy and legislation could help ensure against emerging problems and harness migration to economic development. Cities in Kazakhstan need proper urban development planning. The central government can help local authorities increase their understanding of migration. This would include identifying which urban areas are likely to receive an influx of migrants, mapping the distribution of potential migration flows in urban areas, estimating the number of potential migrants in specific areas, and understanding the relationships between migration and other urban phenomena (Rashid and Ghani, 2009). Migration issues could be linked to such considerations as: the development of the rental market; a recalibration of registration so that migrants have equal access to public services; the creation of conditions for newcomers to establish their own businesses; and continuous professional education for adults, to improve their chances of employment. Kazakhstan may wish to assess Austria's housing policy, which focuses on price-controlled rental units, to ensure that urban housing is affordable for migrants (Amann and Mundt, 2005). The Austrian government has created a legal framework that balances rights and obligations between the city authorities, companies that manage private housing and the incoming migrants. Migrant-oriented urban policy packages for large cities should differ from urban policy packages covering smaller towns, but it should be acknowledged that internal migration affects not only cities but also towns and villages. As young people leave, village populations will begin to age, with implications for the labour market and services for the elderly, as demonstrated in OECD countries like Japan.[27]

Develop a registration system that motivates migrants to register

Kazakhstan could make it a top priority to develop a registration system that makes it easier for migrants to register at their actual place of residence and makes it possible to compile accurate data on migration flows for urban planning. National authorities may wish to analyse the experience of the Baltic Sea countries in improving the system of public service provision to migrants by delinking it from registration status and using the existing identification number system (INS) instead (Tukmadieva, 2015). This has already been applied in the case of the health service, where emergency aid is provided upon presentation of ID. The experience could be extended to the provision of other public services. The reform could build on the existing state database of individuals (Russian: *ГБД ФЛ*), to which all competent local and national administrations would have access. This reform would require co-ordination between the Ministry of Interior Affairs and the Ministry for Information and Communication, and the adoption of new legislation.

The United Kingdom offers another relevant example. Since internal moves are not recorded formally there, information from the National Health Service Central Register (NHSCR) and GP Patient Registers are used as a proxy for estimates of the population of England and Wales. This data is considered to be a good proxy for internal migration, since when they move, most patients will eventually register with a new GP. This is complemented by data from the Higher Education Statistics Agency (HESA), improving the estimates of internal migration by students.[28] Better internal migration statistics and scientific knowledge are important for both the development and implementation of migration and urban policies. Improving the accuracy of population registration can become an important part of the development of an electronic government system to support the work of *akimats* with up-to-date information about citizens and newcomers (OSCE, 2009).

Support urban planning and development in small cities

The national government can help local governments improve living conditions and make post-industrial towns attractive to young people and business start-ups by providing state grants for innovation and experimentation. The central government could shift its focus to dealing with the factors that prompt internal migration for employment. Policies and special programmes could be adopted to identify the net migration loss to regions, so that each oblast and *rayon* can better plan how to develop its economy and labour market. The central government may wish to: i) promote job creation, raising the resources for depressed regions; ii) support the families migrants leave behind, especially children; iii) encourage migrants to return to their place of origin and provide them support for reintegration; and iv) improve social infrastructure and improve access of rural population to basic social services. Kazakhstan may wish to analyse the experience of the US StartupNation initiative in the formerly bankrupt city of Detroit.[29] The national government can help single-industry based towns provide better economic opportunities for young people, by improving adult education, continuing education and professional training. The School of Continuing and Professional Education (SPCE) of the University of Central Asia, located in the single-industry based town of Tekely (Almaty oblast), in co-operation with the Almaty oblast and Tekeli *akimat,* has started to train young people to retain them as the local workforce.[30] According to SPCE alumni feedback, including ethnic Kazakh repatriates, the training programmes helped them find new working places in Tekeli without moving away.

Notes

1. In the period from 1996 to 2016, Astana's population increased from 289 700 to 880 200 (official website of the Akimat of Astana City: http://astana.gov.kz/en/).

2. Single-industry based towns, called *monotowns*, became part of the national policy agenda with the introduction of the Programme of Single-Industry Based Towns (*monotowns*) 2012-2020. The *monotowns* were further integrated into the recently introduced "RDP 2020".

3. For example, examination and approval of the GSOT took slightly less than a year, whereas the "ISTD of Almaty agglomeration till 2030" submitted for examination at the end of 2015, was approved in January 2016. The "ISTD of Astana Agglomeration Until 2030", submitted almost the same time as the "ISTD of Almaty Agglomeration Until 2030", is still currently under examination.

4. These professional meetings take place based on needs (Urban Design Council, 2016). If there is a plan to build new large-scale developments (hotels, multistory housing complexes, entertainment centres, etc.), these projects have first to pass through professional public reviews. The UPC examines general plans and other urban design projects, playing the role of the professional expert group. Different institutions involved in city development delegate the members of the UPC. *Akimats*, along with *maslikhats*, accept them after internal assessment of the candidates.

5. There are the Rules on Construction, Maintenance of the Municipal Property (roads and communal system); Rules on Development and Protection of Greening (trees and other plantations) within the City Limits; Rules on Maintenance of Housing and related Communal Infrastructure; and the Rules on Historical, Cultural Monuments and Natural Reserves.

6. Most of the city *akimats* only publish the approved general plan schemes: layouts of the general plan of Astana available at: http://astanagenplan.kz/genplan/index.html; layouts of the general plan of Karaganda available at: http://karaganda-akimat.gov.kz/ru/og_genplan.

7. Committee for Land Management, part of the Ministry of National Economy, returned to the supervision of the Ministry of Agriculture in May 2016.

8. The territories of Astana, Almaty and Shymkent now have an area of 71 000, 76 000 and 116 000 hectares respectively.

9. The national legislation does not restrict city *akimats* to use GIS to create the duty plans, but it allows the city authorities to work with manually corrected duty plans that may exist on paper only. In accordance with the rules of management and providing information from the State Urban Registry of the Republic of Kazakhstan, approved by order of the Minister of National Economy of the Republic of Kazakhstan dated 20 March 2015, No. 244. In accordance with the Rules of the Management of Urban Development and Process of Approvals in Construction,

approved by order of the Minister of National Economy of the Republic of Kazakhstan dated 30 November 2015, No. 750 (paragraph 10).

10. For further information, see: OECD (2017), *The Governance of Land Use*, forthcoming.

11. More information is available at: www.refina-info.de/en/.

12. *Up-zoning* involves the rezoning of areas of previously lower density uses to higher uses. *Mixed-use zoning* policy, unlike traditional exclusionary zoning, establishes standards for blending various uses, such as residential, commercial, civic and light industrial, with the aim of achieving high-density, compact urban development. *Minimum density zoning* specifies the minimum allowable development density or floor area ratio, rather than the maximum density found in most traditional zoning ordinances, with the aim of encouraging compact development through the increased density minimum (Silva and Acheampong, 2015).

13. For further information see: https://strategy2050.kz/en/news/308/.

14. Many municipalities in South Africa are using the urban development line (UDL) as a tool to control urban development. However, as the case of Durban (Durban Outer West Region) shows, the UDL may also become a demarcation of social inequality, separating suburban areas into luxury gated communities and informal settlements. Outer West Spatial Development Plan, www.durban.gov.za/Resource_Centre/reports/Framework_Planning/Documents/Outer_West_SDP_Report_2013_2014.pdf.

15. See: "New Shymkent-city under construction in South Kazakhstan", retrieved 20 August 20, 2016, from: www.kazpravda.kz/en/news/economics/new-shymkent-city-under-construction-in-south-kazakhstan/.

16. JSC Real Estate Fund (state holding Samruk-Kazyna), JSC Kazakhstani mortgage company (state-owned holding Baïterek).

17. See JSC Real Estate Fund "Samruk-Kazyna" (2015) for further details.

18. The planning institutes can be created based on existing capacity. For example, the urban planning company Project Institute "Kazgiprograd-1" LLC is a private company that was formed instead of the Soviet Planning Institute – Kazgiprograd. Now it is one of the leading companies trying to develop general plans based not only on demographic indicators, but economic and environmental issues related to urban development.

19. For further details, see the City of Sheffield's Local Growth Fund Investment Strategy, www.sheffield.gov.uk/planning-and-city-development/regeneration/local-growth-fund.html (accessed 1 September 2016).

20. The State Committee on Statistics of Kazakhstan, 2009 Census Data, www.stat.gov.kz/ (retrieved 5 September 2016).

21. According to data presented at the roundtable dedicated to the migration processes in Kazakhstan in Astana in 2010: "Social and economic consequences of migration: The vulnerability of migrants and the need for integration in Central Asia", based on the personal participation of Madina Junussova (OECD consultant).

22. Akimat of Astana City, "Astana Statistics in 2014", http://astana.gov.kz/ru/ (accessed 15 February 2014).

23. The Constitution of the Republic of Kazakhstan (adopted at the national referendum on 30 August 1995 and amended in 2 February 2011); Law on Migration of People No. 477-IV, dated 22 July 2011.

24. Newcomers agree to be paid in cash and accept any low-paid unofficial jobs. For further information, see: Abdih, Y. and L. Medina (2013). Many migrants and city commuters are earning money by providing direct services such as street trading or taxi service, without registering their businesses. For further information, see: Zhusupova, A. (2013).

25. New peripheral settlements appeared due to unauthorised occupation of the land such as "Shanyrak" and "Buckeye" in Almaty City, and "Ondiris" in Astana City. See media commentary: "Residents of the outskirts of Astana ask to legalize their homes" [Жители окраины Астаны просят легализовать их дома], retrieved 5 August 2016, from: http://rus.azattyq.org/a/zhiteli-okrainy-astany-prosyat-legalizovat-doma/25440063.html.

26. A *dacha* is a cottage with a small garden that used to serve as a weekend home for many citizens in Soviet times. The former *dachas* in Kazakhstan are used as housing for many city migrants. According to the official Census, they house 1.1% of the total urban population. For further details, see: Smailova, A. et al. (2010).

27. In the absence of adequate regional public transport, people living in rural areas and small towns around large cities (e.g. Almaty) commute daily, using private cars (see subsection on transport). The remotely located single-industry based towns and villages are losing their young and adult population, as they move to seek professional education and jobs. See: Musabaev, T.T. (2013), "Master Plan for the Organisation of the Territory of the Republic of Kazakhstan", White Paper, Valery, Astana.

28. For further information on population estimates methodology in the United Kingdom, see: http://webarchive.nationalarchives.gov.uk/20160105160709/ and www.ons.gov.uk/ons/guide-method/method-quality/specific/population-and-migration/pop-ests/index.html.

29. "Got a great idea? Let Hatch Detroit get you going", retrieved from: https://startupnation.com/startupnation-radio/got-a-great-idea-let-hatch-detroit-get-you-going/.

30. For further information, see: School of Professional and Continuing Education (SPCE), www.ucentralasia.org/Schools/Spce (accessed November 2016).

References

ADB (2014), "Kazakhstan: Alternative Urban Infrastructure Financing Modalities", *Technical Assistance Consultant's Report* (Project 46487-001), available at: www.adb.org/projects/documents/kaz-alternative-urban-infrastructure-financing-modalities-final-report-tacr.

ADB (2012), *Sector Assessment – Country Partnership Strategy: Kazakhstan 2012-2016*. www.adb.org/sites/default/files/linked-documents/cps-kaz-2012-2016-ssa-03.pdf.

Abdih, Y. and L. Medina (2013), *Measuring the Informal Economy in the Caucasus and Central Asia*, IMF Working Paper: Middle East and Central Asia Department, www.imf.org/external/pubs/ft/wp/2013/wp13137.pdf.

Alexander, C. (2007), "Soviet and post-Soviet planning in Almaty, Kazakhstan", *Critique of Anthropology*, Vol. 27/2, pp. 165-181.

Akimat of Aktau City (2015), "Программа развития территории города Актау на 2016-2020 годы" [Programmes of Territorial Development of Aktau 2016-2020], Aktau.

Akimat of Aktobe City (2015), "Программа развития территории города Актобе на 2016-2020 годы" [Programmes of Territorial Development of Aktobe 2016-2020], Aktobe.

Akimat of Almaty City (2016), Financial Activity of the Almaty City, Akimat Report, available on www.economika.astana.kz/ru/node/42814 (accessed 2 May 2016).

Akimat of Almaty City (2013), "Программа развития территории города Алматы 2011-15" [Programme of Development of the Almaty City for 2011-15], Almaty.

Akimat of Almaty City (2011), "Программа развития территории города Астаны 2011-15 [Programme of Development of the Almaty City for 2011-15], Almaty.

Akimat of Astana City (2015), "Report on the Implementation of Astana Development Programme for 2011-15", www.economika.astana.kz/ru/node/42814 (accessed 2 May 2016).

Akimat of Astana City (2012), "The approved budget of Astana for 2013-15", www.economika.astana.kz/ru/node/42814 (accessed 2 May 2016).

Akimat of Astana City (2011), "Regulations of the state institution department of economy and budget planning of Astana City", www.economika.astana.kz/ru/node/42814 (accessed 2 May 2016).

Akimat of Astana City (2010), "Программа развития территории города Астаны 2011-15" [Programme of Development of the Astana city for 2011-15], Astana.

Akimat of Astana City (2001), "Генеральный план города Астана до 2030 года" [General Plan of Astana 2030], approved by the Government of the Republic of Kazakhstan, 15 August, No. 1064.

Akimat of Atyrau City (2015), "Программа развития территории города Атырау на 2016-2020 годы" [Programmes of Territorial Development of Atyrau 2016-2020], Atyrau.

Akimat of East-Kazakhstan Oblast (2015), "Программа развития территории Восточно-Казахстанской области на 2016-2020 годы [Programmes of Territorial Development of East-Kazakhstan Oblast 2016-2020], approved 9 December, No. 32/421-V Usk-Kamenogorsk.

Akimat of Kentau Town (2014), "Комплексный план развития города Кентау Южно-Казахстанской области на 2015-17 годы" [Comprehensive Plan of Development of Kentau of South-Kazakhstan Oblast 2015-17], Kentau.

Akimat of Kyzylorda Oblast (2015), "Программа развития территории Кызылординской области на 2016-2020 годы" [Programmes of Territorial Development of Kyzylorda Oblast 2016-20], approved 10 December, No. 323, Kyzylorda.

Akimat of Pavlodar City (2015), "Программа развития территории города Павлодар на 2016-2020 годы" [Programmes of Territorial Development of Pavlodar 2016-2020], Pavlodar.

Akimat of Pavlodar City (2007), "Budget of the city of Pavlodar in 2007", approved by Pavlodar city maslikhat from December 21, No. 55/3 [Бюджет города Павлодар на 2007 год, принят решением маслихата города Павлодара от 21 декабря 2007 года No. 55/3]

Akimat of Shymkent City (2016), "Концепция социально-экономического развития города Шымкент до 2020 года" [Concept of socio-economic development of Shymkent city 2020], Shymkent, http://shymkent.gov.kz/ru/page/69 (accessed 15 July 2016).

Akimat of South-Kazakhstan Oblast (2016), "Программа развития территории Южно-Казахстанской области на 2016-2020 годы" [Programmes of Territorial Development of South-Kazakhstan Oblast 2016-2020], approved 9 December 2015, No. 32/421-V, Shymkent.

Akimat of Turkestan Town (2015), "Түркістан қаласының 2016-2020 жылдарға арналған даму бағдарламасы" [Programme of Development of Turkestan town 2016-2020], Turkestan.

Akimat of Uralsk City (2015), "Программа развития территории города Уральск на 2016-2020 годы" [Programmes of Territorial Development of Uralsk 2016-2020], Uralsk.

Akimat of Zhekazgan City (2014), "Regulations on the State Institution Department of Architecture and Urban Planning of the City of Zhezkazgan".

Aldashev, A. and B. Dietz (2011), "Determinants of internal migration in Kazakhstan", Osteuropa Institut Regensburg, *MPRA Paper,* No. 34 922, https://mpra.ub.uni-muenchen.de/34922/1/MPRA_paper_34922.pdf.

Amann, W. and A. Mundt (2005), "The Austrian System of Social Housing Finance", Institut für Immobilien, Bauen und Wohnen GmbH, Vienna, www.iut.nu/FindOutMore/Europe/Austria/Socialhousing_finance_Amman_Mundt.pdf (accessed 9 November 2016).

Andres, D., A. Caldera Sánchez and A. Johansson (2011), "Housing Markets and Structural Policies in OECD Countries", *OECD Economics Department Working Papers*, No. 836, OECD Publishing, Paris, http://dx.doi.org/10.1787/5kgk8t2k9vf3-en.

Aoki, K. (2005), "All the King's Horses and All the King's Men: Hurdles to Putting the Fragmented Metropolis Back Together Again, Statewide Land Use Planning, Portland Metro and Oregon's Measure 37", *Journal of Law and Politics*, Spring/Summer 2005, Vol. 21, Issue 2/3, p. 397.

Arts, J., T. Hanekamp and A. Dijkstra (2014), "Integrating land-use and transport infrastructure planning: towards adaptive and sustainable transport infrastructure", Transport Research Arena, Paris, https://trid.trb.org/view.aspx?id=1316947 (accessed 9 November 2016).

Bayandina, G.D. (2014), "Prospects for Public-Private Partnership in the Municipal Sector: The Study Case of Pavlodar, Kazakhstan", *Actual Problems of Economics,* Vol. 152/2, pp. 219-229.

Blanco, A.G., V. Fretes Cibils and A. Muñoz Miranda (2014), "Rental Housing Wanted. Policy Options for Latin America and the Caribbean", Inter-American Development Bank, Washington, DC, http://10.iadb.org/intal/intalcdi/PE/2014/13900en.pdf (accessed 24 November 2016).

Brilhante, O. and J. Skinner (2015), "Review of some incentive mechanisms being used by some European municipalities to promote sustainable housing", Institute for Housing and Urban Development Studies (HIS) Rotterdam, the Netherlands, www.ihs.nl/fileadmin/assets/ihs/marketing/prospective_students_pages/eco_and_mfui/incentive_mechanism_municipalities_sustainable_construction.pdf (accessed 9 November 2016).

Burges, G. and S. Monk (2008), "Delivering affordable housing through the planning system: challenges and good practice", *Housing, Care and Support*, Vol. 11/3, pp. 4-8, www.emeraldinsight.com/doi/pdfplus/10.1108/14608790200800018 (accessed 27 October 2016).

Calavita, N. and A. Mallach (2010), "An international perspective on inclusionary housing", in N. Calavita and A. Mallach (eds.), *Inclusionary Social Housing in International Perspective: affordable housing, social inclusion, and land value recapture*, Lincoln Institute of Land Policy, Cambridge, Mass, www.lincolninst.edu/sites/default/files/pubfiles/inclusionary-housing-in-international-perspective-chp.pdf (accessed 27 October 2016).

Caruso, I., T. Vitolo and L. Cocchis (2003), "The innovative role of public utilities: A strategy for local development", ERSA 2003 Conference, www.researchgate.net/publication/23730864_The_innovative_role_of_public_utilities_a_strategy_for_local_development (accessed 27 October 2016).

CER, ESCAP, UNDP (2013), "Urbanization in Central Asia: Challenges, Issues and Prospects", Tashkent, www.unescap.org/resources/urbanization-central-asia-challenges-issues-and-prospects (accessed 22 November 2016).

Code of the Republic of Kazakhstan (2008), "Бюджетный кодекс Республики Казахстан" [Budget Code of the Republic of Kazakhstan], No. 95-IV, dated 4 December.

Code of the Republic of Kazakhstan (2007), "Экологический кодекс Республики Казахстан" [Environmental Code of the Republic of Kazakhstan], No. 212-III, 9 January 2007 (with additions dated 28 April 2016).

Code of the Republic of Kazakhstan (2003), "Земельный кодекс Республики Казахстан" [Land Code of the Republic of Kazakhstan], No. 442-II, dated 20 June, (with additions dated to 30 June 2016).

Coulibaly, S. et al. (2012), *Eurasian cities: New realities along the Silk Road*, World Bank Publications, World Bank, Washington, DC.

Danzier, A., B. Dietz and K. Gatskova (2013), "Kazakhstan Migration and Remittances Survey: migration, welfare and the labor market in an emerging economy", Institute for East and Southeast European Studies, VolkswagenStiftung, http://www.ios-regensburg.de/fileadmin/doc/VW_Project/Booklet-KAZ-web.pdf (accessed 20 October 2016).

Delion, M.L. et al. (2015), "Zoning and urban planning: Understanding the benefits", *Doing Business 2015*, www.doingbusiness.org/reports/case-studies/2014/zoning-urban-planning (accessed 27 October 2016).

Friedrich Ebert Stiftung (2007), "Financing access to basic utilities for all", Second Regional Multi-stakeholder Consultation, Meeting Report, Lusaka, Zambia, www.un.org/esa/ffd/wp-content/uploads/2014/09/ZambiaMeetingReport.pdf (accessed 17 November 2016).

Governmental Decree of the Republic of Kazakhstan (2016), "Межрегиональная схема территориального развития Алматинской агломерации" [Interregional Scheme of Territorial Development of Almaty Agglomeration], No. 302, dated 24 May, https://tengrinews.kz/zakon/pravitelstvo_respubliki_kazahstan_premer_ministr_rk/stroitelstvo_i_arhitektura/id-P1600000302/ (accessed 7 June 2016).

Governmental Decree of the Republic of Kazakhstan (2014), "Программа развития регионов до 2020 года" [Regional Development Programme 2020], No. 728, dated 28 June, http://online.zakon.kz/Document/?doc_id=31584094#pos=29;-284 (accessed 20 May 2016).

Governmental Decree of the Republic of Kazakhstan (2009), No. 2082, "Утверждение правил ведения Государственного градостроительного кадастра Республики Казахстан" [Adoption of the rules of the State Urban Cadastre of the Republic of Kazakhstan], dated 11 December 2009, available at: http://online.zakon.kz/Document/?doc_id=30533020#pos=8;-273 (accessed 5 May 2016).

Governmental Decree of the Republic of Kazakhstan (2004), No. 452, "Корректировка генерального плана города Алматы" [Integration of change in the general plan of Almaty City], dated 22 April, available at: http://egov.kz/cms/ru/law/list/P020001330 (accessed 20 March 2016).

Government of the Republic of Kazakhstan (2003), "Land Code of the Republic of Kazakhstan", No. 442-II dated 20 June, Земельный кодекс Республики Казахстан (with additions dated to 30.06.2016).

Government of South Australia (2013), "Building a stronger South Australia: Integrated transport and land use plan (factsheets)", Department of Planning, Transport and Infrastructure, http://trove.nla.gov.au/work/186995998?selectedversion=NBD52180140 (accessed 18 October 2016).

Guest, P. (1994), "The impact of population change on the growth of mega-cities", *Asia-Pacific Population Journal*, Vol. 9/1, pp. 37-56.

JSC Real Estate Fund "Samruk-Kazyna" (2015), "Годовой отчет о деятельности" [Annual Report], https://fnsk.kz/main (accessed 4 July 2016).

Junussova, M.A. and K. Muldagalieva (2015), "The planning practice in Kazakhstan" in J. Ryser and T. Franchini (eds.), *International Manual of Planning Practice*, International Society of City and Regional Planners, The Hague, pp. 736-746.

Kuramyssova, A. (2015), "Demand for public housing increasing in Kazakhstan", *The Astana Times*, http://astanatimes.com/2015/03/demand-public-housing-increasing-kazakhstan/ (accessed 4 July 2016).

Law of the Republic of Kazakhstan No. 242-II (2001), "Об архитектурной, градостроительной и строительной деятельности в Республике Казахстан" [On Architectural, Town Planning and Building Activities in the Republic of Kazakhstan], (with additions dated to 07 April 2016).

Law of the Republic of Kazakhstan No. 2572-XII (1993), "Об административно-территориальном устройстве Республики Казахстан" [On administrative-territorial structure of the Republic of Kazakhstan], (with additions dated to 29 March 2016).

Leigh, N.G. and E.J. Blakely (2013), *Planning Local Economic Development: Theory and Practice*, SAGE Publications, Incorporated.

Linn, J. (2014), "Urbanization, Regional Development, and Decentralization", in Aitzhanova, A. et al. (eds.), *Kazakhstan 2050: Toward a Modern Society for All*, Nazarbayev University, National Analytical Centre, Oxford University Press, Group Centennial International, Astana, pp.187-223.

Linn, J.F. (2014), "Kazakhstan 2050: Exploring an ambitious vision", *Global Journal of Emerging Market Economies*, Vol. 6/3, pp. 283-300.

Makhmutova, M. (2012), "Internal migration of young people in Kazakhstan: Case study of Almaty", Public Policy Research Centre and Soros Foundation-Kazakhstan.

Ministry of National Economy (2016), "Sustainable development of the cities through efficient urban planning", presentation for the UN-Habitat Meeting in Prague.

Ministry of National Economy (2014), "Методика по разработке Стратегического плана развития Республики Казахстан, Прогнозной схемы территориально-пространственного развития страны, государственных и правительственных программ, стратегических планов государственных органов и программ развития территорий" [The methodology for the development of the strategic plan of the Republic of Kazakhstan, the predictive scheme for spatial development of the country, government programmes, strategic plans of state bodies and territorial development programmes].

Musabaev, T.T. (2013), "Master Plan for the Organization of the Territory of the Republic of Kazakhstan", White Paper, Valery, Astana.

Nazarbayev, N. (2014), "Kazakhstan's Way – 2050: Common aim, common interests, common future", address of the President of Kazakhstan to the nation, www.strategy2050.kz (accessed 5 June 2016).

NGO Green Salvation (2014), *Letter to the President of the International Olympic Committee*, www.greensalvation.org, retrieved in February 2016.

OECD (2016), *Multi-dimensional Review of Kazakhstan: Volume 1. Initial Assessment*, OECD Publishing, Paris, http://dx.doi.org/10.1787/9789264246768-en.

OECD (2015a), *The Metropolitan Century: Understanding Urbanisation and its Consequences*, OECD Publishing, Paris, http://dx.doi.org/10.1787/9789264228733-en.

OECD (2015b), *OECD Urban Policy Reviews: Mexico 2015: Transforming Urban Policy and Housing Finance*, OECD Publishing, Paris, http://dx.doi.org/10.1787/9789264227293-en.

OECD (2015c), *OECD Urban Policy Reviews: China 2015*, OECD Publishing, Paris, http://dx.doi.org/10.1787/9789264230040-en.

OECD (2014a), *OECD Regional Outlook 2014: Regions and Cities: Where Policies and People Meet*, OECD Publishing, Paris, http://dx.doi.org/10.1787/9789264201415-en.

OECD (2014b), *Kazakhstan: Review of the Central Administration*, OECD Publishing, Paris, http://dx.doi.org/10.1787/9789264224605-en.

OECD (2014c), *Regulatory Policy in Kazakhstan: Towards Improved Implementation*, OECD Publishing, Paris, http://dx.doi.org/10.1787/9789264214255-en.

OECD (2013), *OECD Urban Policy Reviews, Chile 2013*, OECD Publishing, Paris, http://dx.doi.org/10.1787/9789264191808-en.

OECD (2012), *Recommendation of the Council on Principles for Public Governance of Public-Private Partnerships*, https://www.oecd.org/governance/budgeting/PPP-Recommendation.pdf.

OECD (2010), *Regional Development Policies in OECD Countries*, OECD Publishing, Paris, http://dx.doi.org/10.1787/9789264087255-en.

OECD (2007), *OECD Principles for Private Sector Participation in Infrastructure*, OECD Publishing, Paris, http://dx.doi.org/10.1787/9789264034105-en.

OECD (2006), *Competitive Cities in the Global Economy*, OECD Publishing, Paris, http://dx.doi.org/10.1787/9789264027091-en.

OECD (2005), *Encouraging Public-Private Partnerships in the Utilities Sector: the role of development assistance*, DAF/INV/WP(2004)4/ANN4, OECD, www.oecd.org/investment/investmentfordevelopment/34843203.pdf.

OECD (1999), *Urban Policy in Germany: Towards Sustainable Urban Development*, OECD Publishing, Paris, http://dx.doi.org/10.1787/9789264173194-en.

Organization for Security and Co-operation in Europe, OSCE (2009), *Guidelines on Population Registration*, Warsaw, OSCE/ODIHR, www.osce.org/odihr/39496?download=true (accessed 27 October 2016).

Peppercorn, I. and C. Taffin (2013), *Rental Housing: Lessons from International Experience and Policies for Emerging Markets*, Directions in Development, The World Bank, Washington, DC.

Presidential Decree of the Republic of Kazakhstan (2013), "Концепция по переходу Республики Казахстан к зеленой экономике [Concept for transition of the Republic of Kazakhstan to Green Economy], No. 577, dated 30 May, www.strategy2050.kz (accessed 15 June 2016).

Presidential Decree of the Republic of Kazakhstan (2011), "Прогнозная схема территориально-пространственного развития страны до 2020 года" [Forecast Scheme for Spatial-Territorial Development of the Republic of Kazakhstan 2020], No. 118, dated 21 July, http://adilet.zan.kz/rus/docs/U1100000118 (accessed 10 May 2016).

Presidential Decree of the Republic of Kazakhstan (2009), "О системе государственного планирования в Республике Казахстан" [On the system of State planning in the Republic of Kazakhstan], No. 827, dated 18 June, www.economy.kz/sgp/2030/ukaz2.doc (accessed 10 October 2014).

Prybylovsky, P. (2016), *Real Estate: Kazakhstan's Growing Sector*, EDGE, www.edgekz.com/real-estate-kazakhstans-growing-sector/.

Rashid, M. and I. Ghani (2009), "The importance of internal migration in the context of urban planning decision making", ICBEDC, Penang Malaysia, www.academia.edu/719393/the_importance_of_internal_migration_in_the_context_of_urban_planning_decision_making.

Robson, B. and I. Deas (2008), "Defining the Objectives of Local Development Strategies", in *Making Local Strategies Work: Building the Evidence Base*, OECD Publishing, Paris, http://dx.doi.org/10.1787/9789264044869-3-en.

Rode, P. et al. (2014), "Accessibility in Cities: Transport and Urban Form", *NCE Cities Paper 03*. LSE Cities, London School of Economics and Political Science, http://newclimateeconomy.report/2015/wp-content/uploads/2016/04/LSE-Cities-2014-Transport-and-Urban-Form-NCE-Cities-Paper-03.pdf.

Rojas, E. (2012), "The Contribution of Urban Institutes to the Governance of Urban Areas: challenges and opportunities in Antofagasta, Chile", report prepared for the OECD Territorial Review of Antofagasta, Chile (unpublished).

Ryser, J. and T. Franchini (eds.) (2015), "International manual of planning practice", International Society of City and Regional Planners, The Hague.

Sharipova, D. (2015), "Who gets what, when and how? Housing and informal institutions in the Soviet Union and post-Soviet Kazakhstan", *Central Asian Affairs*, Vol. 2/2, pp. 140-167.

Silva, E. et R. Acheampong (2015), "Developing an Inventory and Typology of Land-Use Planning Systems and Policy Instruments in OECD Countries", *OECD Environment Working Papers*, No. 94, OECD Publishing, Paris, http://dx.doi.org/10.1787/5jrp6wgxp09s-en.

Smailova, A. et al. (2010), "Housing characteristics of the population in Republic of Kazakhstan, Results of the National Population Census 2009" [Жилищные характеристики населения в Республике Казахстан, Итоги национальной переписи населения 2009 года в Республике Казахстан], Statistical Yearbook, Astana, p. 361.

SN RK 3.01-00-2011 "Инструкция о порядке разработки, согласования и утверждения градостроительных проектов" [Instruction on the Development, Co-ordination, Approval and the Design Documentation for Construction].

SNIP RK 3.01-01-2008 "Градостроительство. Планировка и застройка городских и сельских населенных пунктов" [Urban Planning and Construction of Urban and Rural Settlements].

SN RK 1.05-01-2011 "Государственный градостроительный кадастр" [State Urban Design Cadastre of the Republic of Kazakhstan].

Stead D. and H. Geerlings (2005), "Integrating transport, land use planning and environment policy", *Innovation: The European Journal of Social Science Research*, Vol.4/18, pp. 443-453, www.tandfonline.com/doi/pdf/10.1080/13511610500384194.

Transport for Quality of Life (2011), "Thriving cities: Integrated land use and transport planning", PTEG, www.urbantransportgroup.org/system/files/20112706ptegthrivingcitiesreportforwebfinal.pdf (accessed 27 October 2016).

Transportation Research Board (2004), "Transit-Oriented Development in the United States: Experiences, Challenges, and Prospects", Federal Transit Administration, Washington, DC, http://onlinepubs.trb.org/onlinepubs/tcrp/tcrp_rpt_102.pdf (accessed 27 October 2016).

Tukmadieva, M (2015), "Ways of reforming the population registration system by the place of residence in the Republic of Kazakhstan" [Пути реформирования системы регистрации населения по месту проживания в Республике Казахстан], Programme for young researchers in the field of public policy, Soros Foundation-Kazakhstan [Программа для молодых исследователей в области публичной политики Фонда Сорос-Казахстан].

Tutubaev A. (2010), "Legal aspects of state control in the field of architecture and urban planning in the Republic of Kazakhstan", dissertation, D. A. Kunaev University.

UITP (2013), "Financing Public Transport", Geneva, www.uitp.org/sites/default/files/Financing%20public%20transport.pdf (accessed 22 November 2016).

UK Government (2006), "Delivering Affordable Housing", Communities and Local Government Department, London, www.gov.uk/government/uploads/system/uploads/attachment_data/file/15789/152897.pdf (accessed 27 October 2016).

UNDP (2016), "Unlocking Energy Efficiency in Kazakhstan", www.kz.undp.org/content/kazakhstan/en/home/ourwork/our_stories/unlocking-energy-efficiency-in-kazakhstan/ (accessed 22 November 2016).

UNDP (2010), "Promoting energy efficiency in buildings: Lessons learnt from international experience", *Environment and Energy*, http://thegef.org/sites/default/files/publications/EEBuilding_WEB_2.pdf (accessed 21 November 2016).

UNECE (2008), "Environmental Performance Reviews: Kazakhstan Second Review", Committee on Environmental Policy, United Nations, New York and Geneva.

UNECE (2016), "CIS Cities: Towards a Sustainable Future – The Commonwealth of Independent States Regional Report", UNECE, UN-Habitat, www.unece.org/index.php?id=42438 (accessed 27 October 2016).

White, M. and P. Allmendinger (2003), "Land Use Planning and the Housing Market: A Comparative Review of the US and the UK", *Urban Studies*, Vol. 40/5, pp. 953-972.

Wong, C. and A. Schulze Baing (2010), "Brownfield residential redevelopment in England: what happens to the most deprived neighbourhoods?", Joseph Rowntree Foundation, https://www.jrf.org.uk/sites/default/files/jrf/migrated/files/brownfield-residential-redevelopment-full.pdf (accessed 17 September 2016).

Zabirova, A. (2004), "Rural-to urban and city-to-city migrations in Kazakhstan: motives and results", *Ethnic Relations and Population Migration*, Central Asia and the Caucasus, Vol. 27/3, pp. 71-78, http://cyberleninka.ru/article/n/rural-to-urban-and-city-to-city-migrations-in-kazakhstan-motives-and-results (accessed 27 October 2016).

Zhusupova, A. (2013), "The phenomenon of self-employment in Kazakhstan as a reflection of the specifics of socio-economic development", the Institute of World Economics and Politics (IMAP) at the Foundation of the First President of the Republic of Kazakhstan, Almaty, http://iwep.kz/files/attachments/article/2013-12-04/doklad_-_samozanyatost-na_pechat-arzygul.pdf (accessed 27 October 2016).

Chapter 3

Governing urbanisation in Kazakhstan

This chapter examines urban governance in Kazakhstan. It begins with an assessment of the main challenges of the current system of inter-governmental relations and offers possible alternatives to improve co-ordination across levels of government and among national policy actors. It also explores local government finance and the way the current arrangements for managing local public finance act in detriment of urban development. It formulates some recommendations to ensure that local governments have access to resources to pay for urbanisation. The chapter proposes some recommendations for strengthening civil service reform with a particular focus on subnational levels of government. Finally, it concludes with proposals to cultivate dialogue with citizens and make them active contributors to the urban planning process.

Kazakhstan is undergoing a gradual process of urbanisation. Its major cities are also modernising, as their institutions make the transition from a young post-Soviet country to an established independent nation. If urbanisation is to be effective, it should ensure prosperity, social cohesion and environmental protection, but how to guarantee those benefits presents a major challenge. Existing institutions, state budgets, and administrative and cultural practices are not fully ready to transform urbanisation into one of Kazakhstan's major assets. Given the traditional concentration of skills and resources in Kazakhstan's central government, the resources, responsibilities and capacities available to local governments are limited.

The local government structure and public administration

The success of national urban policies depends to a large extent on how well organised the different levels of government are in implementing policy. The underlying issue is not whether Kazakhstan has the right local government structure, but rather how well-co-ordinated the different levels of governments are, and the equity and efficiency in the distribution of responsibilities, decision-making powers and resources for urban development that each level of government is granted.

A complex multilevel governance arrangement

The 1995 Constitution of Independent Kazakhstan establishes that the local bodies of public administration include oblast, rayon and city *maslikhats*; oblast, rayon and city *akimats* (local executive branch); and rural *akims* (local executive). The *maslikhats* are the organs of local self-government. As mentioned in Chapter 1, Kazakhstan has three levels of subnational governments (SNGs): regional (*oblast*) that include the two main cities (*sity*) (Almaty and Astana), district (*rayons*), and municipal (*auls*). In addition, there are 27 single-industry towns ("monotowns"), a heritage of the Soviet past. Some are undergoing economic difficulties and need to diversify their economy.

According to the 2001 Law on Local Public Administration in Kazakhstan, the oblasts (regions) and the cities of Almaty and Astana are headed by a regional/city *akim* (regional governor) appointed by the president, but have a regional *maslikhat* (regional/city council) elected by universal suffrage. The *akim* represents the president and government of Kazakhstan and is the head of the local executive body, and is responsible for implementing state policy within the local territory. At the intermediate level, the executives (*akim*) are appointed by the regional governor (or by the mayor in the cities of republican significance) while they have a directly elected council (city or district *maslikhat*). At the local or municipal level (settlements, villages and cities of district significance), the election of local *akims* has been carried out since 2013 through indirect suffrage by local-level councils (direct election by citizens is planned at some point in the future). The local representative body, or *maslikhat*, is elected by the inhabitants of the oblasts or *rayon* (for a city of oblast value). It expresses the will of the citizens, determines measures to implement this will, and controls their implementation in accordance with legislation. Villages and small towns do not have *maslikhats* (Makhmutova, 2006; Bhuiyan, 2010).

Weak local self-government

Kazakhstan is in the process of strengthening statehood by forming an accountable government. For this purpose, the government intends to empower citizens to participate in the decision-making process, by developing local governance and strengthening the role of public councils under state agencies and *akimats.*[1] However, as in the other countries of Central Asia, the principle of centralised management in Kazakhstan is still dominant, which detracts from the development of local self-government (UNECE, 2016). Kazakhstan's strong central government is used to supervising urban, regional as well as national development projects. The public administration machinery of subnational levels of government has consequently not been developed to assume greater responsibilities. Local authorities have weak institutional capacity to deliver local public services and to promote local development (Bhuiyan, 2010). Despite recent decentralisation efforts, SNGs are still closely controlled by the central government and lack adequate financial, budgetary, administrative and legal resources.[2] Kazakhstan's model of local government mixes elements of both a centralised and a decentralised system. The state apparatus continues to play a key role in regional development and reflects the strong vertical hierarchies, and the leaders of local territories are accountable only to their superiors from higher levels of government, rather than directly to the people (Kazakova, 2015). Thus, the decisions of the central government are not always based on the actual conditions of local economies. The president of the republic appoints *akims* of oblasts and of the cities of Astana and Almaty, who are nominated by the prime minister. The power of the president over *akims* supersedes the power of the government, in the sense that their tenure continues at the president's discretion. The president also has the power to dismiss *akims*. An *akim's* tenure expires when a new president takes office, but the *akim* continues to work until the president makes a new appointment. Lower-level *akims* are nominated by the *akims* of the echelon above. For example, the *akims* of Almaty and Astana nominate the *akims* of the city *rayons*.

The *akim* provides regulatory and legal decisions, as well as regulations on administrative and managerial matters and on urgent and individual problems. The actions of the *akimat* and *akim* are binding on the whole territory of the administrative and territorial unit. The validity of the *akimat's* acts and decisions can be suspended completely or partially by the president, the government of Kazakhstan, a higher-level *akimat* or *akim*, or the *akimat* or *akim* themselves, as well as by court decisions (Makhmutova, 2006). *Maslikhats,* or local councils, are elected for a four-year term directly by the citizens of the representative territories and approve the "comprehensive development plan" of their region or city. However, Kazakova (2015) argues that *maslikhats* have no real power over the local state administration and perform a ceremonial role. OECD (2016a) found that the 1995 Constitution reaffirmed the hierarchical organisation of the state and the subordination of local executive bodies to the central government, with local executive bodies as extensions of the central government. Local executive bodies exercise only those powers and responsibilities that central government confers on them.

Since 2013, rural *akims* have been elected through local councils (*maslikhats*), which includes 2 533 *akims* of rural districts and villages, and 50 *akims* of towns of regional significance. According to the government, this number makes up 91.7% of *akims* at all levels who have direct contact with citizens. However, their *akimats* are extremely weak in their administrative and operational capacity, with limited budgets and human capital. Even if they are working at grassroots level, they do not always have the means to deliver public services. Moreover, the remaining 8% of local authorities (the two cities of republican significance and the 38 oblast-level cities), where authorities are still centrally appointed, account for 50% of the population of the country (over 8.7 million people) and 87% of the urban population. The central government thus needs to work on two fronts: enhancing the administrative and operational capacity of subnational governments at all levels to improve service delivery, and in the long term, pursuing reforms for the election of *akims* of all cities, including those of republican significance.

A deconcentrated but centralised system of government

Urban development takes place in a setting where responsibilities are distributed across different governments. An urban governance structure will be effective if cities can take decisions commensurate with the problems they face in their respective territories and in relation to other levels of government. In the case of Kazakhstan, at least three important aspects of subnational governance arrangements are worth noting:

- *Unclear assignment of responsibilities across levels of government.* The Budget Code of the Republic of Kazakhstan sets out the distribution of responsibilities across levels of government.[3] However, there are significant overlaps in expenditure powers. Despite several reform attempts to provide greater clarity in the division of responsibilities, there are still many areas of uncertainty. For example, housing and utility services, transport and communications, and energy saving and energy efficiency are urban-related areas for which all levels of government seem to bear some responsibility. In education, for instance, local governments are responsible for financing schools. However, given the different types of school, and the division of responsibilities between national and regional governments, the system is highly complex. One example is the "Almaty Green Growth Project", which has suffered from ongoing debate about who is to administer it, since the oblast *akimat* and the city *akimat* both have responsibility and interests in the initiative. This makes expenditure ineffective, blurs accountability and destabilises intergovernmental relations.
- *Central government still has control over local decisions*. This is manifested in the appointment of *akims* by the upper executive power and the degree of dependence on transfers from the upper level of government. The superior *akims*, the prime minister and finally the president determine appointments to political positions. The *akims* are vertically subordinated to the government, which limits their interest in solving local problems. In general, they are not interested in gaining popular support or for what purpose. The fact that *akims* at oblast and *rayon* levels can be dismissed at any time at the president's discretion is an indication of the control over SNGs.

  Efforts have been made to increase the accountability of local administrations to citizens through the introduction of the *maslikhats* (representative bodies) at oblast and *rayon* levels, and the elections of rural *akims*. However, these measures have had only a limited effect, since *maslikhats* have relatively little influence over the services provided in their localities and limited control over the level of financing; *akimats* are accountable to upper government levels and not to the *maslikhats*; and in rural areas there are no *maslikhats*. Moreover, *akims* are assessed based on centrally defined key performance indicators (KPIs), such as inflation control. This limits their ability to implement locally based policies to satisfy local needs. The "Kazakhstan 2050" strategy clearly states that decentralisation should not involve a lessening of vertical authority, or decrease executive discipline and order. OECD (2017) has found that *maslikhats* rarely play the role in oversight and accountability provided for them in Article 86 of the constitution, and play only an advisory role in the review of the local budgets, since the final decision rests with the *akimats*.

- The different efforts to reform the intergovernmental structure have led to a significant deconcentration of administrative functions to subnational levels of government. This means that there has been some transfer of authority and responsibility from central government to subnational levels, while maintaining the same hierarchical level of accountability from the local units to the central government ministry or agency. For example, tax collection is conducted by local agencies of the central government tax committee that are not accountable to any local authority. Nonetheless, deconcentration can be seen as the first step in a newly decentralising government to improve service delivery in the medium to long term.

Intergovernmental relations are based on hierarchical subordination

Intergovernmental relations should ensure that all mechanisms are set up for co-ordinating the work of all spheres of government in providing services and promoting development.

Central control over local decisions is considerable

A feature of Kazakhstan's system of local government is the subordination of lower levels of government to the level immediately above (OECD, 2017). As shown in Table 3.1, below the central government, each tier of government is subordinate to the one above it. This arrangement consolidates central control over local decisions and minimises the accountability of local executive bodies. This is amply illustrated in the cascading appointments of local executive body leadership, from the president on down to the local level, resulting in what is described as a "dominant vertical" (Linn, 2014).

Table 3.1. **Territorial structure of SNGs in Kazakhstan**

<table>
<tr><td colspan="5">Central government</td></tr>
<tr><td>First tier</td><td rowspan="4">Cities of republican significance (2)</td><td colspan="3">Oblast (14)</td></tr>
<tr><td>Second tier</td><td rowspan="3">Cities of oblast significance</td><td colspan="2">Rayons (177)</td></tr>
<tr><td>Third tier</td><td rowspan="2">Cities of rayon significance</td><td>Settlements</td></tr>
<tr><td>Fourth tier</td><td>Towns and villages</td></tr>
</table>

Note: Arrows show direction of influence. Central government has direct influence over oblasts and cities of republican significance.

Source: OECD (2017), adapted from The World Bank (2012), "Eurasian Cities: New Realities along the Silk Road", Europe and Central Asia Reports, The World Bank, Washington, DC.

These intergovernmental arrangements leave cities little room to decide on their own priorities and look for innovative local solutions to urban challenges. They have limited scope to regulate urban issues affecting their jurisdictions. Local administrative decisions on issues such as land use planning and management, environmental protection, local economic development and zoning normally need to be approved by upper levels of government, which are not always fully aware of the needs of the cities, settlements and villages. This subordinate relationship also affects how goods and services are procured. Greater flexibility in public service delivery is needed, because administrative autonomy over procurement processes is limited. This relationship even affects the way local governments manage their public workforce. There is little flexibility over civil service and employment policies. One problem is a lack of discretion over pay policy, since staff are paid from the money received from transfers. Administrative departments do not work in concert with their peers, but follow regulations, and instructions from equivalent departments at the higher level of government. Accountability is to the employer, in this case, the upper level of government. This leaves little room for accountability to citizens.

Possibilities for co-operation among regions and cities are very restricted

Official incentives for horizontal co-ordination among cities or among regions are non-existent. The governance arrangements – budget, administrative and political – prevent cities from working in co-ordination in projects that could lead to economies of scale. Budgets are not used to finance common projects such as transport or roads across cities. Roads are built only up to the geographic limits of the city or city administration. Legal obstacles, for instance the Budget Code, prevent the use of budgets for investment projects across cities or even regions. Under the current rules, each territory requires an administrator, but two administrators are not permitted to manage a project, so the project must be conducted under the auspices of the central government. No flexibility is granted to tailor the governance arrangements to the local area, and local co-operation is lacking. *Akims* have no incentives to work together; and since they are appointed and assessed by *akims* at the upper level, their relationships appear to be more competitive than co-operative. It is true that vertical co-ordination is mostly guaranteed through the way vertical relations work across levels of government. Small urban centres must be aligned with policies issued by the central government that may not reflect local needs. Moreover, small urban centres do not have the financial and operational capacity to implement centrally defined policies and strategies.

Nonetheless, in 2012, the national government implemented a three-year interregional pilot programme in East Kazakhstan. The President of the Republic stipulated that interregional co-operation should be emphasised. Co-operation agreements were signed to exchange products, and education and health care services among four regions. According to the Ministry of National Economy, trade volumes among the participating regions have increased as a result of the programme. Some oblast-*akimats* have signed Memorandums of Understanding to exchange experience, employment and trade, for example between the oblasts of Akmola and Almaty. Discussions to extend the programme are ongoing.

Enabling the governance environment for urbanisation

To prepare the ground for urbanisation and to put cities on a solid, functioning basis, Kazakhstan may wish to consider the following recommendations, based on the experience of OECD member countries.

Enhance local self-government and strengthen participatory forms of development

Efforts to improve urban governance should focus on strengthening local self-government and integrating urban communities into the decision-making process of urban development projects. Citizens should be provided with the opportunity to influence the executive branch. The key to this process is to give local *maslikhats* more responsibility for oversight of the *akim* and his local administration, and make them more accountable to the people. *Maslikhats* are key actors in reinforcing local self-government. They should be able to require *akimats* to implement laws, policies and programmes they have approved and hold the *akim* and his officials to account for their performance. In this respect, it is important to ensure that the *maslikhats* are able to assume their role as legislators.

Akims should be accountable to *maslikhats* for planning, financing, and the efficiency and effectiveness of service delivery. This would increase the democratic basis of SNGs. Kazakhstan should be commended for its reform calling for the election of rural *akims*, to strengthen local self-government. Building on this reform, Kazakhstan may consider, in the long term, the election of *akimats* at all levels (including those of Astana and Almaty) through the *maslikhats*, rather than appointment by the central government. A reform of this kind would increase the responsiveness of local governments to their citizens through democratic institutions, since members of the *maslikhat* are publicly elected. The aim would be to reinforce the weak local authorities and councils. This would be comparable to the Netherlands, where mayors are indirectly elected. In the United Kingdom, city mayors are also indirectly elected, but there have been efforts to strengthen democratic practices and in Bristol, London and Liverpool, citizens now directly elect mayors. Mayors who are directly elected have been determined to be better at sharing power with their councils, have effectively had more authority, and given more direction and a better performance in terms of internal management and of the quality of services provided (Finding, 2015). In Turkey, for example, mayors and municipal councils are publicly elected, but the central administration oversees mayors and has the power to remove from office local administrators who are being investigated or prosecuted for offences related to their duties (Union of Municipalities of Turkey, 2015). OECD (2017) notes that the election of *akims* will help build ties with local communities that have been undermined by the practice of appointing *akims* with little to no connection to their region or city.

Box 3.1. **Chile's municipal reform**

In 2014, Chile initiated a process to reform its municipal system. The objective of the reform is to transition to autonomous local governments, able to manage their own resources in an effective and efficient way, and contribute to inclusive economic and social strategic development of its citizens. The reform has four strategic aims:

- *Modernisation* – which focuses on the development of municipal human resources and the installation of a management model of municipal innovation, performing research and analysis.
- *Equity* – which concentrates on the diversity of each municipality, aiming to identify the differences in each municipality, in order to define the action that every municipality needs to take.
- *Autonomy* – which seeks to strengthen the autonomy of the municipalities through more powers, duties and responsibilities, to exercise effective and efficient management.
- *Accountability* – which aims at better management of financial resources, including the installation of a Council for General Government Internal Audit.

The specific objectives of the reform are to: i) establish a framework of fiscal responsibility for municipalities; ii) better manage resources and competences; iii) strengthen municipal human resources; iv) community participation and v) strategic planning through a model of municipal innovation management. Chile's national government established an Inter-Ministerial Committee for Municipal Modernisation as a decision-making, strategic body to implement the reform; and a Technical Advisory Committee for Municipal Modernisation to produce studies and make proposals for municipal modernisation. The technical committee is composed of a wide range of actors from academia, municipal organisations, think tanks, public employee organisations and so on.

Source: Ministry of Interior of Chile, Under-secretariat of Regional Development (SUBDERE), "From a State Administration to a Local Government", PowerPoint presentation; SUBDERE (2014); "Protocolo de Acuerdo para la Modernización Municipal', information provided by SUBDERE.

To enhance reforms for strengthening *rayon*-level governments, Kazakhstan could draw inspiration from the municipal reform in Chile, another unitary country. Its intent is to give Chilean municipalities the tools to become agents of local development, based on the problems, challenges and assets of each municipality (Box 3.1 above). Two main lessons emerge from the Chilean reform that Kazakhstan may wish to consider: i) strengthening municipal governments should be an inclusive process, in which a wide range of actors take part in the discussions; and ii) Chile, as a unitary country, has realised that if the country is to develop, it needs municipalities with strong administrative capacities that are accountable to voters. The reform is not intended to change the country's unitary system but aims for municipal governments with more flexibility and autonomy to manage their own resources and priorities.

Pursue reforms towards greater decentralisation with a more strategic edge

Increasing the process of decentralisation would give more freedom to SNGs to solve their own problems. The vision of "Kazakhstan 2050" envisages a more decentralised government system. As noted above, a deconcentrated system of government could facilitate the move towards actual decentralisation (see also Linn, 2014). Decentralisation should allow SNGs to assume control over the resources they administer and to become more accountable to citizens. The experience of OECD countries suggests that decentralisation needs to be sensitive to the existing cultural, political and institutional arrangements in a given country; it is not a one-off policy change but an ongoing process where the end point, accountable and efficient local governments, may take decades to achieve (Charbit, 2011).

Kazakhstan's decentralisation policy requires a decentralisation strategy. Decentralisation needs to be a flexible process, allowing the central/local dynamics to evolve and taking into consideration the potential instability of the political framework (Work, 2002). There should be a clear design for its implementation, with defined roles for the various management levels and linkages between them. A situation where local players do not have the authority to take decisions cannot lead to good governance. The capacities of SNGs for decentralisation should be fully assessed prior to implementation, and this process should build on existing institutional arrangements. In this sense, it is essential for Kazakhstan to carefully phase in the decentralisation process so that local capacities match local responsibilities (Linn, 2014). An asymmetric decentralisation of responsibilities can be an interesting way forward in devolving responsibilities to subnational governments, as is the case in Colombia (OECD, 2016b). Asymmetric governance approaches involve risks, in terms of creating institutional complexity and preferential treatments, but at the same time, they are ways to better take into account various territorial, political or cultural situations, as in OECD countries like France, Italy, Spain, Sweden and the United Kingdom. The central government could consider devolving more responsibilities to the more qualified oblasts and cities, and it can also identify sectors that can potentially be more efficiently managed at the municipal level. If competences are to be devolved, oblasts and cities need to comply with specific criteria defined by the national government. Moreover, Kazakhstan will need to ensure broad participation in the decentralisation process if it is to be successful. Support for decentralisation must be carefully mobilised among all critical actors, and the private sector must be recognised as a critical partner in the process. Decentralisation can facilitate empowerment and encourage creative solutions. For example, in Lublin, Poland, the Local Initiatives Programme has shown that participatory planning and community-based development processes adapted to the dynamics of the local economy can ensure the sustainability of the revitalisation effort with limited public input (Box 3.2).

Box 3.2. **Poland: Lublin's Local Initiatives Programme**

In Poland, the city of Lublin has succeeded in creating a framework to structure the interface between the municipality and the community, relying on participatory processes, partnership and empowerment. In 1990, the Urban Planning Unit of the city initiated a participatory process to engage residents in the development of their neighbourhood and to rehabilitate older districts. The new approach was initiated in two lower-income districts, Bronowice and Kosminek. In 1994, the Local Initiatives Programme was scaled up, to guarantee its continuity as a key environmental improvement strategy. The programme ensures that public and private stakeholders engage in cost-sharing partnerships to develop infrastructure and finance environmental improvements. Lublin has created an enabling environment for private investment in housing and microenterprises. In two years, 137 houses were renovated in the two pilot areas; 120 people started working in microenterprises, and several buildings have been converted to commercial use.

Source: UNESCO. For further information, see: www.unesco.org/most/easteur4.htm.

OECD (2016a) notes that decentralisation will enhance multi-level governance, referred to as the continuous interaction between governmental actors. In this case, it is necessary for Kazakhstan to establish the independent mechanisms for dispute resolution between levels of government, taking into consideration local circumstances; at present, resolution of disputes generally involves the central government and limited consideration of the local context.

Kazakhstan's authorities may wish to supplement the powers of local executive bodies to monitor heating, electricity, water supply and sanitation. This can be done independently or with the support of external auditors. As part of this process, city residents will need full and timely access to all the information, activities, policies and decisions of local self-government. The key issue in managing urban infrastructure is related to the limited powers and accountability of local authorities for infrastructure development. However, not all government functions should be fully decentralised. Critical functions should be retained at central government level if they are necessary to achieve the goals of the central government and they cannot be sustained at the local level, or if performance of the function falls short and is not cost-effective at the local level. Decentralisation should also be accompanied by the adequate provision of financial resources.

Adopt mechanisms for urban co-ordination to facilitate joint investments and develop metropolitan thinking

Lack of co-ordinated action among cities limits urban development and can lead to free-riding, where some cities refrain from action in the expectation that they will benefit from the actions of others. Thus, OECD (2015a) argues that identifying the incentives that shape the behaviour of people and institutions is critical to making co-operation and co-ordination operational. The experience of OECD countries suggests that contractual arrangements and financial transfers are key tools for co-operation and co-ordination. Contractual arrangements have been widely used as an instrument for carrying out joint action for regional development across levels of government, and OECD countries are also applying them at a metropolitan scale. The central government would need to commit to giving specific advantages to metropolitan areas in exchange for stronger co-operation among municipalities. Financial transfers could be designed to incentivise co-operation. For example, Mexico established a "metropolitan fund", the national government's way of transferring resources to cities for joint investment projects (OECD, 2015c). France established the inter-communality grant to municipalities willing to levy a joint business tax with neighbouring municipalities (OECD, 2015a). The United Kingdom introduced the "City Deals" agreements to give local areas specific powers and freedoms to help regions support economic growth, create jobs and invest in local projects.[4]

As Chapter 1 shows, the economic influence of some urban cores extends beyond their administrative borders, constituting a functional urban area (FUA). If productivity is to improve, these will need adequate governance arrangements, since several administrative authorities will be in play. One alternative for Kazakhstan's main FUAs is to think in metropolitan terms, co-ordinating service delivery across the metropolitan area and sharing costs. Kazakhstan may consider an urban governance reform at least for its largest cities, Astana, Almaty, Shymkent, Aktobe and even Turkestan, giving them the possibility to co-ordinate budgets, transport and spatial planning, and water and waste management with their respective neighbouring municipalities (villages, towns, etc). The idea would be to reduce the negative spill-overs across local boundaries and achieve economies of scale. Since local administrations are not autonomous, one option would be to adopt a one-tier, consolidated model of governance, setting up a metropolitan government with powers to deliver and raise revenues across the metropolitan area. Turkey's model of metropolitan municipalities offers one example of overcoming fragmentation and better aligning policies; it was first implemented in the three largest cities and subsequently expanded to others (Box 3.3). Another option would be a two-tier model with an upper tier providing for services that are region-wide and lower tiers providing for local services. This would be comparable to Barcelona, which has one metropolitan council and 36 lower tiers, and London, where the Greater London Authority includes 32 boroughs. The problem is that this model would only add to the already confusing and complex governance structure and to the costs and duplications of functions.

Box 3.3. **Turkey's metropolitan municipalities**

The concept of a metropolitan municipality was first introduced in 1984 for Istanbul, Ankara and Izmir, the three largest cities in Turkey. There are currently 30 metropolitan municipalities. The boundaries of metropolitan municipalities were extended to those of the respective provinces, and special and village administrations were abolished. The metropolitan municipality, as the sole local government in such provinces, took on the local government services for the entire province. It is responsible for rural and urban administration, and 77% of the total national population lives within the metropolitan boundaries.

The rationale for their introduction was that it was not possible to align services such as urban transport, infrastructure, water and sewerage networks, environmental and even land development of the various municipalities in the same space. Technically and for economies of scale, it is necessary to plan and manage the services for the entire urban space. A single administration is needed to plan and execute these services effectively and economically.

Source: Union of Municipalities of Turkey (2015), "Local Governments in Turkey", Ankara, www.tbb.gov.tr/online/yayinlar/local_government_inturkey/files/publication.pdf.

The urban governance system

The "Kazakhstan 2050: New Political Course of the Established State" has as an ultimate goal to make Kazakhstan one of the 30 most developed countries in the world.[5] National authorities have prioritised the establishment of a market economy in the political agenda, along with efforts to modernise public institutions and improve governance arrangements. The experience of OECD countries has shown that urban policies are a critical source of development and a tool for reducing inequality. They should thus be an integral component of development strategies.

Kazakhstan does not have a dedicated urban policy

Kazakhstan has no comprehensive strategic document clearly outlining the policy priorities of urbanisation, the role cities will play in the development process, and the institutional processes that will enable cities to build upon their assets and potential to achieve long-term sustainability. Urban development issues are referred to in the "Regional Development Programme until 2020" (RDP), in essence a public utilities programme. Several key national documents note the importance of regional, not urban, development, such as the "Kazakhstan 2050" strategy (and the "Concept of Joining the Top 30 Developed Countries"), the "Forecast Scheme of Territorial and Spatial Development of the Republic of Kazakhstan until 2020" and the "General Scheme of Organisation of the Territory until 2030."

The RDP aims to create favourable conditions for social and economic capacity building in the regions, by ensuring the sound organisation of the territory and providing incentives to concentrate population and capital in the economic growth centres. The RDP gives priority to infrastructure development in the economic growth centres, such as hub cities, agglomerations, regional centres, towns and single-industry cities (monotowns) and towns. The programme intends to improve living standards (infrastructure development of energy and heat sources, gas, heat, electricity and water supply and sewerage systems), build economic capacity and encourage the development of regions according to their functional type and economic potential. In addition, the RDP correlates with the key sector priorities specified in the effective national and sectoral programmes, in particular "Water Resource Management", "Business Roadmap 2020", "Employment Roadmap 2020", and "Agribusiness 2020".

Kazakhstan does not seem to have fully grasped the potential of urbanisation as a national development opportunity. The overall understanding the role of cities in national development is very limited. The RDP has no specific focus on the development of cities. Urban development is regarded as part – and not as a complement – of the regional policy of the country. Before 2016, there were plans for the development of the urban agglomerations, but they stalled because of the financial difficulties the country is now facing. Only the action plans for Shymkent and Aktobe, and interregional action plans for Astana and Almaty City are in place. Monotowns also have a comprehensive development plan. Long-term planning for investment projects on infrastructure such as transport, for instance, still presents a challenge. Cities are only allowed to plan for periods of three or four years, rather than 10- to 15-year periods. Almaty City has a general plan with a long-term focus (30 years) but the plans mainly concern cadastre and land-use planning. Neither intermediary planning cycles nor specific planning for transport issues have been adopted, to increase productivity and well-being. The efficiency of the transport systems, diversity of housing options, accessibility of schools, hospitals and working centres, and the quality of the environment are issues that are not clearly addressed in government's strategic planning documents.

The success of Kazakhstan's development will, to a large extent, depend on how well government is organised to govern the urbanisation process. The challenge is to develop policies, strategies, and instruments that will: improve the competitiveness of cities; make cities more sustainable and not impose the cost of development on the surrounding regions; encourage innovative, inclusive and flexible decision-making processes; build a balanced urban system that supports the needs and opportunities of medium-sized as well as large cities, and encourages effective networking between cities.

Urban development is still largely based on sectoral plans

The lack of a national urban policy is reflected in the mix of narrowly designed sectoral programmes mostly aiming for physical development of urban infrastructure. Urban development takes place in a setting where economic, social, environmental and physical development policies are disconnected from each other. The RDP has been greatly influenced by the prevailing sectoral policy approach in the central government. Between 2011 and 2014, the RDP was transformed from an urban and regional development programme into a collection of specific sectoral policies that had already existed, such as: the "Programme for the Development of Single-Industry Towns", "Modernisation of Housing and Communal Facilities 2011-2020", "Ak Bulak programme 2011-2020", and "Affordable Housing 2020 Programme". These sectoral policies were put together as part of the RDP, without any preliminary assessment of their efficiency. For instance, until recently, the "Ak Bulak" programme focused exclusively on supplying drinking water and did not include any assessment of the possible impact of subjecting the sewage system to increasing volumes of water. Now, most cities' sewage systems lack the capacity to cope with the growing amount of wastewater. The new mix of programmes, lacking internal coherence, was rolled out in a very brief period.

In cities, planning and co-ordinating work across departments is limited by the budget rules and the administrative organisation of the *akimats*. In general, each deputy *akimat* is in charge of its own departments, and reaching consensus on cross-cutting issues that require the intervention of several departments and budget lines is highly complex. Some issues are under the jurisdiction of the national government. For instance, in Almaty, transport policy is weakly integrated with other sectoral priorities such as the environment, because measuring air quality is the exclusive responsibility of the national government. The national government has the obligation to reduce the level of emissions, but its plans and strategies are not translated to the city level. Kazakova (2015) argues that one of the main problems of local governance is a formal approach to the planning process, as the work is often done without reference to real-life situations and without prior analysis and predesigned and well-calculated strategies.

National ministries responsible for developing and pursuing national policies still operate within their sectoral confines. The sectoral policies are usually implemented through provision of special national transfers for conducting certain projects in the selected localities. There is no evidence that former policies and programmes are assessed before being updated or discontinued, and financial concerns often carry more weight in deciding whether a programme should continue. The end of a national programme usually leads to the end of financial support provided to the cities. Today, the continuation of the RDP is under consideration because of the current budget deficit. The national government announced a financial cut-off of future activities included in the programme after 2016. At present, activities involving low-interest loans, through programmes such as "Business Road Map 2020" and "Road Map of Employment 2020" are funded by the National Fund. However, such minor restructuring of financial support, including short-term subsidies for urban development, do not create the opportunities for developing cities' strategic capacities to sustain urban development in the long term.

Weak co-ordination among central agencies is holding back urban development

In Kazakhstan's central government, a number of ministries are responsible for urban development issues. They all have implicit or explicit shared responsibility and authority for issues related to urban development. The problem, as in many OECD countries, is to ensure co-ordination and collaboration among all these upper-level actors. Moreover, the leadership of regional and urban development policy has been unstable. In 2013, the creation of the Ministry of Regional Development (MRD) was announced. This had all the levers for developing and implementing comprehensive urban and regional development policies, except for the allocation of revenue authority and budgetary transfers to SNGs. It was expected that MRD would facilitate the co-ordination and integration of fragmented government policies. However, in 2014, an administrative reform led to the MRD's merger with the Ministry of National Economy (MNE).

Box 3.4. **Kazakhstan's Ministry of National Economy**

The Decree of the President "On the reform of public administration of Kazakhstan" of 6 August 2014, No. 875, established the Ministry of National Economy (MNE). This is an institution with wide-ranging powers in public management that reports to the prime minister. To support the implementation of high-level documents, the ministry is responsible for the development, implementation, monitoring and evaluation of the "National Strategy 2020", developed in support of the "Kazakhstan Vision 2030" and "Vision 2050". The ministry serves as the government's technical advisor on the strategy's design, roll-out and performance assessment, and engages with government organisations to co-ordinate the implementation of strategic plans.

The MNE also has a wide range of responsibilities for formulating policies in the fields of public governance; tax; budget and customs policy; public and publicly guaranteed debt; state investment policy; public-private partnerships; business competition protection and restriction of monopolistic activity; international economic and financial relationships; management of state assets, including the development of the system of public governance; mobilisation and migration; e-government policy; and development of a green economy. With the 2014 administrative reform, the MNE acquired the functions of the Ministry of Economy and Budget Planning, except for its functions in the area of budget planning; the Ministry of Regional Development; in the formation and development of the state managerial reserve from the Ministry of Emergency Situations; Statistics Agency; Agency on Regulation of Natural Monopolies; Agency for Competition Pro (Anti-monopoly Agency); and the Agency for the Protection of Consumer Rights.

Source: Government of Kazakhstan.

The MNE is the central public agency in charge of formulating, implementing and co-ordinating regional development policy at the national level. Its task is to align regional and budget programmes. Its Committee for Construction, Housing, Public Utilities and Land Resource Management is in charge of leading implementation of the "Regional Development Programme until 2020". It could be argued that merging the MRD into the MNE a year after its creation did not position urban development issues prominently in the political agenda and in public awareness.

Table 3.2. **Central government bodies involved in urban development in Kazakhstan**

Government body	Responsibilities
Ministry of National Economy	National executive agency in charge of: regional development; private sector promotion; architecture, urban planning, construction; housing and public utilities; the supply of water, sewerage, electricity, heat and gas in residential areas; land management; geodesic and cartographic activities.
Ministry of Investments and Development	Provides guidance in areas such as: industrial development; scientific and technological development; investment policy and promotion of a favourable investment climate; sustainable and multipurpose subsoil use; government control of use of underground water; energy efficiency; tourism; railway, road and inland water transport.
Ministry of Health and Social Development	Health care; labour; migration and social protection.
Ministry of Education and Science	Human capital development; implementation of education and science policy to enhance competitiveness and ensure sustainable social and economic growth.
Ministry of Energy	Environmental protection and environmental management; protection, control and supervision of the sustainable use of natural resources; solid household waste management; renewable power development; control of green economy policies.
Ministry of Internal Affairs	Intergovernmental co-ordination for crime prevention, enforcement of public order and maintenance of public security, and internal migration.
Ministry of Finance	Intergovernmental co-ordination in budget planning, budget performance, accounting and financial reporting on national and local budget performance; accounting and financial reporting of the National Fund; public procurement; national assets. Takes part in tax and customs policy.
Ministry of Agriculture	Water management; land-use management; management of natural reserves.
Ministry of Culture and Sports	Inter-ethnic harmony, development of languages and national symbols.

Source: Answers provided to the OECD background questionnaire by the Ministry of National Economy of Kazakhstan.

The large number of actors involved in urban policies poses a co-ordination challenge, as it is necessary to ensure policy consistency to ensure positive outcomes. However, the OECD Review of the Central Administration in Kazakhstan found co-operation weaknesses across central ministries. The problem is that relations between ministries are confined within the framework of their respective strategic plans. Once their strategic objectives have been set, ministries operate within sectoral silos, and there is little exchange of information at the level of policy implementation and monitoring. OECD (2014a) noted that although there have been some improvements in the collaboration across ministries in central government, there are still significant barriers for co-operation and collaboration, such as: i) incompatibility of systems and other restrictions on sharing information across ministries; ii) different organisational cultures; iii) the division of whole-of-government budget into separate ministerial allocations; iv) public managers who only have experience within a single ministry, (due to frequent staff turnover, there is weak institutional memory); and v) accountability structures that focus mainly on ministry-specific issues. The fragmented nature of the government may in turn inhibit resolution of problems and issues that cross departmental boundaries.

Urban development requires clear policy direction, in line with the New Urban Agenda and the UN SDGs

Kazakhstan would benefit from adopting a comprehensive urbanisation policy framework that clearly formulates policy direction, concepts and strategies of urban and spatial development (i.e. urban governance, urban economy strategies, local self-government powers, urban budgets, financing instruments for urban infrastructure and so on). The "New Urban Agenda" and the "UN Sustainable Development Goals" (SDGs) could be a guiding source. As UN-Habitat states, a national urban policy provides the general framework to orient public interventions in urban areas and is a reference for sectoral ministries and service providers, as well as for legislative institutional reform (Box 3.5). Developing an integrated urban policy framework could be key to promoting development in the three major cities, Almaty, Astana and Shymkent, by channelling core investments into their development. However, it is important that the urban policy framework foresees a gradual support for the development of small and medium-sized towns that could also become poles of sustainable growth. This decision should be based on the available resources, capabilities and potential of cities and regions (CER, ESCAP, UNDP, 2013). By adopting an explicit urban policy framework, Kazakhstan would be following the path of several OECD countries, such as Australia, Chile, France, the Netherlands and Poland, which have formulated extensive and explicit national urban policies. Their experience shows that a national urban policy framework gives more room for manoeuvre for the cities and sometimes regions to pursue initiatives for urban development and gives more national attention for bottom-up initiatives of development. A national urban policy framework encourages cities to come up with original initiatives of development and may even influence the urban policy agenda.

Kazakhstan could make sure that the development of a national urban policy contributes to the achievement of UN Sustainable Development Goals (SDGs) – in particular Goal 11 on making cities inclusive, safe, resilient and sustainable.[6] The SDG 11 and its goals, which cover housing, transport, urban planning, environment and safety, could be used as a guideline to build a national urban policy framework. The key questions should be how these targets could be achieved in Kazakhstan, how they could be translated into concrete actions at city level, and how the national government can support cities to achieve them.

Box 3.5. **The development of a national urban policy**

The development of a national urban policy is the key step in providing a new direction for urban space and territoriality. It will also be vital in providing a course of action for urban development. The National Urban Policy should provide an overarching co-ordinating framework to deal with the most pressing issues related to rapid urban development, including slum prevention and regularisation, access to land, basic services and infrastructure, urban legislation, delegation of authority to subnational and local governments, financial flows, urban planning regulations, urban mobility and urban energy requirements, as well as job creation. The development of a national urban policy should: i) identify urban development priorities; ii) guide future development; iii) enhance co-ordination; and iv) increase co-ordinated investments.

Source: UN Habitat, National Urban Policies, http://unhabitat.org/urban-initiatives/initiatives-programmes/national-urban-policies/.

Adopting an explicit and comprehensive programme of urban development would require an increased role for local authorities at the *oblast*, *rayon* and even town levels, which should become co-ordinating centres for directing investment to the selected cities that can drive growth (CER, ESCAP, UNDP, 2013). Without a co-ordinated effort by central government and SNGs, distributing productive forces to create growth poles could be fruitless, and the potential of leading cities could be diminished. OECD work has shown that the most competitive regions also have the most competitive cities. Since cities and regions have common interests, conflict between urban and regional policy should not be add odds. Australia's National Urban Policy offers an example of the scope and strategic character of such an instrument (Box 3.6).

Box 3.6. Australia's national urban policy and the "Smart Cities Plan"

In April 2016, Australia's prime minister presented a new national urban policy, the "Smart Cities Plan". This sets out the government's vision for cities and a plan to maximise their potential. It is intended to inform planning and investment in the country's largest cities as well as its smaller regional cities and is based on three pillars:

1. *Smart Investment*, which emphasises financing mechanisms in projects that meet broader economic and city objectives, such as accessibility, jobs, affordable housing and healthy environments. Infrastructure funding is treated as a long-term investment, and the plan is to ensure that projects create opportunities for urban renewal and raise private capital. Using innovative financing approaches such as value capture, the government aims to leverage the balance sheet and deliver more essential infrastructure sooner.
2. *Smart Policy*, which proposes a "City Deals" mechanism to unlock public and private investment in key economic centres. By incentivising reforms, i.e. regulatory reform and decreasing government fragmentation at the metropolitan level, the government expects to generate additional benefits for the economy, making cities better places to live and do business. Data collection and analysis of the cities' performance is to be conducted to measure the success of the policies and respond to new needs.
3. *Smart Technology*, which focuses on embracing new technology with the potential to revolutionise how cities are planned and operate, and how the economy runs. The government aims to make use of new technology in transport, communications and energy efficiency, to improve the sustainability of cities and drive innovation.

One notable aspect of the *Smart Cities Plan* is that it calls for the active participation of the private sector and other stakeholders, particularly in terms of financing for investment. The plan was subject to an eight-week comment period and its website actively encouraged feedback from the public.

Source: Commonwealth of Australia (2016), *Smart Cities Plan*, Department of the Prime Minister and Cabinet, https://cities.dpmc.gov.au/smart-cities-plan (accessed 22 November 2016).

Diversify mechanisms for horizontal co-ordination at the central level for urban policy

OECD (2014a) has already recommended solidifying mechanisms for horizontal collaboration among ministries, including by creating ministerial posts for cross-cutting issues, strengthening accountability frameworks for horizontal activities, and developing rotations for government managers and policy communities to reinforce the capacity of the central government. The same recommendations apply to national urban development, but they might be complemented with the following actions:

Grant the leadership of regional and urban development a strong mandate, to provide stability

To drive urban policy initiatives, Kazakhstan might do well to create a central urban and regional development policy body with a long-term national vision. Two options could be suggested: the first to reinstall the Ministry of Regional Development as the Ministry for Urban and Regional Development, with responsibility for linking urban and regional policy objectives to broader governmental goals and co-ordinating urban policy. Many OECD countries have a central body for regional and urban development, including Chile (Ministry of Housing and Urbanisation), France (Ministry of Housing and Habitat), Mexico (Secretariat of Agrarian, Territorial and Urban Development), Spain,

(Ministry of Public Works and Urbanisation) and the United States (Secretariat of Housing and Urban Development). The new Ministry of Urban and Regional Development would focus on urban, regional and decentralisation issues at the ministerial level, and co-ordinate planning and implementation across the many government agencies currently engaged in the area. A second option would be to reorganise the Directorate of Regional Development and Local Self-Government and the Committee for Construction, Housing, Public Utilities and Land Resource Management, both within the MNE, and ensure they work in close co-ordination. A new Directorate General for Urban and Regional Development could be established, focusing on strategy, planning, policy formulation, and monitoring and evaluation of implementation, rather than getting into the daily operational work, which could be delegated to agencies and SNGs.[7]

The central body for urban and regional development should act within a policy framework giving it a clear mandate for its activities. It should also have a medium and long-term action plan to achieve government's goals in the area and to assess how well they succeed. It must assume a co-ordination role in implementing regional and urban policies, by providing guidelines, technical support and feedback, mostly to SNGs. Its oversight role should not necessarily be transaction-oriented, but may instead rely on strategic monitoring and measurement of results and risks. It is important that this body have the financial and human resources to conduct its activities in a professional way, and it should have the mandate and capacity to formulate urban policy.

Promote cross-sectoral planning for urban policy development

To facilitate cross-sectoral planning for urban development, Kazakhstan authorities need to ensure that each sector has a comprehensive understanding of the other sectors' roles, responsibilities, legal authorities and assets. The MNE, as the lead body held accountable for regional and urban development, has a key role to play in ensuring that different sectors are consulted when conducting urban planning. The experience of OECD countries suggests that for horizontal co-ordination to achieve results, it must be carried out across the different levels of government by government itself. High-level committees, working groups and bilateral partnerships are set up to supervise co-ordination. Kazakhstan could draw inspiration from the experience of Sweden's National Board of Housing, Building and Planning, a platform for greater collaboration, co-ordination, knowledge development, dissemination of knowledge and exchange of experience for sustainable urban development. This is an important link between practice and politics at the local, regional and national level, and it is a meeting place for local and regional initiatives. The platform is co-ordinated by the Swedish Energy Agency and the Swedish Agency for Economic and Regional Growth, as well as the Swedish Transport Administration.[8]

Kazakhstan could also invest in establishing network-based arrangements for urban development as a major co-ordination mechanism across policy sectors. It may be necessary to have a formal specification of the leadership and decision-making role of the co-ordinating body, MNE, in the legislation or in a Memorandum of Understanding (MoU). A MoU could be established with each participating agent in the network, to encourage delivery of concrete results, establish their accountability and work collectively to achieve shared objectives. The political support of the President's Administration Office would play a key role in ensuring commitment from different actors. Kazakhstan's central government may also consider establishing, with the political support of the prime minister, a National Urban and Regional Development Co-ordination Council. This would include a decision-making hierarchy for achieving better results in urban development and develop a co-ordinated urban strategy and common targets, agreed upon across government. These national co-ordinating arrangements and structures would be an extension of the accountable lead body (the MNE) that manages them and could be used as platforms for agreeing and reviewing national regional and urban development policies and programmes; mobilising resources, co-ordinating multisectoral partnerships; and consulting with a wider group of stakeholders. The hierarchy would include three levels, as shown in Table 3.3. The Co-ordination Council's key contribution would be to ensure that policies are designed and implemented in a clear, open and transparent manner conducive to policy integration, thereby contributing to sustainable development.

Table 3.3. **Proposal for a National Urban and Regional Development Co-ordination Council for Kazakhstan**

Secretariat	Body	Role
	Urban and Regional Development Executive Committee Representation at ministerial level of the ministries of: National Economy, Investment and Development, Health and Social Development, Education and Science, Energy, Internal Affairs, Finance, Civil Service and Anti-Corruption, President's Administration Office	*Its role would be to agree on, co-ordinate and communicate top-level strategies on regional and urban development among ministries. It should align all actors on a long-term vision of regional and urban development with specific roles. The Executive Committee could assess how the Regional Development Programme is contributing to the "Kazakhstan 2050" strategic directions. The participation of the President's Administration Office would help to communicate high-level political support. It could meet three to four times a year and be chaired by MNE.*
Co-ordination Secretariat Provided by the lead regional and urban lead body: Ministry of National Economy (MNE) which may have a dedicated unit in charge of the organisation of the works of the Co-ordination Council.	**Urban and Regional Development Managers' Working Group** Representation at technical level/ senior managers from the ministries of: National Economy, Investment and Development, Health and Social Development, Education and Science, Energy, Internal Affairs, Finance, Civil Service and Anti-Corruption	*This would be the hub for cross-sectoral co-ordination for regional and urban development. It could meet monthly and comprise senior managers from each ministry/agency with responsibilities for day-to-day urban development related-issues. It should co-ordinate the implementation of the Regional Development Programme, conduct reviews, identify priorities, and promote and monitor a co-ordinated country-wide programme of activities. It could establish technical working groups to assist its activities. It should also follow up on actions of the different parties involved under the framework of the agenda of regional and urban development. Officials of the largest cities (Astana, Almaty, Shymkent and Turkestan) and private actors may be invited to some meetings when important urban/infrastructure projects are discussed, for example Almaty's new tram line, or the preparations for the Astana World Expo 2017. The MNE should chair.*
	Urban and Regional Advisory Group Experts and scientific organisations	*This would be a consultative body including all main regional and urban development stakeholders, including the private, business, academia and experts. It could meet twice a year, with the MNE as Chair.*

To meet the objectives of the Co-ordination Council, the decisions taken in the executive committee and the working groups should be binding. The findings and recommendations that the Council provides could be used to revise the Regional Development Programme and other related programmes. The Co-ordination Council could monitor how all participants contribute to the main cross-cutting urban and regional development priorities. To strengthen cross-sectoral planning for urban development, it would be critical to identify gaps in existing legal authorities and tools for co-ordinated response to urban planning, involving several sectors. It may also be necessary to develop communication plans involving agencies and organisations in different sectors.

Create platforms to share best practices, promote regional/urban development and present a collective voice on subnational matters

Interviews for this review revealed that there is no formal platform or forum where local executives get together to discuss common problems and share experiences and best practices on urban development. It would be relevant for local executives (*akims*) to have the possibility of meeting regularly with their peers from other *oblasts* or *rayons* to create networks for local development. Across OECD countries, a wide range of associations of subnational executives exist, some for regional authorities (governors), others for municipal presidents (mayors) and others exclusively for cities. Kazakhstan could, for example, create an association of cities composed of the 38 large cities of *oblast* significance and 47 cities of district significance; Astana and Almaty should also be invited to join. Such an association would advocate the interests of its members towards central government; advise and inform its members about developments of importance to local government; and facilitate an exchange of experience between its members on urban development issues, as well as on issues of practical day-to-day management. In some OECD countries, such associations organise training courses for members, which could be important in Kazakhstan's cities as part of the efforts to improve capacity. Another option could be the creation of an association of the 27 monotowns, whose aim would be to assess the effectiveness of the Monotowns Development Programme, share experiences and learn from each other. Box 3.7 presents some examples of municipal or governors associations in OECD federal and unitary countries that Kazakhstan could use as an inspiration.

Box 3.7. **Associations of governors and municipalities in OECD countries**

In **the United States**, the National Governors Association (NGA) is a bipartisan organisation of the nation's governors that promotes visionary leadership, shares best practices and speaks with a collective voice on national policy. Governors convene at NGA twice a year. NGA has a Centre for Best Practices that helps governors and their key policy staff develop and implement solutions to governance and policy challenges in their states.

In **the United Kingdom**, Core Cities is an association of the 10 economically important cities in the country that does not include London. The 10 Core Cities urban areas deliver 28% of the combined economic output of England, Wales and Scotland (26.5% of the UK economy) and have a population of almost 19 million people, 30.7% of the combined English, Welsh and Scottish population (29.8% of the UK's population). The association works as a voice for its cities, maintaining dialogue with the government, members of Parliament, national agencies and business representatives, to create a policy environment for cities to thrive. It provides a forum to share and explore ideas and best practices, driving improvement and efficiency.

In **Turkey**, the Union of Municipalities of Turkey is the sole nation-wide local government association that represents municipalities. It protects the interests of municipalities, provides guidance, assists in development efforts, conducts lobbying on behalf of the municipalities, provides training to municipal staff and promotes inter-municipal co-operation, exchange of information and expertise. It also assists its members through free distribution of software used in municipal services, emergency financial and /or material assistance, and advice on legal matters.

Box 3.7. **Associations of governors and municipalities in OECD countries** (*cont.*)

In **Norway**, *KS*, an association founded in 1972, includes all 428 municipalities and 19 counties as well as over 500 public enterprises. Its vision is to have an independent and innovative local government sector. Its activities include consultation with government, regional development, training and development programmes for elected councillors and administrative staff, the promotion of sustainable community development and local democracy.

Source: National Governors Association, www.nga.org/cms/home.html; Core Cities, www.corecities.com; Union of Municipalities of Turkey www.tbb.gov.tr/online/yayinlar/local_government_inturkey/files/publication.pdf; Norway's KS, www.ks.no/.

Promote information sharing between regional and urban development actors, reinforcing horizontal integration

Given the large number of institutions involved in regional and urban development, Kazakhstan may consider taking steps towards greater horizontal integration by sharing processes and practices. There is enormous potential for quality improvement and savings through the horizontal integration of policy execution through, for instance, e-government projects based on common portals. In the short term, Kazakhstan may consider following the Danish example of focusing on virtual "seamless interaction", which leaves the institutional arrangement as it is but guarantees easy communication across government bodies and easy access for citizens to government services (Box 3.8). For ministries to be willing to share information, a clear presidential instruction and follow-up would be essential. The President's Administration Office may need to assume the role of a facilitator of information sharing across ministries.

Box 3.8. **Denmark's horizontal integration initiatives**

In **Denmark**, emphasis has been placed on using ICT to create seamless horizontal government. Horizontal integration across government through enhanced ICT standard setting by the Ministry of Finance, facilitating communication between all government units (central and local). The use of common e-government components across the public sector or within selected domains can not only increase efficiency (and in some cases significantly cut costs) but also help make the public sector more transparent to citizens and businesses. A strict condition for the development of e-government initiatives in Denmark is to show that they can lead to savings.

Source: OECD (2012), *Value for Money in Government: Denmark 2011*, OECD Publishing, Paris, http://dx.doi.org/10.1787/9789264130746-en.

Strengthening accountability for urban development across ministries and agencies

Strengthening accountability for urban development is critical for designing incentives for collaboration and effective joint action. It is thus important, as OECD (2014a) has noted, to focus the conception and development of policy proposals on collective ministerial responsibility, to serve the broader public interest and to work across institutional lines to develop the best possible policy. There should be a balance in fulfilling individual accountabilities to their stakeholders and collective responsibilities to the broader public interest. To reinforce accountability, ministries should be clearly briefed on their areas of responsibility and how they are expected to contribute to cross-cutting issues such as urban development. The mandates and performance agreements of ministers and their deputies could explicitly reflect the need to work together and with central agencies. They could then manage the Regional Development Programme and related programmes and plans, in order to optimise the capacity of government to set, implement and monitor regional and urban policies to contribute to the performance of the President's Agenda and the "Kazakhstan 2050" strategy. It is important that collaboration across ministries and central agencies be strategic rather than issues-based and take a whole-of-government approach. Ministries should be given the possibility to innovate by finding different ways to address policy issues in concert.

Continuously refine legislation on urban development

To facilitate subnational governments' task in the urbanisation process of Kazakhstan, continuous efforts are needed to refine legislation on urban and regional development, in particular the Law of 16 July 2001, "On Architectural, Urban Planning and Construction Activities in the Republic of Kazakhstan". The aim would be to improve procedures for registering and record-keeping on, for instance, internal migration, to help optimise the development of urban infrastructure, the design of adaptation programmes and social planning. Legislation should also be revised to help build an urban statistical system to provide reliable data on a wide range of issues, such as urban infrastructure, migration, employment, housing and commuting patterns. Legislation could also be revised to build the linkages between large cities on the one hand and medium and small cities on the other. This would give a legal incentive to boost co-ordination among subnational governments to invest in common urban infrastructure and public service provision.

Data collection for public policy monitoring and assessment needs to be enhanced

To promote sustainable, inclusive urban development, policy making should be based on hard evidence (data). Kazakova (2015) argues that Kazakhstan needs to improve the efficiency of data collection at the city level and to provide reliable quantitative analyses of urban issues. These should be the basis for realistic, efficient urban development planning, regular monitoring and objective assessment. For example, building databases on cities and facilitating the access to information, city authorities and civil society organisations could have critical input in modernising urban infrastructure, improving the quality of public services and looking for sources of funding. Data at city level will also stress the main priorities for cities to focus on, as well as where the local public administration should focus in terms of professional training of civil servants.

The lack of monitoring and assessment of policies during their implementation phase is another major stumbling block in pursuing efficient urban policy. The national government adopts new programmes without examining the effects of the previous ones. This has negative consequences for the effectiveness of spending, as no targeted corrections can be taken during policy implementation. Moreover, policy makers do not always have at their disposal information (facts, indicators) upon which to draw conclusions for decision making. The information may not always be readily available to public servants and the public. To monitor and assess urban policies, an integrated statistical database on urban demography, migration, the economy and other indicators of well-being is needed. These data should be regularly updated and made accessible on a website managed by the Statistics Committee. Developing performance indicators can build capacity and improve subnational spending efficiency through competition and learning among *oblasts* and *rayons*. Norway's KOSTRA system, for example, has helped Norwegian municipalities (Box 3.9) provide municipalities with a tool for internal planning, budgeting and benchmarking. It has also helped the central government assess whether municipalities are complying with national standards and regulations and evaluate their needs for federal funding.

Box 3.9. **KOSTRA, Norway's data reporting and information system**

Norway's KOSTRA system is an OECD-area best practice. KOSTRA (Local Governments-State-Reporting) is a national system that provides information on the use of resources by the municipal and county authorities. It is based on consecutive data records and annual reports to Statistics Norway by local authorities. The data includes financial data and data on service provision. Statistics Norway compiles these with other data, such as population figures, and generates key figures for priorities, coverage rates and productivity/efficiency regarding public services. The key indicators are published online in a format that makes it possible to compare the use of resources by similar municipalities. This helps local authorities identify areas where resources can be used more effectively.

KOSTRA integrates information from local government accounts, service statistics and population statistics. It includes indicators of production, service coverage, needs, quality and efficiency. The information is easily accessible online and facilitates detailed comparison of the performance of local governments. The information is frequently used by local governments, as well as by the media and researchers. Although individual local governments could use KOSTRA more efficiently (e.g. by systematic benchmarking), the system has helped facilitate comparisons of municipalities, promoting "bench-learning" or "bench-marketing".

Source: Government of Norway, (2007), *KOSTRA (local governments-State-Reporting)* www.regjeringen.no/en/dep/kmd/subjects/municipal-economy/kostra-municipality--state-reporting.html?id=1233, (accessed 21 July 2016); and OECD (2010b), *Finland: Working Together to Sustain Success*, OECD Publishing, Paris, http://dx.doi.org/10.1787/9789264086081-en.

Paying for urbanisation

Good urban governance depends to a large extent on the quality of the financial mechanisms available to cities. It is essential that cities have significant resources of their own. Moreover, a clear distribution of responsibilities is the base for determining responsibility for expenditures, an issue many countries find problematic. According to the World Bank (2014), generally, the central government should be involved in overall policy, setting standards and auditing; state governments should have oversight functions; and local governments should be involved in the provision of infrastructure and services.

A dependency on central government transfers

In general, Kazakhstan's SNGs lack the financial resources to carry out their comprehensive development plans. The structure of the intergovernmental finance system inhibits the decentralisation of decision making and provision of services.

Funding of public services is left to inter-governmental transfers and vertical programmes

In Kazakhstan, SNGs' total revenue represented 9.5% of GDP and 37.2% of public revenue in 2013. This is lower than in OECD countries, where subnational government revenue represents 16% of GDP and 42.3% of public revenue on average (OECD, 2016c). A large portion of subnational revenue consists of transfers from the national budget, which represent one-third of total revenues of the central government (OECD, 2017, forthcoming). Research shows that 13 of Kazakhstan's 16 regions depend on subsidies from the national government, indicating a shortage of internal financial resources and a lack of incentives to develop their own tax base (Kysykov, 2013). Table 3.4 shows that almost 40% of SNGs' total revenue is self-generated – mainly tax-sharing arrangements – while almost 60% is transfers.[9] Across OECD countries, the average is 44% and 38% respectively; in OECD unitary countries, such as Iceland, Sweden and New Zealand, tax revenue as a percentage of local revenue ranges from more than 50% to less than 15% in Estonia, the Netherlands, Turkey and the United Kingdom, (OECD, 2016c).

Table 3.4. **Revenue of Kazakhstan's SNGs**

	Subnational revenue		
	% GDP	**% general government** (same revenue category)	**% subnational government**
Total revenue (2013)	**9.5**	**37.2**	**100**
Tax revenue	3.7	17.8	38.7
Grants and subsidies	5.6	-	59.4
Other revenues	0.2	-	1.9

Source: OECD/UCLG (2016), "Subnational Governments around the World: Structure and Finance", OECD, Paris, www.uclg-localfinance.org/sites/default/files/Observatory_web_0.pdf.

Kazakhstan's SNGs receive all kinds of transfers, including: inter-governmental grants, subsidies, subventions, donations and sharing of tax revenues. In 2012, on average, 49% of the transfers granted to SNGs were non-targeted (non-earmarked), 47% were targeted (earmarked) and 4% were loans from upper level governments. However, targeted transfers vary from year to year and from region to region. The Budget Policy Department within the MNE is responsible for managing the inter-budget relationship between the national budget and the oblast budgets. It decides on the general transfers (non-earmarked) from national to regional budgets to satisfy the needs of the region. General transfers are decided through a formula that projects revenues and expenses. The level of expenditure is largely calculated on the basis of the previous year's data, with adjustment for inflation. The existing methodology for calculating transfers of a general character is mostly based on revenues from previous years and does not allow oblasts and cities to augment their own resources.

The 16 oblast governments have the right to obtain specific transfers and loans from the Ministry of Finance. For example, Almaty received specific transfers from the national budget to build the underground and the facilities for the university games. Specific transfers (earmarked) cannot be used to compensate for budget deficits and are approved depending on the importance of the project in meeting social, education, health and housing construction objectives. Specific transfers are determined by the Ministry of Finance. A variety of other earmarked transfers exist, the largest being the targeted investment transfer to fund regional and local infrastructure and exceptional expenditures (e.g. hosting a large international sporting event). All in all, in 2013, capital grants accounted for 28% of transfers, whereas 72% were current grants.

The methodology for revenue redistribution across regions lacks clarity

The most important taxes go to the central government budget and are distributed to regional governments. Regions contribute to the budget at different levels, and it is necessary to equalise their budget income. In Kazakhstan, the disparities in regional development are the basis of the unequal revenue position of local budgets and thus determine the essential role of interbudget relations, such as subsidies and earmark transfers. Transfers to SNGs thus include funds from the equalisation of *oblasts*' tax revenues to reduce disparities. On the whole, general (non-earmarked) budget transfers are based on a complex system of formulas that tries to capture the difference in the cost of providing public services in each *oblast*, district or city. This system has three major features: i) it is has no component that takes into account the performance assessment of subnational budget spending or the quality of public services delivered by subnational governments (user satisfaction, etc.); ii) it leaves considerable discretionary power to the national and the *oblast* levels, to adjust the level of budget transfers to the lower level of government; and iii) all other things (such as density and population) being equal, a higher official urbanisation rate leads to higher budget transfers, and the status of city of oblast significance can also unlock additional budget transfers.

Box 3.10. **Methodology to determine general (non-earmarked) transfers in Kazakhstan**

This methodology applies for general (non-earmarked) transfers from the national budget to oblasts, Almaty City and Astana (TL2), and also from the *oblast* level to district (*rayons*) and the 38 cities of oblast significance (TL3). Forecast revenues and expenditures are determined for a three-year period, and general transfers are simply the difference between forecast revenues and forecast expenditures. If forecast revenues exceed forecast expenditures (in the case of "donor" regions), the difference is withdrawn and allocated to the budget of the superior level (from oblast to the national budget, or from districts/cities of *oblast* significance to the oblast level). Forecast revenues are largely determined by the relative economic development of territories/cities and their tax base. All things being equal, higher forecast expenditures translate into more budget transfers (or decreased budget withdrawals for donor regions).

Coefficients are supposed to reflect objective cost differences in public service delivery between oblasts, districts and cities of oblast significance. Different coefficients are applied to each expenditure item. For instance, there is a coefficient for urbanisation, based on the official urbanisation rate, to compensate for the higher cost of service delivery in urban areas.

Source: Ministry of National Economy (2014), Order No. 139, available (in Russian) at: http://adilet.zan.kz/rus/docs/V1400010068#z35 and Budget Code, available at: http://adilet.zan.kz/eng/docs/K080000095.

Revenue in excess of forecast expenditure of a local budget is withdrawn and paid into the budget of the central government. Since 1999, oblasts with high revenue-generating capacity have a part of their income deducted and paid into the national budget. These so-called "donors", Astana, Almaty, Atyrau and Mangystau, help to subsidise low-income *oblasts*. The consequence has been to discourage initiative on the part of local authorities, undermining their interest in expanding their own tax base and improving tax collection (Kysykov, 2013). The calculation is done during the annual budget process, based on oblasts' projected expenditures and revenues. When an oblast's expenditure exceeds revenues, it receives additional funds (subsidies). If it produces extra revenues, oblasts are subject to withdrawals, retaining only the amounts they need to finance their expected expenditure. Estimates are largely derived from historical trends and inflation. The weakness of this arrangement is that the methodology used by the

MNE is not understood by all SNGs and changes every three years. Interviews suggest that the problematic feature of the methodology is the coefficient used to determine the amount of money withdrawn from "donors" to the national budget. Moreover, OECD (2017, forthcoming) has noted that this mechanism does not take into account a region's actions or particularities, and acts as a disincentive for using resources efficiently. In addition, the lack of clarity may leave room for mismanagement. Almaty, for instance, had a budget of KZT 1.3 trillion (about USD 3.9 billion) in 2015, of which KZT 1 billion was paid into the national budget and the rest kept for the city budget. Projects like the new Almaty airport are financed through the national budget. To increase its revenues under the current fiscal framework, Almaty would need to diversify its economy by attracting innovative technologies through initiatives such as the Techno Park and the industrial park. In 2015, Astana became a donor to the national budget. Each year, the number of jobs in the city has risen, as have city revenues.

The intergovernmental transfer system needs to be restructured to promote a metropolitan strategy…

Ensuring that SNGs have enough resources for urban development requires restructuring the intergovernmental transfer system. However, it is important that Kazakhstan focus on developing a metropolitan strategy and recognise the wide disparities in economic development and income in its different regions and cities. One option would be to redesign the transfer system to make it asymmetrical, with the largest and more developed regions and cities treated under a regime different from other local governments'. "Donor" regions and/or the four largest cities would be gradually weaned from transfers, while ensuring that they had enough authority to impose taxes and user charges. A hard budget constraint with no "back door" for financing deficits would be part of this strategy. The aim would be to shift the financing of infrastructure investment in the largest urban areas from transfers towards debt finance, where borrowing was supported by locally raised revenues. Transfers are unlikely to disappear entirely as a financing source, as there will always be externalities, and local budgets may not be high enough to pay for urban infrastructure such as transport and the expansion and maintenance of public utilities. The goal would be to reduce non-targeted grants dramatically and focus the central government's attention on other regions and cities. With a separate regime, it would be possible for the central government to transfer resources to areas that rely more on grants. This could also allow the central government to provide incentives for regional taxes and greater tax effort. Turkey, for example, has an intergovernmental transfer model with predefined criteria and weights. The allocation is based on formulas that cover population, area and development level of the municipalities.[10]

To restructure the intergovernmental transfer system, two essential reforms would be necessary. The first would be to explicitly grant regions and cities, particularly the largest ones, the authority to set taxes and fees and modify the rates. Almaty, Astana, Shymkent and Aktobe, for example, could be granted greater fiscal autonomy, greater ability to levy own taxes, collect own revenues and borrow for capital expenditure, reducing their dependence on transfers by comparison with other urban areas. They should also have greater responsibility for local services, and will need a governance structure that allows them to levy taxes and provide certain services (such as public transport) on a metropolitan-wide scale. The Tax Commission could still collect the taxes and fees on behalf of those governments – as it has the technical capacity to do – but resources should be sent to the local government. The second reform needed is to allow local governments to borrow not only from the budget of higher-level governments but from the national capital market, carefully monitored by the Ministry of Finance.

...and the monitoring of the use of earmarked grants in the implementation of national urban objectives

Kazakhstan's central government may wish to consider collecting performance information on the use of earmarked grants given to SNGs, to analyse how local actions contribute to national urban development strategy. This performance information could be used to improve programmes or redefine minimum standards in service delivery. Central government authorities may wish to link the monitoring of performance closely to the attribution of grants, as part of the budget cycle. The experience of OECD countries suggests that linking this closely is often necessary to make sure that funds are used as intended and that central government authorities can be made to account for the results obtained. With close linkage, information about unsatisfactory results can be used not only to adjust the programme or the minimum standards but also to adjust the financing grants themselves, by extending them to cover new services or by limiting them and reallocating the funds.

Box 3.11. **European Union Cohesion Policy 2014-2020**

In 2013, the European Union (EU) defined long-term objectives for growth and jobs ("Europe 2020 Strategy") to better align policy to achieve the agreed targets on employment, education, poverty, innovation and research and climate (renewable energy, energy efficiency and greenhouse gas emissions). Given their share of the EU budget (more than one-third), cohesion policy instruments are critical for boosting Europe's economic competitiveness, promoting social cohesion, and creating more and better jobs.

Commission and member states set out the commitments to concrete actions to deliver Europe 2020 objectives. Minimum allocations are fixed for a number of priority areas on which the EU has set itself goals. For example, in more developed regions, at least 80% of European Regional Development Fund (ERDF) resources at national level have to be allocated to the shift towards a low-carbon economy (energy efficiency and renewables), research and innovation, ICTs and the improvement of the competitiveness of SMEs. This amount will be 60% in transition regions and 50% in less developed regions, reflecting their broader development needs.

Partnership Agreements for each member state are tailored within a single European reference framework, for co-ordination between the funds and other EU instruments in the Common Strategic Framework. A number of framework conditions must be in place before the funds are disbursed (for instance, the proper functioning of the procurement systems) to ensure that investments are made in the most effective manner. Progress towards objectives is closely monitored and measured against a set of milestones agreed upon as part of a performance framework. The Commission can also release additional funds contingent on performance. A clear focus on sustainable urban development requires that at least 5% of the European Regional Development Fund resources be allocated for "integrated actions" on sustainability managed by cities. The Commission also calls for innovative action in sustainable urban development and makes European Structural Fund human capital investment in cities easier. Territorial co-operation among regions is encouraged (whether cross-border, transnational or interregional), since it offers clear added value.

Source: European Commission (2013), "Q&A on the legislative package for EU Cohesion Policy 2014-2020" Press release database, http://europa.eu/rapid/press-release_MEMO-13-678_en.htm?locale=EN.

A further advantage of performance information is that it provides a good base from which to involve regional actors. This can help in many ways, from obtaining local information on problems and ideas for solutions, to giving local actors a stake in the outcome. Moreover, if *oblast*- and *rayon*-level governments have revenue-raising power, co-funding grants linked to performance targets can help to obtain subnational commitment to the objectives set by central government on urban development. Co-funding can be helpful in encouraging responsible behaviour, since people will generally take better care of funds to which they have contributed themselves. Kazakhstan authorities may wish to look at the European Union Cohesion Policy 2014-2020 as an example of a co-funding grant linked to performance targets.

SNGs have limited taxing power

In Kazakhstan, SNGs do not have enough incentives to broaden their tax base to increase their own resources. Large differences obtain across regions and cities: Aktau generates 80% of its revenue, while South Kazakhstan oblast only produces 18%. SNGs in Kazakhstan are more dependent on the central government for resources than many OECD countries. Figure 3.1 shows that SNGs' tax revenues amounted to 3.7% of GDP and 17.8% of public tax revenue in 2013, whereas in OECD unitary countries, the percentage was 4.8% and 20% respectively. On average, in OECD countries, SNGs' tax revenue as a percentage of GDP was 7%, and 31.6% as a percentage of public tax revenue in 2014.

Figure 3.1. **Subnational government tax revenue as a % of public tax revenue and GDP, 2014**

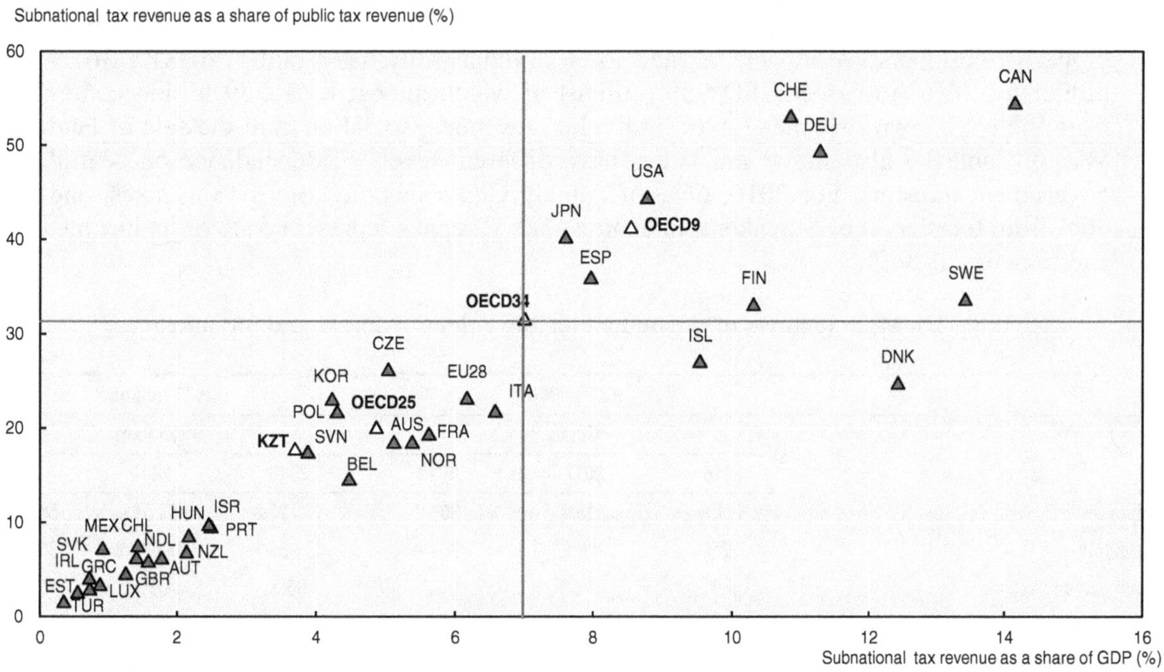

Notes: 2013 Mexico, Chile, New Zealand and Kazakhstan; 2012 Australia; 2011 Turkey.

OECD25: OECD unitary countries; OECD9: OECD federal countries; OECD34: OECD member countries.

Source: OECD (2016c), *Regions at a Glance 2016*, OECD Publishing, Paris; and OECD/UCLG (2016), "Subnational Governments around the World: Structure and Finance", OECD, Paris, www.uclg-localfinance.org/sites/default/files/Observatory_web_0.pdf.

Local governments in Kazakhstan do not have the authority to determine tax rates or the basis for taxation. SNGs have little taxing power over rate or base. SNGs (*rayons*) can only revise the land tax rate within a margin of 20%, depending on the characteristics of the land, and set the rate of minor local taxes. There is no formula to define revenues at the local level. Most of SNGs' tax revenues are shared taxes: personal income tax (40% of SNG tax revenue) and social tax based on payroll (30%). Social tax, personal income tax and excise duties make up more than half of local tax revenue (75% in 2015). Land and property taxes represent 15% of SNGs' tax revenue, and excise 7%. Additional taxes are levied, for example on transport or environmental emissions.

All taxes are collected centrally, and the responsibility for tax collection falls to the Tax Committee of the Ministry of Finance and its territorial divisions. These committees remit all tax revenues and other obligatory payments to the national budget. The committees do not report to any local government authority but are subordinate to the tax committee in the government level immediately above. Redistribution of shared taxes is made through an equalisation mechanism. The current decentralisation programme is expected to increase the financial autonomy of lower-level governments by assigning new shared taxes and own-source tax revenues.

The main feature of the taxation system is that the national government's revenue comes mainly from nonstable taxes subject to global fluctuation, such as the price of oil. Whereas in OECD countries, income tax is a principal source of revenue for the national budget (for instance, 50% of the U.S. federal budget comes from income tax), income tax in Kazakhstan only accounts for 7.3% of the total revenue of the state budget (Kysykov, 2013: 91). The oblast-level governments, on the other hand, generate their revenue from stable taxes connected directly to their territory (taxes on real estate, transport taxes, property taxes, personal income tax and so on). Almaty City has a budget of KZT 361.9 billion for 2016 (just over USD 900 million) of which almost KZT 239 billion comes from the city's own revenues (taxes, individual revenues, social tax and the sale of land assets). Table 3.5 also shows that cities have different levels of dependence on central government transfers. For 2016, 66% of Almaty City's income comes from taxes, and 30% from transfers. For Shymkent, in contrast, tax revenues represent 51% of its income, and transfers 49%.

Table 3.5. **Main features of the budget for the cities of Almaty and Shymkent**

	KZT billion			KZT million		
	Almaty			Shymkent		
	2016	2017	2018	2016	2017	2018
Receipts	**361.9**	**315.9**	**297.9**	**86 725.9**	**53 311**	**56 136.1**
Tax revenues	239	286.2	269.8	43 850.2	37 682.8	38 990.3
Non-tax revenues	1.7	1.5	1.7	95.8	97.7	99.9
Proceeds from sales of fixed assets	12.7	2.6	2.6	311	322	322
Income transfers	108.5	25.6	23.8	42 468.9	14 769	16 542.9
Receipt of loans					439.5	450

Note: The budget for Almaty includes loans under "Transfers".

Source: Budget for Almaty, *akimat* of Almaty, http://almaty.gov.kz/page.php?page_id=2837&lang=1&article_id=27610. Budget for Shymkent provided by the *akimat* of Shymkent.

According to the Ministry of Finance, the tax revenues of SNGs in general have increased in the last four years from 37% as a percentage of total income in 2012 to 42% in 2015, while income transfers have fallen from 60% to 54% in the same period

(Figure 3.2). Meanwhile, the percentage of revenue self-generated by local governments has fallen (Kysykov, 2013). Between 2001 and 2010, the share of SNGs' self-generated revenue fell by more than 50%, making them more dependent on transfers from the national government (Figure 3.3). The declining share of self-generated revenue in subnational budget revenue is attributed to changes in budget and tax legislation.

Figure 3.2. **Share of tax revenues and transfers in local budgets in Kazakhstan**

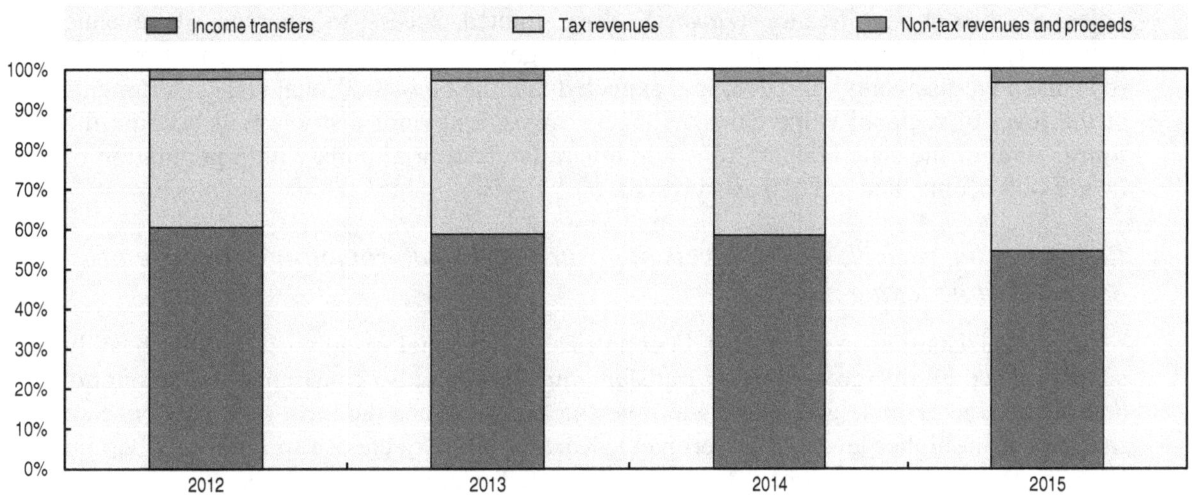

Note: Tax revenues include individual income tax, social tax and excise.

Source: Ministry of Finance of the Republic of Kazakhstan, National Accounts.

Figure 3.3. **Percentages of national and subnational budgets in state budget revenue, excluding transfers**

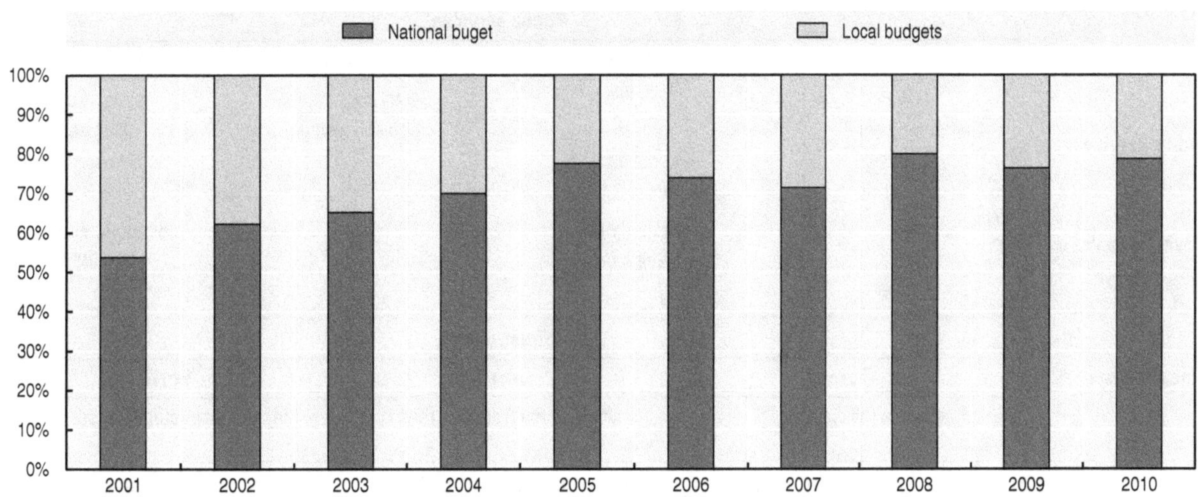

Source: Kysykov, A. (2013), "On overcoming the subsidy dependence of regional budgets".

Kazakhstan's legislation does not recognise the concept of local taxes (Bhuiyan, 2010). As the tax receipts allocated to SNGs are stable, local authorities are unable to exert much influence on the formation of their own budget revenue. The amount of tax accruing to local budgets depends only indirectly on the degree of development of production and entrepreneurship, investment capacity or restructuring of regional economies. This limits the possibility for increasing self-generated revenue (Kysykov, 2013).

In 2013, the Law of Local Self-Governments and the presidential decree on self-governments were passed. The main principle of self-government is to ensure that local *akims* – *rayon* cities of regional significance, villages and major rural settlements – have the financial independence to satisfy the needs of citizens in their territory. *Akims* of cities of district significance (*rayons*) were granted access to sources of revenue previously allocated directly to the *oblast* budget (for example fines, and taxes on roadside advertisements). In 2018, it is expected that the budget of local self-governments at the level of regional value cities, villages, towns, and rural districts will become the fourth level of the state budget in the administrative territorial units with a population of over 2 000 people, and in 2020 everywhere.[11]

Redistributing revenue across levels of government and promoting better use of SNGs' existing taxing power

In Kazakhstan, as in many OECD countries, subnational resources are often heavily supplemented by intergovernmental transfers, but they can also constrain local autonomy and discourage revenue generation and investment. To reduce the level of dependence on transfers from higher levels of government, Kazakhstan may choose to reallocate certain kinds of taxes from the national to the local level. Taxes levied by SNGs should fall on local residents or non-residents (commuters and visitors) who benefit from the services. Table 3.6 provides guidance on how different revenue tools can be used to finance infrastructure and public services.

Table 3.6. **Revenue tools to finance public services and infrastructure**

	Public services			
	Private	**Public**	**Redistributive**	**Spill-overs**
Public services	Water Sewers Garbage Transit	Police Fire Local parks Street lights	Social assistance Social housing	Roads / transit Culture Social assistance
Revenue tools	User fees	Property tax Sales tax	Income tax	Intergovernmental transfers

	Infrastructure		
Fiscal tools	**Taxes**	**User fees**	**Borrowing**
	Short asset life (official cars, computers)	Identifiable beneficiaries (transit, water)	Major infrastructure (roads, bridges)

Source: Slack, E. (2014), "Governance and finance of large metropolitan areas: Which institutional setting is needed to secure metropolitan economic growth?", presentation to the fifth Halle Forum on Urban Economic Growth, Halle, Germany.

Kysykov (2013) argues that one of the taxes that would be economically rational to reallocate to local governments is the value added tax (VAT) on domestically manufactured and imported goods, as it constitutes a small portion of the revenue of the republic's budget (approximately 11.6%) and has the most evenly distributed tax base. However, the experience of countries like Brazil suggests that such a move has its risks.

Brazil has adopted a fully developed VAT to replace a state-based cascading tax on consumption. Each of the 26 federal states set their own indirect tax rates. The result has been a complex system often criticised for being unfair, anticompetitive and costly. The Brazilian federal states do not have the autonomy to tax factor income, as is the case in the United States or Canada, and have used the VAT extensively as an industrial policy instrument, granting tax exemptions to attract economic activity, particularly investment, which has resulted in distortions in economic decisions (Sen et al., 2014). Using the VAT as a tax-sharing mechanism is also complicated in Kazakhstan by the fact that the data needed to share revenues (i.e. data on consumption by SNGs that would be needed to distribute VAT revenues) may not be available or reliable. Subnational surcharges could be the most appropriate means of providing Kazakhstan's SNGs with their own marginal revenues, especially when administrative resources are scarce. This is the course of action followed by some Canadian provinces, which rely on surcharges on national taxes. Surcharges provide almost as much fiscal autonomy as independent taxation, but are much simpler; they provide more autonomy than tax sharing (McLure et al., 2000). However, they do not provide for redistribution among SNGs, so grants will be needed.

The design of the local tax instruments is another reason for the limited revenue of SNGs in Kazakhstan. *Oblasts* and *rayons* collect revenue through user charges and property tax, but these cannot be levied at high enough rates to cover the expenditures of the urban areas. Although in principle property tax has most of the characteristics of a good local tax, in practice this is a relatively minor source of revenue (Bahl et al., 2013). There are different explanations for this, including its unpopularity with citizens, the administration of the tax, and the demanding process of property valuation. The large intergovernmental transfers also allow governments not to raise property tax rates. In Kazakhstan, most *rayon*-level governments and even the two cities of republican significance do not have the technological capacity and the personnel to administer property tax. In OECD countries, some cities have been able to identify properties and keep track of improvements with computerisation and satellite photography, which are not available to cities in Kazakhstan. Properties are assessed infrequently and at rates well below market value. Kazakhstan authorities may wish to consider trying different approaches to define the tax base. Property tax is concentrated in the largest cities, such as Almaty, Shymkent and Astana, and, as typical in emerging economies, property tax is more important in metropolitan areas than in secondary cities. Kazakhstan may also adopt a system where *akimats* in urban areas can charge a land tax – where land has a higher market value – and rural *akimats* a property tax. Alternatively, like Brazil and South Africa, Kazakhstan could explore moving to a capital value system where tax is levied on both land and improvements and away from rental systems and site-value systems (McCluskey and Franzsen, 2013). The property value base might be reached with several other forms of taxation, like property transfer taxes, capital gain taxes on land, various kinds of special assessments and the sale of government land.

The vehicle tax is another tax available to cities that is underutilised. City authorities in Kazakhstan could be allowed to use variations of the tax. Motor vehicle taxes can take the form of licenses to operate; a tax on the estimated value of the vehicle; a sales tax on motor fuel, tolls or parking; and restricted permit charges. Aside from the potential to raise substantial amounts of revenue, higher motor vehicle taxes might have beneficial economic and environmental outcomes, particularly in cities like Almaty and Shymkent.

A more efficient and clearer property taxation in rural and urban areas is essential

Kazakhstan has at least one reason to reform property taxes: to increase revenue from property taxes for SNGs, in particular cities. Including rural land in this reform would also improve tax collection for villages and towns that require public services. One way to approach this would be by giving favourable treatment to rural land and properties under the property tax system. This could be done in a variety of ways: lower assessments, lower tax rates on farms or farm tax rebates. Rather than assessing rural land at market value, which reflects the highest and best use, it could be assessed at its value in current use, based on its selling price if it were to continue to be used as a farm. Favourable treatment of rural land is usually designed to preserve it from conversion to urban use. Kazakhstan may draw inspiration from the Ontario Farm Property Class Tax Rate Programme in Canada. The farm tax rate is set by provincial law at only 25% of the residential tax rate established by the local government.[12] Even when land is being used as farmland while awaiting urbanisation, new values are phased in gradually, with increases triggered when the land is being registered for subdivision and when a building permit has been issued. In Kazakhstan, even if taxes are collected centrally, an effective barrier to rural land taxation could be the high administrative cost. The differential between rural and urban tax may still be too high to preserve rural land from conversion into urban use. In Kazakhstan, a simple uniform tax on rural land is probably the better option initially, while its administrative capacity develops.

Box 3.12. **Property tax reform in Colombia and the United Kingdom**

Property tax reform in **Colombia** involved the amalgamation of four taxes (the property tax, park and forest tax, tax on socio-economic strata, and surcharge on the formation of cadastre) into one unified property tax. Municipalities were permitted, if they wished, to introduce self-assessment (*autoavaluo*) as the tax base. Tax rates were increased to 1.6% of the base for land for purposes other than simple possession of the property and 3.3% for property not used for the performance of an economic activity.

In the **United Kingdom**, the poll tax was replaced by a property tax on residential property (the council tax). Although the base for the earlier property tax was rental value, the base for the council taxes market value. Each property is assigned to one of eight valuation bands. There is no individual valuation. The idea behind banding is to determine the relative values of properties within a particular area at a particular time. Subsequent changes are not taken into account in the banding. The tax rate differs for each band, with higher rates applying to properties in the higher bands.

Source: Bird, R. and E. Slack (2002), "Land and Property Taxation: A Review", The World Bank, http://www1.worldbank.org/publicsector/decentralization/June2003Seminar/LandPropertyTaxation.pdf (accessed 27 October 2016).

One way of increasing property taxation revenue in urban areas would be to modernise the cadastre. In OECD countries, reforms to implement an *ad valorem* property tax (Hungary) and update the cadastre of urban properties (Mexico) have been central in a context of shrinking local self-revenue and reliance on central government transfers, which are unpredictable and in decline. Updating the cadastre to value property more accurately would be an expensive and difficult task for SNGs in Kazakhstan, given the limited capacity and expertise and the financial resources needed. Kazakhstan may instead draw inspiration from the Mexican programme to update cadastres. The Mexican National Statistics Institute (INEGI), with the financial support of the development bank

(BANOBRAS), has successfully helped to update the cadastre in some municipalities and increase the property tax collection by 40% (OECD, 2015c). A fiscal fund was also adopted to reward tax collection increases. A similar programme for Kazakhstan could be designed and piloted in some middle-sized cities before being implemented on a wider scale. The Statistics Committee could play a leading role to complement and ensure technical capacity, as cities may not have the expertise to appraise the value of properties in their territory. Other options are Colombia's unified tax or the United Kingdom's valuation bands (Box 3.12 above). The approach will depend on the type of reform Kazakhstan is to implement.

To make the most of property tax, cities in Kazakhstan need to ensure that certain preconditions are met. The availability of technical expertise, the existence of a cadastre, a land registration system, and solid administrative infrastructure are key preconditions. Canada's experience suggests that the introduction of tax relief programmes such as phase-ins, deferrals for seniors, and capping of tax increases for some classes of property, to cushion the impact of reforms are preconditions for a successful reform (Bird and Slack, 2002). Kazakhstan could even introduce a centralised assessment system to make the system less vulnerable to changes at the local level. One critical condition for a property tax reform in Kazakhstan would be to increase the capacity to administer the tax at the local level, as many cities may lack experience with property taxation. Information to support the fiscal cadastre on a consistent, nation-wide basis needs to be unified and shared across and among levels of government and the public. Political support from central government would be a key element underpinning any property tax reform.

Making better use of borrowing

Borrowing is an effective way to finance urban projects with a long life and that produce revenue, but governments should be vigilant not to over-borrow.

Borrowing is allowed for SNGs, but under strict limitations

Local governments in Kazakhstan have the right to borrow to cover budget deficits (Budget Code Article 47). At the request of the oblast *akims* and the *akims* of Almaty and Astana, the Ministry of Finance may provide budget loans from the national budget. Similarly, *rayon*-level *akims* can borrow from the *oblast* budget (Makhmutova, 2006). In the recent economic crisis, borrowing has been restricted, as the currency devaluation resulted in a tripling of the national debt. The major obstacle to local borrowing is the absence of reliable medium-term and long-term budget planning at the local level, because of the uncertainty surrounding the government policy concerning the allocation of taxes between the national and local budgets and the rate of budget withdrawals (Makhmutova, 2006).

Since April 2016, the Budget Code has allowed the 14 oblasts (regions) and the cities of Almaty and Astana to issue bonds, to cover their budget deficits and to finance the construction of public social housing.[13] The Ministry of Finance strictly controls this practice (including regarding the exact use of borrowed funds), and cities are not allowed to issue bonds to access capital markets. Quotas for annual local borrowing and total local debt are fixed annually by the Budget Law. In 2009, the government determined new subnational government borrowing limits (in a given fiscal year, annual payment and debt servicing costs were not to exceed 10% of the local budget revenues, and total debt 75% of local budget revenues). SNGs' total liabilities are very limited, at 0.5% of GDP and 4.1% of total public liabilities in 2012 (Table 3.7) and interviews for this Review suggested that the situation has so far remained unchanged. In Astana, loans for the construction of the light-rail transit system were obtained from international banks with government guarantees.

Table 3.7. **Debt of Kazakhstan's SNGs**

	Outstanding debt	
	% GDP	% general government
Subnational government outstanding debt (2012, OECD definition)	0.5%	4.1%

Source: OECD/UCLG (2016), *Subnational Governments Around the World: Structure and Finance*, OECD Publishing, Paris.

Borrowing options for SNGs to finance urban infrastructure need to be increased

Borrowing is arguably the most efficient way to pay for public assets that have a long life and generate revenue.[14] By matching payment for infrastructure with the time pattern of benefits received, governments can capture the return from infrastructure investments while deferring the payment (Bahl et al., 2013: 21). Limiting the possibility of SNGs to borrow from capital markets prevents many governments from accessing extra funding to finance infrastructure. One option for Kazakhstan would be to allow its larger cities (Almaty, Astana and Shymkent, for instance) to borrow from the national capital market. They are in a better position to make use of debt markets to fund long-lived public assets and have a stronger and more diversified economic base than smaller cities and monotowns.

There are at least four points Kazakhstan authorities might consider if they wish to strengthen the use of debt by local governments. First, SNGs must have a strong base of own-source financing. Treating these regions and cities under a different transfer regime and granting them more power to set and collect taxes and fees would be essential. If local agencies have instruments for managing local budget revenues, local borrowing for capital investment would be expedient (Makhmutova, 2006). If infrastructure is to be maintained and debt obligations are to be met, regional and city governments need to be able to control their level of budgetary resources. Next, debt should be exclusively used to finance capital projects with a long life, and not to cover budget gaps for current expenditure. The third critical aspect would be to impose a hard budget constraint on borrowers, to eliminate the possibility of a costly bailout by higher levels of government. A central-government-mandated borrowing framework would need clear rules about who can borrow, how much, for what purpose, from whom, with what instruments and with what restrictions. The central government would have the task of monitoring compliance with the framework. Finally, providing loans to local governments for the renewal of urban infrastructure through central government programmes is a viable way to overcome the lack of funding. However, as Turkey's experience suggests, it may require a specific institution providing technical and financial support to SNGs. Such an institution could also help make project selection and prioritisation more transparent. Mexico's BANOBRAS (National Bank of Works and Public Services)[15] and Turkey's IlBank (Bank of Provinces)[16] are examples of development banks that provide financing to local governments for investment projects and that could be of inspiration to Kazakhstan. These banks finance public investment in infrastructure and public services that contribute to social development and competitiveness.

Encouraging accountability and fairness in public finances

In Kazakhstan, the operating system of local finances does not create incentives for accountability for ensuring local public services or promote the development of entrepreneurship and higher living standards. Local authorities are accountable only to higher-level government bodies and do not serve at the will of citizens (Makhmutova, 2006).

SNGs expenditure is relatively high, but spending is deconcentrated

Kazakhstan's SNGs are key investors; but since most of the spending is deconcentrated, they act only as paying agents. In 2013, SNGs' expenditure accounted for 9.4% of GDP (17% average in OECD countries) and 46.3% of public expenditure (40% in OECD countries in 2014) (Table 3.8). This situation is similar to OECD unitary countries with limited competencies and spending capacity, such as Chile, Greece, Ireland, New Zealand and Turkey. However, the situation contrasts with Japan and Nordic countries, where local expenditure is an important share of public expenditure. In Denmark, subnational government expenditure accounts for 36% of GDP and 64% of public expenditure.

Table 3.8. **Expenditure of Kazakhstan SNGs**

Expenditure	% GDP	% General government (same expenditure category)	% Subnational government
Total expenditure (2013)	9.4	46.3	100
Current expenditure	6.8	-	72.3
including staff expenditure	2.0	61.9	20.0
Capital expenditure	2.6	63.7	27.7
including investment	2.6	63.7	27.7

Source: OECD/UCLG (2016), "Subnational Governments Around the World: Structure and Finance", OECD/UCLG, Paris, www.uclg-localfinance.org/sites/default/files/Observatory_web_0.pdf (accessed November 2016).

The 2005 Budget Code introduced fixed expenditures for the *oblast* and *rayon*. All tax rates are the same in the country. *Oblast* budgets are to finance expenditures including general public service, defense, public order and security, education, health care, social welfare, housing and utilities, culture, sports, tourism, agriculture, water resources, forestry and environmental protection, architecture and construction, transport and communication and regulation of economic activity. Table 3.9 shows that education, health care and housing are the main spending items in Almaty City. Under the Budget Code, cities cannot budget more than they can spend and are penalised if they do not spend all the money allocated to them. This gives them no incentives to spend wisely, since spending is understood merely as "disbursement", and results in poor contracts for investment projects and poor works, with limited resources. Major events of international or national significance, such as the Asian Winter Games or the Expo Astana 2017, are covered by the national budget; the *oblasts'* budget is not used to pay for these events. *Akimats* should be responsible for their own revenues, but there is no capacity for governments to do so.

Table 3.9. **Almaty City budget by sector, 2016**

in KZT million

Sector	Amount
Education	52 974.7
Health	21 741.5
Social protection	5 545.1
Housing and utilities	17 561.3
Energy	5 373.3
Environmental measures	1 222.9
Transport infrastructure	11 693.6
Culture and information	4 975.6
Sports and tourism	10 898.5

Source: Almaty City *Akimat*, http://almaty.gov.kz/page.php?page_id=2837&lang=1&article_id=27610.

The Budget Code does not facilitate horizontal co-ordination across cities, as there are no incentives for metropolitan projects.[17] It only provides for a vertical relationship across levels of government. *Maslikhats* approve the budget and its distribution in cities of *oblast* significance (*rayon*-level cities). The *akimat* is in charge of its execution. A "revision commission" not related to the *akimat* or *maslikhat* is responsible for controlling how money is spent and can take disciplinary measures if money is spent without a clear purpose. It functions as an accounting committee of the regional level.

The system of local finances does not encourage accountability for public service delivery

The dependence of SNGs on the budget transfers from the upper level of government, and the fact that all taxes are collected by the central government and subsequently redistributed, restrict local decision-making and priority-setting. Executives of *oblast* and *rayons* are appointed rather than elected, which compromises their accountability towards citizens and their need for public services. As in other countries with the same system, such as China, appointed officials tend to be accountable to the authority that hires them and not to citizens or any other body of local representation. Since the *oblast* governor and the *akims* of cities of republican significance can only be removed by the president, their responsibility for the outcome of their work depends on their good will. The national government, not the citizens, assess their performance. The same situation applies at the rayon level, particularly in the cities of regional significance, as the city *akims* are appointed by the *oblast*-level government.

The process of fiscal decentralisation has been uneven. Expenditure but not income has been decentralised. This process began in the 1990s, when social expenses were assigned to SNGs to maintain national budget deficits at the level demanded by the International Monetary Fund (Makhmutova, 2006). Moreover, subnational authorities, and cities in particular, cannot determine how their budgets are spent. The system for allocating charges between levels of the budget system turns local authorities not into partners of the government – who ensure financing and perform important duties – but into clients petitioning for resources. Although *maslikhats* are invited to participate in the discussions, this exercise is rather a *post-factum* consultation on local programmes and budgets.

Promoting local self-government mechanisms by giving maslikhats *a larger role in the budget process*

Step 98 of the "100 Concrete Steps to Implement Five Institutional Reforms" refers to the introduction of independent budgets for local governments in rural districts, *auls*, villages and towns. It considers the adoption of mechanisms to allow citizens to participate in discussing the best way to spend the budget. Building on Step 98 and the Law of 23 January 2001, No. 148, "On the Local Government and Self-Government of the Republic of Kazakhstan," the national government could design a mechanism that promotes a system of checks and balances in managing the budget at subnational levels of government. A key part of the system should be giving *maslikhats* – as citizens' representatives – the responsibility not just for approving but for discussing, monitoring and evaluating execution of the budget. The rationale is that they are the representative bodies in the system of the local public administration and that, since their members are elected, they are the accountable institution of local self-government. The *maslikhats* at *oblast* and *rayon*-levels of government should make sure that the budget is spent wisely and on projects that are priority for citizens' well-being.

The *maslikhats* should be able to encourage *akimats* to discuss urban development and economic challenges of the region or city in an open, informative manner. The experience of OECD countries suggests that executives are unlikely spontaneously to improve accountability, except in response to some kind of external prompting. This explains why legislatures in most OECD countries have a larger budgetary role than they had a decade earlier (Schick, 2002; Anderson, 2009). To have an independent position on public finances and budgetary issues, *maslikhats* need to be given the political capacity to reject salient elements in the *oblasts* or *rayons*' budgets. This issue needs to be discussed and supported by the central government. To be able to encourage more accountability from the *akimats*, *maslikhats* need help in understanding complex budget issues and processes. *Maslikhats* require reliable, unbiased information to participate constructively in formulating the budget and to be able to hold *akimats* accountable. One way to move forward in this respect is to create an independent research unit that can provide information to put the *maslikhat* on a more equal footing with the *akimat* on public finance issues. This information is critical, because of the scrutiny it can generate into the *akimat*'s budget office. Some of the core functions of this independent research unit would be to produce economic forecasts, baseline estimates, analysis of the *akimat's* budget proposals, analysis of policy proposals, tax analysis and policy briefs with both long and medium-term perspectives. It could also publish annual reports on the budget execution on behalf of the *maslikhats*. Creating such units would be out of reach for many SNGs in Kazakhstan, as they would require financial resources, but the experiences of the Legislative Analyst's Office in California and the Independent Budget Office in New York City show that it is possible to set one up with a relatively modest investment (Anderson, 2009). However, once it is established, the unit must operate in a credible, impartial manner. Initially, Kazakhstan may create an independent research unit in every *oblast* and consider the creation of a unit in some of the medium-size cities of *rayon* significance in the future.

Assigning clear responsibilities for expenditure, to enhance efficiency and accountability

Urban development takes place in a setting where responsibilities are distributed among different levels of government. SNGs must know exactly what they are responsible and accountable for if it is to be possible to accurately assess the adequacy of the revenue and tax assignment to different levels of government and the need for a system of intergovernmental transfers. Administrative, policy and expenditure responsibilities will have to be clearly spelled out. As Kazakhstan's unitary system becomes more decentralised, it will be important to revise and clarify the assignment of responsibilities for expenditure for each level of government, to prevent inefficient provision of public services, reduce unproductive overlap and avoid duplication of authority and even legal challenges. Since SNG budgets are tight, the lack of clear assignments has reduced provision of public services. If this problem is not addressed, financial constraints will continue to dictate the responsibilities of each government, resulting in institutional instability and poor service delivery.

The Budget Code presents a detailed distribution of expenditure responsibilities, but leaves room for overlapping responsibilities. Many of the revenue responsibilities remain vague. In revising the Budget Code to clarify expenditure responsibilities, Kazakhstan authorities may think about grouping roughly congruent services at the budget level of the *rayon* (i.e. street lighting, waste removal), *oblast* (i.e. rural-urban roads, waste disposal) and cities of republican status (i.e. intercity highways and environmental policy). Kazakhstan should avoid an unwieldy mix of deconcentration and decentralisation of government activities. One way to examine the adequacy of expenditure assignments is to analyse how well the actual assignment of responsibilities fits the fundamental rules for the ideal assignment of responsibilities in a decentralised system of governance (McLure and Martinez-Vázquez, 2000). Kazakhstan's authorities may want to consider that responsibility for the provision of services should be at the lowest level of government compatible with the size of the benefit area associated with those services. Leaving the supply of public services with wider benefit areas, such as transport, to smaller units of government is likely to result in inefficient under-provision of services. When transferring responsibilities to local governments, Kazakhstan may wish to ensure that the functions are relevant to the communities.

Decentralisation efforts should include a reflection on the areas where cities are likely to have a comparative advantage in the design, development, implementation and evaluation of urban policies. Action by city governments is particularly valuable where policies need to be tailored to local circumstances and responsive to local constituencies. Central and *oblast* levels of government are best positioned to act where economies of scale are possible, where cross-jurisdictional co-ordination is necessary, and where standardised approaches are needed to avoid free-riding. It may be advisable for the national government of Kazakhstan to assume responsibility for national public services, international affairs, monetary policy, regulation, transfers to persons and businesses, fiscal policy co-ordination, regional equity, redistribution and preservation of an internal common market. However, some central functions, such as regulation of the financial sector and the environment, may be effectively shared with subnational levels of government. *Oblast*-level governments may have a dominant responsibility for education, health, social insurance, inter-municipal issues and oversight of lower-level governments. All local services could be assigned to *rayon*-level governments. Certainly, there will be areas of shared responsibility, but the role of each level of government should be clarified. Chile's ongoing decentralisation process, for example, has led the central government to recentralise education. A function normally conducted by municipalities is now in the process of being taken over by the central government, to liberate municipal resources for regional development.

An analysis of the distribution of expenditure responsibilities across levels of government in OECD countries reveals a general pattern that Kazakhstan authorities might consider (see Table 3.10). However, there is no best way to decide which level of government should be responsible for which service. This has to be judged in terms of how well it achieves the goals or objectives set by government in its decentralisation strategy (McLure and Martinez-Vázquez, 2000).

Table 3.10. **Breakdown of responsibilities across SNG levels: A general scheme**

Municipal level	Intermediary level	Regional level
• A wide range of responsibilities: – General clause of competence – Eventually, additional allocations by the law • Community services: – Education (nursery schools, pre-elementary and primary education) – Urban planning and management – Local utility networks (water, sewerage, waste, hygiene, etc.) – Local roads and city public transport – Social affairs (support for families and children, elderly, disabled, poverty, social benefits, etc.) – Primary and preventive health care – Recreation (sport) and culture – Public order and safety (municipal police, fire brigades) – Local economic development, tourism, trade fairs – Environment (green areas) – Social housing – Administrative and permit services	• Specialised and more limited responsibilities of supramunicipal interest • Assistance for small municipalities • May exercise responsibilities delegated by the regions and central government • Responsibilities determined by the functional level and the geographic area: – Secondary education or specialised education – Supramunicipal social youth welfare – Secondary hospitals – Waste collection and treatment – Secondary roads and public transport – Environment	• Heterogeneous and more or less extensive responsibilities depending on countries (in particular federal vs unitary) • Services of regional interest: – Secondary/higher education and professional training – Spatial planning – Regional economic development and innovation – Health (secondary care and hospitals) – Social affairs, e.g. employment services, training, inclusion, support to special groups, etc. – Regional roads and public transport – Culture, heritage and tourism – Environmental protection – Social housing – Public order and safety (e.g. regional police, civil protection) – Local government supervision (in federal countries)

Source: OECD (2016c), *Regions at a Glance 2016*, OECD Publishing, Paris, http://dx.doi.org/10.1787/reg_glance-2016-en.

Kazakhstan's government has been conducting functional reviews of all national ministries. Linn (2014) argues that as part of this process, a systematic analysis should be carried out of the extent of overlap of functions between the central and subnational government bodies (*oblast* and *rayon*), with a view to assigning clear and non-duplicative functions to each level of government. While conducting a distribution of responsibilities, Kazakhstan's authorities need to ensure that local governments have sufficient capacity to wield information, decision-making and allocation powers that other levels of government do not have. At the same time, it is necessary to guarantee that all levels of government are held accountable for the decisions they take, and that they do not get into debates that will confuse responsibilities or cloud the transparency of information.

Strengthening the capacity of subnational public administrations

Kazakhstan SNGs have a pressing need to improve the skills and competences of politicians and local civil servants. Many face a real shortage of personnel. This lack of capacity compromises the delivery of public services and effective investment in urban development projects. In several OECD countries, capacity building, in terms of human resources and financial support, has often been cited as the principal obstacle to decentralisation. Reinforcing SNGs' capacity should be a key priority as decentralisation progresses.[18]

SNGs need to build capacity

The capacity of Kazakhstan's SNGs, mostly *rayon*-level cities and cities of oblast significance, to deliver urban development projects is an issue of concern. SNGs have little room for manoeuvre to adapt their workforce to local needs. Civil servants in the country are governed by the same rules, codes and laws. *Akimats* have little leverage to influence working conditions and remuneration levels, as they are all decided at the central level. The experience of OECD countries has shown that a successful urbanisation policy is also largely dependent on the quality of human capital in the public administration. An efficient civil service, with high standards of behaviour, is associated with a better quality of policies and policy stability (Scartascini and Tommasi, 2012).

Across OECD countries, the proportion of staff employed at subnational level of government is an indicator of the level of decentralisation of public administrations. In general, larger shares of government employees at subnational level indicate that more responsibilities are delegated to regional and local governments. As Figure 3.4 shows, most countries have more employees at the subnational level than at the central level of government. Federal states employ less than one-third of all government employees at the central level, indicating higher levels of decentralisation. In comparison, Kazakhstan, as a unitary country, employs less than 10% of government employees at central level (Table 3.11). Even federal employees in Germany, Canada and the United States have higher levels of employment at central level. It must be noted that even if 90% of government employees are in SNGs, it does not mean that the country is decentralised. The fact that local authorities, like the *akims*, are appointed by central government, or the oblast government in the case of *rayons,* means that the subnational administrations are deconcentrated units of central government, rather than autonomous self-governments. Government employees at subnational levels can thus be considered central government employees.

Table 3.11. **Distribution of public employees between central government and SNGs**

	2012	2013	2014	2015
Central government	8 281	8 796	8 747	9 536
SNGs	78 606	81 424	82 183	89 782
Total	**86 887**	**90 220**	**90 930**	**99 318**

Source: Answers to the OECD background questionnaire provided by the Ministry of National Economy.

Figure 3.4. **Distribution of general government employment across levels of government, 2011**

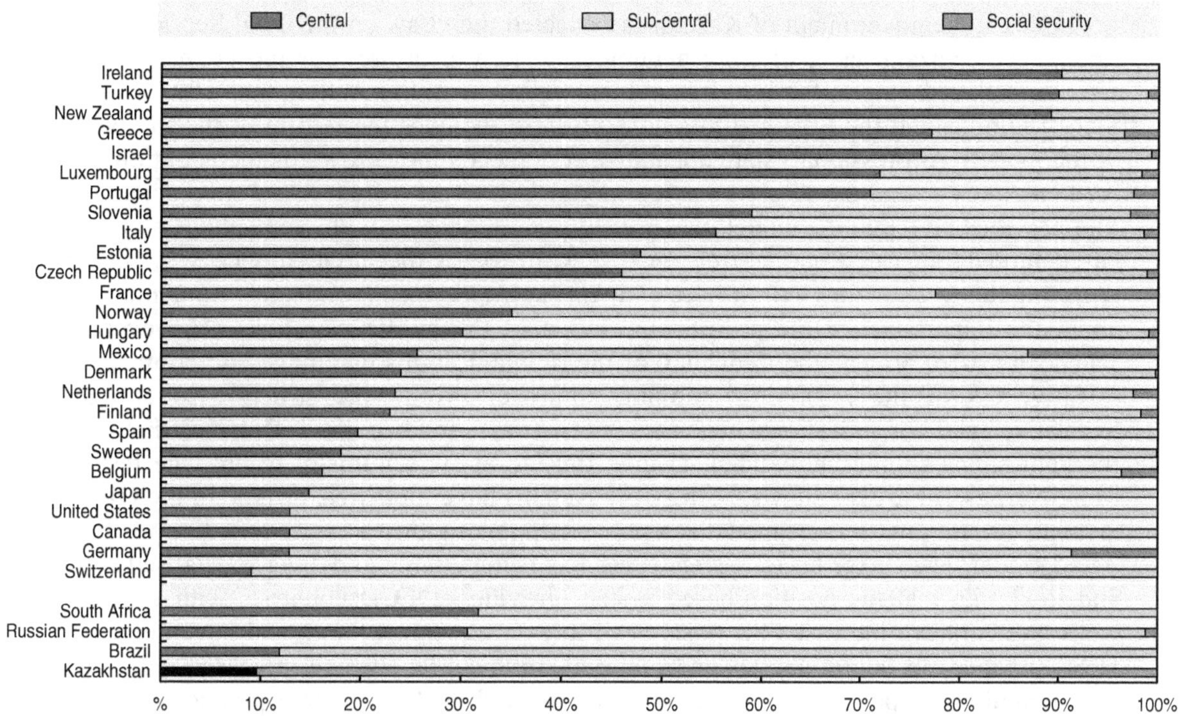

Note: Information for Kazakhstan is for 2015.

Sources: OECD (2013a), *Government at a Glance 2013*, OECD Publishing, Paris, http://dx.doi.org/10.1787/gov_glance-2013-en; Information for Kazakhstan provided by the Ministry of National Economy of the Republic of Kazakhstan.

Kazakhstan's cities in general need to improve the capacity (in both technical expertise and managerial capacity) of public servants. Almaty, for instance, lacks urban transport planners and managers, limiting its capacity for medium-term strategic planning of transport networks. City *akimats,* in general, lack qualified staff to run the Urban Zoning Registry (UZR), limiting its use for land-use management, and staff with financial management and marketing skills to assess and management investment projects. Brief training is provided to existing staff, but is often insufficient, and administrative duties prevent meaningful long-term training. Pay levels make it difficult to attract and retain skilled and highly qualified staff, as civil servants (i.e. urban planners) in key cities such as Almaty are paid USD 300 per month, compared to USD 600-800 in the private sector. Lack of technical capacity makes it difficult to implement general plans in many cities.

The civil service as a whole has a problem of personnel and talent management that appears to require an adjustment in the way competencies are defined and assessed. Kazakhstan requires a clear competence management framework to ensure the skills, knowledge and behaviour that result in good performance at individual and organisational level. Competences should be linked to different elements of human resource management (HRM), in the recruitment and selection of staff, training and development, and succession or career planning. Several models are used in OECD countries, but Kazakhstan may wish to review the French model, known as Employment, Workforce and Competency Planning (*Gestion prévisionnelle des emplois, des effectifs et des compétences* or GPEEC), as it shows how recruitment methods may incorporate competences without abandoning the established principle of selection through competitive examination.

Civil service reforms towards a career-based system

In 2015, the government of Kazakhstan enacted the "Law on the Civil Service of the Republic of Kazakhstan", offering a number of new measures for the country's civil service, such as hiring of foreigners in public employment. In addition, the "100 Concrete Steps to Implement the Five Institutional Reforms" includes the reform of the formation of the modern (professional) state apparatus. It depicts a move towards the adoption of a predominantly career-based civil service model in a quest to renew the state apparatus. The previous civil service model was mostly position-based, with elements of a career-based model. To carry out the reform, the Ministry of the Civil Service was set up, replacing the Agency for Civil Service and Anti-corruption, and sending a strong message about the importance of the professionalisation of the public workforce. However, as Janenova (2016) argues, the frequency of the reorganisations may have compromise the effectiveness of the reform. In moving employees from one structure to another, legislative and organisational changes need time to become effective. Frequent reorganisations should be avoided, to give time to allow a ministry to produce results. Moreover, as Table 3.12 shows, both HRM systems have their weaknesses. In the OECD area, no current civil service model is a pure example of either a career-based or position-based model. The career-based system is seen as being unable to deliver specialised skills and flexibility that the position-based system provides. OECD countries with a career-based system have increased the posts open to external competition, and have delegated HRM practices to line ministries and lower hierarchical levels, and increased individual accountability for performance. Kazakhstan may wish to follow these practices once its own career-based system is better established.

Table 3.12. **Comparing the strengths and weaknesses of civil service systems**

	Classic career-based system		Classic position-based system	
	Relative strengths	**Weakness**	**Relative strengths**	**Weakness**
Entry into the civil service	• Fairness ensured by competitive examinations or diplomas • Whole-government collective values guaranteed by similar pre-entry training for different categories of civil servants	• Weak cross-hierarchical values: differing values and culture depending on hierarchical level of the groups. • Weak assessment at entry of an individual's drive for results. • Collective values and culture weakened by division of staff in coherent but closed groupings of different status.	• Fairness ensured by open and competitive process for each position. • More collective values across staff of different status.	• Possible biases at entry, with a lack of transparency in the recruitment process. • Weak common values at entry into core public service.
Promotion	• Limited possibilities of unfair management by separation of the grade (acquired with time in the civil service) and the specific post.	• Lack of transparency on appointment to different posts (due to weak individual staff assessment).	• Fairness ensured by strong individual performance assessment.	• When processes are not transparent, possible patronage in promotion (grades and posts being mixed). • More difficult cross-departmental appointments.

Source: OECD (2005), *Modernising Government: The Way Forward*, OECD Publishing, Paris, http://dx.doi.org/10.1787/9789264010505-en.

Under the new civil service system, public servants are expected to stay in the public service more or less throughout their working life. The model places a strong emphasis on career development but limits the possibilities for entering the civil service at mid-career. Mandatory competition has been introduced for entrance to and promotion in the administrative civil service. Indeed, initial entry is at grassroots level, based on academic credentials and a civil service entry examination. The aim is to allow every citizen with the potential and the right set of skills the opportunity to enter civil service employment. The competition is conducted by the public agency with a vacant position or by the Ministry of the Civil Service, in an open or closed form, after the competition has been advertised in the national media. The process involves three stages: i) a test on knowledge of the law; ii) assessment of personal qualities; and iii) an interview in state agencies on specialised (sectoral) knowledge. Once recruited, people are placed in positions as required, at the government's discretion. This may include moving staff from one ministry to another and from one area of specialisation to another.

Promotions are to be granted based on competition among internal candidates, who take precedence over external candidates. A candidate will need specific expertise, work experience in lower positions and continuous training. If no ideal candidate is found, the competition is opened to the wider civil service, and eventually to external candidates. The aim is to facilitate the promotion of public servants, since in the past, external candidates had preference. Under the career-based model, a public servant's progress depends to a large extent on how he/she is viewed by the organisational hierarchy, a powerful lever for moulding behaviour to conform to group norms. At SNGs, the situation is similar. Local civil servants are selected based on two main criteria: their qualifications and how they are perceived by the *akimat*.

The management of senior public servants is run under a separate system. The positions involved include 500 professional manager positions (corps A) of the 99 000 positions nationwide (corps B), which belong to the senior civil servants known as the reserve corps of civil servants. Heads of central agencies, inspectors, committee chairmen, heads of administration and governors of regions and towns are part of this group. City *akims* are not included in this group. There is a separate selection procedure to join the reserve. Candidates have to pass an interview with a HR Policy Commission at the national level. When there is a vacancy, the official authorised to conduct the recruitment can select the new official from the reserve pool. Another aspect of the civil service reform is the introduction of a training system of civil servants. It increases the role of the Academy of Public Administration as a training centre; the Graduate School of Public Policy of Nazarbayev University also has a role as the provider of professional programmes in public policy and public administration and as a research centre on public policy.

A career-based model is found in OECD countries such as France, Greece, Hungary, Japan, Korea, Luxembourg and Spain. The main lesson for Kazakhstan, based on the experience of these countries, is that a career-based system runs against the trends in the wider job market, where it is considered less able to deliver specialised skills and flexibility than the position-based approach. This does not mean that Kazakhstan should move to a position-based system, since both systems have strengths and weaknesses, but authorities must be aware that the challenge is to establish a civil service responsive to the needs and specialised skill demands of contemporary Kazakhstan (and the skills required for urban development).

Kazakhstan's civil service operates under a "command movement" principle, which means that when heads of a government agency move to a new post, an entire cadre of people loyal to them move too, forcing a reshuffling of government officials (Janenova, 2016). The new law attempts to minimise the transfer of officials when new political appointments occur; these transfers will only be permitted within the same government body, and transfers between government bodies will be conducted on a competitive basis only. The Civil Service Law guarantees the continuation of employment of administrative civil servants if a government body is reorganised or liquidated and protects them from unjustified dismissal resulting from a change in government. Nonetheless, the Law has its limitations, as newly appointed heads of public administration organisations put pressure on administrative civil servants to vacate their positions "voluntarily". Interviews for this Review indicated that both political and administrative civil servants at all levels are not so much accountable to citizens but to those who have the power to hire and fire them. This prevents the continuation of experienced staff in public employment, compromising capacity.

The new civil service law pays special attention to ethics and moral issues. In 2015, a new Ethics Code was introduced to deal with conflicts of interest. This set up a new position, the "ethics commissioner", for civil servants to consult on ethical issues.[19] The National Bureau of Anti-Corruption was established in the Ministry of the Civil Service with the functions of prevention, detection, suppression and investigation of corruption offences. Janenova (2016) points out the need for a cultural change in government and of a renewal of ethical and moral values of civil servants, to be able to create a professional civil service.

Enhancing SNGs' capacity requires a professional public workforce

There is no "right" way of designing a human resource management system; it all depends on the culture and business needs of the organisations and the context in which they operate. Kazakhstan has just embarked on a series of reforms to professionalise its public workforce, and the reforms need to be fully implemented and give them time to mature and produce results. The following suggestions are intended to complement and reinforce the reforms in place.

Invest in developing capacity for strategic workforce planning

The government workforce is in constant flux, due to flows in and out of public employment. Kazakhstan's decentralisation measures, giving more responsibilities to SNGs, are changing their needs for skills and competencies. The national labour market is also in constant flux, making it harder for government to attract and retain highly skilled people. Workforce planning is an essential tool for Kazakhstan's government, for anticipating future developments and maintaining a well-structured workforce of an appropriate size, able to meet the changing needs of the public service in a cost-efficient manner. A distinction has to be made between the short-term or *operational* dimension of workforce planning, and the longer term or *strategic* dimension. In the short term, there is a direct link between workforce planning and operational decisions. In the longer term, workforce planning is instead linked to strategic decisions about the positioning of the government organisations a number of years into the future. Workforce planning is not necessarily the same as central or top-down planning. Adequate workforce planning can be developed in any organisation, centralised or decentralised, and by any level of government. At the very least, the Ministry of the Civil Service should have the responsibility to: i) track numbers of employees, costs and competencies; and ii) develop a framework for holding ministries and agencies accountable for workforce planning and, at a later stage, to SNGs. If workforce planning is to be effective, flexibility is needed in managing the pool of workers. Workforce planning need not be overly sophisticated. Its purpose is to avoid approximate, "back-of-the-envelope" calculations about future staff needs and encourage professional linking of human resource management to the agencies' strategic needs. The Ministry of the Civil Service could develop a framework for workforce planning that allows for the establishment of government-wide analysis and targets of workforce size, competencies and allocation across sectors. This is especially important in the career-based system, where employees are usually employed for their entire working life in specific career groups.

Increase managerial flexibility by delegating human resource management responsibilities to SNGs

To help SNGs, in particular cities of oblast significance, to adapt their workforce to better meet their needs, the central government could delegate to them responsibility for HRM, to increase managerial flexibility and improve their performance and responsiveness. *Akims* would be in a better position to meet their targets if they were given the possibility to adapt the public workforce to their business needs, adjusting working conditions and even levels of remuneration. A complete delegation of authority for HRM may not be needed, but SNGs should at least be given the option to determine how many employees they need, and which mix of skills they have. Closely related to this is the authority to decide when to use purchase services and contractors instead of hiring more full-time staff. Appropriate financial regulations would be needed to back up this function. Another function that could be delegated is not recruiting as such, but the specification of the required competencies and criteria, which is essential to complement manpower planning. Staff training and development could also be handed down, since these constitute normal management functions. The central government might, however, want to establish minimum standards for recruitment, selection criteria and competency frameworks. All SNGs also need to be able to motivate their employees: to reward them for good performance and behaviour and to sanction misconduct and unsatisfactory behaviour. This can be achieved in many different ways, but some control over monetary rewards is probably indispensable.

Kazakhstan's central government may wish to analyse the convenience of delegating responsibility for setting pay levels to SNGs, at least to the level of cities of oblast significance. If SNGs, and cities in particular, want to attract and retain a talented workforce and compete with the private sector, they need to offer competitive remuneration and working conditions. Some flexibility over pay may help adapt pay levels to the market situation in each city. This will result in pay differentials across different governments and cities, but not necessarily across individuals. The experience of OECD countries in this respect is wide and mixed. One issue for consideration is affordability, and whether SNGs have the resources to pay competitive salaries. This issue needs to be considered during the decentralisation process. Moreover, delegating pay setting to SNGs will be demanding, both for the centre that has to learn how to govern a decentralised process appropriately, and for SNGs that have to learn how to manage the pay-setting process. The experience of OECD countries suggests that delegating pay setting can have positive effects on the performance of local public administrations, but these cannot be taken for granted. A lack of adequate preparations may delay or prevent the desired outcomes: adequate training for managers, adequate monitoring arrangements and financial management, and a cultural reorientation of the

Ministry of the Civil Service as it shifts from setting pay to supervising decentralised pay setting.

Delegating authority for HRM to subnational levels of government will never be complete. The central government would need to keep a certain level of authority to monitor its development, to hold *akimats* to account for their handling of their delegated authority. The Ministry of the Civil Service that traditionally controls HRM in central and subnational levels of government would need to redefine its role and functions. Its role could be more strategic and less managerial, as seems to be the case so far, and as is typical of OECD countries such as Finland, Ireland, Japan, the United Kingdom and the United States. It could co-ordinate HRM across levels of government and even across central ministries and agencies.

If Kazakhstan opts for a delegated HRM system across levels of government, this will have to be accompanied by development of managerial capacity and competence on HRM issues at the subnational level. Ensuring that the HRM function in all *akimats* is performed by professionals and that senior managers are properly trained in management is a must for successful delegation of HRM authority.

Link performance management of personnel to the strategic goals of ministries and government as a whole

Until recently, civil servants in Kazakhstan have not been subject to performance reviews. However, the "100 Concrete Steps to Implement Five Institutional Reforms" include measures to transition to labour results in the state apparatus. State employees will be assessed through annual individual plans; ministers and oblast-*akims* through specific indicators of quality of public services, quality of life and attracted investment. Government agencies are assessed through the implementation of strategic plans; and members of the government through macroeconomic indicators. This plan for assessing individual and organisational performance is a good start. Kazakhstan authorities may nevertheless wish to keep in mind that the ultimate aim of performance management is to allow operational managers to work with their staff to align their individual needs, interests and career aspirations with the organisation's business needs. The focus should be in the future, on what the employee needs to be able to do, and how he/she can do things better (OECD, 2008).

Kazakhstan's government may wish to build a performance management system that considers that the effective performance of an organisation depends on the contributions of activities at all levels. For example, whether or not *akims* achieve the objectives set in the indicators for quality of public services will depend on their competence, managerial flexibility, regulatory issues and financial resources, which should be considered in the assessment, rather than simply the indicator itself. Ultimately, the national government needs to help subnational administrations achieve their goals. Similarly, the administration should help individual employees develop their capacity to perform. Focus on performance is not just a matter of achieving targets and implementing plans, but assessing them in relation to other employees, organisations, levels of government or policy sector. The performance management system should be based on the strategic goals and business plans of government as a whole and of each organisation or level of government. Employees should know how their performance contributes to the overall performance of the organisation. It is important that good performance be rewarded and poor performance be addressed appropriately. Public sector managers should be trained in performance management and assessment. Their ability to manage and promote good performance should be a key element in recruiting managers and assessing their performance.

Some discussions have centred on establishing a performance-related pay (PRP) system. In this respect the experience of OECD countries is a warning signal to Kazakhstan. Performance assessment is inherently difficult in the public sector, owing to the complex set of goals and restrictions, and the lack of suitable quantitative indicators. Whether performance-related pay will have a positive impact on staff is strongly dependent on how well individual and team objectives can be identified, and on the extent to which they are based on performance rather than standard job criteria. Kazakhstan would need to make sure that transparency, clear promotion mechanisms, trust of top and middle management, and a strong performance management system are features of the administrative culture before introducing a performance-oriented pay culture. PRP policies could be counterproductive in an inadequate management framework, and in such situations increase problems linked to trust and contribute to corruption and patronage. Perhaps a way forward would be to focus on the senior managers group (corps A) as a distinctive group in the civil service.

Enhance the training and competence management of central and subnational civil servants

Training courses for civil servants on issues such as municipal governance, local budgets, inter-budgetary relations, personnel management, tax collection and administration, management of urban infrastructure and interaction with citizens could help bridge the gap between existing skills and the competencies needed to implement urban policies and programmes. The training programmes should ensure that civil servants have the right mix of skills and expertise to deliver effective services and avoid providing training on issues unrelated to the job. The Ministry of the Civil Service must ensure that civil servants at all levels of government have access to appropriate training throughout their careers in government. Beyond accrediting the skills of existing and future staff, the Ministry of the Civil Service and its counterparts in SNGs should provide their staff with formal and informal training to develop their skills. Kazakhstan may develop a schema of the skills needed for government. Since public servants can be moved to any sector or level of government, it is important to ensure they have the basic skills for government and enhance the professionalism of the public workforce. Kazakhstan could draw inspiration from the United Kingdom's Capabilities Plan for the Civil Service, which mostly concerns how to train individuals and develop their competences (Civil Service, 2013). The Academy of Public Administration, which provides professional training for public employees from national and regional governments, has a critical role to play in training and could lead such a scheme, given its vast experience in training. If new legislation is passed, officials from the national government travel to the regions to explain the new legislation, and in some cases, organise practical workshops to train local public employees. *Oblasts* and *rayons* have their own training centres for professional advancement.

To make training more strategic, SNGs, with the assistance of the Ministry for the Civil Service, could invest in competence management. This has the potential to effectively identify gaps in employees' current skills and help them map out training and development plans. Belgium has introduced "development circles" focused on building competencies to achieve personal and organisational goals. A crucial element is the individual training plan made for each public servant. The development circle consists of four phases: function discussion, planning discussion, performance review and assessment interview. Kazakhstan could also explore introducing certified training. Its goal is to develop the competencies of public servants in order to meet the needs of the organisation (OECD, 2011). Belgium and Mexico, for instance, have introduced the certification of competencies in order to value experience and give validity to training. This certification could be used to participate in promotion contests or to apply for positions in other sectors. A national evaluation centre is normally in charge of this certification. In Kazakhstan, it could be done by the Academy of Public Administration or any university, at the request of the Ministry for the Civil Service.

A periodic rotation of public employees could be used to broaden their experience…

The OECD (2014a) Review of the Central Administration in Kazakhstan has already proposed introducing rotational programmes for policy and programme managers, to give them multiple ministerial and central agency experience. For policy and programme managers from the MNE with direct responsibility for regional and urban policy, rotational programmes could also include secondments in SNGs, mainly at rayon level, to share expertise and get a better understanding of the reality of those cities. The programme should also allow officials in charge of urban planning to be assigned to other cities or to the MNE. Establishing reasonable time limits for every assignment (two to four years) could also enable policy continuity while advancing collaboration. The programme could be co-ordinated by the MNE through the National Analytical Centre (NAC), with the Ministry of Civil Service and Anti-Corruption. OECD experience shows that such rotational assignments can achieve collaboration-related results, such as developing participants' collaboration skills and building inter-ministerial and multilevel networks. Similar programmes have been introduced in Canada, the United Kingdom and the United States. Leadership development in the UK civil service is managed through the Fast Stream Programme. This is a rotational scheme that allows civil servants to take on a range of positions involving direct contact with the public, providing them with insight into the policy-making process and direct leadership experience. This is supplemented by formal training courses, regular feedback and performance reviews, mentoring, e-learning as well as preparations for professional qualifications.

… but this should be accompanied with clear career paths and job categories

The experience of OECD countries suggests that the structure and management of job categories and career paths have important implications for workforce flexibility and for cost-efficient staffing. An effective system should allow the government of Kazakhstan to structure employment and deploy staff optimally to meet organisational needs and adapt to changing requirements. It should provide sufficient flexibility, in terms of staff mobility within ministries and across levels of government, to meet employers' needs and enhance career opportunities for staff. A good system should also ensure that the public service can recruit and retain the talent it needs by offering sufficiently interesting and attractive jobs and career opportunities, one of the main problems at *oblast* and *rayon* levels of government. Developing a good system for Kazakhstan would require an in-depth technical discussion that is beyond the scope of this review, but the experiences of Ireland and Japan could provide some ideas on how some OECD countries with a career-based system are addressing this issue. However, while structuring its new system, Kazakhstan needs to make sure to open up opportunities for career progression and develop a job classification system to introduce more transparency into the remuneration system.

Box 3.13. **Organisation of job categories and career paths in Ireland and Japan**

Ireland and **Japan** are examples of career-based systems in which most jobs are grouped into service-wide grades that form a career and pay ladder. Recruitment tends to be mainly or exclusively at entry level, with promotion linked to a series of grades. A clear distinction needs to be made in these systems between salary progression within the grade, which is not a promotion in the real sense of the term, and functional promotion to a post with higher responsibilities. In Ireland, specialist and departmental grades have tended to grow over time, leading to fragmentation and inflexibility, and careers have in practice tended to be managed on a departmental basis, thus reducing mobility. Changes have aimed at increasing flexibility and mobility, for example by integrating some specialist grades and opening up competition for promotion to higher grades. In Japan, careers tended to be managed on a departmental basis, but since 2009, the career system based on grading was changed to a career system based on standard competencies for standard positions of job categories. Promotions are now mainly based on competency assessment (in addition to performance assessment) using standard competencies as criteria. Service-wide pay grades are now only used for pay.

Source: OECD (2010), *OECD Reviews of Human Resource Management in Government: Brazil 2010 Federal Government*, OECD Publishing, Paris, http://dx.doi.org/10.1787/9789264082229-en.

Create a forum for the exchange of knowledge and experience

The creation of a permanent platform to share information and experiences and develop policy options on urban challenges has proved a useful mechanism for improving policy making and civil servants' competencies. Such a forum could benefit from engaging regional experts, academics, civil servants, professionals, businesses, NGOs and international donor organisations. A forum for policy dialogue and structured exchange of ideas and views on urban development issues would enhance networking and a new working culture of co-operation. Urban Toronto in Canada, the University of Chicago Urban Network in the United States, and the Viet Nam Urban Forum (VUF) are examples of platforms for networking and discussion on key urban issues among agents from different backgrounds. The membership of the VUF, for instance, chaired by the Ministry of Construction, includes public, private and nonprofit organisations (universities, think tanks and so on) and even international organisations. The VUF, a platform for discussion on urban issues, regularly reviews and reports to stakeholders on the state of ongoing urban development programmes. It also contributes to a deeper understanding of urban upgrading projects. Donors use the Forum to present their views and the findings of the projects they finance. Kazakhstan could draw inspiration from these experiences to build a similar platform (*Kazakhstan Urban Forum*), where national, *oblast*, *rayons* and national and international expert groups discuss urban issues and search for co-operative strategies. This would add transparency and ownership in building a vision for the national urban network.

Box 3.14. **Viet Nam Urban Forum**

The Viet Nam Urban Forum (VUF) was established in 2003, based on a consensus of government authorities and international and domestic organisations. It is led by the Ministry of Construction of Viet Nam, which is also in charge of urban development in the country. Its mission is "to promote dialogue for sharing of experiences and knowledge among government agencies, associations, unions, scientific/professional, social/political organisations and nongovernmental organisations, entities and individuals of all economic sectors and the donor agencies, with the aim of actively contributing to the formulation and implementation of policies on urban development and

Box 3.14. **Viet Nam Urban Forum** (*cont.*)

management, and improving the effectiveness of urban development and management activities in Viet Nam". The VUF works as a network/platform for discussion between all these stakeholders, and is divided into seven member groups, as follows: multilateral donor organisations, bilateral donor organisations, government ministries and agencies, professional associations and academic institutions, cities, private sector corporations and NGOs. Currently, the VUF has 150 members and plans to expand to 200 by 2020.

The VUF is organised around three types of events and activities: i) annual events, consisting of the Annual Conference (General Assembly) and the Viet Nam Urban Day; ii) conferences, workshops and seminars based on thematic discussions; and iii) producing policy recommendations. It provides an interesting opportunity to bring to the table local governments, national government and international partners to work on urban green growth.

Source: OECD (2016d), *Green Growth in Hai Phong, Viet Nam*, OECD Green Growth Studies, OECD Publishing, Paris, http://dx.doi.org/10.1787/9789264260207-en.

Ensuring equal opportunities

Kazakhstan is working to improve equal opportunities in the public sector, and recently approved a Concept of Gender Policy. More could be done: in the public sector, women are predominantly employed in administrative-level positions, and only 10% of vice ministers and secretaries and 11.4% of elected authorities at subnational level are women. Kazakhstan has never had a female *akim*. Ensuring equal opportunity is a challenge for Kazakhstan, so that it can make best use of the talent available in the population. This will require political commitment at the highest levels of government and promoting policies that favour a balance between work and personal life. Kazakhstan needs to design inclusive and gender-sensitive policies. In the research conducted for this Review, no evidence emerged that gender was part of the political agenda to strengthen the capacity of the public service. Promoting merit in accessing public employment, as stated in Kazakhstan's public employment reform, is a way of ensuring equal opportunities, as is choosing the best person for the job, regardless of gender, age, ethnic background, sexual orientation and religion. This principle, however, could be stated clearly in all strategic government documents. In pursuing equal opportunities in government, Kazakhstan might adopt the 2015 "OECD Recommendation of the Council on Gender Equality in Public Life" to mainstream gender equality in the design, development, implementation and evaluation of relevant public policies and budget (OECD, 2016f).

Professionalise the human resource management function at all levels of government

The management of the public workforce and the implementation of the new civil service model have to be entrusted to human resource management (HRM) professionals. The Ministry of the Civil Service and its counterparts in subnational levels need to be staffed with experts. So far, HRM departments are in the hands of personnel trained in the Soviet era, and their understanding of HRM is limited to the daily paper work. Most of these staff will need to be retrained to acquire the skills necessary to modernise the management of the public workforce. In some cases, they might be reallocated to areas where tasks are more in line with their skills. This could open the opportunity to bring in people with more modern skills to senior positions. Regional centres for training of HRM staff could be created to train staff from district and rural levels where there is limited capacity to implement HRM policy reforms.

Kazakhstan requires the HRM function to be strategic. The Ministry of the Civil Service needs to develop an understanding of how HRM can help meet the strategic goals of government. HR experts need to have access to a range of career paths, similar to those for other professionals. In other words, the HR career path must make it possible for HR professionals to stay in their positions, move sideways to gain broader experience, take on more responsibilities, or (temporarily) move out of the public service. The Ministry of the Civil Service may consider developing a profile for the HR profession as a primary tool for improving HRM capability. The experience of the United Kingdom's Cabinet Office in setting HR professional standards as part of its Professional Skills for Government Agenda provides some inspiration. The key task is to define what is expected of HR professionals and how to measure their performance. The HR Professional Standards set out the requirements for HR professionals in four key areas: i) knowing the business; ii) demonstrating HR expertise; iii) acting as a change agent; and iv) building personal credibility (Civil Service, 2016).

Cultivating dialogue with civil society

In Kazakhstan, the parallel evolution of citizens' participation in urban development and the capacity of SNGs will define how far urban development can be sustainable and indeed improve people's well-being.

Information rather than consultation leaves little room for the participation of civil society

Interviews for this review consistently revealed concern about the ability of Kazakhstan's civil society to participate in decision making on issues such as urban planning, water management, air quality and waste management. It emerged that the interests of local communities are not always taken into account and, as UNECE (2016) points out, this should be the main criterion of effective management. The practice of consulting with the public is not fully regulated or even enforced. There seems to be a common practice of informing citizens about authorities' plans and decisions on urban development issues rather than a consultation process where people's views, ideas, and concerns are considered. A similar situation occurs in countries such as Chile (OECD, 2013b), China (OECD, 2015b), Mexico (OECD, 2015c) and Viet Nam (OECD, 2016d). Conflicts between local authorities, citizens and the private sector (e.g. housing developers) are common once the urban development plans have been approved. The reason is that citizens and the private sector were not consulted in advance. This detracts from the public investment plans, since in some cases the execution is delayed and may not even respond to the real needs of the communities.

The central and local governments in Kazakhstan seem to be aware of the importance of public participation in improving the urban environment. Step 97 of the "100 Concrete Steps to Implement the Five Institutional Reforms" reflects central government's acknowledgement of the need to enhance citizen participation in the decision-making process through the development of self-regulation and local self-government. However, little evidence emerged on how this was being implemented. When a city general plan is developed, a public hearing is held to allow citizens to participate in discussions and air their comments. Cities have the duty to inform residents about the general plans and get feedback from them. Some developments in urban planning, such as the General Plan for

Astana, newly revised for the 2017 World Expo, are experimenting with new forms of public consultation and participation. This is important, as these experiences can be the foundation for civic action in major cities.

Interviews for this review suggest that public participation in urban development is limited. The problem seems to be that there is, to some extent, a lack of interest from citizens, due to the mistrust of government in general; no methodology makes public participation an integral part of the urban planning process and implementation; citizens do not perceive a benefit from taking part in these exercises; and local government officials are not trained to engage with the community. Citizens are not interested in the technicalities of the general plans but on more practical issues such as what will be demolished, for example. The limitation is that the general plans are highly technical, and ordinary citizens lack the knowledge to understand them. *Akimats* thus rely on different fora for the discussion of general plans. For instance, the general plan for the city of Astana was discussed in the union of urban planners. Although these fora may help improve the technical aspects of the master plans, they would still lack the social aspect and the input of all those who are to be impacted by its implementation.

It has been suggested that people may be more willing to discuss more concrete plans at the neighbourhood level. In Almaty City, citizens' participation in urban issues seems to be more active. The city government advertised the amendments to the general plan in on the press and online, and public hearings are being held. Local authorities reported receiving over a thousand requests and proposals from citizens on improvements to the city. Local authorities use social media to communicate with citizens. Changes at the neighbourhood level are approved by the local *maslikhat*, whereas changes to the general plan need to be approved by the central government. The awareness of social accountability for public service delivery is slowly growing (Bhuiyan, 2010).

Making urban neighbourhoods effective and meaningful partners in urban development

The central and subnational governments could consider the following recommendations to support Step 97 of the "100 Concrete Steps to Implement Five Institutional Reforms".

Encourage public participation as part of the urban planning process with strong public leadership

The experience of OECD countries suggests that in order to enhance local self-governments, make better public investment decisions, and meet citizens' needs in an effective manner, it is necessary to consult with citizens and make them active stakeholders in the urban planning and implementation process. One of the lessons from the reconstruction process after the earthquake in Abruzzo, Italy, is that it is essential to encourage public participation to help decision making, because the regional development strategy needs to understand and reflect the community's vision (OECD, 2013c). Many past experiences have shown that when communities are allowed and supported to embark on a participatory process, they can provide input in complex strategic decision making and facilitate a lasting recovery in the case of natural disasters or urban improvement projects in general. OECD countries' experience suggests that citizens' participation in urban development issues should be from early stages of the process. This helps avoid reaching the final stages of a project that citizens do not support or recognise as their own.

One of the successful factors of community engagement in urban development issues has been the strong and sustained leadership of local authorities and even national authorities in the process. *Akims* and senior public managers should express at the outset commitment to the process and the principles of the purpose and scope of the exercise. One way to start would be by understanding what people value about the city and engaging on these terms. It is recommended that *akims* and senior officials from different levels of government engage in regular discussions about the process. International experience suggests that measuring the key outcomes of a region's strategy is critical for monitoring progress, increasing accountability and motivating citizens and policy action (OECD, 2013c).

A deliberative and pro-active approach to engaging with citizens

Kazakhstan authorities need to actively seek the opinions of interested and affected groups throughout the formulation and implementation of policy. Consultation can help gather information to arrive at better urban policies, and stakeholder participation facilitates feedback on the design and effects of regulations and policies. Consultation on urban planning allows citizens to engage directly or indirectly in specific urban development issues. National and subnational authorities may wish to promote more participatory urban planning processes, with citizens participating in forums, public hearings or send opinions by mail or online. The public councils, as considered in the Law on 2 November 2015, "On Public Councils", are a promising start for increasing public participation in decision making, including discussions on budget programmes and territorial development programmes. Although the use of public councils is in its early stages, they should be part of the process towards strengthening local self-governments, and enhancing transparency. Moreover, free access to meetings of the *akimats* and *maslikhats* could be a way to build trust and inform citizens. This is the case in Turkey, where municipal council meetings are public; citizens and the press may freely observe the meetings. Meetings of the municipal council commissions are open to relevant professional organisations, civil society organisations and others. Turkey's "citizens' assemblies" which consist of representatives from professional organisations, universities, trade unions and others, form opinions that are communicated to the relevant municipal council. These assemblies have been seminal in raising the awareness of citizens and municipal administration in protecting the rights of the city, implementing the principle of decentralisation and ensuring sustainable development.

Box 3.15. **Pro-active participation in policy making**

The European citizens' initiative allows EU citizens to participate directly in the development of EU policies, by calling on the European Commission to make a legislative proposal. A citizens' initiative is possible in any field where the Commission has the power to propose legislation, for example environment, agriculture, transport or public health. A citizens' initiative has to be backed by at least one million EU citizens, coming from at least seven of the member states, with a minimum number of signatories (1 million). Citizens' initiatives cannot be run by organisations, but they can promote or support initiatives provided that they do so in full transparency. The Commission will adopt a formal response spelling out what action it will propose, if any, and the reasons why it is or is not doing so, but it is not obliged to propose legislation as a result of the initiative.

In Switzerland, citizens can request changes to the constitution by collecting 100 000 signatures of eligible voters within a period of 18 months. Their proposals may take the form of a general proposition or a fully drafted constitutional text, which cannot be modified by either the parliament or the government.

Source: European Commission, "The European Citizens Initiative", accessed at: http://ec.europa.eu/citizens-initiative/public/basic-facts; and OECD (2013d), "Investing in trust: Leveraging institutions for inclusive policy making", background paper, www.oecd.org/gov/ethics/Investing-in-trust.pdf.

Making public deliberation a key component of the urban planning process ensures that the opinions of those concerned have an influence on the decision process. A deliberative model would be consistent with a government committed to an urban planning process based on genuine community engagement and consultation. A broad range of stakeholders would need to be involved in its design, development and implementation, following the example of OECD cities such as Perth, Calgary, Vancouver and Phoenix. *Akimats* could identify spaces for community deliberation, whether physical or online, and they could organise meetings to discuss progress. Managing urban planning strategy would require integration across multiple policy areas, and broad-based support from the community.

Growing interest in local partnerships and greater civic involvement are a recurring theme in urban policy in OECD countries. Most national governments see partnerships – among cities as well as between public and private parties – virtually as a precondition for effective national urban policies. However, it is important that public participation does not turn into an obstacle to urban projects. In some cases, citizens who have opposed plans have taken the case to court to block infrastructure projects. This indicates how important it is to get citizens involved in public deliberations from the earliest stages.

Develop and adopt a wide range of engagement tools

The current apathy of citizens in local governance must be reformed by a constructive process of engaging citizens in local reform (Kazakova, 2015). For that purpose, local communities need to be given a variety of tools and mechanisms to participate in resolutions adopted by the *akimats*. To engage the broader public, focus groups, media campaigns and an interactive website could be considered. The operation of civil society in Kazakhstan is expressed through family or neighbourhood units. This means that there is a mechanism for dealing with local issues and social provision. Neighbourhood development processes could be explored to explain the impacts on local communities both during development and implementation. Nonetheless, the planning of a city or region needs to engage with organisations above neighbourhood level. For instance, collection and disposal of solid waste and sewage in Almaty, Astana and Shymkent can lead to large-scale environmental and social problems that require civil participation as well as state action.

Akimats and *maslikhats* together could organise workshops to discuss opportunities for urban development and develop scenarios with other stakeholders. Special strategies for targeting groups that are hard to reach (the disabled, youth and the elderly) would be implemented to ensure their participation in public events and forums. *Akimats* could make use of community outreach officers. Forums of expert panels could encourage informed debate on key issues among academic and opinion leaders.

Improve accessibility, quality and disclosure of information

Building on the Law on Access to Information, Kazakhstan may ensure access to quality information to ensure the meaningful participation of civil society in urban development. *Akimats* could make sure that citizens have timely access to useful, easy-to-understand information on different urban development plans. Investment in resources – skills and funds – to provide information for gathering and sharing key outcomes of the urban policy may be necessary. Targets of accountability, transparency and dialogue with private stakeholders and civic society, as well as multisectoral planning can improve *akimats*' capacity. Policy evaluation can play a decisive role in offering insights on conditions and bottlenecks in the implementation of policies and in suggesting how to revise goals, reallocate resources and identify tools that deliver results.

Notes

1. Steps 97 and 99 of the "100 Concrete Steps to Implement Five Institutional Reforms".

2. Kazakhstan's long-term foreign and local currency sovereign credit rating by international rating agencies such as Standard & Poor's has been lowered, due in part to the country's limited institutional and governance effectiveness, owing to the highly centralised political environment.
www.standardandpoors.com/en_AP/web/guest/article/-/view/sourceId/20018335.

3. A common feature of CIS countries is that most often local authorities have no clear division of functions, powers, competencies and responsibilities. The Commonwealth of Independent States (CIS) was established in 1991, and it has 10 permanent members and one associate member: Armenia, Azerbaijan, Belarus, Kazakhstan, Kyrgyzstan, Moldova, Russia, Tajikistan, Turkmenistan (an associate member), Ukraine and Uzbekistan (UNECE, 2016).

4. For more information, see: www.gov.uk/government/collections/city-deals.

5. For further information regarding the "100 Concrete Steps to Implement Five Institutional Reforms", see: www.mid.gov.kz/en/kategorii/100-konkretnyh-shagov-0 and Kazakhstan 2050 Strategy Leads to Government Restructuring: http://carnegieendowment.org/2013/02/21/undefined/fis2.

6. For further information, see: UN Sustainable Development Goals, www.un.org/sustainabledevelopment/sustainable-development-goals/.

7. This idea was exposed by Linn (2014) as a task for the newly established Ministry of Regional Development.

8. For further information on Sweden's National Board of Housing, Building and Planning see: www.boverket.se/en/start-in-english/planning/platform-for-sustainable-cities/.

9. Interviews for this review at the Ministry of Finance suggested that, on average, 30% of SNGs' revenue is self-generated while 70% is transfers. According to Kysykov (2013: 82), in 2010 transfers from the republic's budget accounted for 61.7% of the total revenue of local budgets.

10. For further information, see: www.tbb.gov.tr/en/local-authorities/municipal-finances.

11. For further information, see: https://vlast.kz/novosti/19245-finansovye-polnomocia-organov-mestnogo-samoupravlenia-budut-rassireny.html.

12. For further details, see: www.omafra.gov.on.ca/english/policy/ftaxfacts.htm.

13. See Article 44 of Kazakhstan's Budget Code.

14. In the European Union, the share of investments financed through debt has nearly doubled since the beginning of the global financial crisis (Hulbert, C. and C. Vammalle, 2014).

15. For further information on BANOBRAS, see:
www.banobras.gob.mx/quienessomos/Paginas/Inicio.aspx.

16. For further information on IlBank, see: www.ilbank.gov.tr/.

17. Kazakhstan Budget Code, Art 42. 2. The relationships of the republican budget with budgets of regions (the cities of regional importance) and the budgets of districts (the cities of regional importance) with each other are not allowed in the budget process.

18. It is beyond the scope of this review to produce a detailed analysis of the human resource management arrangements at national and local levels of government. Some general assessment and recommendations are formulated here to raise awareness of the pros and cons of the career-based model and provide some practical suggestions to improve the system.

19. OECD is currently conducting an Integrity Study of Kazakhstan, which will include an-depth analysis of anti-corruption issues. Hence, to avoid duplication, this Review will not go into detail on these issues.

References

Aitzhanova, A. et al. (eds.) (2014), *Kazakhstan 2050: Toward a Modern Society for All*, Nazarbayev University, National Analytical Centre, Oxford University Press, Group Centennial International, Astana.

Anderson, B. (2009), "The changing role of parliament in the budget process", *OECD Journal on Budgeting*, Vol. 9/1, pp. 1-11, http://dx.doi.org/10.1787/budget-v9-art2-en.

Bahl, R., J. Linn and D. Wetzel (eds.) (2013), "Governing and Financing Metropolitan Areas in the Developing World", in *Financing Metropolitan Governments in Developing Countries*, The Lincoln Institute of Land Policy, Massachusetts, pp. 1-30.

Bergvall, D. et al. (2006), "Intergovernmental transfers and decentralised public spending", *OECD Working Papers on Fiscal Federalism*, No. 3, OECD Publishing, Paris, http://dx.doi.org/10.1787/5k97b11z2hxw-en.

Bhuiyan, S.H. (2010), "Decentralization and local governance in Kazakhstan", *International Journal of Public Administration*, Routledge, Vol. 33/12-13, pp. 658-672, doi: 10.1080/01900692.2010.514445.

Bird, R. and E. Slack (2002), "Land and Property Taxation: A Review", The World Bank, http://www1.worldbank.org/publicsector/decentralization/June2003Seminar/LandPropertyTaxation.pdf (accessed 27 October 2016).

CER, ESCAP, UNDP (2013), "Urbanization in Central Asia: Challenges, Issues and Prospects", Tashkent, www.unescap.org/resources/urbanization-central-asia-challenges-issues-and-prospects.

Charbit, C. (2011), "Governance of Public Policies in Decentralised Contexts: The Multi-level Approach", *OECD Regional Development Working Papers*, No. 2011/04, OECD Publishing, Paris, http://dx.doi.org/10.1787/5kg883pkxkhc-en.

Civil Service (2016), "Civil Service Human Resources Function", www.gov.uk/government/collections/civil-service-human-resources-function.

Civil Service (2013), "Meeting the Challenge of Change: A Capabilities Plan for the Civil Service", www.gov.uk/government/uploads/system/uploads/attachment_data/file/307250/Civil_Service_Capabilities_Plan_2013.pdf.

Commonwealth of Australia (2016), *Smart Cities Plan*, Department of the Prime Minister and Cabinet, https://cities.dpmc.gov.au/smart-cities-plan (accessed 22 November 2016).

European Commission (2016), "The European Citizens Initiative", http://ec.europa.eu/citizens-initiative/public/basic-facts (accessed 27 October 2016).

Finding, S. (2015), "Who governs Britain – democracy in action? Directly elected mayors in England", *Cahiers du MIMMOC*, http://mimmoc.revues.org/2288 (accessed 22 November 2016).

Government of Norway (2007), *KOSTRA (local governments-State-Reporting)* www.regjeringen.no/en/dep/kmd/subjects/municipal-economy/kostra-municipality--state-reporting.html?id=1233 (accessed 21 July 2016)

House of Commons, Public Administration Select Committee (2007), "Skills for Government, Ninth Report of Session 2006-07", Vol. 1, www.publications.parliament.uk/pa/cm200607/cmselect/cmpubadm/93/93i.pdf (accessed 27 October 2016).

Huerta Melchor, O. (2008), "Managing Change in OECD Governments: An Introductory Framework", *OECD Working Papers on Public Governance*, No. 12, OECD Publishing, Paris, http://dx.doi.org/10.1787/227141782188.

Hulbert, C. and C. Vammalle (2014), "A Subnational Perspective on Financing Investment for Growth I – Measuring Fiscal Space for Public Investment: Influences, Evolution and Perspectives", *OECD Regional Development Working Papers*, 2014/02, OECD Publishing, Paris, http://dx.doi.org/10.1787/5jz5j1qk8fhg-en.

Idrissova, A. (2014), "Civil Service Reforms in Kazakhstan and its Influence on Modernization", *International Journal of Social, Behavioral, Educational, Economic, Business and Industrial Engineering*, Vol. 8/3, pp. 800-803, http://waset.org/publications/9997893/civil-service-reforms-in-kazakhstan-and-its-influence-on-modernization (accessed 27 October 2016).

Janenova, S. (2016), "New Trajectories of Civil Service Reform in Kazakhstan", *The Astana Times*, 16 February, http://astanatimes.com/2016/02/new-trajectories-of-civil-service-reform-in-kazakhstan/ (accessed 27 October 2016).

Kazakova, A. (2015), *Modern urbanisation analysis and prospects in Kazakhstan*, Central Asian Bureau for Analytical Reporting, http://cabar.asia/en/alexandra-kazakova-modern-urbanization-analysis-and-prospects-in-kazakhstan/ (accessed January 2017).

Kysykov, A. (2013), "On overcoming the subsidy dependence of regional budgets", *Problems of Economic Transition*, Routledge, Vol. 56/8, December, pp. 75-92, http://dx.doi.org/10.2753/PET1061-1991560805 (accessed 14 October 2016).

Linn, J. (2014), "Urbanization, Regional Development, and Decentralization", in Aitzhanova, A. et al. (eds.), *Kazakhstan 2050: Toward a Modern Society for All*, Nazarbayev University, National Analytical Centre, Oxford University Press, Group Centennial International, Astana, pp. 187-223.

Makhmutova, M. (2006), "Local Government Organization and Finance: Kazakhstan" in Anwar Shah (ed.), *Local Governance in Developing Countries*, The World Bank, International Bank for Reconstruction and Development, pp. 275-302.

McCluskey, W. and R. Franzsen (2013), "Property Taxes in Metropolitan Cities", in Bahl, R., J. Linn and D. Wetzel, (eds.), *Financing Metropolitan Governments in Developing Countries*, Lincoln Institute of Land Policy, Massachusetts, pp. 159-181.

McLure, C. and J. Martínez-Vazquez (2000), "The assignment of revenues and expenditures in intergovernmental fiscal relations", The World Bank, Washington, DC, http://www1.worldbank.org/publicsector/pe/PEAMMarch2005/AssignmentRevenues.pdf (accessed 14 October 2016).

Ministry of National Economy (2014), Order No. 139, available (in Russian) at: http://adilet.zan.kz/rus/docs/V1400010068#z35 and Budget Code, http://adilet.zan.kz/eng/docs/K080000095_).

NAC of Nazarbayev University (2012), "Policy Brief on the Course of Decentralization Reform and Inter-budget relation in the Republic of Kazakhstan in 2001-2012", NAC, Astana.

OECD (2017), *OECD Territorial Reviews: Kazakhstan*, OECD Publishing, Paris, forthcoming.

OECD/UCLG (2016), "Subnational Governments around the World: Structure and Finance", OECD, Paris, www.uclg-localfinance.org/sites/default/files/Observatory_web_0.pdf .

OECD (2017), Decentralisation and Multi-level Governance in Kazakhstan, forthcoming.

OECD (2016a), *OECD Territorial Reviews: The Metropolitan Region of Rotterdam-The Hague, Netherlands*, OECD Publishing, Paris, http://dx.doi.org/10.1787/9789264249387-en.

OECD (2016b), *Making the Most of Public Investment in Colombia: Working Effectively across Levels of Government*, OECD Multi-level Governance Studies, OECD Publishing, Paris, http://dx.doi.org/10.1787/9789264265288-en.

OECD (2016c), *OECD Regions at a Glance 2016*, OECD Publishing, Paris, http://dx.doi.org/10.1787/reg_glance-2016-en.

OECD (2016d), *Green Growth in Hai Phong, Viet Nam*, OECD Publishing, Paris, http://dx.doi.org/10.1787/9789264260207-en.

OECD (2016e), *Multi-dimensional Review of Kazakhstan: Volume 1. Initial Assessment*, OECD Development Pathways, OECD Publishing, Paris, http://dx.doi.org/10.1787/9789264246768-en.

OECD (2016f), *2015 OECD Recommendation of the Council on Gender Equality in Public Life*, OECD Publishing, Paris. http://dx.doi.org/10.1787/9789264252820-en.

OECD (2015a), *Governing the City*, OECD Publishing, Paris, http://dx.doi.org/10.1787/9789264226500-en.

OECD (2015b), *OECD Urban Policy Reviews: China 2015*, OECD Publishing, Paris, http://dx.doi.org/10.1787/9789264230040-en.

OECD (2015c), *OECD Urban Policy Reviews: Mexico 2015: Transforming Urban Policy and Housing Finance*, OECD Publishing, Paris, http://dx.doi.org/10.1787/9789264227293-en.

OECD (2015d), *OECD Economic Surveys: Mexico*, OECD Publishing, Paris, http://dx.doi.org/10.1787/eco_surveys-mex-2015-en.

OECD (2015e), *The Metropolitan Century: Understanding Urbanisation and Its Consequences*, OECD Publishing, Paris, http://dx.doi.org/10.1787/9789264228733-en.

OECD (2014a), *Kazakhstan: Review of the Central Administration*, OECD Public Governance Reviews, OECD Publishing, Paris, http://dx.doi.org/10.1787/9789264224605-en.

OECD (2014b), *Spain: From Administrative Reform to Continuous Improvement*, OECD Public Governance Reviews, OECD Publishing, Paris, http://dx.doi.org/10.1787/9789264210592-en.

OECD (2014c), *How's Life in Your Region? Measuring Regional and Local Well-being for Policy Making*, OECD Publishing, Paris, http://dx.doi.org/10.1787/9789264217416-en.

OECD (2014d), *Recommendation of the Council on Effective Public Investment across Levels of Government*, adopted on 12 March, www.oecd.org/regional/regional-policy/Principles-Public-Investment.pdf.

OECD (2013a), *Government at a Glance 2013*, OECD Publishing, Paris, http://dx.doi.org/10.1787/gov_glance-2013-en.

OECD (2013b), *OECD Urban Policy Reviews, Chile 2013*, OECD Publishing, Paris, http://dx.doi.org/10.1787/9789264191808-en.

OECD (2013c), *Policy Making after Disasters: Helping Regions Become Resilient – The Case of Post-Earthquake Abruzzzo*, OECD Publishing, Paris, http://dx.doi.org/10.1787/9789264189577-en.

OECD (2013d), "Investing in trust: Leveraging institutions for inclusive policy making", background paper, OECD, www.oecd.org/gov/ethics/Investing-in-trust.pdf (accessed 27 October 2016).

OECD (2013e), *OECD Territorial Reviews: Puebla-Tlaxcala, Mexico 2013*, OECD Publishing, Paris, http://dx.doi.org/10.1787/9789264203464-en.

OECD (2013f), *Investing Together: Working Effectively across Levels of Government*, OECD Publishing, Paris, http://dx.doi.org/10.1787/9789264197022-en.

OECD (2013g), *OECD Territorial Reviews: Antofagasta 2013*, OECD Publishing, Paris, http://dx.doi.org/10.1787/9789264203914-en.

OECD (2012), *Value for Money in Government: Denmark 2011*, Value for Money in Government, OECD Publishing, Paris, http://dx.doi.org/10.1787/9789264130746-en.

OECD (2011), *Public Servants as Partners for Growth: Toward a Stronger, Leaner and More Equitable Workforce*, OECD Publishing, Paris, http://dx.doi.org/10.1787/9789264166707-en.

OECD (2010a), *OECD Reviews of Human Resource Management in Government: Brazil 2010: Federal Government*, OECD Publishing, Paris, http://dx.doi.org/10.1787/9789264082229-en.

OECD (2010b), *Finland: Working Together to Sustain Success*, OECD Publishing, Paris, http://dx.doi.org/10.1787/9789264086081-en.

OECD (2008), *The State of the Public Service*, OECD Publishing, Paris, http://dx.doi.org/10.1787/9789264047990-en.

OECD (2005), *Modernising Government: The Way Forward*, OECD Publishing, Paris, http://dx.doi.org/10.1787/9789264010505-en.

Scartascini, C. and M. Tommasi (2012), "How (not) to produce effective policies? Institutions and policymaking in Latin America", in J. Santiso and J. Dayton-Johnson (eds.), *The Oxford Handbook of Latin American Political Economy*, Oxford University Press.

Schick, A. (2002), "Can National Legislatures Regain an Effective Voice in Budget Policy?", *OECD Journal on Budgeting*, Vol. 1/3, http://dx.doi.org/10.1787/budget-v1-art15-en, pp. 15-42.

Sen, T. et al. (2014), "Intergovernmental finance in five emerging market economies", National Institute of Public Finance and Policy, New Delhi, http://fincomindia.nic.in/writereaddata%5Chtml_en_files%5Cfincom14/others/31.pdf (accessed 27 October 2016).

Slack, E. (2014), "Governance and Finance of Large Metropolitan Areas: Which institutional setting is needed to secure metropolitan economic growth?, presentation to the fifth Halle Forum on Urban Economic Growth, Halle Germany, IMFG, University of Toronto, MUNK School of Global Affairs, http://munkschool.utoronto.ca/imfg/uploads/304/slack_presentation_on_governance_and_finance_of_metropolitan_areas_halle_december_11_2014.pdf (accessed 27 October 2016).

Stockholm Environment Institute (2015), "What cities do best: How to maximise the role of cities in a low-carbon future", Bloomberg Philanthropies, Stockholm Environment Institute, www.sei-international.org/publications?pid=2879 (accessed 16 November 2016).

The World Bank (2014), "Intergovernmental Fiscal Relations", *Decentralization and Sustainable Regional Economics*, www.worldbank.org/pulisector/decentralization/fiscal.htm (accessed 16 November 2016).

The World Bank (2012), *Kazakhstan: Targeting Development Transfers*, The World Bank, Washington, DC.

UNECE (2016), "CIS Cities: Towards Sustainable Future – The Commonwealth of Independent States Regional Report", UNECE, UN-Habitat, www.unece.org/index.php?id=42438 (accessed 16 November 2016).

Union of Municipalities of Turkey (2015), "Local Governments in Turkey", Ankara, www.tbb.gov.tr/online/yayinlar/local_government_inturkey/files/publication.pdf (accessed 16 November 2016).

Wilson, J. et al. (2002), "The changing role of local government managers in a transitional economy: evidence from the Republic of Kazakhstan", *International Journal of Public Sector Management*, Emerald Insight, Vol. 15/5, pp. 399-411, http://dx.doi.org/10.1108/09513550210435737 (accessed 14 October 2016).

Work, R. (2002), "Overview of Decentralisation Worldwide: a stepping stone to improve governance and human development", UNDP, 2nd International Conference on Decentralisation: Federalism: The Future of Decentralizing States? 25-27 July, Manila, Philippines, www.cities-localgovernments.org/committees/dal/Upload/library/overviewofdecentralisationworldwide_work_2002.pdf (accessed 22 November 2016).

Yilmaz, S., Y. Beris and R. Serrano-Berthet (2008), "Local Government Discretion and Accountability: a diagnostic framework for local governance", *Social Development Working Papers*, Local Governance & Accountability Series, Paper No. 113, July, The World Bank, http://documents.worldbank.org/curated/en/897941468137384275/pdf/465520NWP0Box31SD1Working1Paper1113.pdf (accessed 24 November 2016).

ORGANISATION FOR ECONOMIC CO-OPERATION AND DEVELOPMENT

The OECD is a unique forum where governments work together to address the economic, social and environmental challenges of globalisation. The OECD is also at the forefront of efforts to understand and to help governments respond to new developments and concerns, such as corporate governance, the information economy and the challenges of an ageing population. The Organisation provides a setting where governments can compare policy experiences, seek answers to common problems, identify good practice and work to co-ordinate domestic and international policies.

The OECD member countries are: Australia, Austria, Belgium, Canada, Chile, the Czech Republic, Denmark, Estonia, Finland, France, Germany, Greece, Hungary, Iceland, Ireland, Israel, Italy, Japan, Korea, Latvia, Luxembourg, Mexico, the Netherlands, New Zealand, Norway, Poland, Portugal, the Slovak Republic, Slovenia, Spain, Sweden, Switzerland, Turkey, the United Kingdom and the United States. The European Union takes part in the work of the OECD.

OECD Publishing disseminates widely the results of the Organisation's statistics gathering and research on economic, social and environmental issues, as well as the conventions, guidelines and standards agreed by its members.

OECD PUBLISHING, 2, rue André-Pascal, 75775 PARIS CEDEX 16
(04 2017 02 1 P) ISBN 978-92-64-26884-5 – 2017

www.ingramcontent.com/pod-product-compliance
Lightning Source LLC
LaVergne TN
LVHW080652011026
849160LV00014B/1392